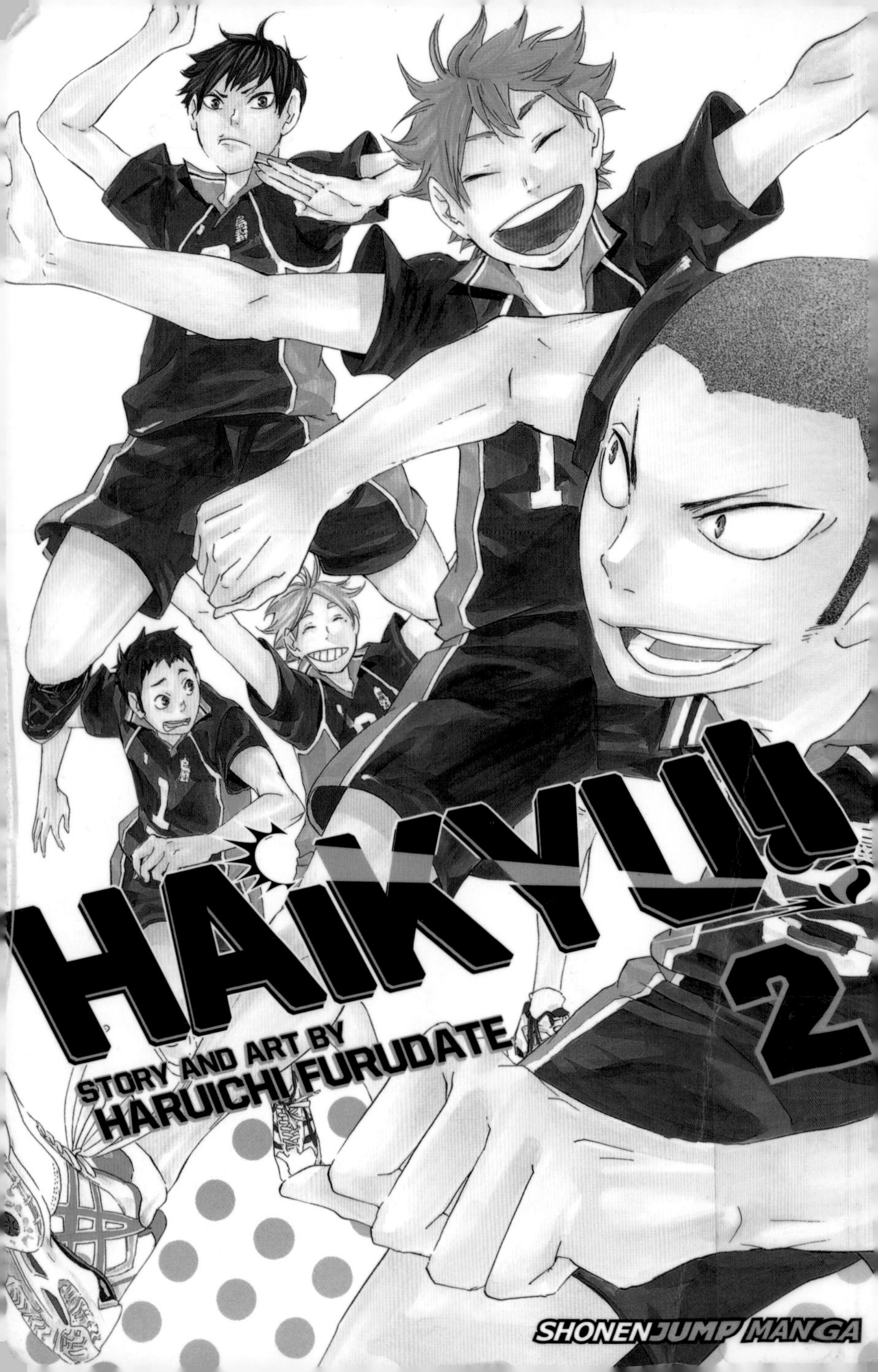
HAIKYU!!
2
STORY AND ART BY
HARUICHI FURUDATE
SHONEN JUMP MANGA

You're Reading the WRONG WAY!

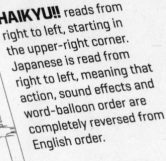

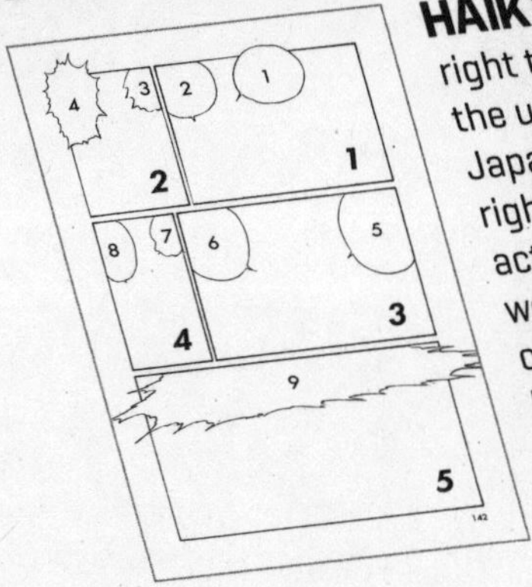

HAIKYU!! reads from right to left, starting in the upper-right corner. Japanese is read from right to left, meaning that action, sound effects and word-balloon order are completely reversed from English order.

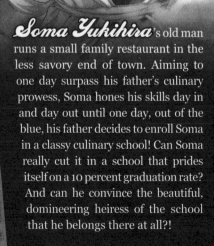

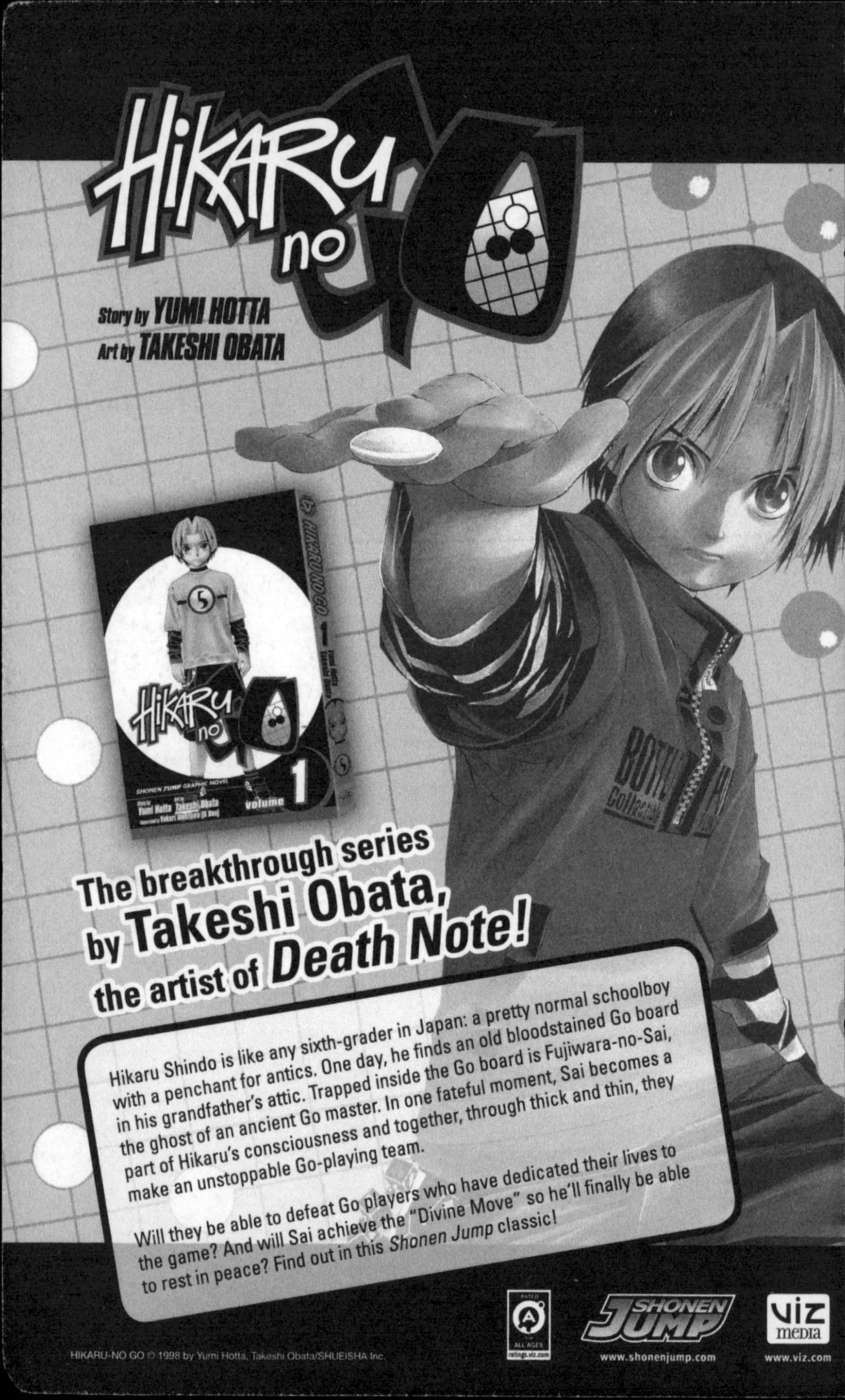
HIKARU no GO
Story by YUMI HOTTA
Art by TAKESHI OBATA
HIKARU NO GO
Yumi Hotta Takeshi Obata
HIKARU no GO
SHONEN JUMP GRAPHIC NOVEL
volume 1
The breakthrough series by Takeshi Obata, the artist of Death Note!
Hikaru Shindo is like any sixth-grader in Japan: a pretty normal schoolboy with a penchant for antics. One day, he finds an old bloodstained Go board in his grandfather's attic. Trapped inside the Go board is Fujiwara-no-Sai, the ghost of an ancient Go master. In one fateful moment, Sai becomes a part of Hikaru's consciousness and together, through thick and thin, they make an unstoppable Go-playing team.
Will they be able to defeat Go players who have dedicated their lives to the game? And will Sai achieve the "Divine Move" so he'll finally be able to rest in peace? Find out in this Shonen Jump classic!
RATED A FOR ALL AGES ratings.viz.com
SHONEN JUMP
www.shonenjump.com
VIZ MEDIA
www.viz.com
HIKARU-NO GO © 1998 by Yumi Hotta, Takeshi Obata/SHUEISHA Inc.

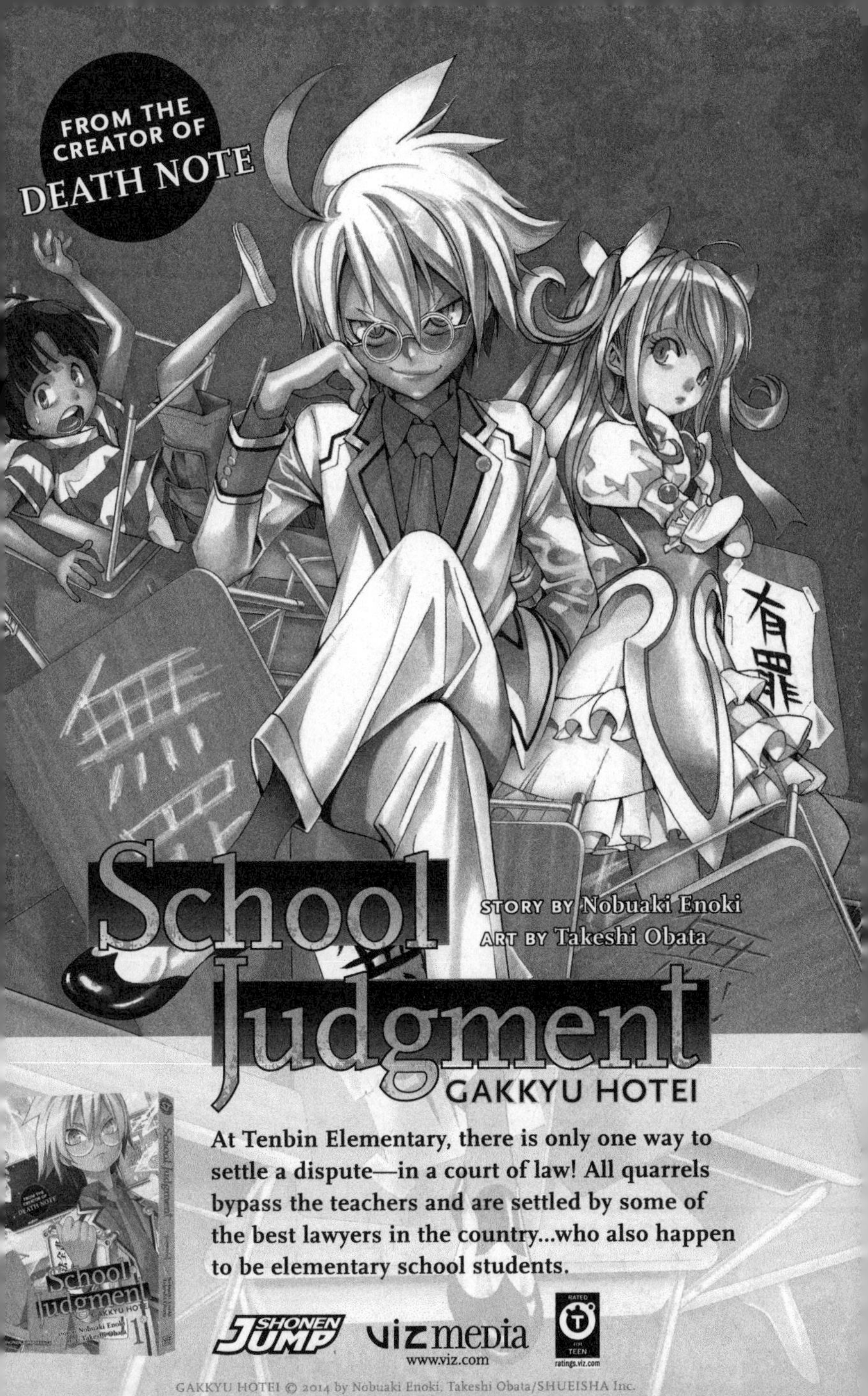
FROM THE CREATOR OF DEATH NOTE
有罪
School Judgment
STORY BY Nobuaki Enoki
ART BY Takeshi Obata
GAKKYU HOTEI
At Tenbin Elementary, there is only one way to settle a dispute—in a court of law! All quarrels bypass the teachers and are settled by some of the best lawyers in the country...who also happen to be elementary school students.
SHONEN JUMP
VIZ media
www.viz.com
RATED T FOR TEEN
ratings.viz.com

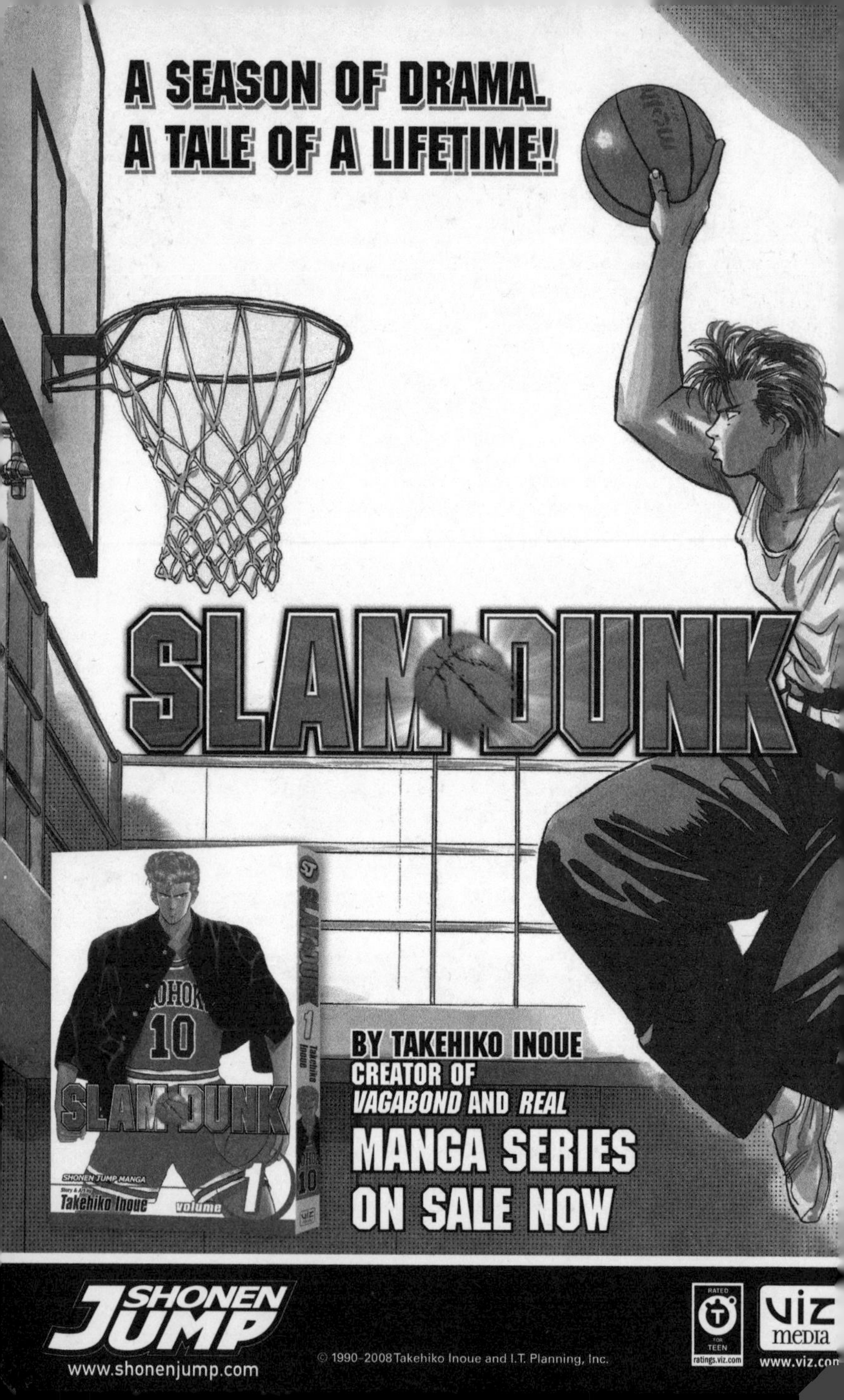
A SEASON OF DRAMA.
A TALE OF A LIFETIME!
SLAM DUNK
SHONEN JUMP MANGA
Story & Art by
Takehiko Inoue
volume 1
BY TAKEHIKO INOUE
CREATOR OF
VAGABOND AND REAL
MANGA SERIES
ON SALE NOW
SHONEN JUMP
www.shonenjump.com
© 1990–2008 Takehiko Inoue and I.T. Planning, Inc.
RATED T FOR TEEN
ratings.viz.com
VIZ media
www.viz.com

SHONEN**JUMP** MANGA

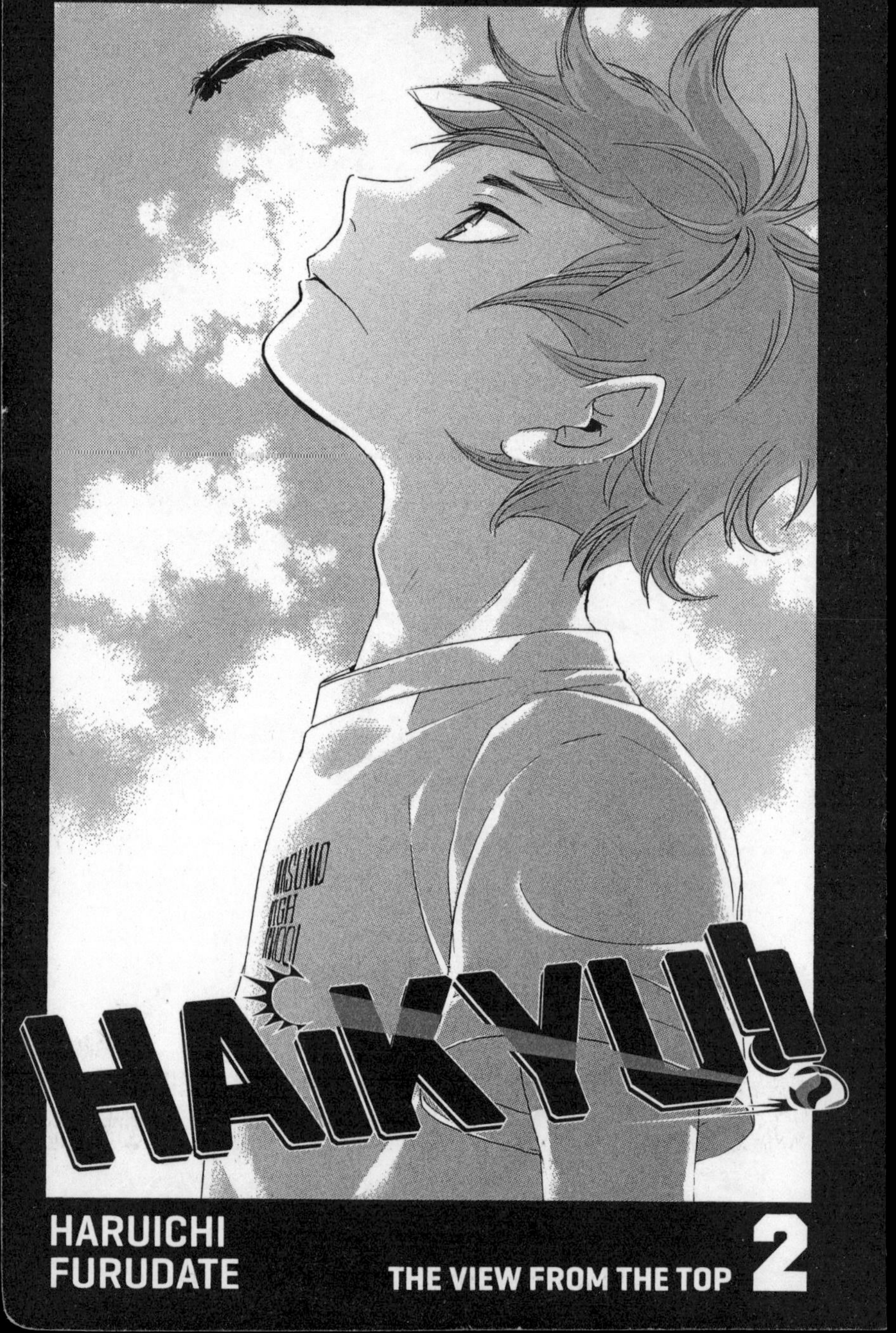

HAIKYU!!

HARUICHI
FURUDATE

THE VIEW FROM THE TOP **2**

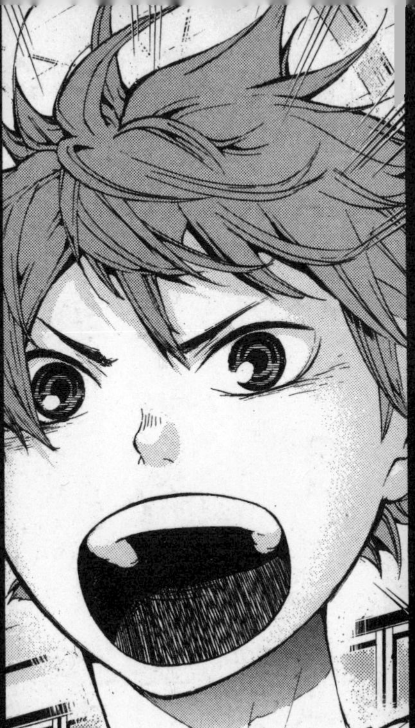

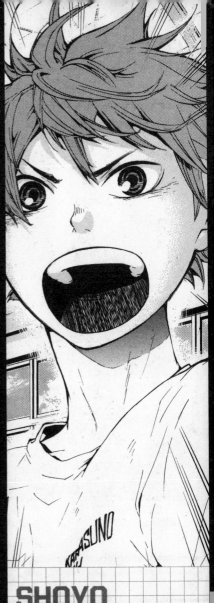

SHOYO HINATA

1ST YEAR / WING SPIKER

Even though he doesn't have the best body type for volleyball, he is super athletic. Gets nervous easily.

TOBIO KAGEYAMA

1ST YEAR / SETTER

His instincts and athletic talent are so good that he's like a "king" who rules the court. Demanding and egocentric.

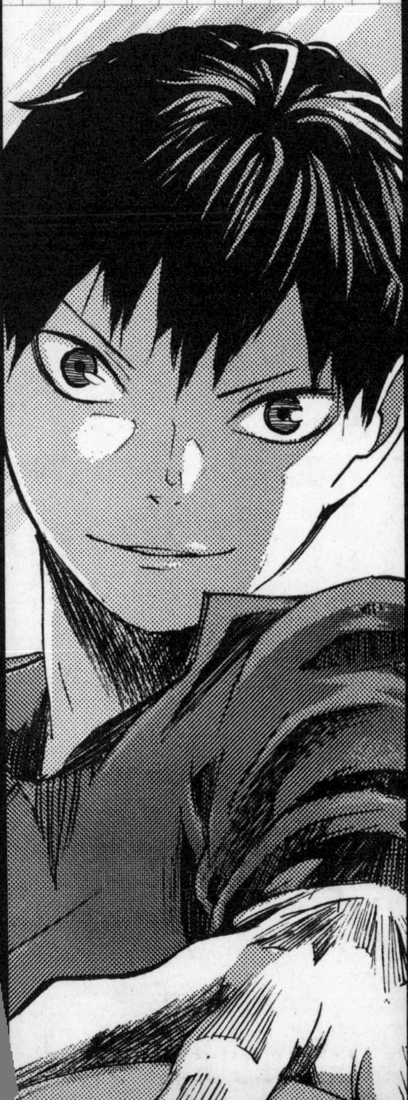

CHARACTERS

Karasuno High School Volleyball Club

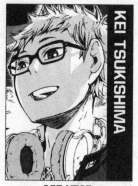

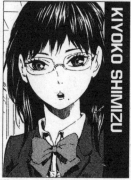

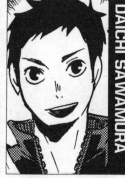

DAICHI SAWAMURA

3RD YEAR (CAPTAIN)
WING SPIKER

KIYOKO SHIMIZU

3RD YEAR
MANAGER

KEI TSUKISHIMA

1ST YEAR
MIDDLE BLOCKER

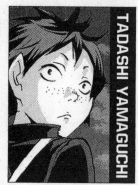

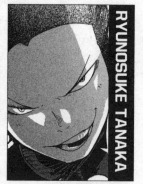

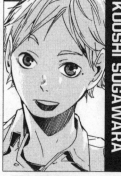

KOUSHI SUGAWARA

3RD YEAR (VICE CAPTAIN)
SETTER

RYUNOSUKE TANAKA

2ND YEAR
WING SPIKER

TADASHI YAMAGUCHI

1ST YEAR
MIDDLE BLOCKER

Ever since he saw the legendary player known as "the Little Giant" compete at the high school national volleyball finals, Shoyo Hinata has been aiming to be the best volleyball player ever! He decides to join the volleyball club at his middle school, and he gets to play in an official tournament during his third year. His team is crushed by a team led by volleyball prodigy Tobio Kageyama, also known as "the King of the Court." Swearing revenge on Kageyama, Hinata graduates middle school and enters Karasuno High School, the school where the Little Giant played. However, upon joining the club, he finds out that Kageyama is there too! The two of them bicker so much they're barred from practice. In order to be allowed back in, they must work together to win a 3-on-3 match against the team's other new first years, but the pair is still having trouble working together...

HAIKYU!!

2 THE VIEW FROM THE TOP

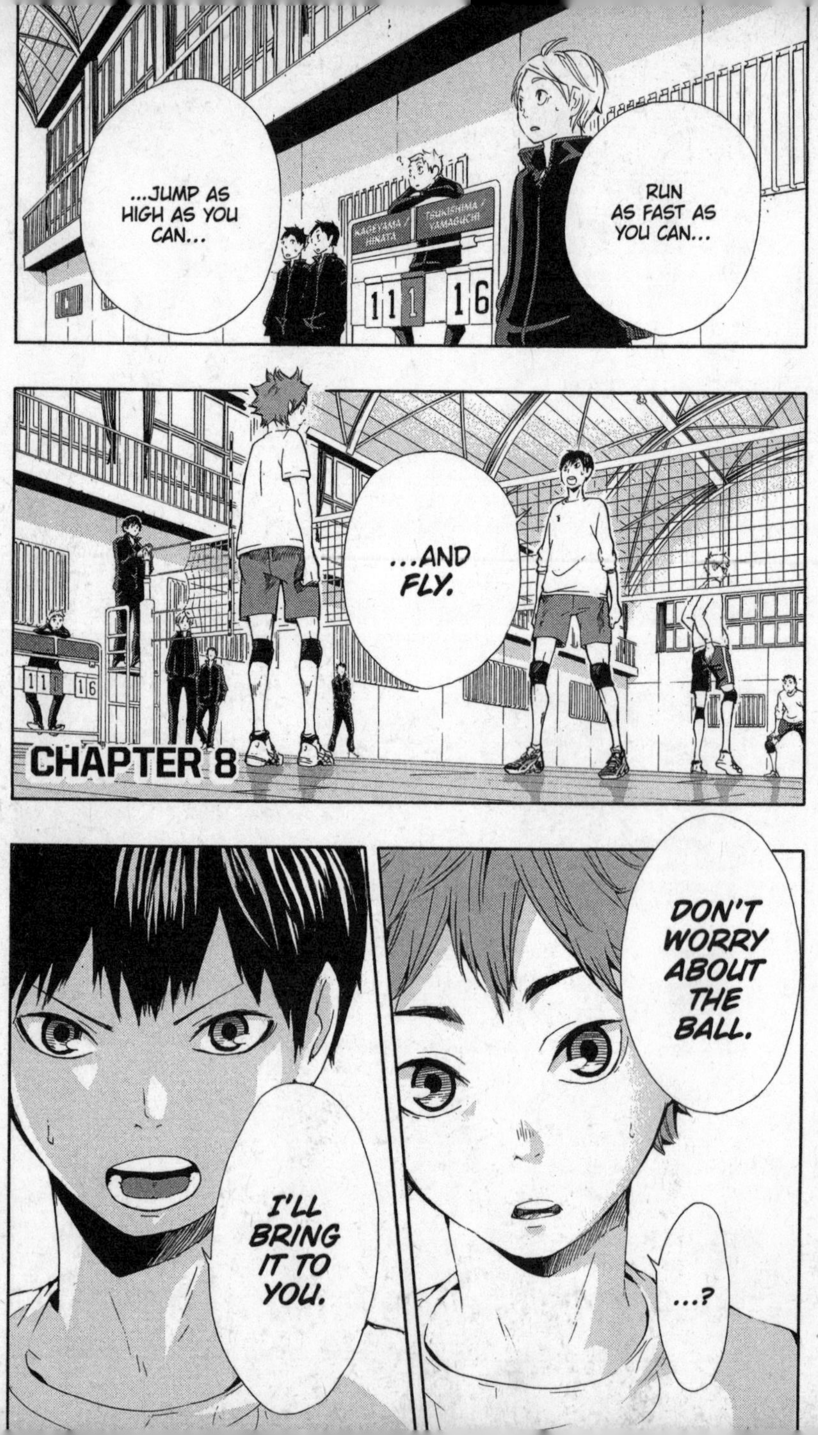
RUN AS FAST AS YOU CAN...
...JUMP AS HIGH AS YOU CAN...
...AND FLY.
CHAPTER 8
DON'T WORRY ABOUT THE BALL.
...?
I'LL BRING IT TO YOU.

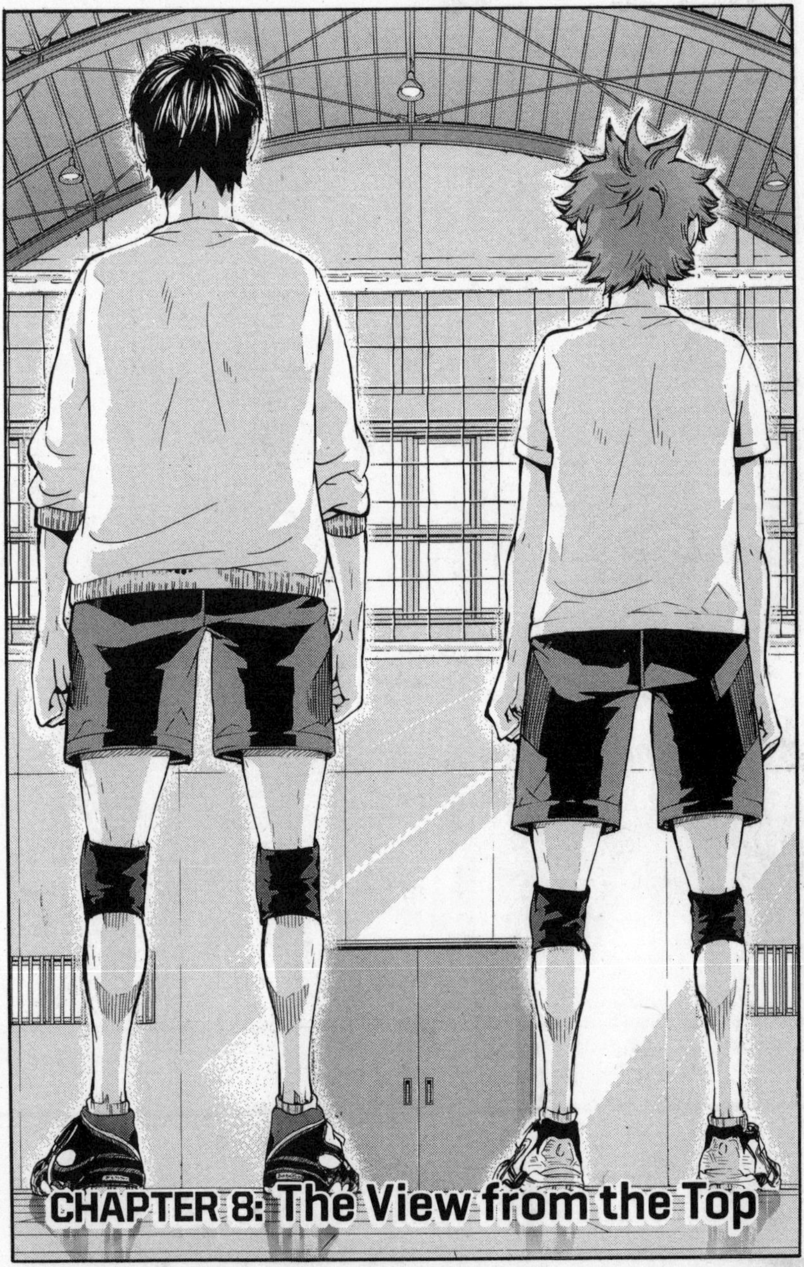
CHAPTER 8: The View from the Top

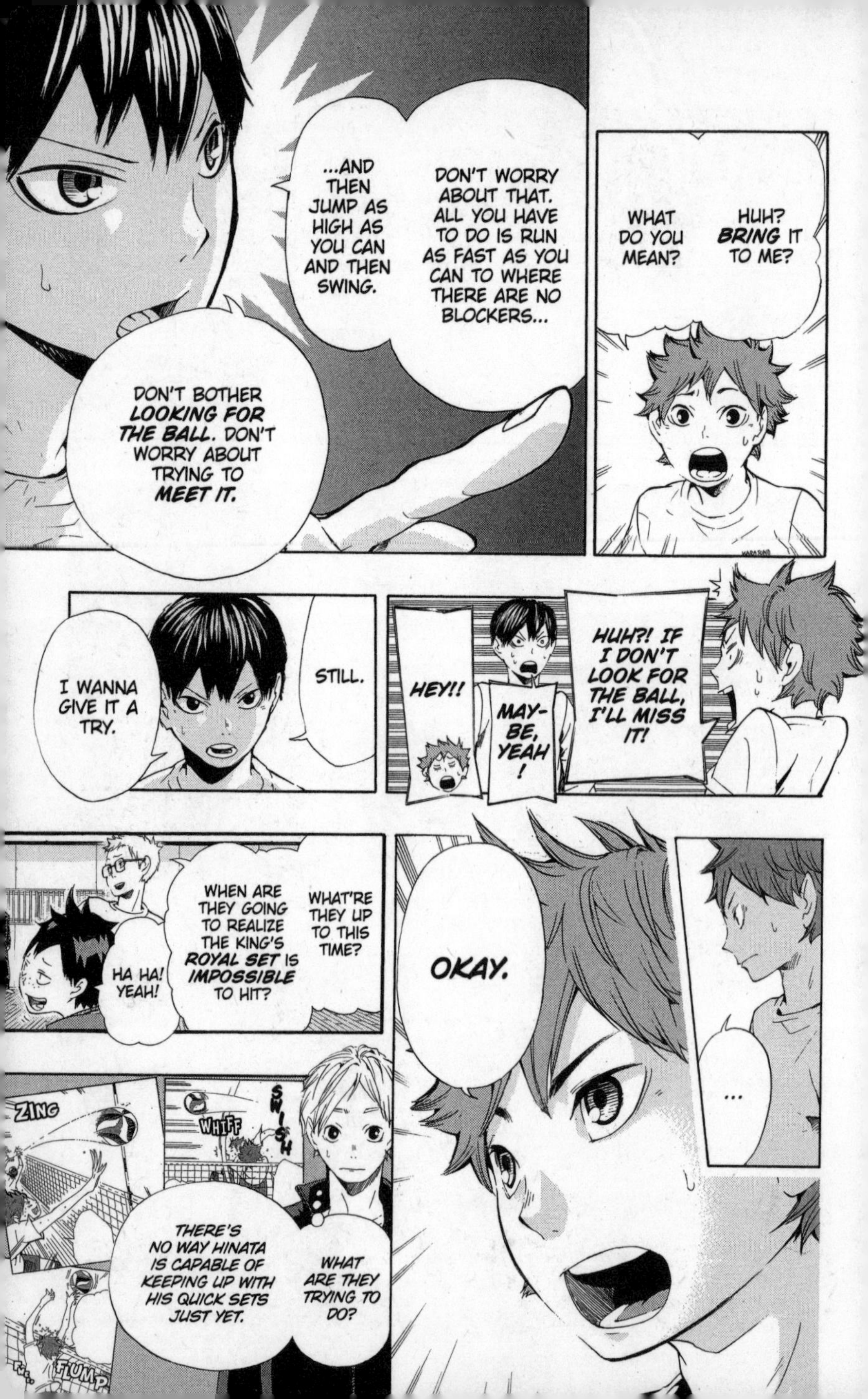
HUH? BRING IT TO ME?
WHAT DO YOU MEAN?
DON'T WORRY ABOUT THAT. ALL YOU HAVE TO DO IS RUN AS FAST AS YOU CAN TO WHERE THERE ARE NO BLOCKERS...
...AND THEN JUMP AS HIGH AS YOU CAN AND THEN SWING.
DON'T BOTHER LOOKING FOR THE BALL. DON'T WORRY ABOUT TRYING TO MEET IT.
HUH?! IF I DON'T LOOK FOR THE BALL, I'LL MISS IT!
MAY-BE, YEAH!
HEY!!
STILL.
I WANNA GIVE IT A TRY.
...
OKAY.
WHAT'RE THEY UP TO THIS TIME?
WHEN ARE THEY GOING TO REALIZE THE KING'S ROYAL SET IS IMPOSSIBLE TO HIT?
HA HA! YEAH!
SWISH
WHIFF
ZING
FLUMP
WHAT ARE THEY TRYING TO DO?
THERE'S NO WAY HINATA IS CAPABLE OF KEEPING UP WITH HIS QUICK SETS JUST YET.

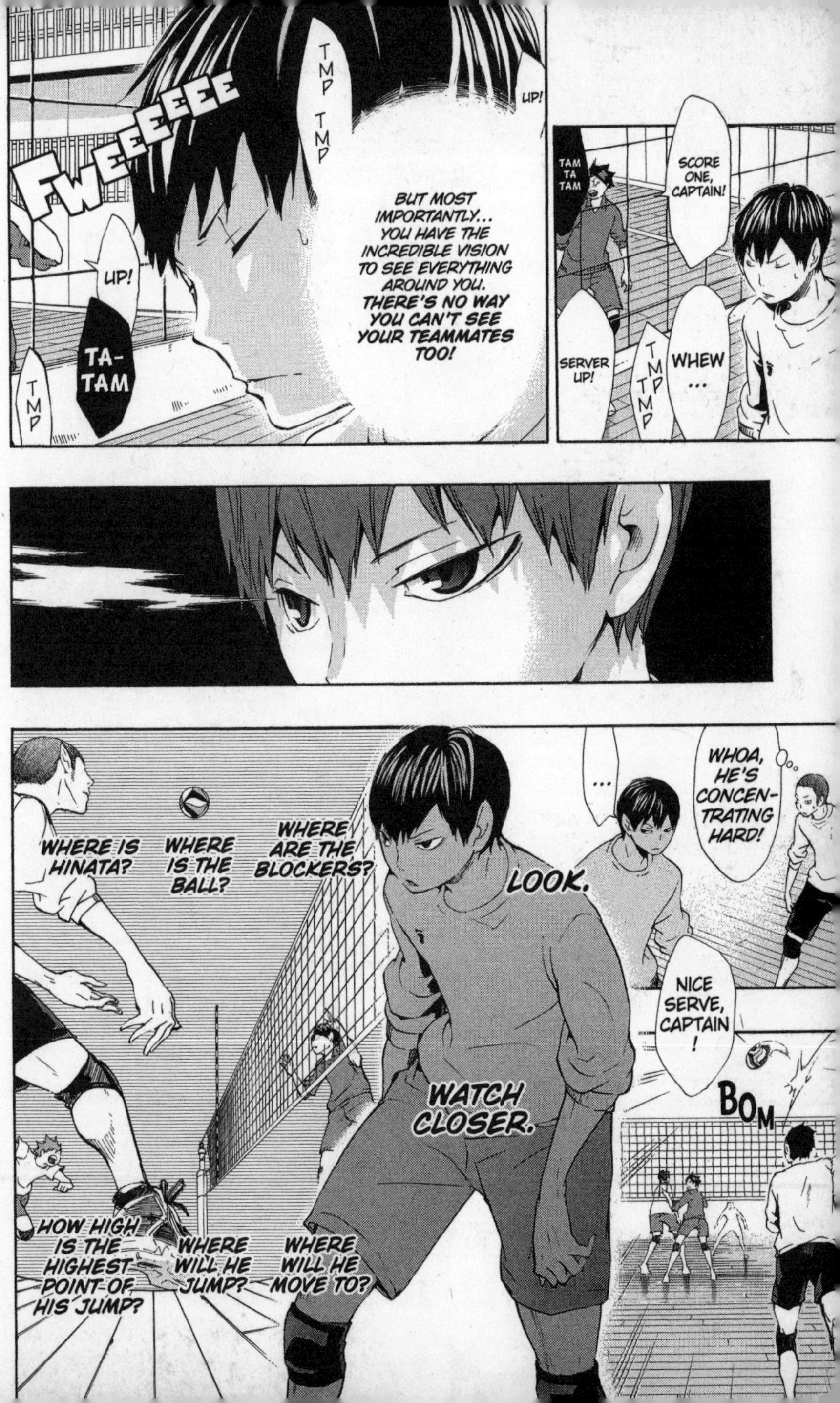
SCORE ONE, CAPTAIN!
TAM TA TAM
WHEW...
TMP TMP
SERVER UP!
UP!
TMP TMP
FWEEEEEE
BUT MOST IMPORTANTLY... YOU HAVE THE INCREDIBLE VISION TO SEE EVERYTHING AROUND YOU. THERE'S NO WAY YOU CAN'T SEE YOUR TEAMMATES TOO!
UP!
TA-TAM
TMP
WHOA, HE'S CONCEN-TRATING HARD!
...
NICE SERVE, CAPTAIN!
BOM
LOOK.
WHERE ARE THE BLOCKERS?
WHERE IS THE BALL?
WHERE IS HINATA?
WATCH CLOSER.
WHERE WILL HE MOVE TO?
WHERE WILL HE JUMP?
HOW HIGH IS THE HIGHEST POINT OF HIS JUMP?

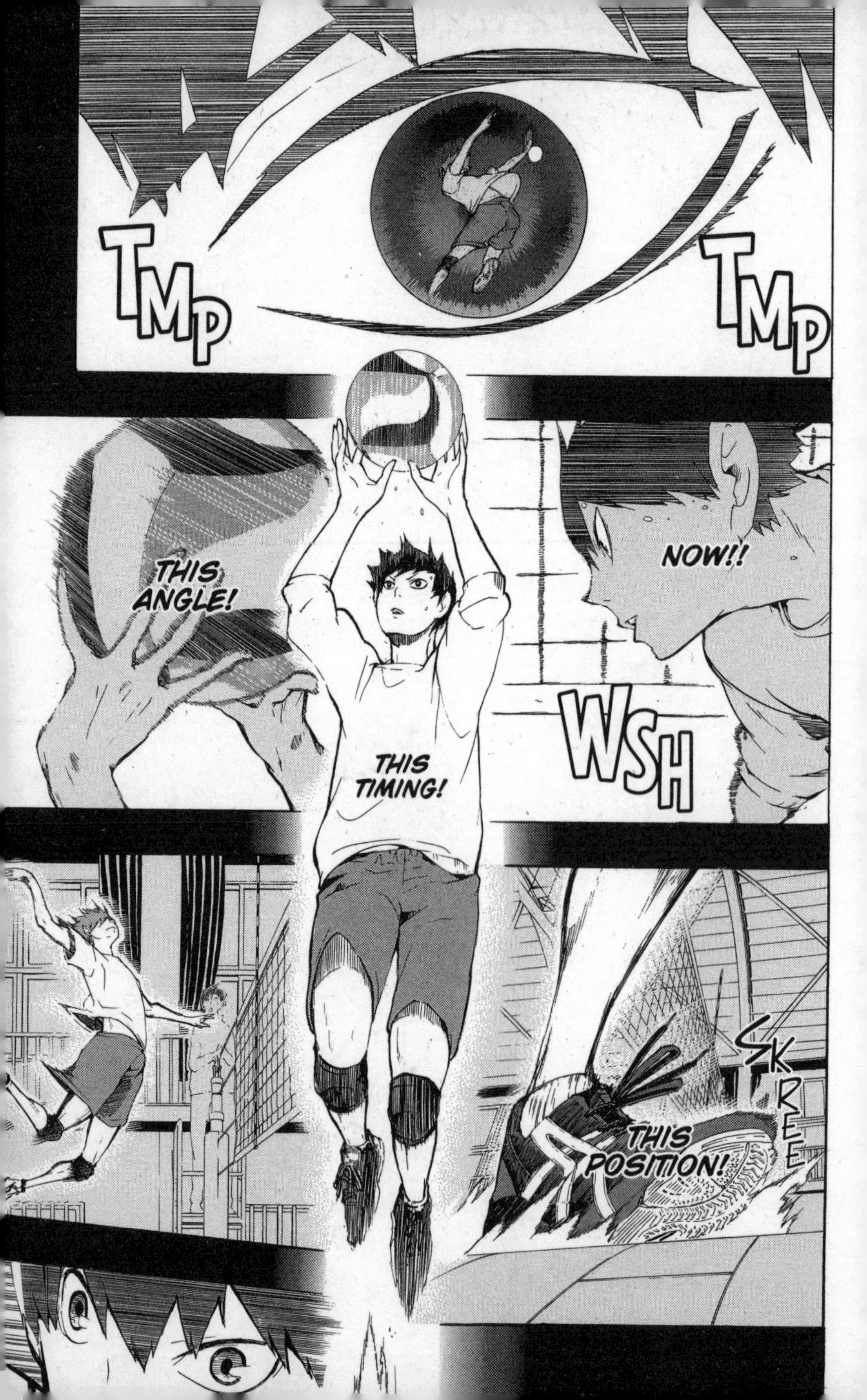
TMP
TMP
NOW!!
WSH
THIS ANGLE!
THIS TIMING!
SKREE
THIS POSITION!

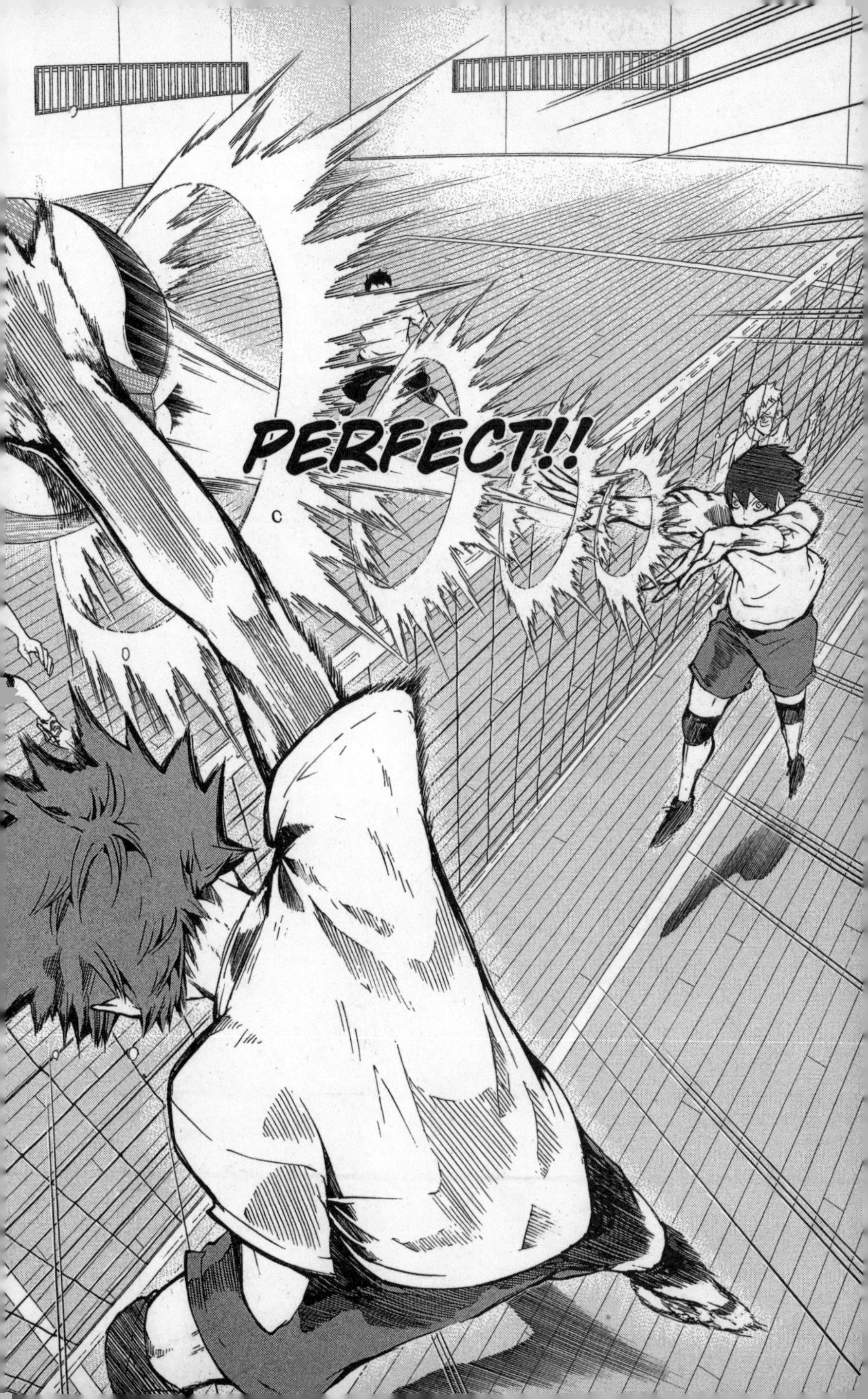
PERFECT!!

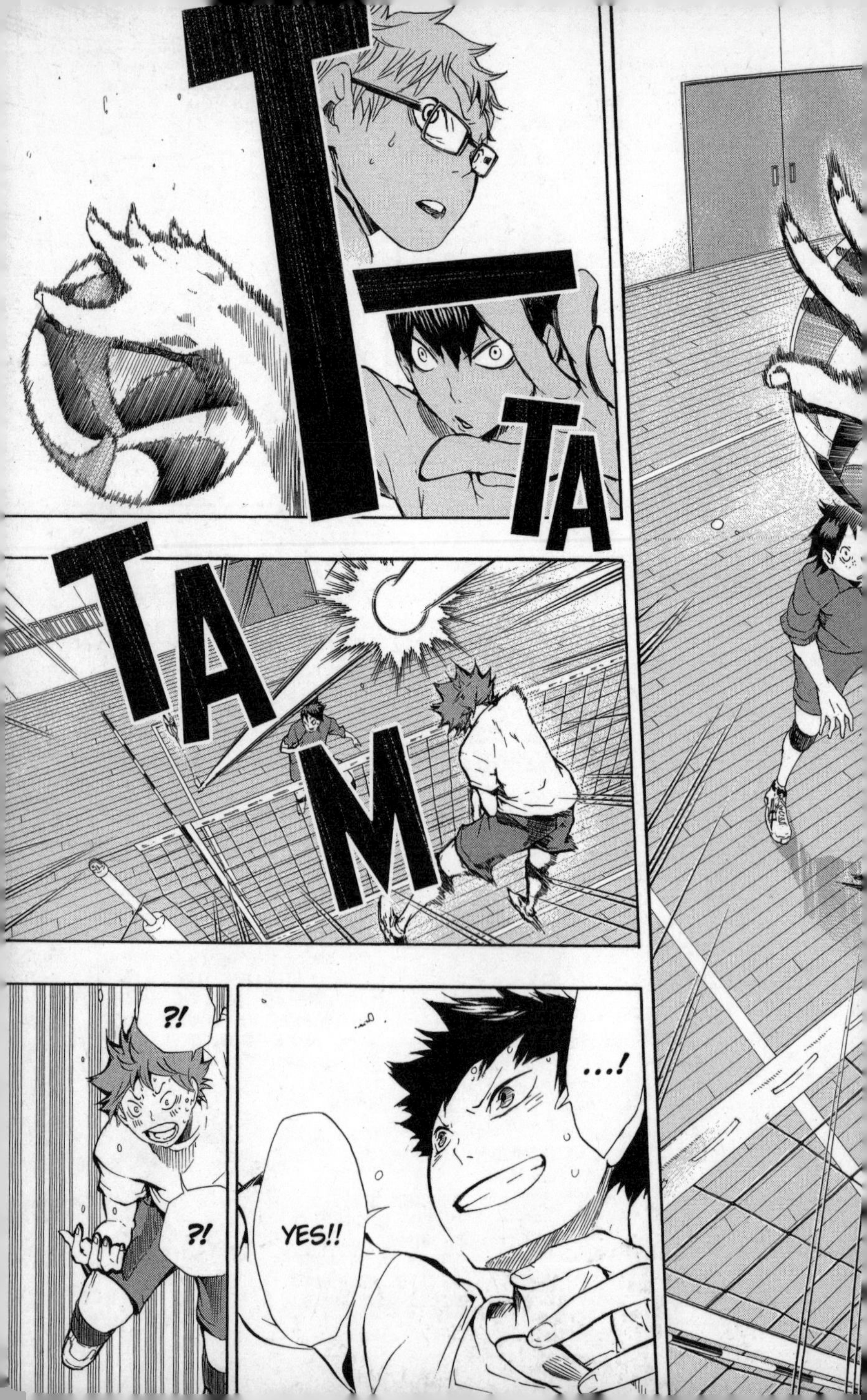
T
—
TA
TA
M
...!
YES!!
?!
?!

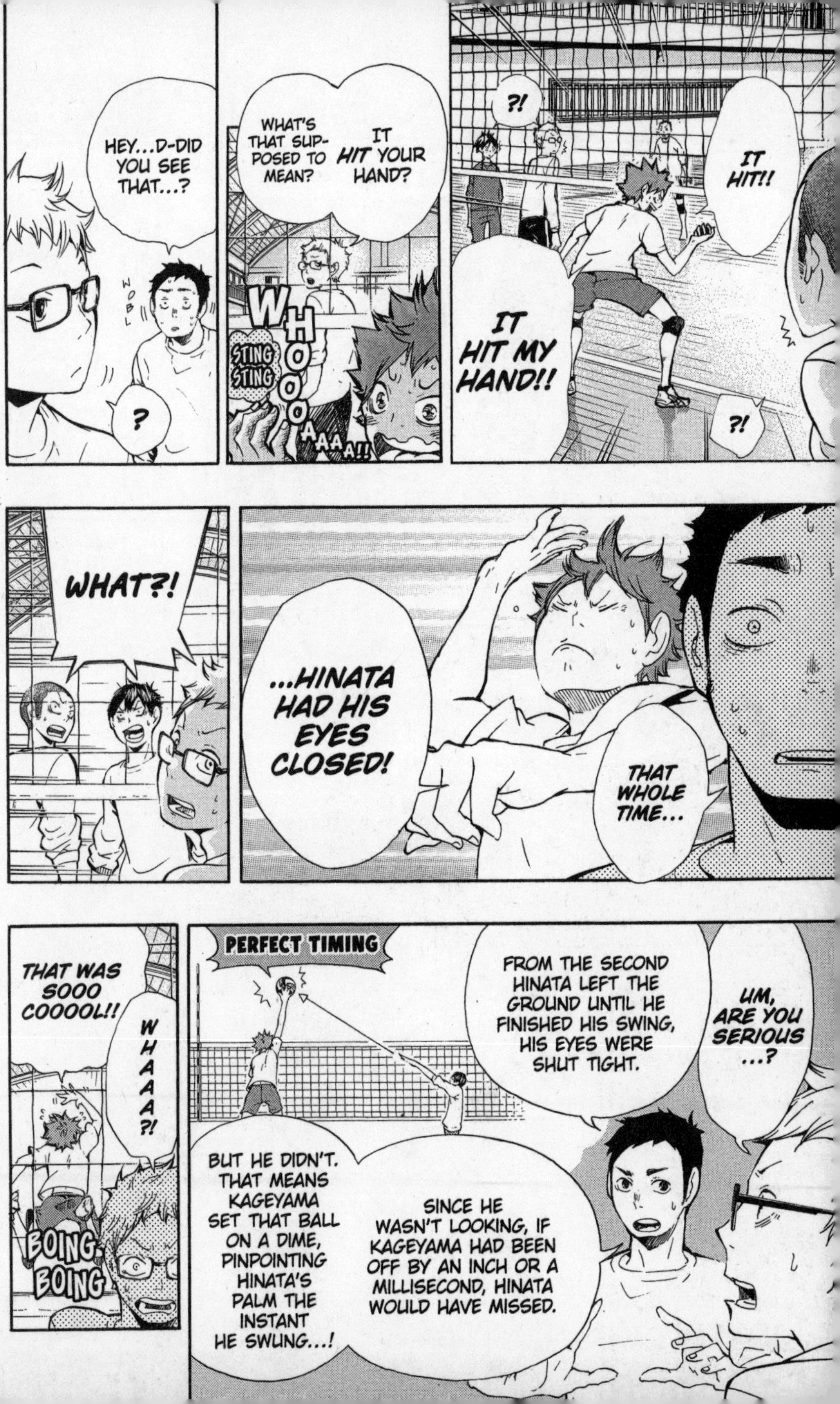
IT HIT!!
?!
IT HIT MY HAND!!
?!
IT HIT YOUR HAND?
WHAT'S THAT SUP-POSED TO MEAN?
WHOOOAAAA!!
STING STING
HEY...D-DID YOU SEE THAT...?
WOBL
?
THAT WHOLE TIME...
...HINATA HAD HIS EYES CLOSED!
WHAT?!
UM, ARE YOU SERIOUS...?
FROM THE SECOND HINATA LEFT THE GROUND UNTIL HE FINISHED HIS SWING, HIS EYES WERE SHUT TIGHT.
PERFECT TIMING
SINCE HE WASN'T LOOKING, IF KAGEYAMA HAD BEEN OFF BY AN INCH OR A MILLISECOND, HINATA WOULD HAVE MISSED.
BUT HE DIDN'T. THAT MEANS KAGEYAMA SET THAT BALL ON A DIME, PINPOINTING HINATA'S PALM THE INSTANT HE SWUNG...!
WHAAAA?!
THAT WAS SOOO COOOOL!!
BOING BOING

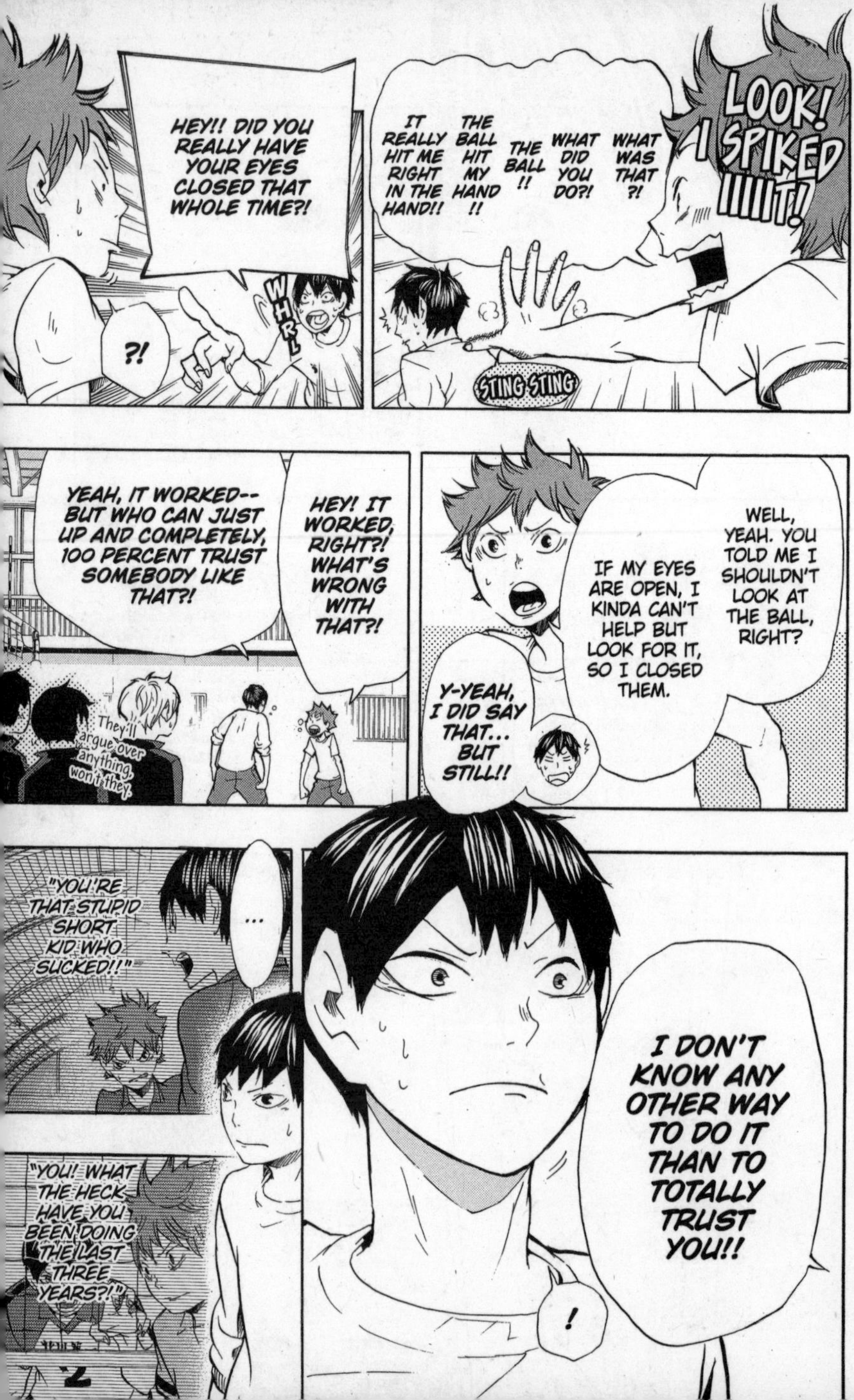
LOOK! I SPIKED IIIIIIT!!
WHAT WAS THAT?!
WHAT DID YOU DO?!
THE BALL!!
THE BALL HIT MY HAND!!
IT REALLY HIT ME RIGHT IN THE HAND!!
STING STING
HEY!! DID YOU REALLY HAVE YOUR EYES CLOSED THAT WHOLE TIME?!
WHRL
?!
WELL, YEAH. YOU TOLD ME I SHOULDN'T LOOK AT THE BALL, RIGHT?
IF MY EYES ARE OPEN, I KINDA CAN'T HELP BUT LOOK FOR IT, SO I CLOSED THEM.
Y-YEAH, I DID SAY THAT... BUT STILL!!
HEY! IT WORKED, RIGHT?! WHAT'S WRONG WITH THAT?!
YEAH, IT WORKED-- BUT WHO CAN JUST UP AND COMPLETELY, 100 PERCENT TRUST SOMEBODY LIKE THAT?!
They'll argue over anything, won't they.
I DON'T KNOW ANY OTHER WAY TO DO IT THAN TO TOTALLY TRUST YOU!!
!
...
"YOU'RE THAT STUPID SHORT KID WHO SUCKED!!"
"YOU! WHAT THE HECK HAVE YOU BEEN DOING THE LAST THREE YEARS?!"

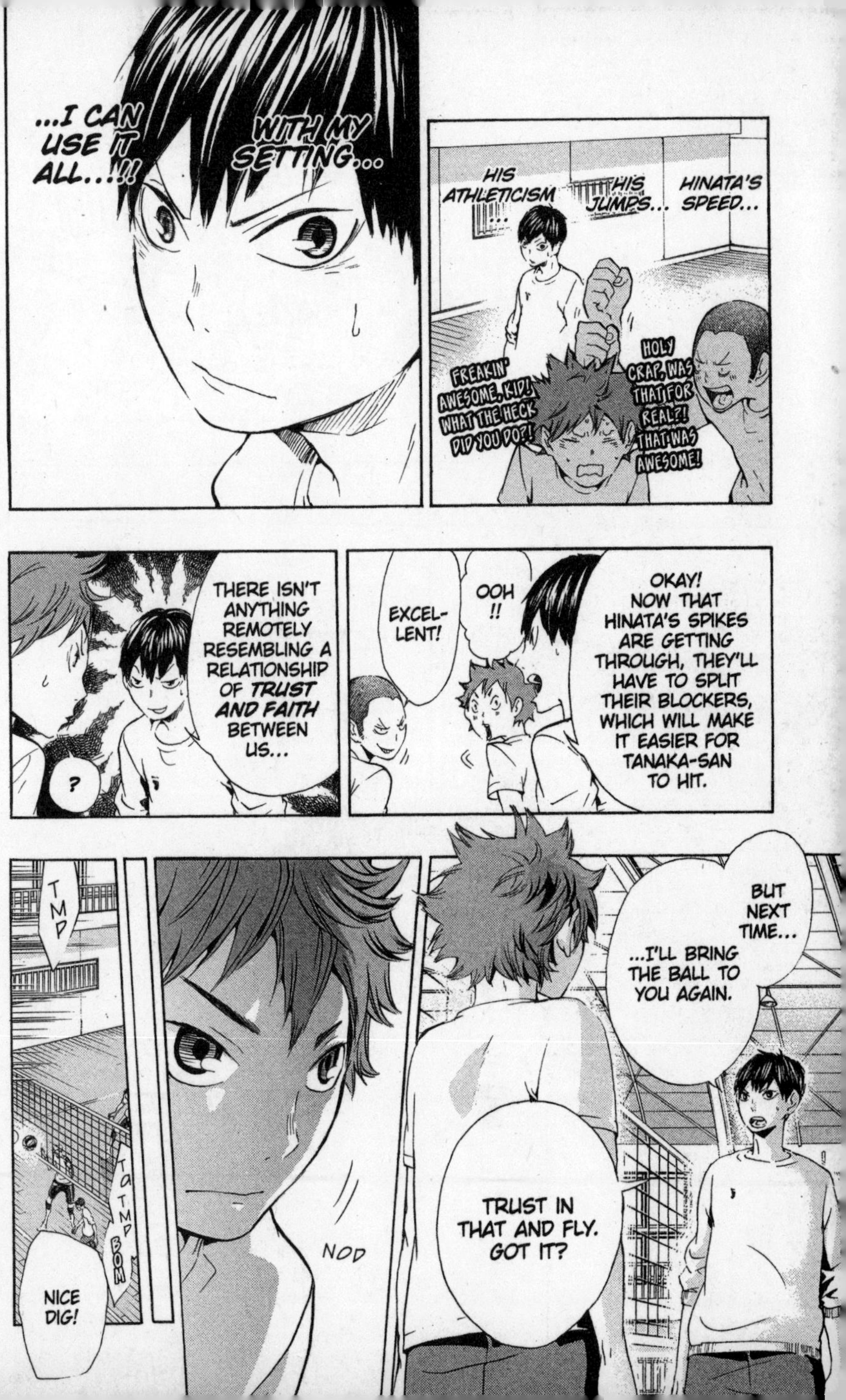
HINATA'S SPEED...
HIS JUMPS...
HIS ATHLETICISM...
HOLY CRAP, WAS THAT FOR REAL?! THAT WAS AWESOME!
FREAKIN' AWESOME, KID! WHAT THE HECK DID YOU DO?!
WITH MY SETTING...
...I CAN USE IT ALL...!!!
OKAY! NOW THAT HINATA'S SPIKES ARE GETTING THROUGH, THEY'LL HAVE TO SPLIT THEIR BLOCKERS, WHICH WILL MAKE IT EASIER FOR TANAKA-SAN TO HIT.
OOH !!
EXCEL-LENT!
THERE ISN'T ANYTHING REMOTELY RESEMBLING A RELATIONSHIP OF TRUST AND FAITH BETWEEN US...
?
BUT NEXT TIME...
...I'LL BRING THE BALL TO YOU AGAIN.
TRUST IN THAT AND FLY. GOT IT?
NOD
TMP
TATMP
BOM
NICE DIG!

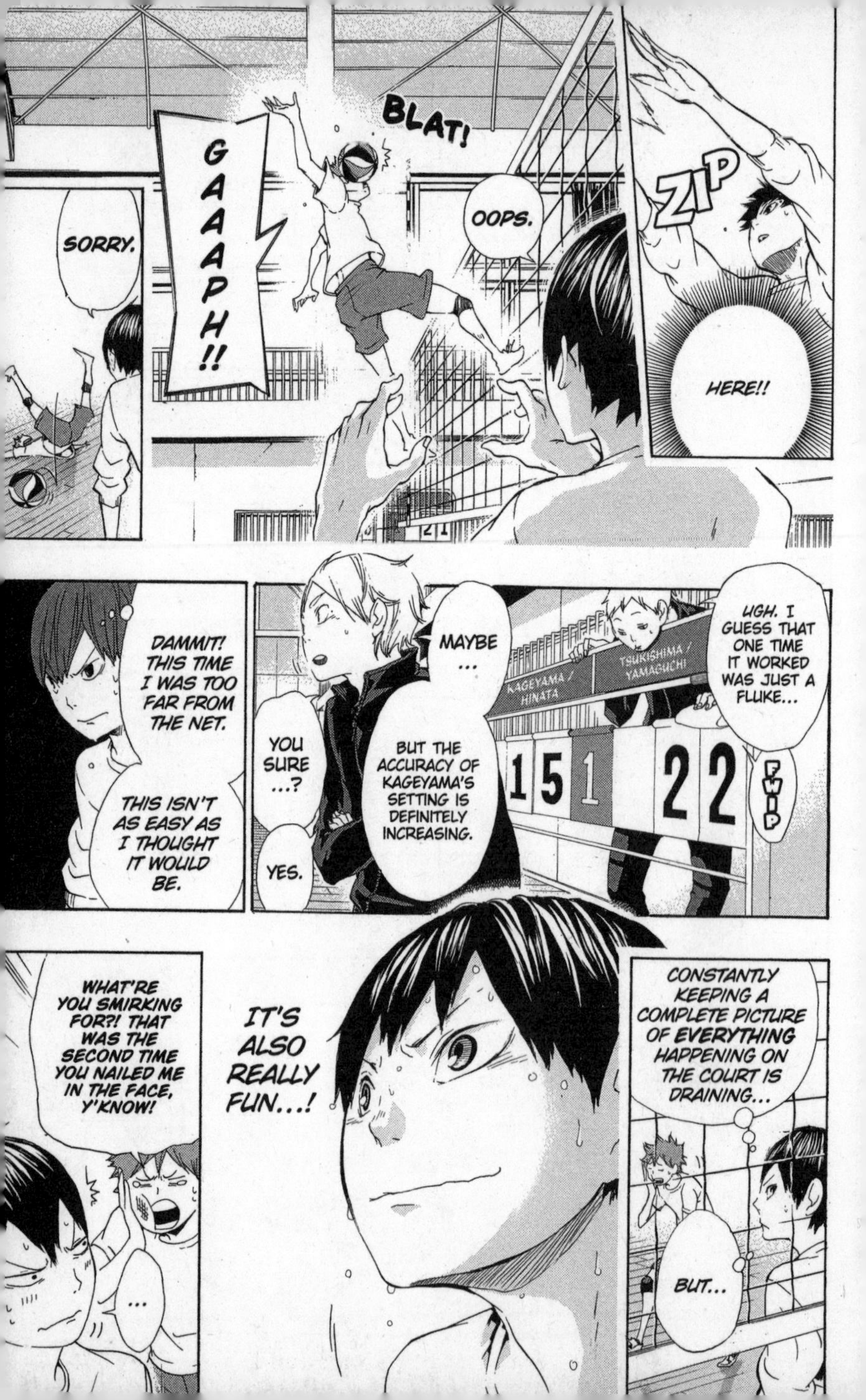
ZIP
HERE!!
BLAT!
OOPS.
GAAAAPH!!
SORRY.
UGH. I GUESS THAT ONE TIME IT WORKED WAS JUST A FLUKE...
TSUKISHIMA / YAMAGUCHI
KAGEYAMA / HINATA
FWIP
MAYBE...
BUT THE ACCURACY OF KAGEYAMA'S SETTING IS DEFINITELY INCREASING.
YOU SURE...?
YES.
DAMMIT! THIS TIME I WAS TOO FAR FROM THE NET.
THIS ISN'T AS EASY AS I THOUGHT IT WOULD BE.
CONSTANTLY KEEPING A COMPLETE PICTURE OF EVERYTHING HAPPENING ON THE COURT IS DRAINING...
BUT...
IT'S ALSO REALLY FUN...!
WHAT'RE YOU SMIRKING FOR?! THAT WAS THE SECOND TIME YOU NAILED ME IN THE FACE, Y'KNOW!
...

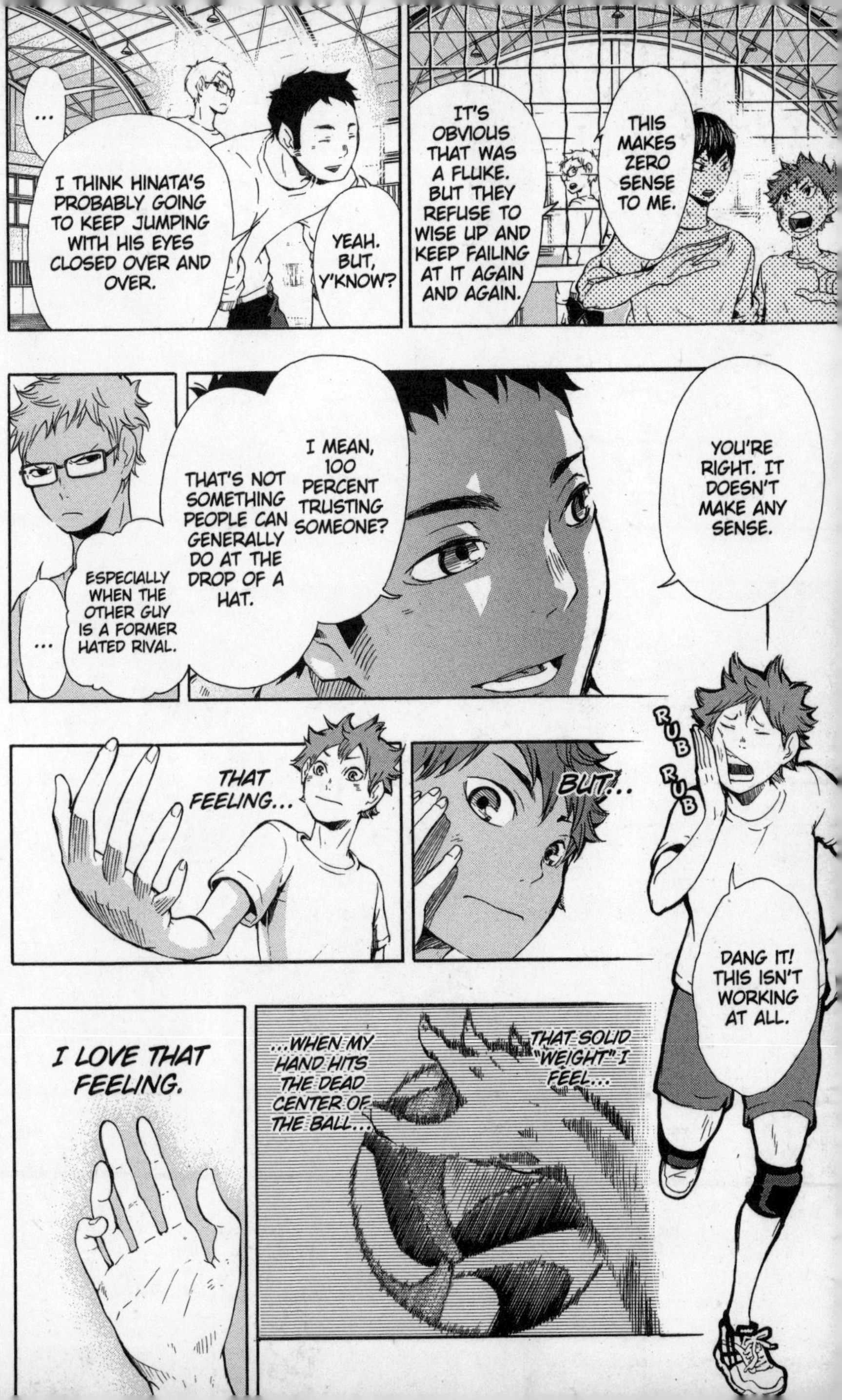
THIS MAKES ZERO SENSE TO ME.
IT'S OBVIOUS THAT WAS A FLUKE. BUT THEY REFUSE TO WISE UP AND KEEP FAILING AT IT AGAIN AND AGAIN.
...
I THINK HINATA'S PROBABLY GOING TO KEEP JUMPING WITH HIS EYES CLOSED OVER AND OVER.
YEAH. BUT, Y'KNOW?
YOU'RE RIGHT. IT DOESN'T MAKE ANY SENSE.
I MEAN, 100 PERCENT TRUSTING SOMEONE?
THAT'S NOT SOMETHING PEOPLE CAN GENERALLY DO AT THE DROP OF A HAT.
ESPECIALLY WHEN THE OTHER GUY IS A FORMER HATED RIVAL.
...
RUB RUB
DANG IT! THIS ISN'T WORKING AT ALL.
BUT...
THAT FEELING...
THAT SOLID "WEIGHT" I FEEL...
...WHEN MY HAND HITS THE DEAD CENTER OF THE BALL...
I LOVE THAT FEELING.

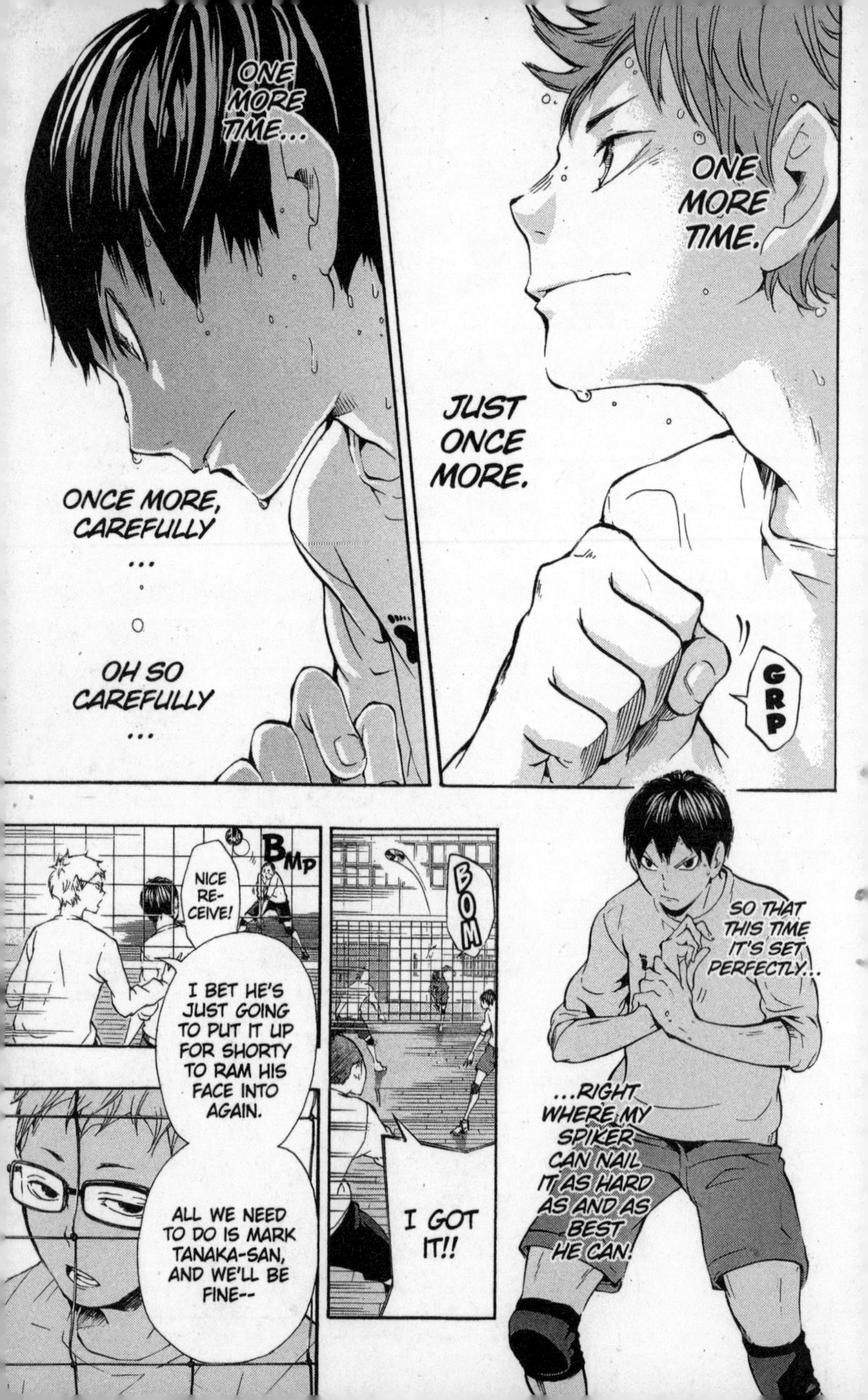
ONE MORE TIME.
JUST ONCE MORE.
GRP
ONE MORE TIME...
ONCE MORE, CAREFULLY ...
OH SO CAREFULLY ...
SO THAT THIS TIME IT'S SET PERFECTLY...
...RIGHT WHERE MY SPIKER CAN NAIL IT AS HARD AS AND AS BEST HE CAN!
BOM
I GOT IT!!
BMP
NICE RE-CEIVE!
I BET HE'S JUST GOING TO PUT IT UP FOR SHORTY TO RAM HIS FACE INTO AGAIN.
ALL WE NEED TO DO IS MARK TANAKA-SAN, AND WE'LL BE FINE--

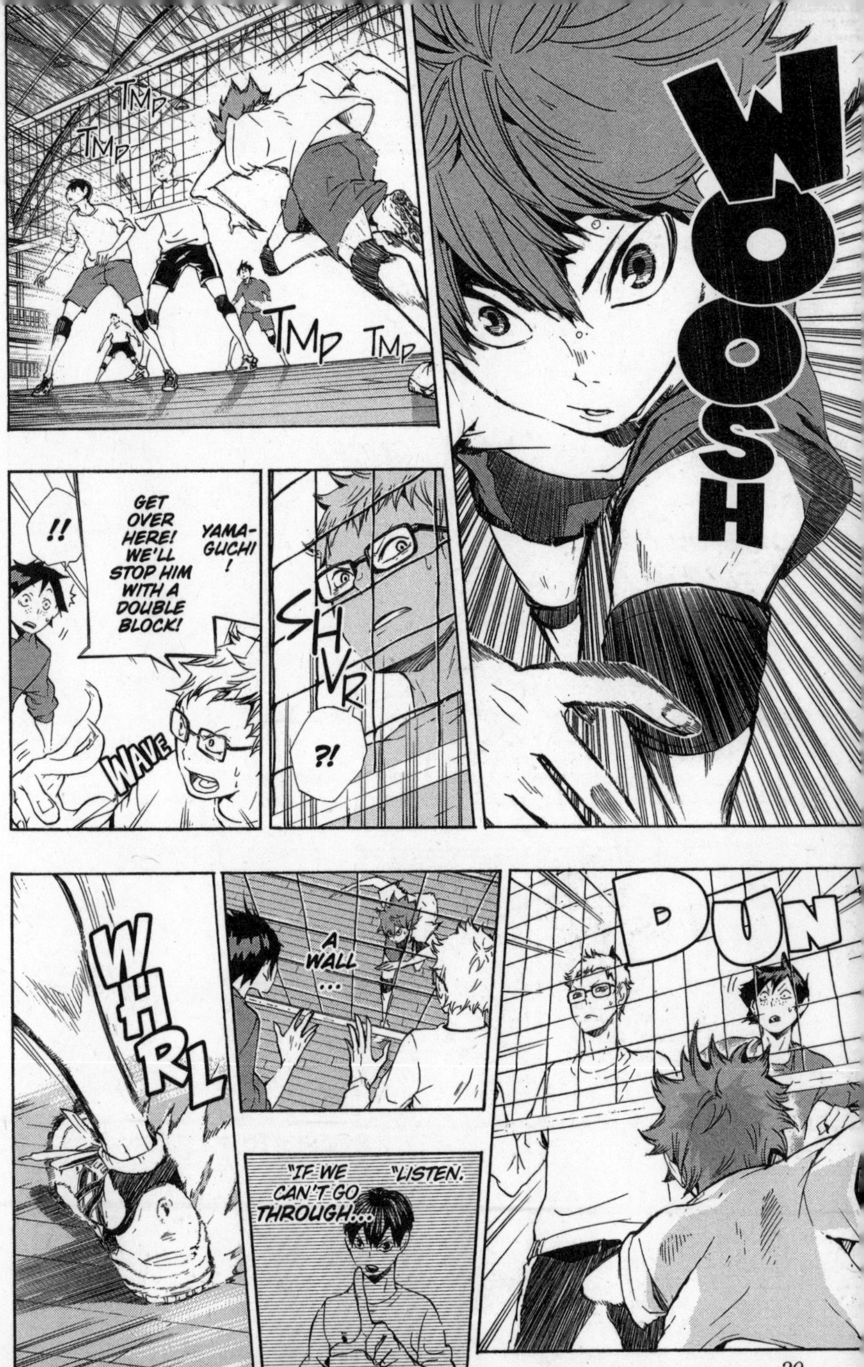
WOOSH
TMP TMP
TMP TMP
SHVR
?!
YAMA-GUCHI!
GET OVER HERE! WE'LL STOP HIM WITH A DOUBLE BLOCK!
!!
WAVE
DUN
A WALL...
"LISTEN.
"IF WE CAN'T GO THROUGH...
WHRL

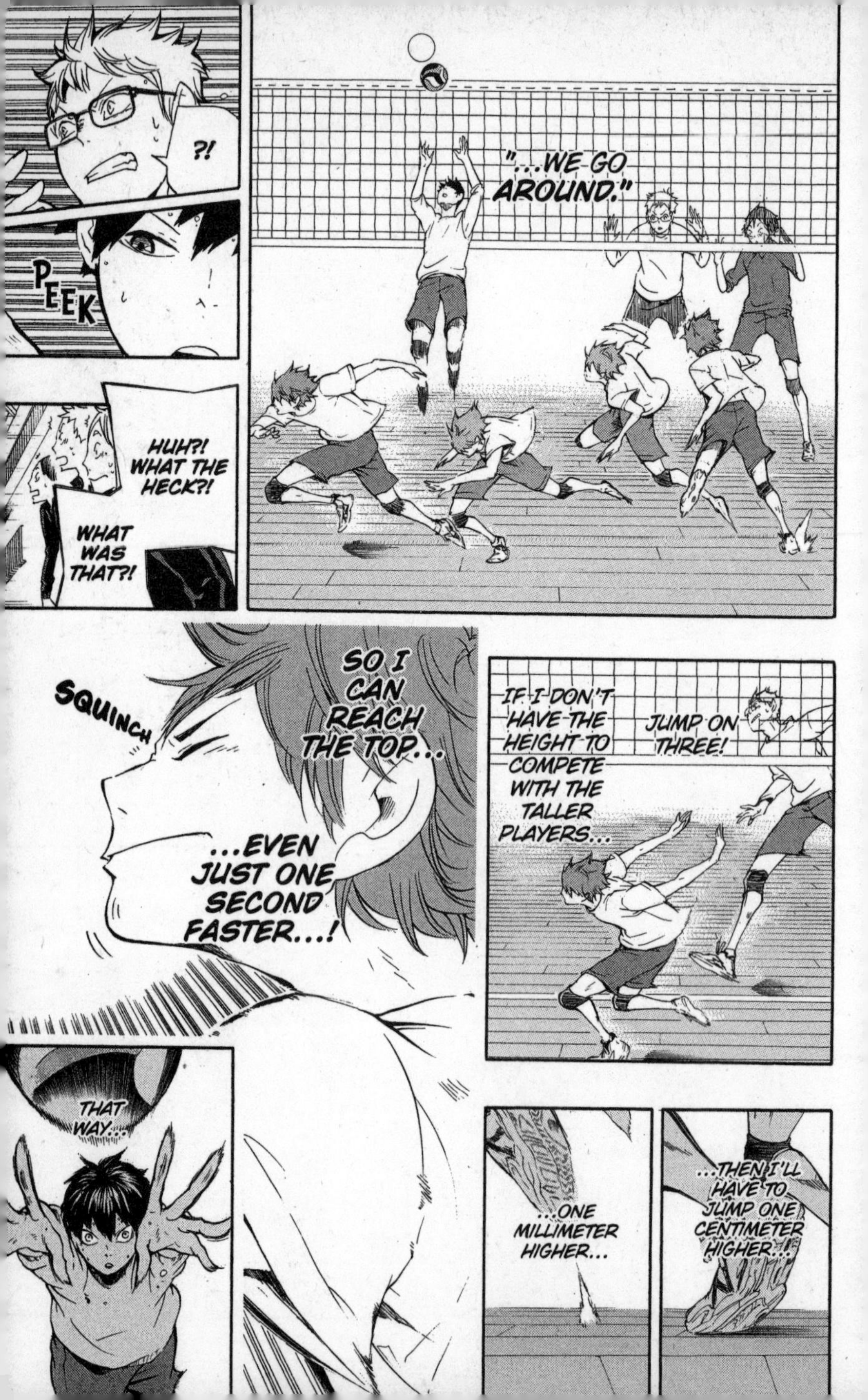
"...WE GO AROUND."
?!
PEEK
HUH?! WHAT THE HECK?!
WHAT WAS THAT?!
IF I DON'T HAVE THE HEIGHT TO COMPETE WITH THE TALLER PLAYERS...
JUMP ON THREE!
...THEN I'LL HAVE TO JUMP ONE CENTIMETER HIGHER...
...ONE MILLIMETER HIGHER...
SO I CAN REACH THE TOP...
SQUINCH
...EVEN JUST ONE SECOND FASTER...!
THAT WAY...

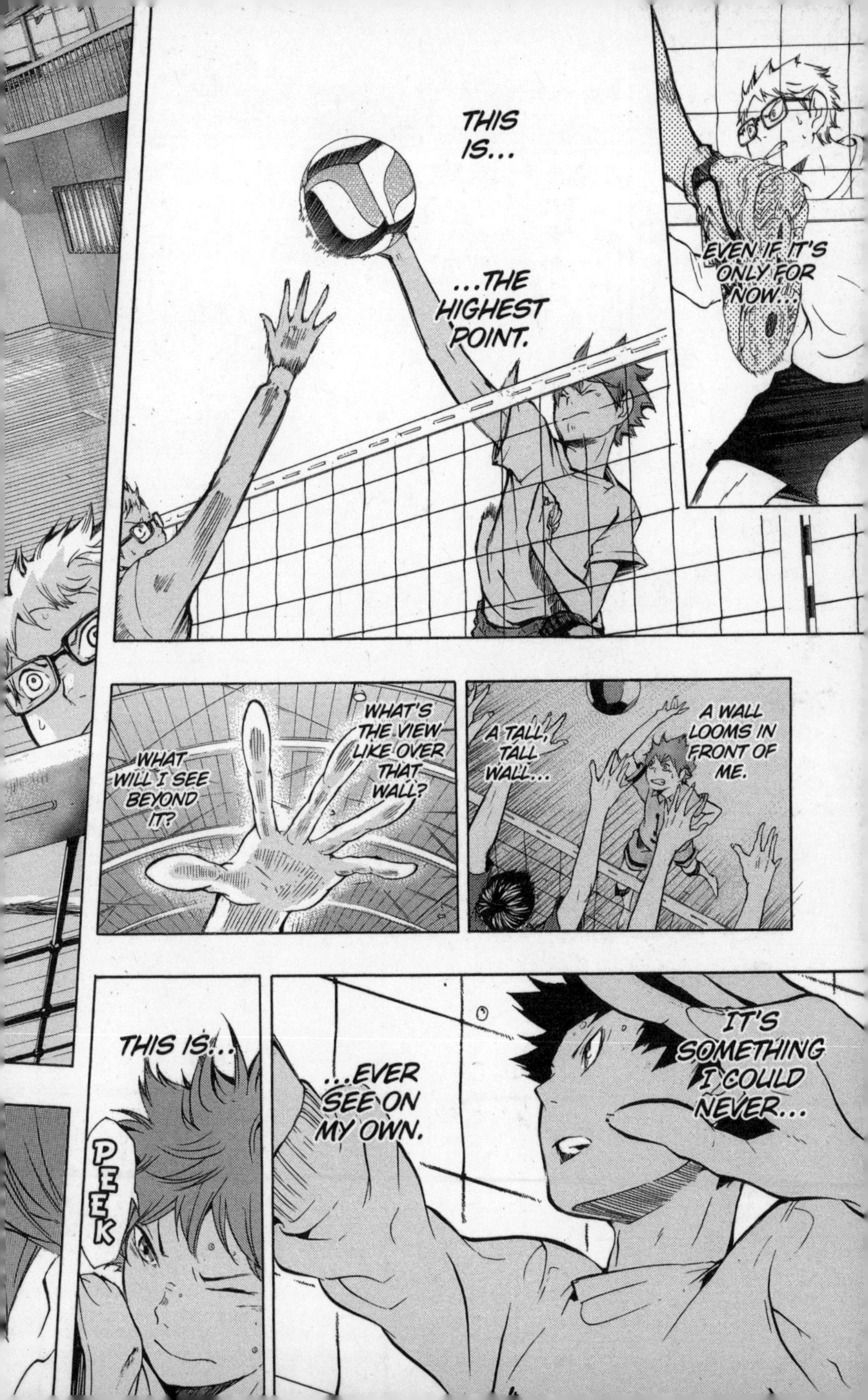
EVEN IF IT'S ONLY FOR NOW...
THIS IS...
...THE HIGHEST POINT.
A WALL LOOMS IN FRONT OF ME.
A TALL, TALL WALL...
WHAT'S THE VIEW LIKE OVER THAT WALL?
WHAT WILL I SEE BEYOND IT?
IT'S SOMETHING I COULD NEVER...
...EVER SEE ON MY OWN.
THIS IS...
PEEK

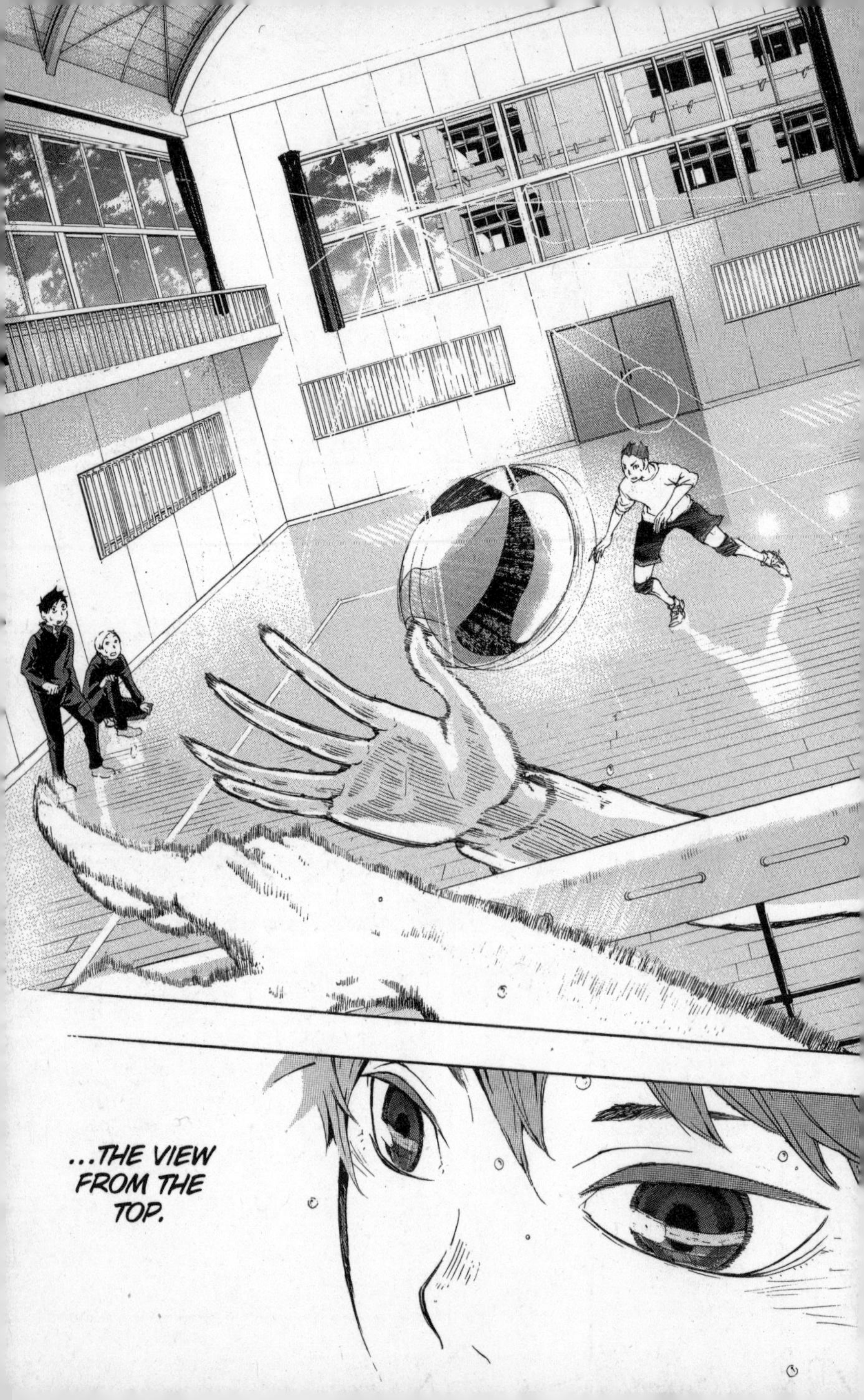
...THE VIEW FROM THE TOP.

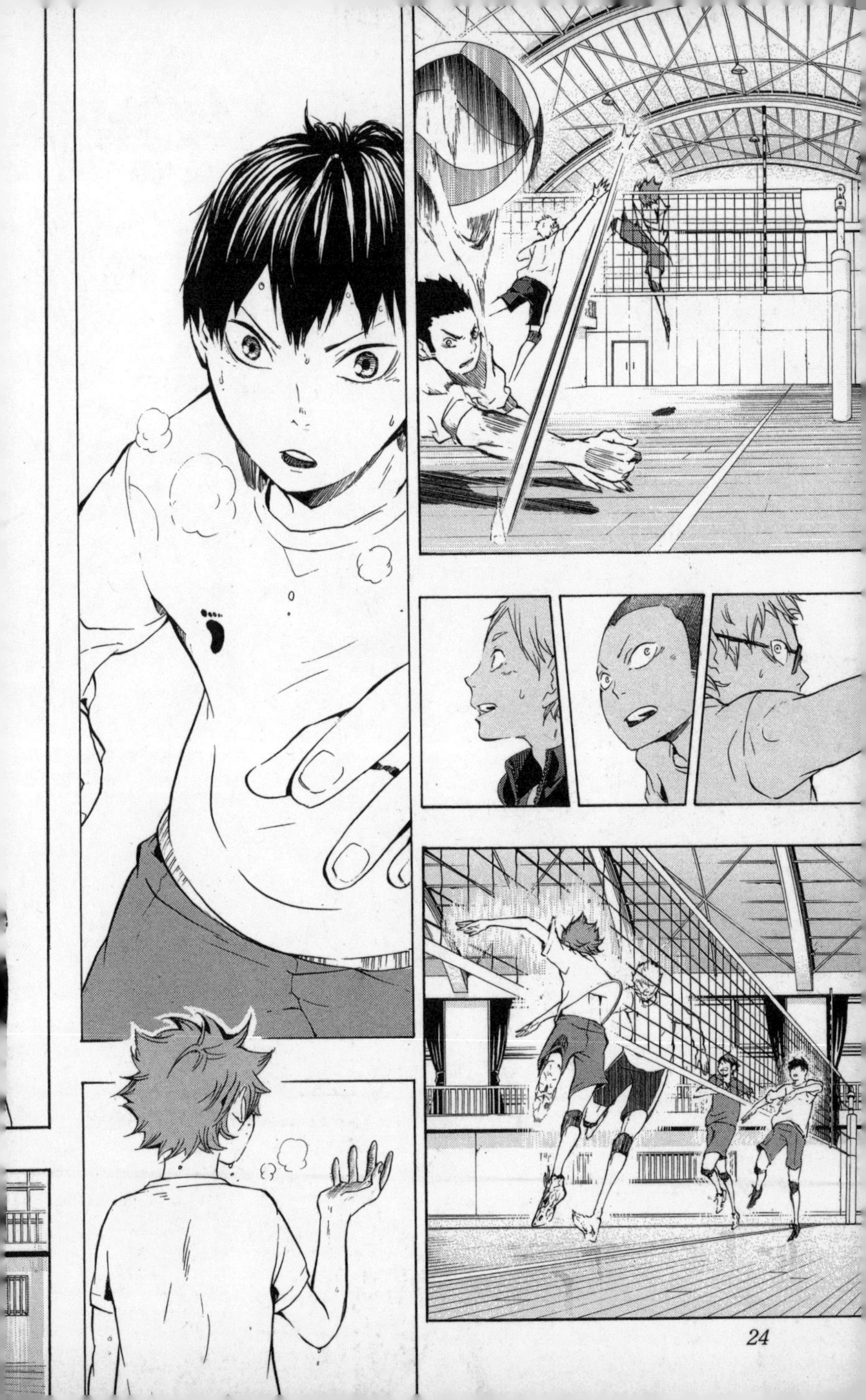

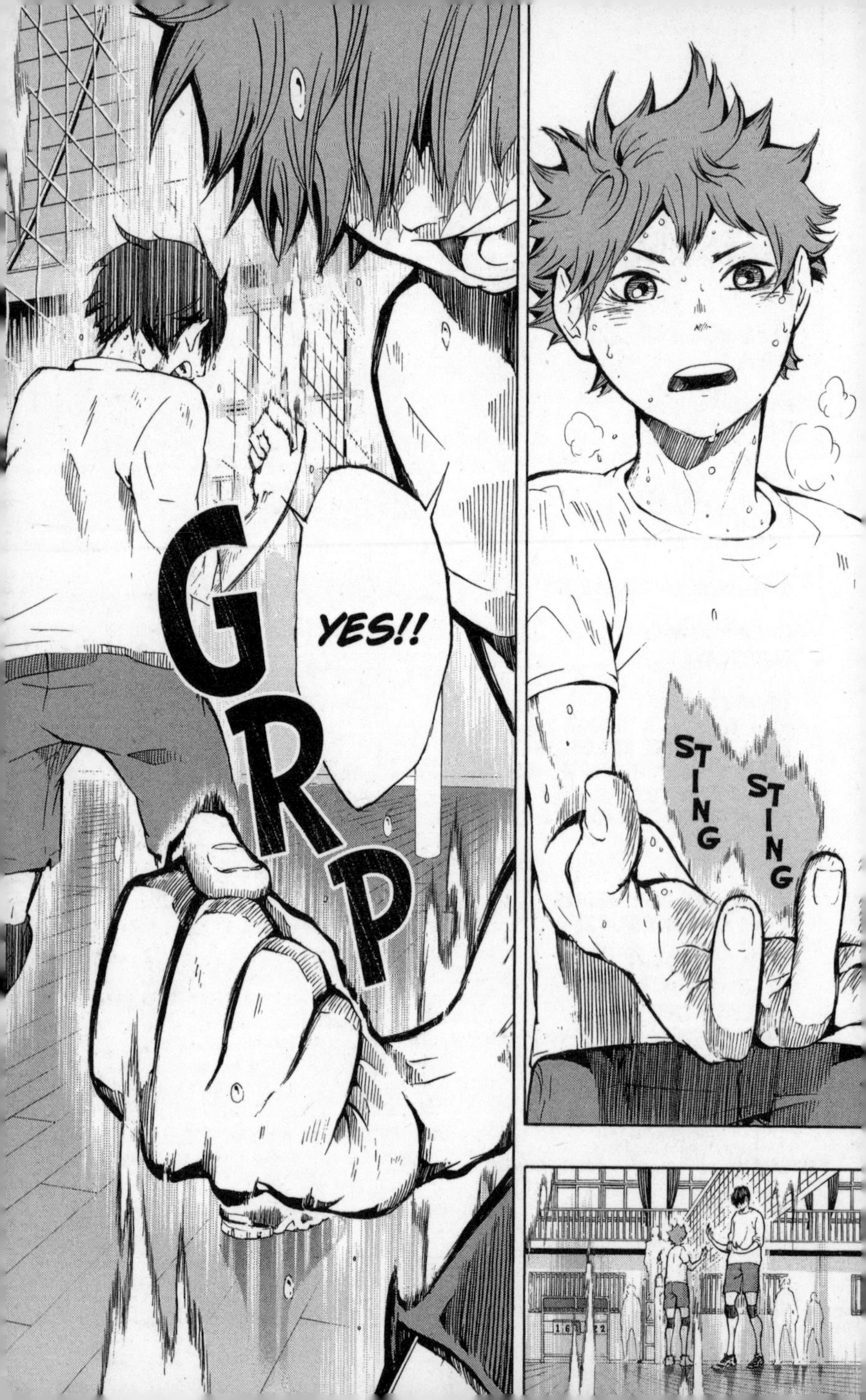
STING
STING
16 22
YES!!
GRP

KEI TSUKISHIMA

KARASUNO HIGH SCHOOL
CLASS 1-4

POSITION:
MIDDLE BLOCKER

HEIGHT: 6'2"
WEIGHT: 151 LBS.
(AS OF APRIL, 1ST YEAR
OF HIGH SCHOOL)

BIRTHDAY: SEPTEMBER 27

FAVORITE FOOD:
SHORTCAKE

CURRENT WORRY:
NOW THAT HE'S IN HIGH SCHOOL, PEOPLE ARE GOING TO START PESTERING HIM AGAIN ABOUT HOW TO READ THE KANJI CHARACTER FOR HIS FIRST NAME.

ABILITY PARAMETERS
(5-POINT SCALE)

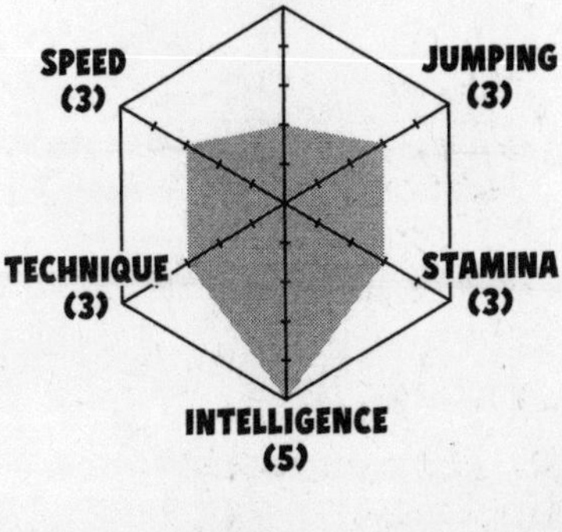
POWER
(2)
JUMPING
(3)
STAMINA
(3)
INTELLIGENCE
(5)
TECHNIQUE
(3)
SPEED
(3)

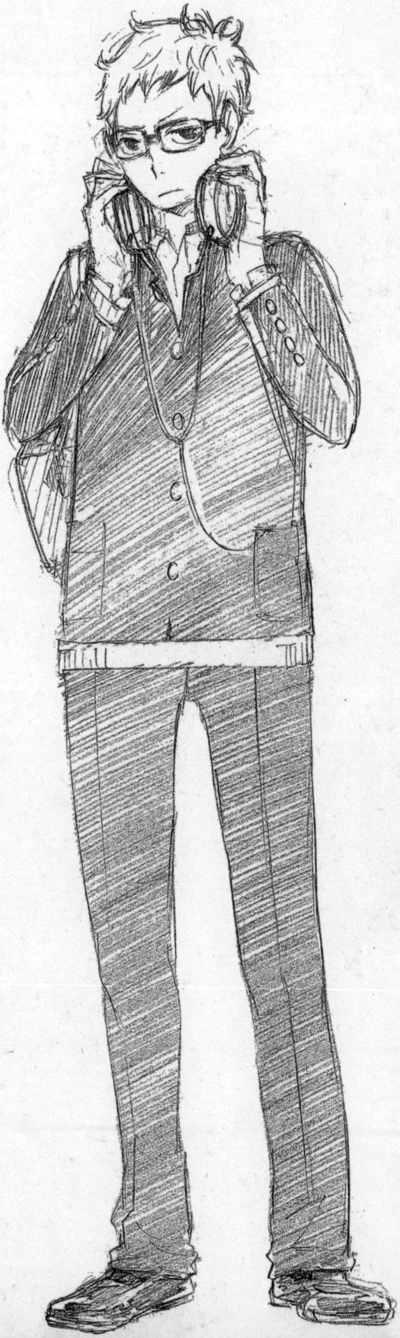

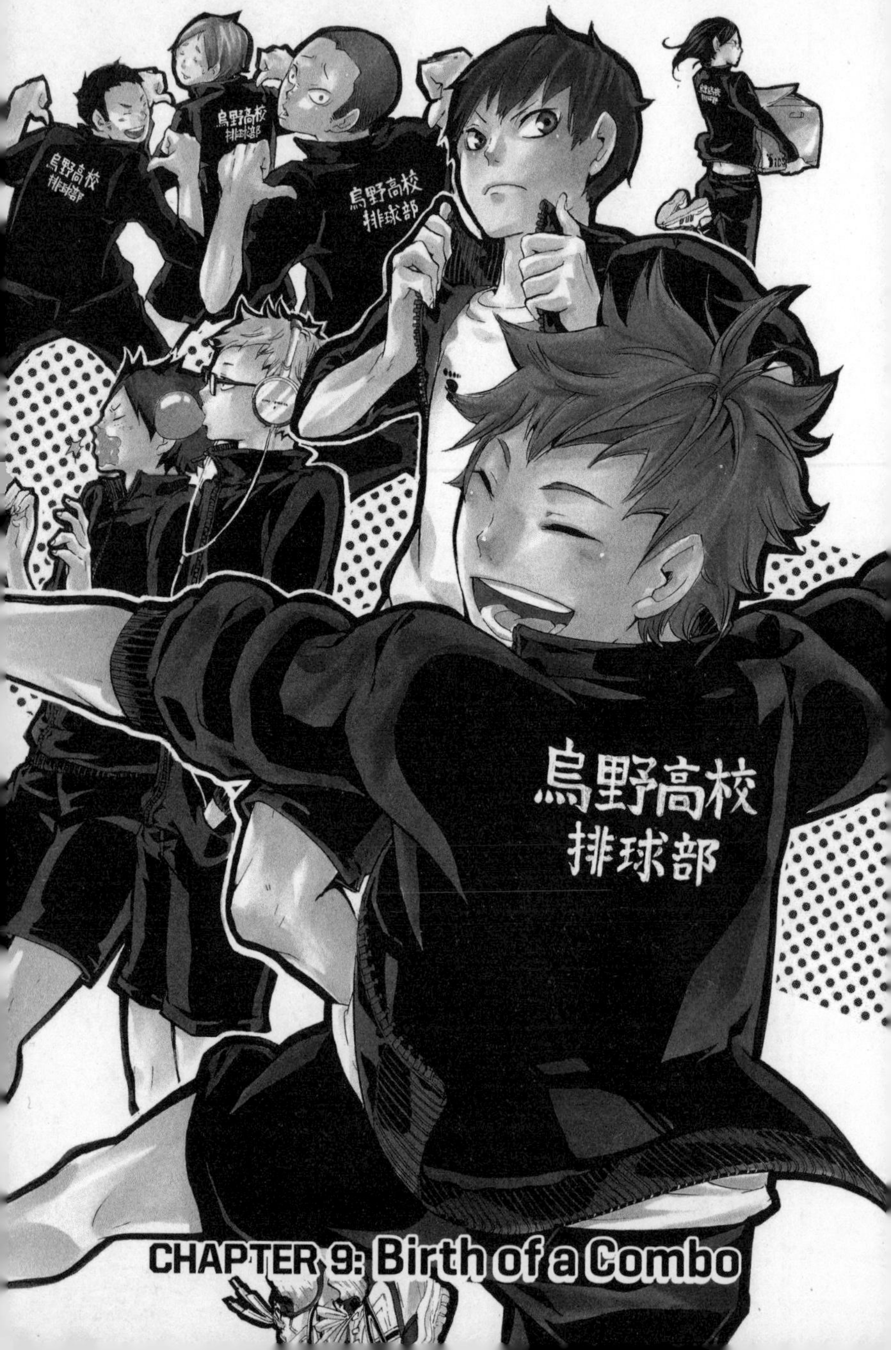
烏野高校
排球部
烏野高校
排球部
烏野高校
排球部
烏野高校
排球部

CHAPTER 9: Birth of a Combo

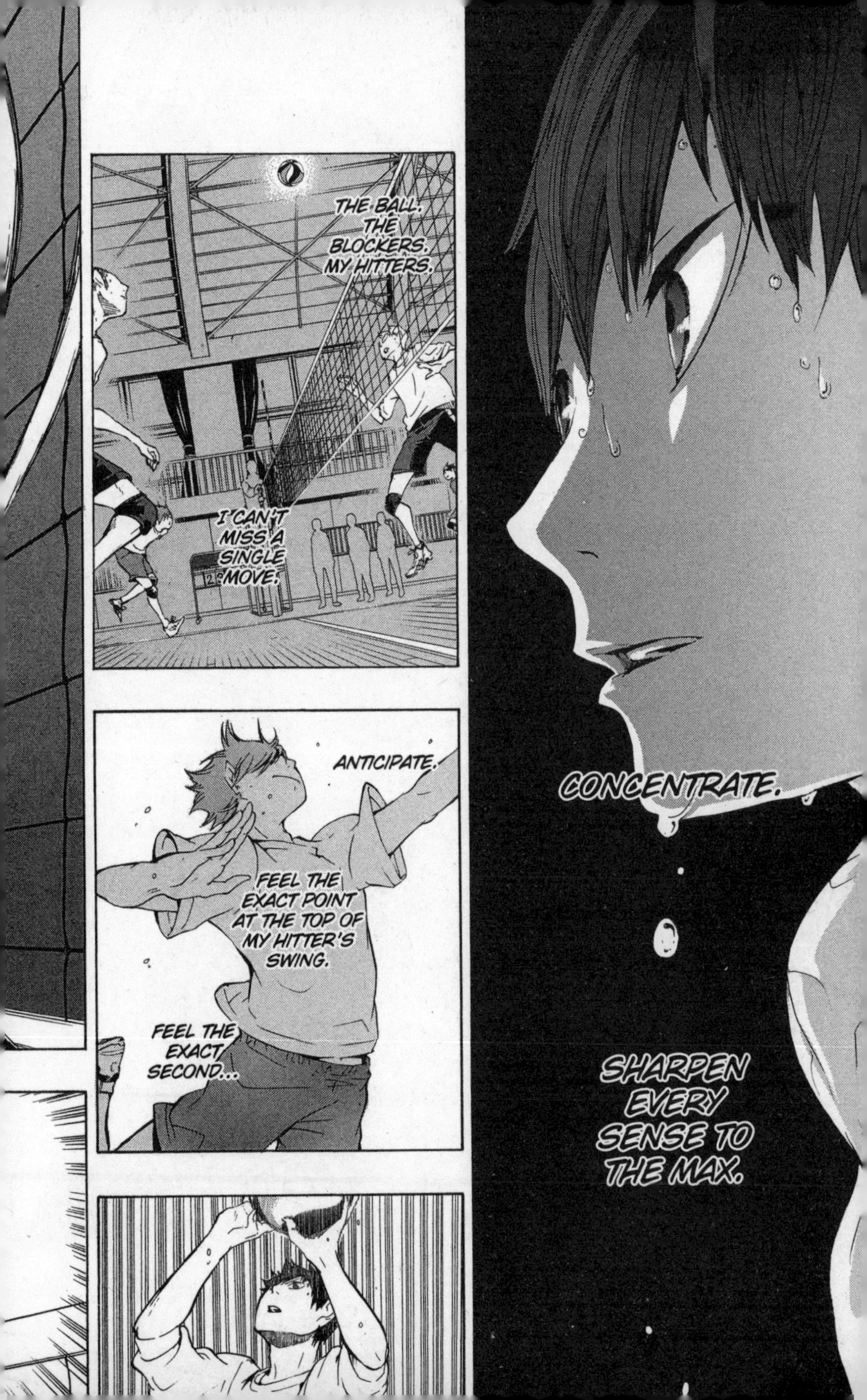
CONCENTRATE.
SHARPEN EVERY SENSE TO THE MAX.
THE BALL. THE BLOCKERS. MY HITTERS.
I CAN'T MISS A SINGLE MOVE.
ANTICIPATE.
FEEL THE EXACT POINT AT THE TOP OF MY HITTER'S SWING.
FEEL THE EXACT SECOND...

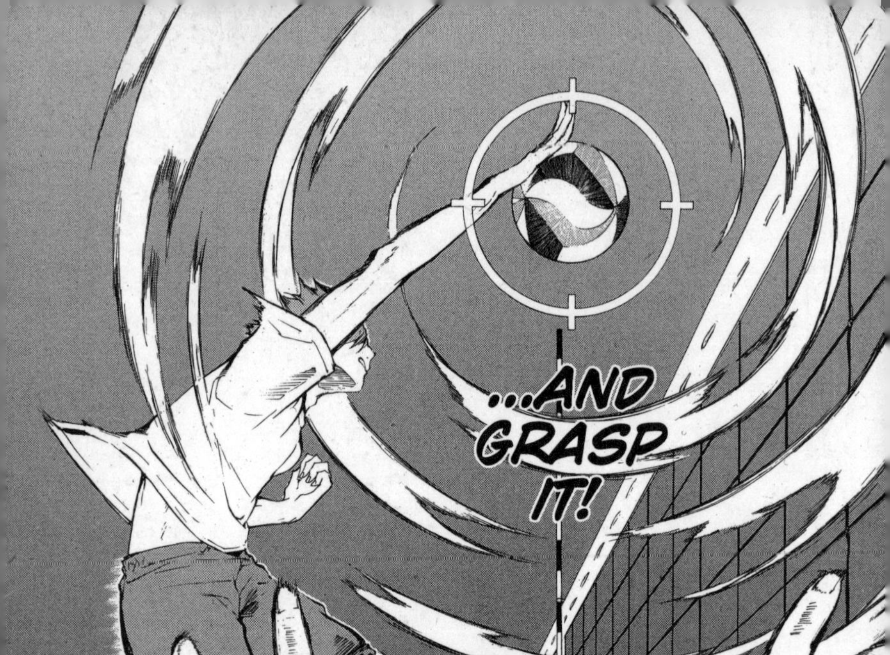
...AND GRASP IT!
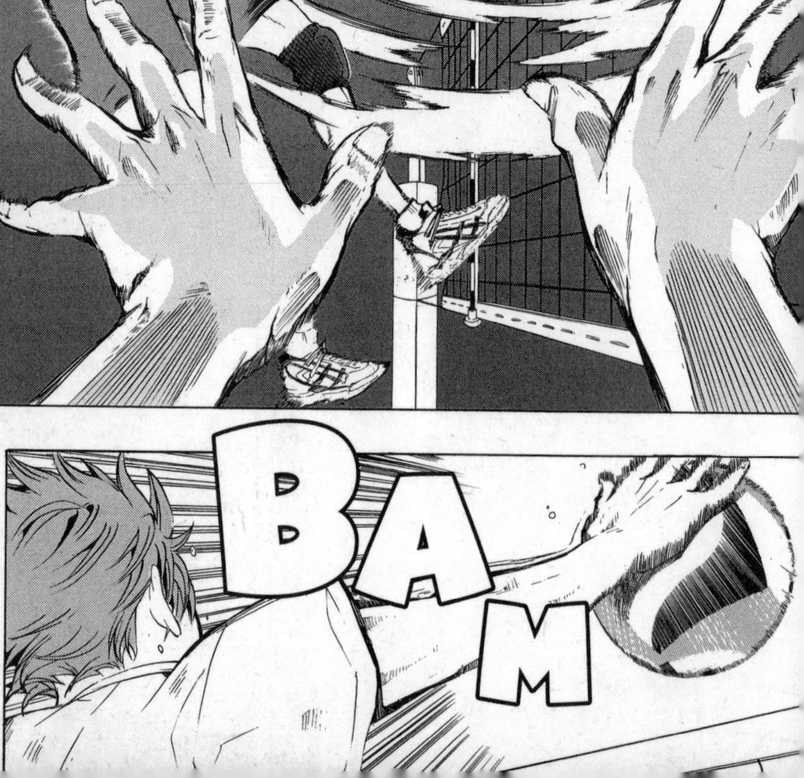
BAM

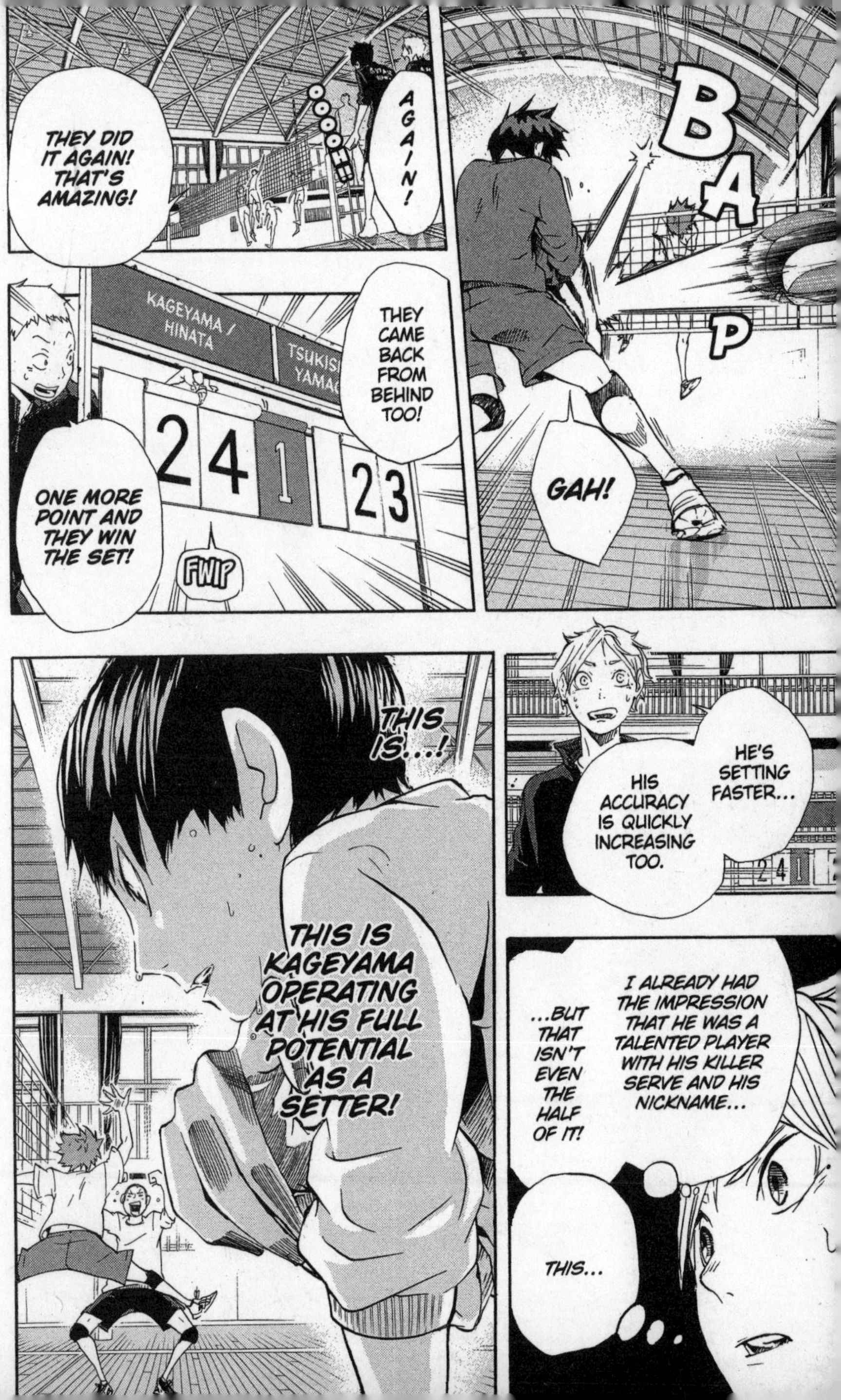
BA
P
GAH!
AGAIN!
OOOOOH!!
THEY DID IT AGAIN! THAT'S AMAZING!
THEY CAME BACK FROM BEHIND TOO!
KAGEYAMA / HINATA
24 1 23
ONE MORE POINT AND THEY WIN THE SET!
FWIP
HE'S SETTING FASTER...
HIS ACCURACY IS QUICKLY INCREASING TOO.
I ALREADY HAD THE IMPRESSION THAT HE WAS A TALENTED PLAYER WITH HIS KILLER SERVE AND HIS NICKNAME...
...BUT THAT ISN'T EVEN THE HALF OF IT!
THIS...
THIS IS...!
THIS IS KAGEYAMA OPERATING AT HIS FULL POTENTIAL AS A SETTER!

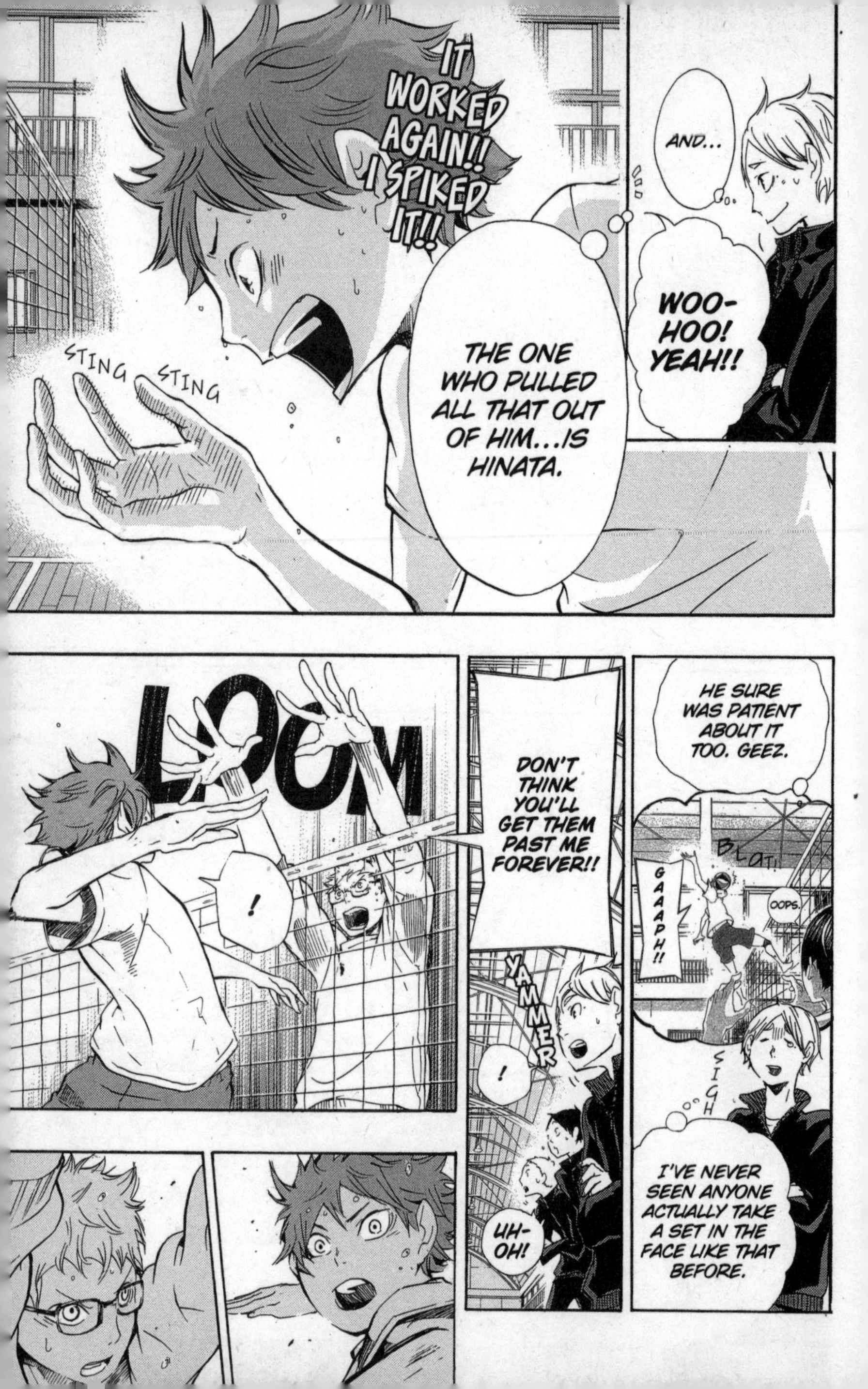
AND...
WOO-HOO! YEAH!!
IT WORKED AGAIN!! I SPIKED IT!!
THE ONE WHO PULLED ALL THAT OUT OF HIM...IS HINATA.
STING STING
HE SURE WAS PATIENT ABOUT IT TOO. GEEZ.
BLAT
GAAAAPH!!
OOPS.
SIGH
I'VE NEVER SEEN ANYONE ACTUALLY TAKE A SET IN THE FACE LIKE THAT BEFORE.
DON'T THINK YOU'LL GET THEM PAST ME FOREVER!!
YAMMER
!
UH-OH!
LOOM
!

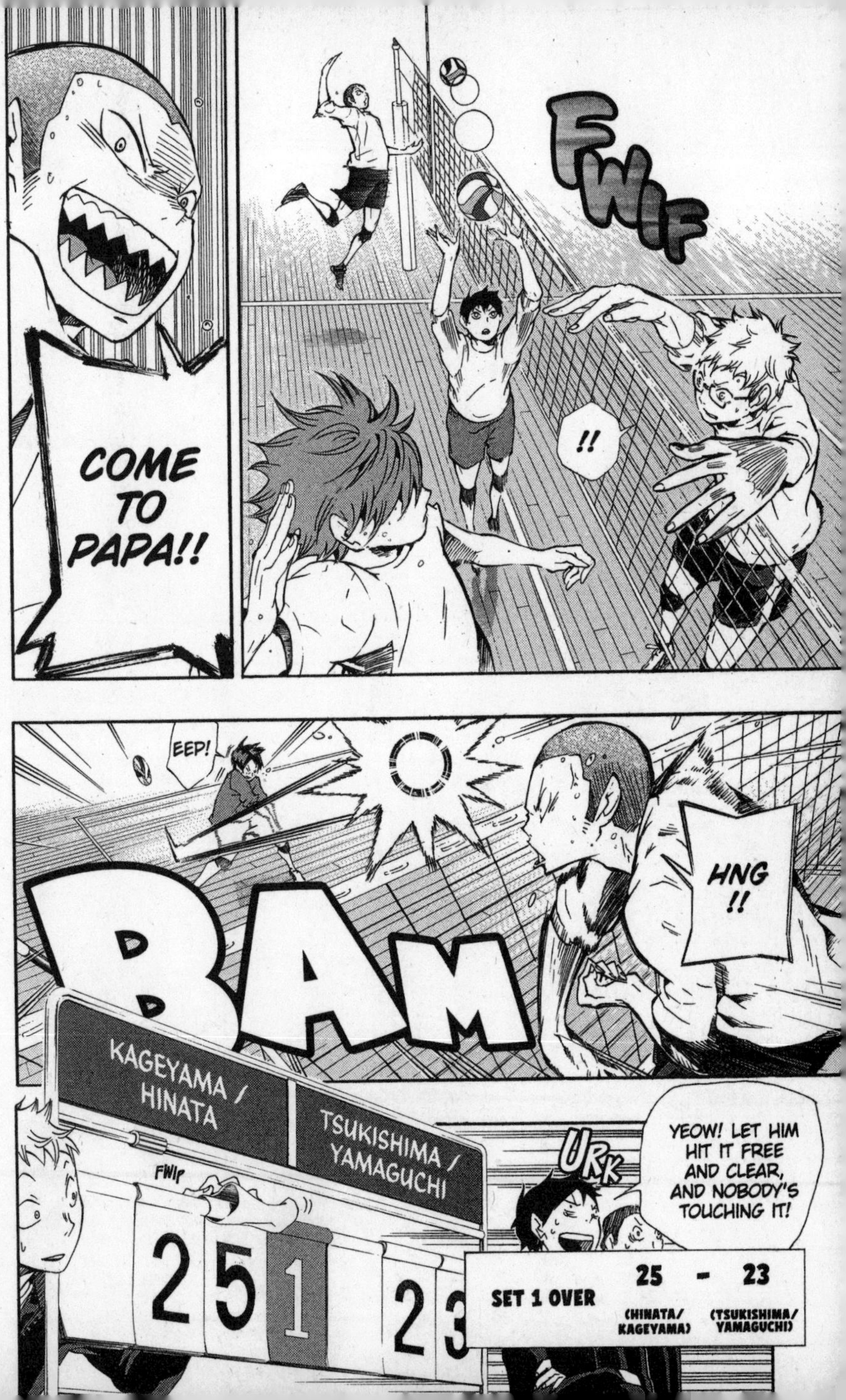
FWIF
!!
COME TO PAPA!!
HNG !!
BAM
EEP!
YEOW! LET HIM HIT IT FREE AND CLEAR, AND NOBODY'S TOUCHING IT!
URK
KAGEYAMA / HINATA
TSUKISHIMA / YAMAGUCHI
FWIP
25 1 23
SET 1 OVER 25 - 23 (HINATA/ KAGEYAMA) (TSUKISHIMA/ YAMAGUCHI)

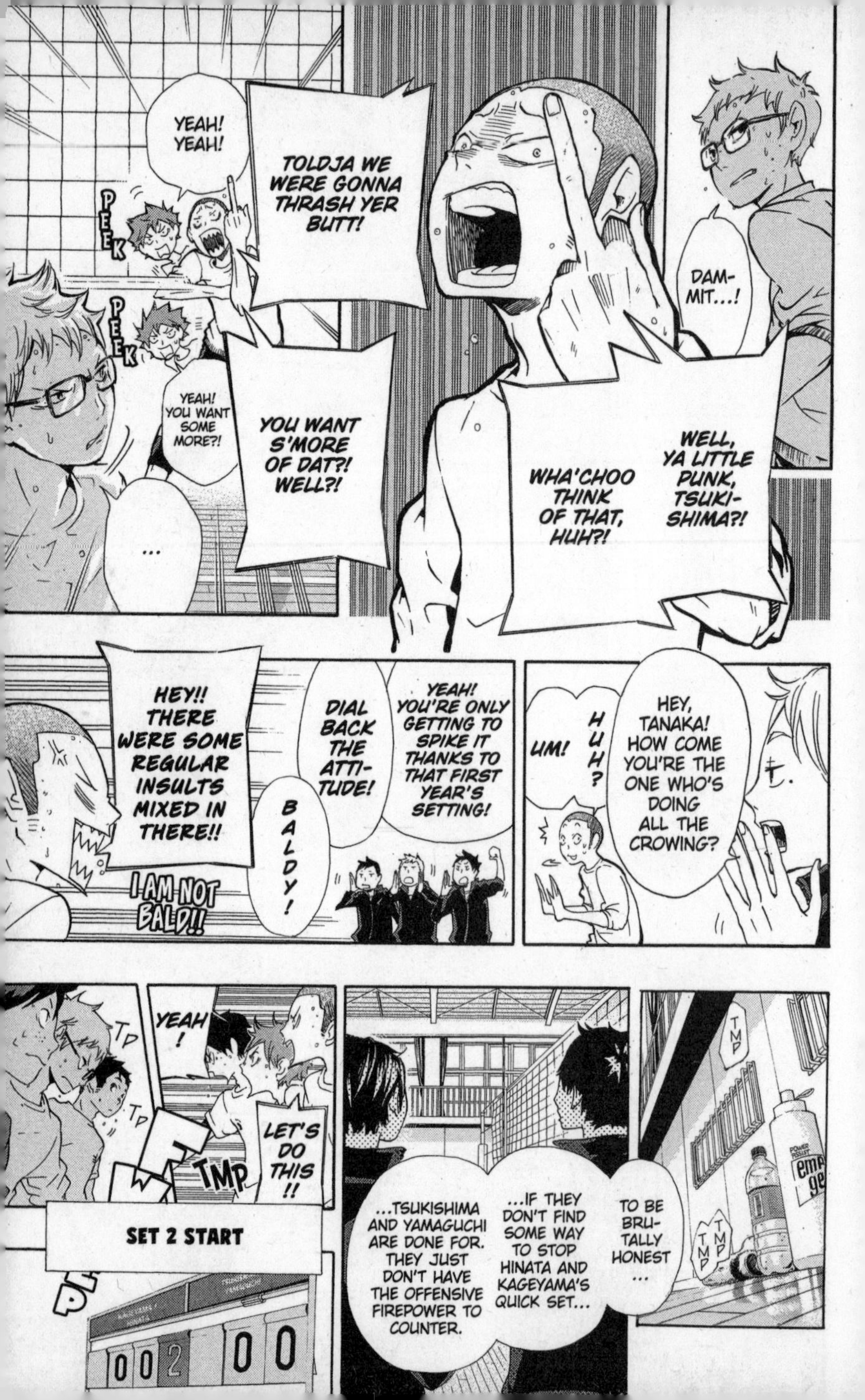
DAM-MIT...!
TOLDJA WE WERE GONNA THRASH YER BUTT!
WELL, YA LITTLE PUNK, TSUKISHIMA?!
WHA'CHOO THINK OF THAT, HUH?!
YOU WANT S'MORE OF DAT?! WELL?!
YEAH! YEAH!
PEEK
PEEK
YEAH! YOU WANT SOME MORE?!
...
HEY, TANAKA! HOW COME YOU'RE THE ONE WHO'S DOING ALL THE CROWING?
HUH?
UM!
YEAH! YOU'RE ONLY GETTING TO SPIKE IT THANKS TO THAT FIRST YEAR'S SETTING!
DIAL BACK THE ATTI-TUDE!
BALDY!
HEY!! THERE WERE SOME REGULAR INSULTS MIXED IN THERE!!
I AM NOT BALD!!
TMP
TO BE BRU-TALLY HONEST...
...IF THEY DON'T FIND SOME WAY TO STOP HINATA AND KAGEYAMA'S QUICK SET...
...TSUKISHIMA AND YAMAGUCHI ARE DONE FOR. THEY JUST DON'T HAVE THE OFFENSIVE FIREPOWER TO COUNTER.
TMP TMP
YEAH!
LET'S DO THIS!!
TP
TP
TMP
SET 2 START
00 2 00

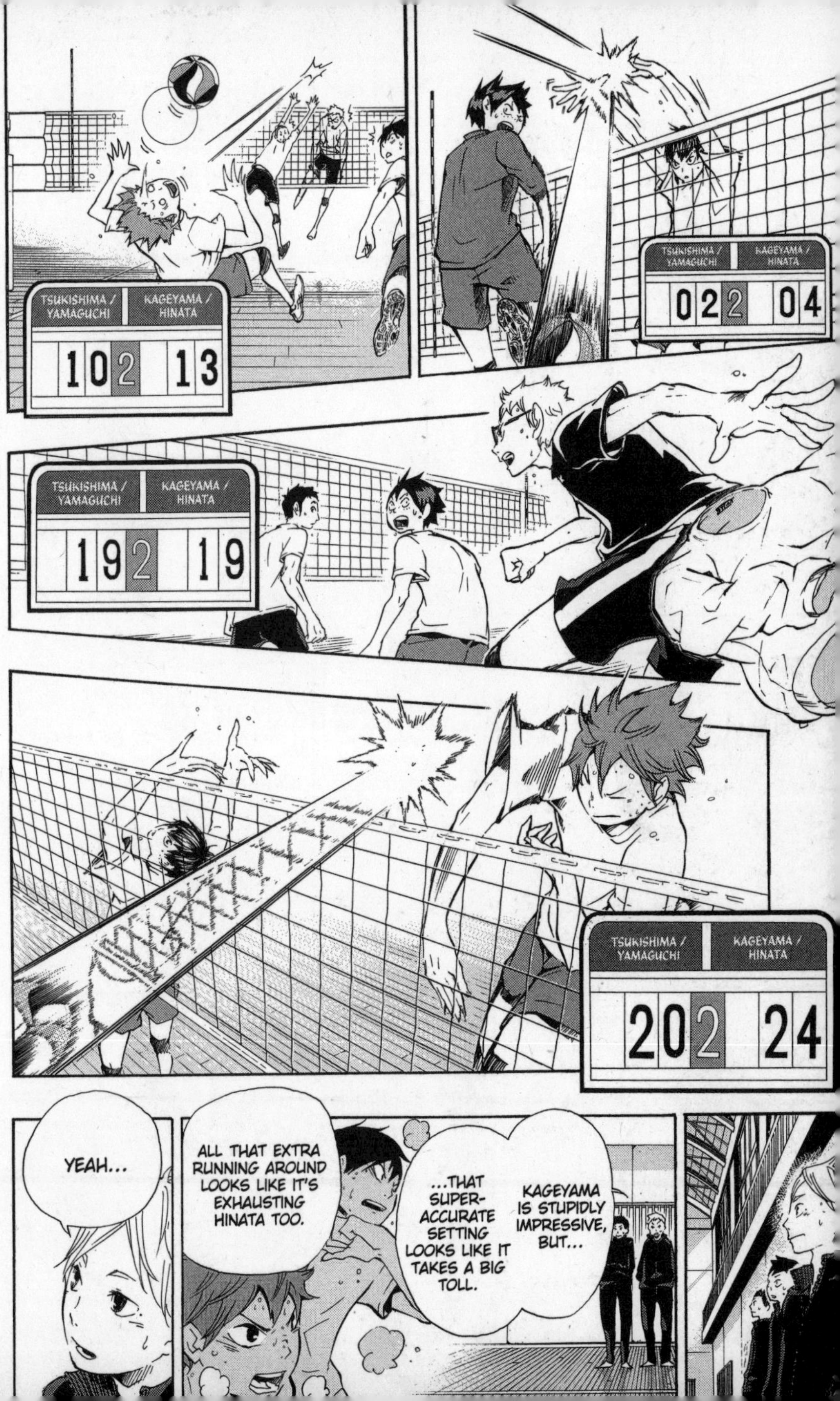
TSUKISHIMA / YAMAGUCHI
KAGEYAMA / HINATA
02 2 04
TSUKISHIMA / YAMAGUCHI
KAGEYAMA / HINATA
10 2 13
TSUKISHIMA / YAMAGUCHI
KAGEYAMA / HINATA
19 2 19
TSUKISHIMA / YAMAGUCHI
KAGEYAMA / HINATA
20 2 24
KAGEYAMA IS STUPIDLY IMPRESSIVE, BUT...
...THAT SUPER-ACCURATE SETTING LOOKS LIKE IT TAKES A BIG TOLL.
ALL THAT EXTRA RUNNING AROUND LOOKS LIKE IT'S EXHAUSTING HINATA TOO.
YEAH...

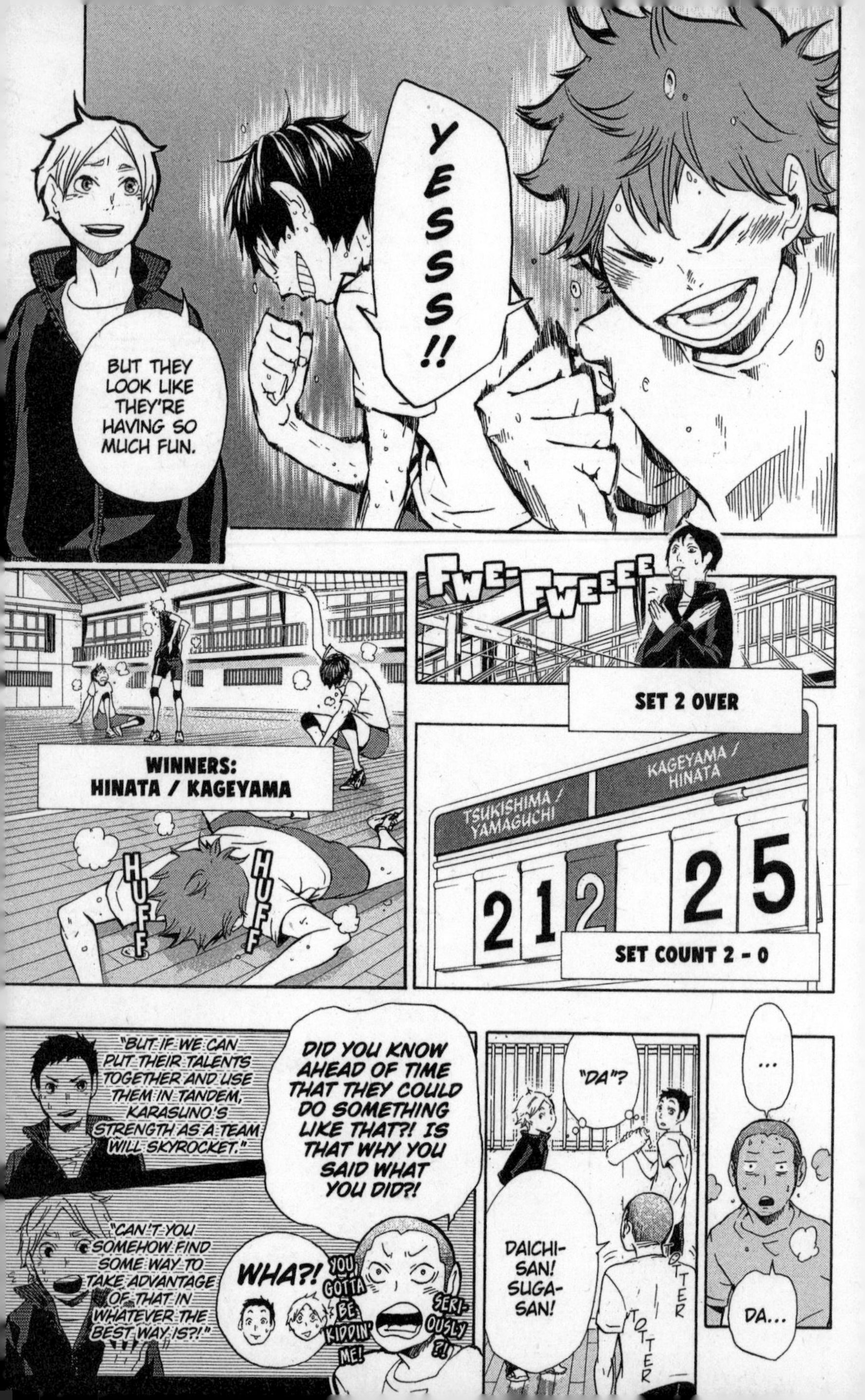
YESSS!!
BUT THEY LOOK LIKE THEY'RE HAVING SO MUCH FUN.
FWE-FWEEEE
SET 2 OVER
KAGEYAMA / HINATA
TSUKISHIMA / YAMAGUCHI
21
25
SET COUNT 2 - 0
WINNERS: HINATA / KAGEYAMA
HUFF
HUFF
...
DA...
"DA"?
DAICHI-SAN! SUGA-SAN!
TOTTER
TOTTER
DID YOU KNOW AHEAD OF TIME THAT THEY COULD DO SOMETHING LIKE THAT?! IS THAT WHY YOU SAID WHAT YOU DID?!
"BUT IF WE CAN PUT THEIR TALENTS TOGETHER AND USE THEM IN TANDEM, KARASUNO'S STRENGTH AS A TEAM WILL SKYROCKET."
SERI-OUSLY?!
YOU GOTTA BE KIDDIN' ME!
WHA?!
"CAN'T YOU SOMEHOW FIND SOME WAY TO TAKE ADVANTAGE OF THAT IN WHATEVER THE BEST WAY IS?!"

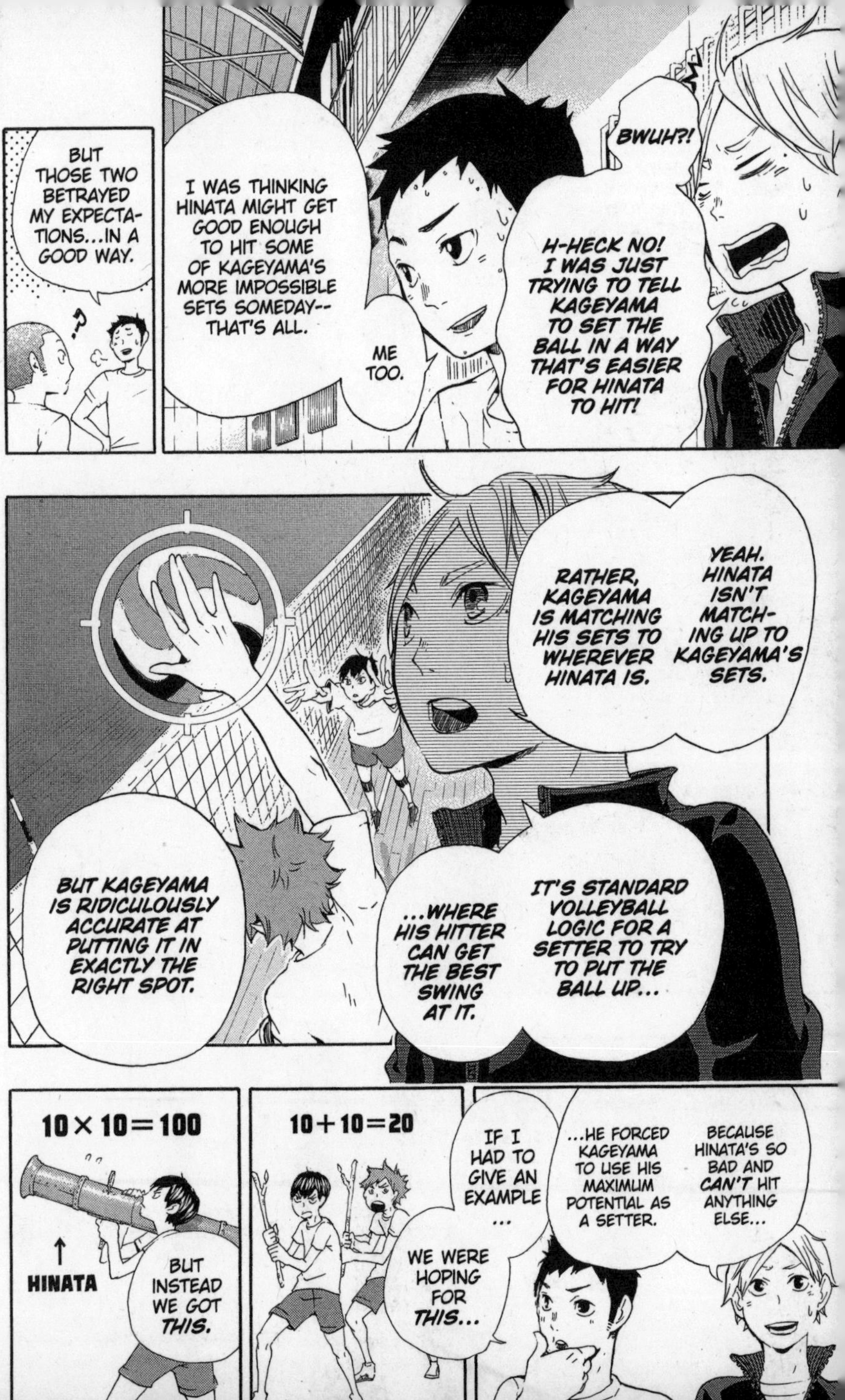
BWUH?!
H-HECK NO! I WAS JUST TRYING TO TELL KAGEYAMA TO SET THE BALL IN A WAY THAT'S EASIER FOR HINATA TO HIT!
I WAS THINKING HINATA MIGHT GET GOOD ENOUGH TO HIT SOME OF KAGEYAMA'S MORE IMPOSSIBLE SETS SOMEDAY--THAT'S ALL.
ME TOO.
BUT THOSE TWO BETRAYED MY EXPECTATIONS...IN A GOOD WAY.
YEAH. HINATA ISN'T MATCHING UP TO KAGEYAMA'S SETS.
RATHER, KAGEYAMA IS MATCHING HIS SETS TO WHEREVER HINATA IS.
IT'S STANDARD VOLLEYBALL LOGIC FOR A SETTER TO TRY TO PUT THE BALL UP...
...WHERE HIS HITTER CAN GET THE BEST SWING AT IT.
BUT KAGEYAMA IS RIDICULOUSLY ACCURATE AT PUTTING IT IN EXACTLY THE RIGHT SPOT.
BECAUSE HINATA'S SO BAD AND *CAN'T* HIT ANYTHING ELSE...
...HE FORCED KAGEYAMA TO USE HIS MAXIMUM POTENTIAL AS A SETTER.
IF I HAD TO GIVE AN EXAMPLE...
10+10=20
WE WERE HOPING FOR *THIS*...
10×10=100
↑ HINATA
BUT INSTEAD WE GOT *THIS*.

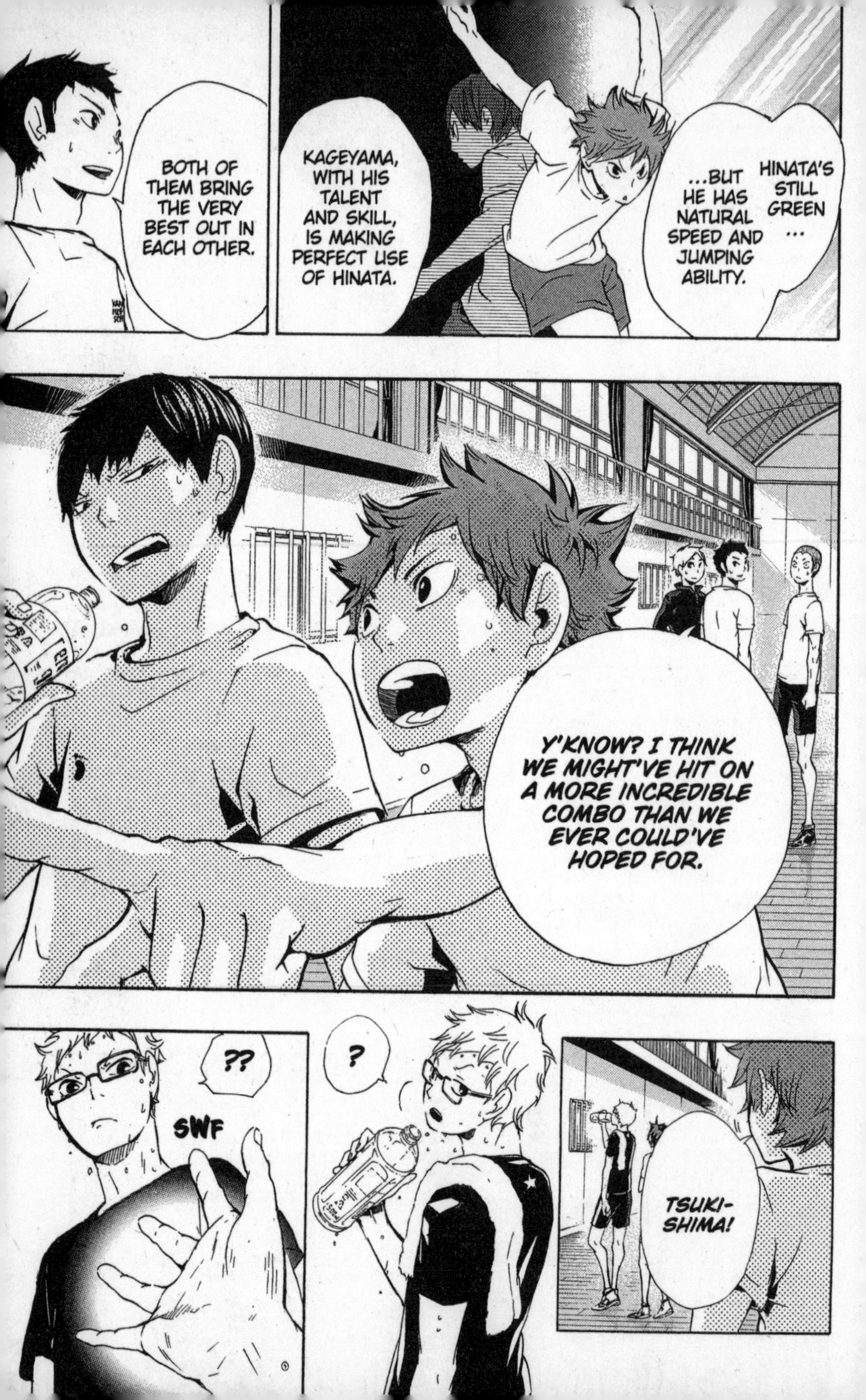
HINATA'S STILL GREEN ...
...BUT HE HAS NATURAL SPEED AND JUMPING ABILITY.
KAGEYAMA, WITH HIS TALENT AND SKILL, IS MAKING PERFECT USE OF HINATA.
BOTH OF THEM BRING THE VERY BEST OUT IN EACH OTHER.
Y'KNOW? I THINK WE MIGHT'VE HIT ON A MORE INCREDIBLE COMBO THAN WE EVER COULD'VE HOPED FOR.
TSUKI-SHIMA!
?
??
SWF

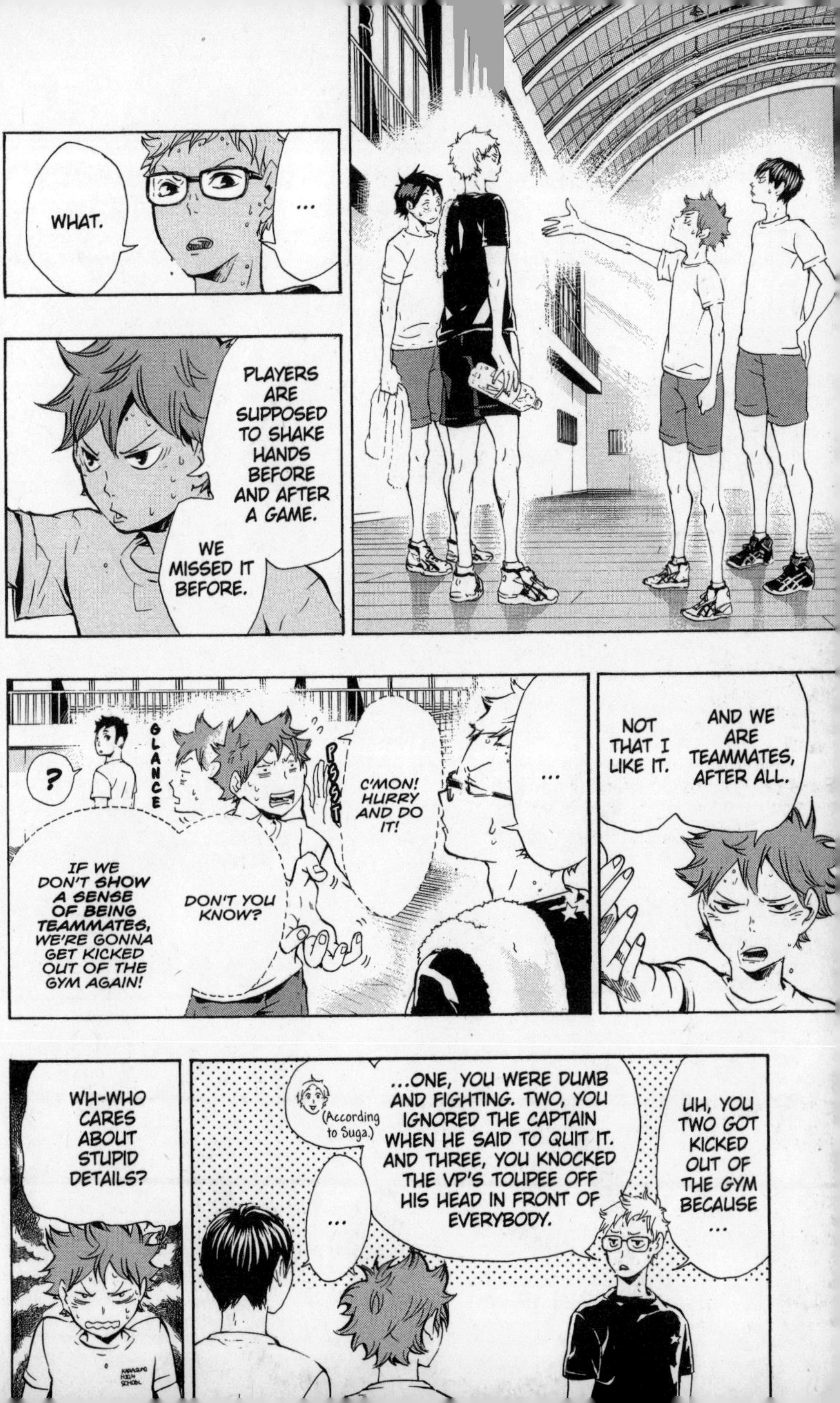

...
WHAT.
PLAYERS ARE SUPPOSED TO SHAKE HANDS BEFORE AND AFTER A GAME.
WE MISSED IT BEFORE.
AND WE ARE TEAMMATES, AFTER ALL.
NOT THAT I LIKE IT.
...
C'MON! HURRY AND DO IT!
PSST
GLANCE
?
DON'T YOU KNOW?
IF WE DON'T SHOW A SENSE OF BEING TEAMMATES, WE'RE GONNA GET KICKED OUT OF THE GYM AGAIN!
UH, YOU TWO GOT KICKED OUT OF THE GYM BECAUSE ...
...ONE, YOU WERE DUMB AND FIGHTING. TWO, YOU IGNORED THE CAPTAIN WHEN HE SAID TO QUIT IT. AND THREE, YOU KNOCKED THE VP'S TOUPEE OFF HIS HEAD IN FRONT OF EVERYBODY.
(According to Suga.)
...
WH-WHO CARES ABOUT STUPID DETAILS?

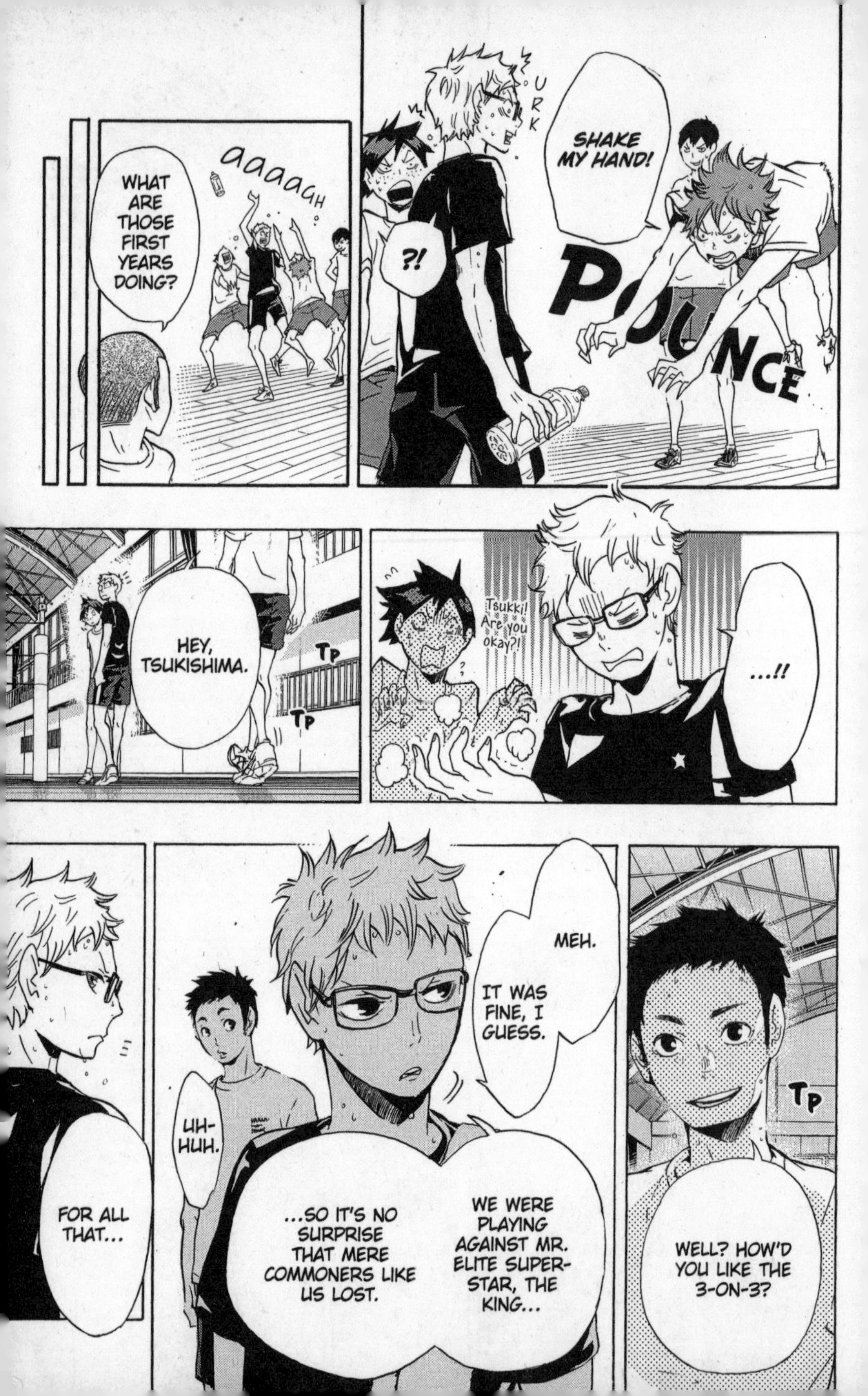
SHAKE MY HAND!
URK
?!
POUNCE
aaaaagh
WHAT ARE THOSE FIRST YEARS DOING?
...!!
Tsukki! Are you okay?!
Tp
Tp
HEY, TSUKISHIMA.
Tp
WELL? HOW'D YOU LIKE THE 3-ON-3?
MEH.
IT WAS FINE, I GUESS.
UH-HUH.
WE WERE PLAYING AGAINST MR. ELITE SUPER-STAR, THE KING...
...SO IT'S NO SURPRISE THAT MERE COMMONERS LIKE US LOST.
FOR ALL THAT...

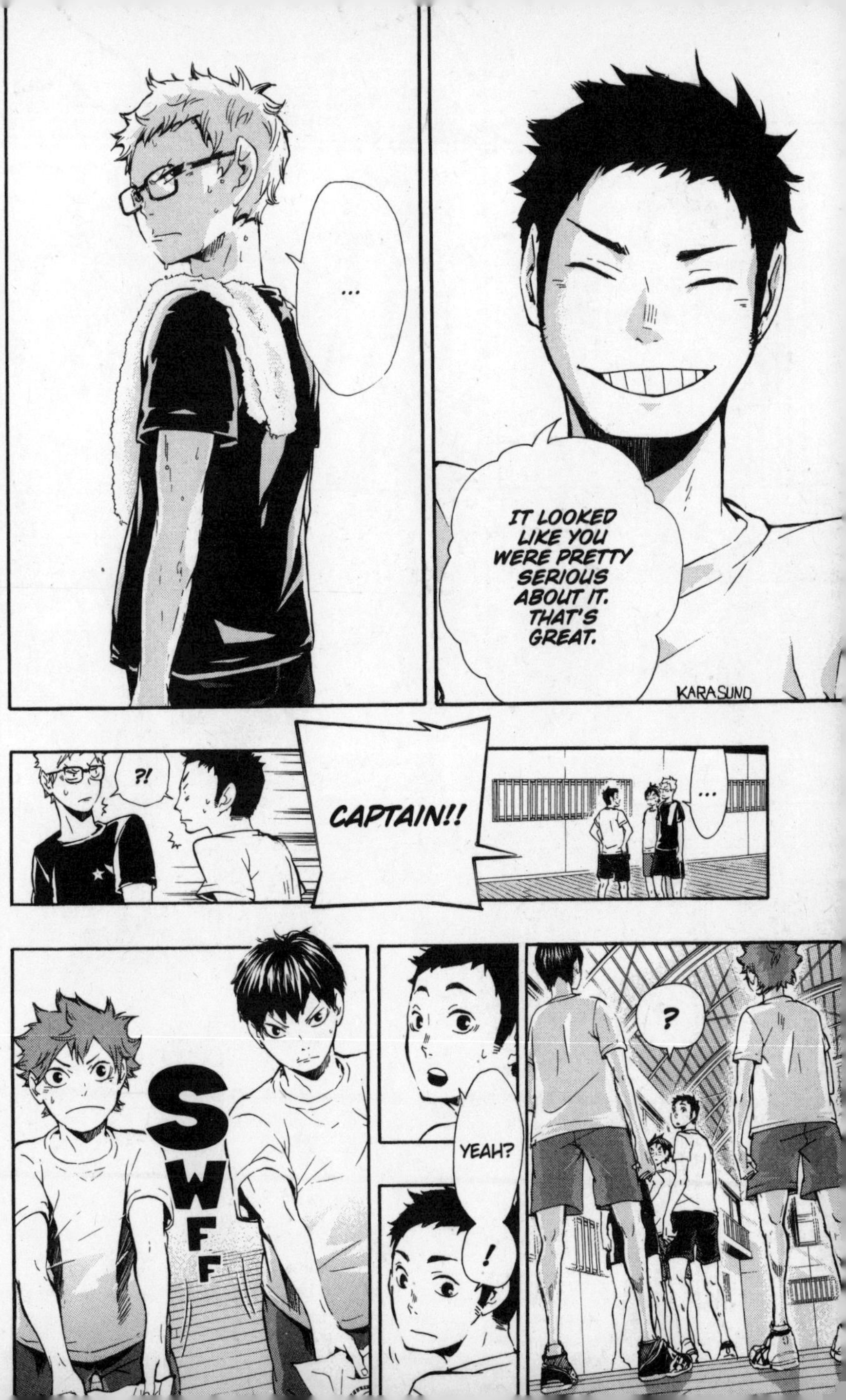
IT LOOKED LIKE YOU WERE PRETTY SERIOUS ABOUT IT. THAT'S GREAT.
KARASUNO
...
...
CAPTAIN!!
?!
?
YEAH?
!
SWFF

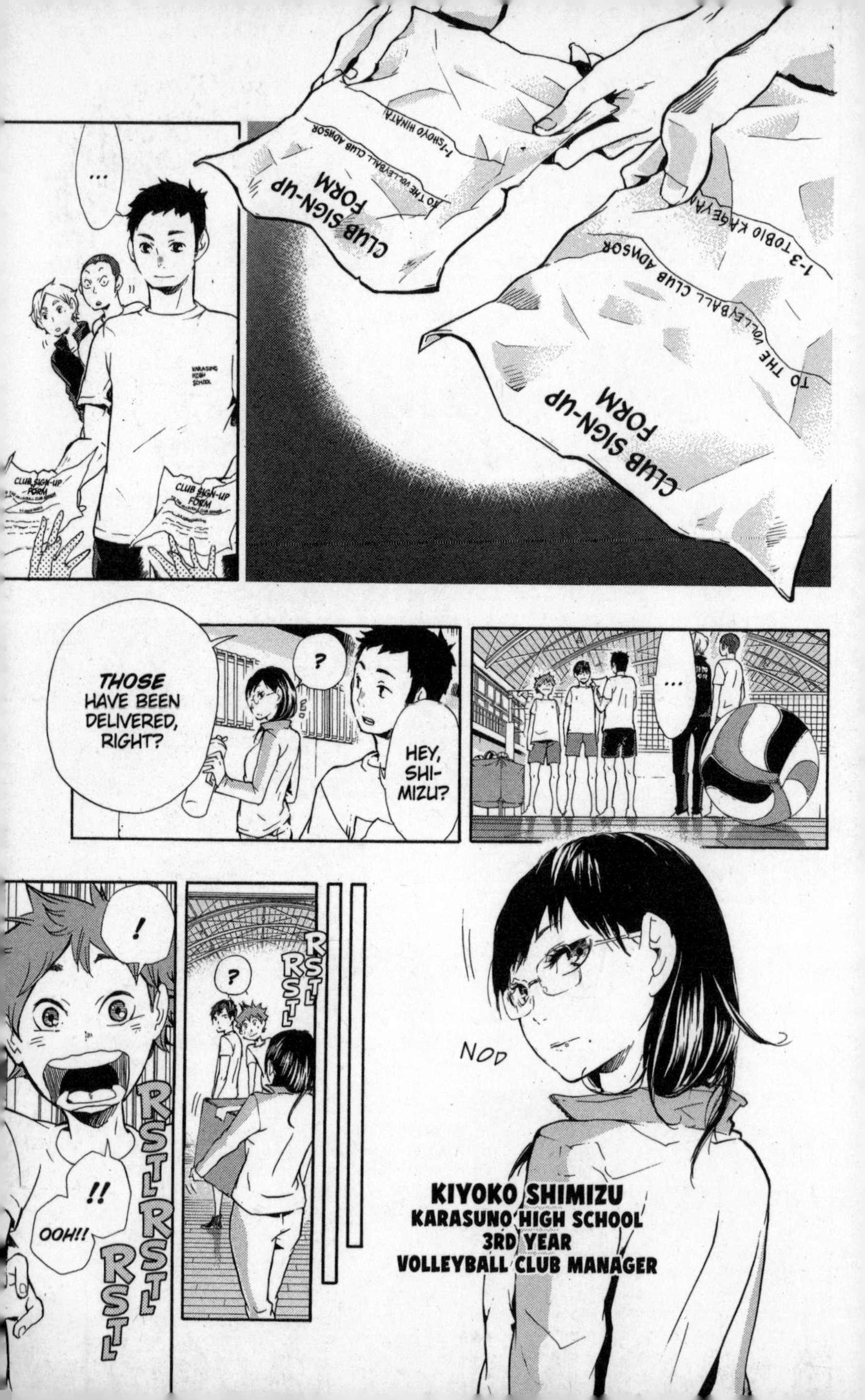
CLUB SIGN-UP FORM
TO THE VOLLEYBALL CLUB ADVISOR
1-1 SHOYO HINATA
CLUB SIGN-UP FORM
TO THE VOLLEYBALL CLUB ADVISOR
1-3 TOBIO KAGEYA
...
CLUB SIGN-UP FORM
CLUB SIGN-UP FORM
KARASUNO HIGH SCHOOL
...
HEY, SHI-MIZU?
?
THOSE HAVE BEEN DELIVERED, RIGHT?
NOD
KIYOKO SHIMIZU
KARASUNO HIGH SCHOOL
3RD YEAR
VOLLEYBALL CLUB MANAGER
RSTL
RSTL
?
!
RSTL
RSTL
RSTL
!!
OOH!!

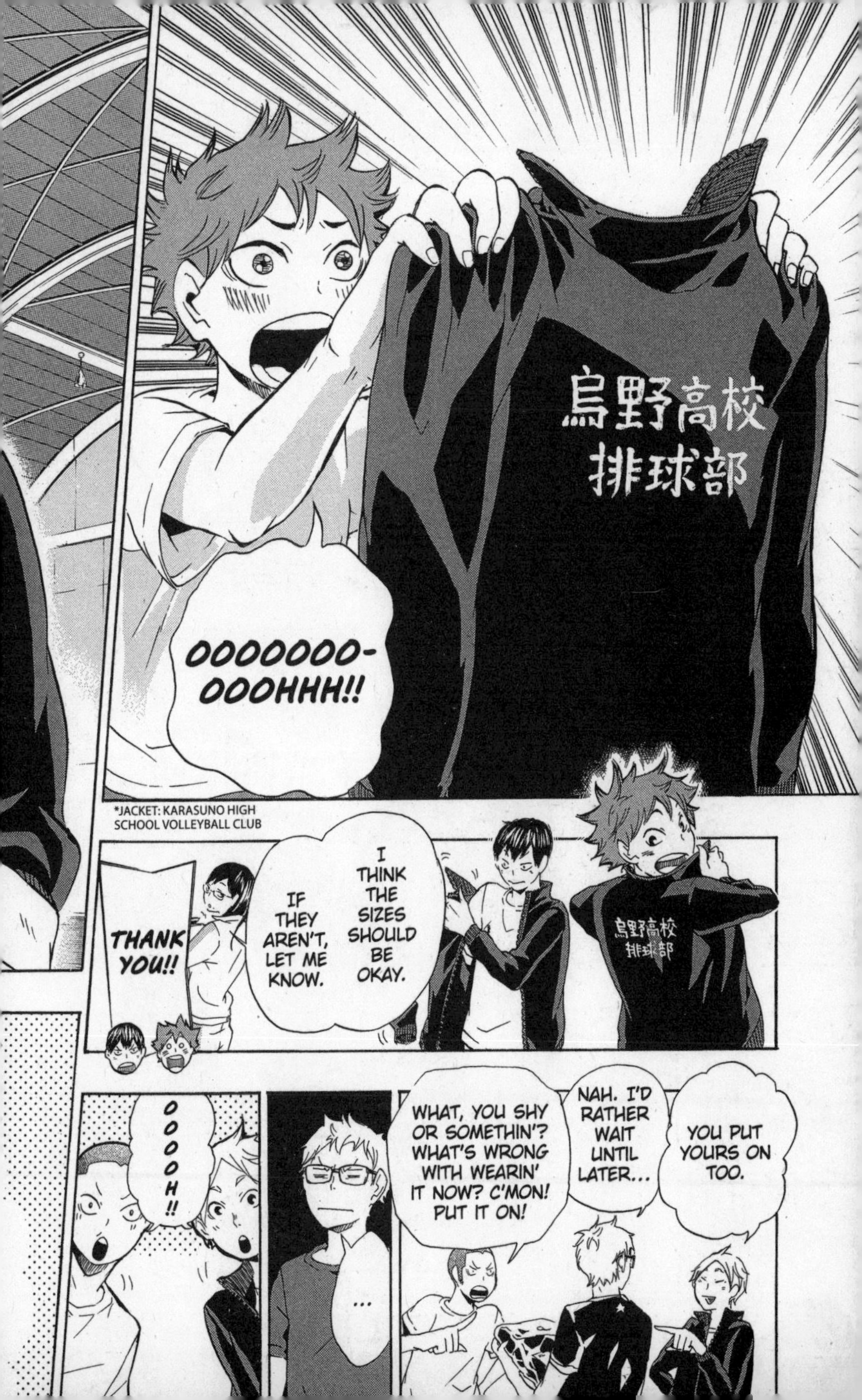

烏野高校
排球部
OOOOOOO-OOOHHH!!
*JACKET: KARASUNO HIGH SCHOOL VOLLEYBALL CLUB
烏野高校
排球部
I THINK THE SIZES SHOULD BE OKAY.
IF THEY AREN'T, LET ME KNOW.
THANK YOU!!
YOU PUT YOURS ON TOO.
NAH. I'D RATHER WAIT UNTIL LATER...
WHAT, YOU SHY OR SOMETHIN'? WHAT'S WRONG WITH WEARIN' IT NOW? C'MON! PUT IT ON!
...
OOOOOH!!

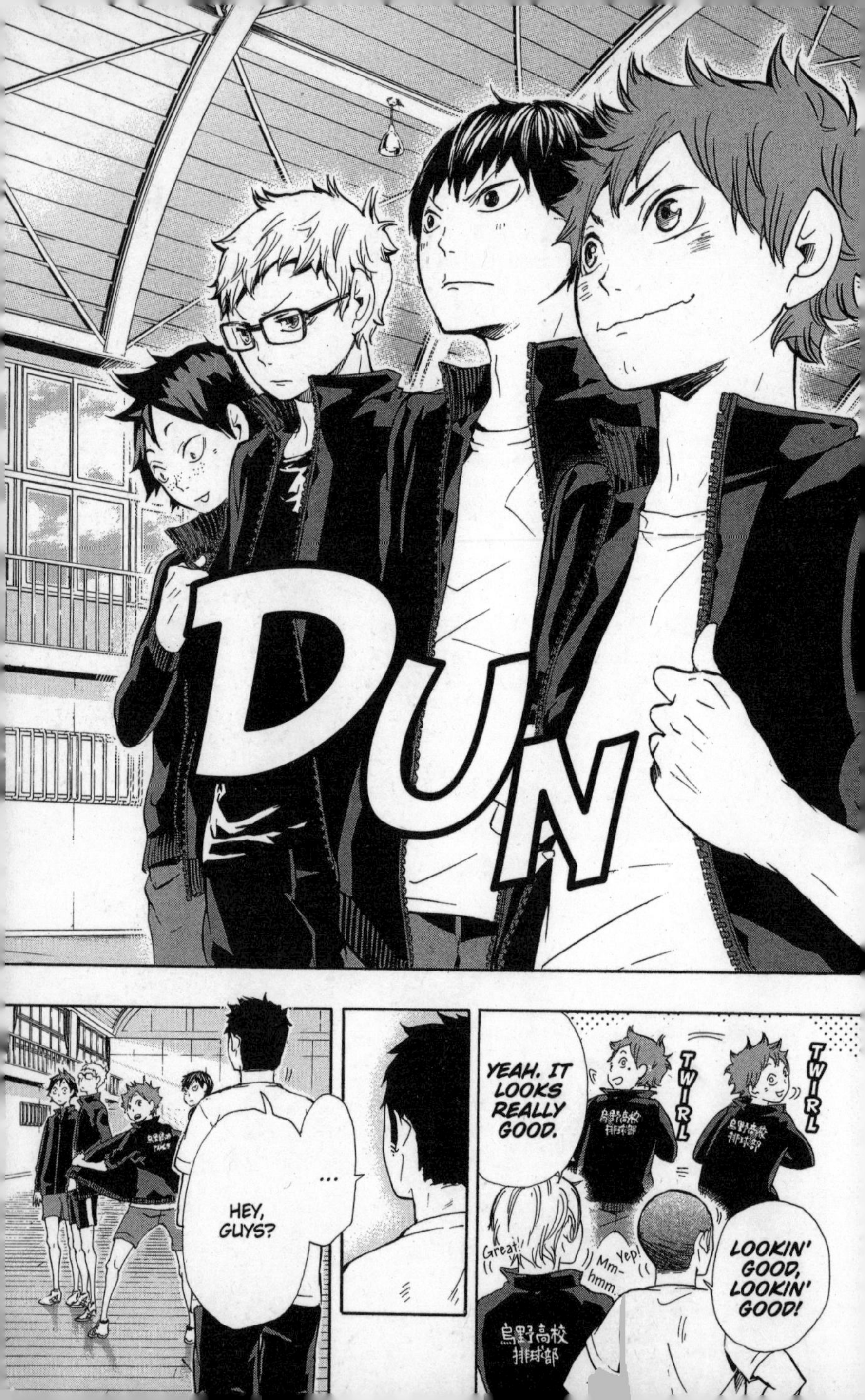
DUN
TWIRL
TWIRL
YEAH. IT LOOKS REALLY GOOD.
烏野高校 排球部
LOOKIN' GOOD, LOOKIN' GOOD!
Yep!
Mm-hmm.
Great!
...
HEY, GUYS?

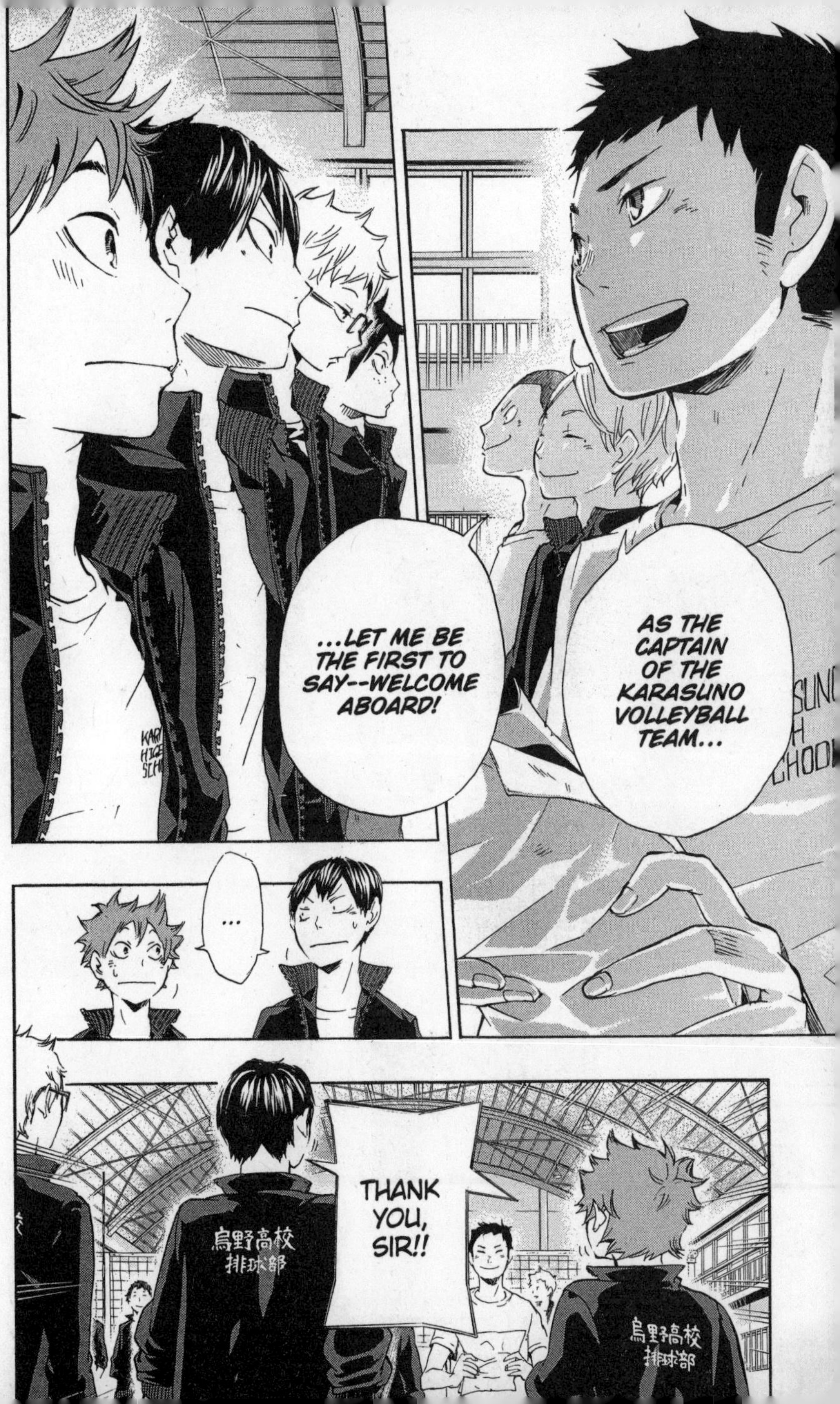
AS THE CAPTAIN OF THE KARASUNO VOLLEYBALL TEAM...
...LET ME BE THE FIRST TO SAY--WELCOME ABOARD!
...
THANK YOU, SIR!!
烏野高校 排球部
烏野高校 排球部

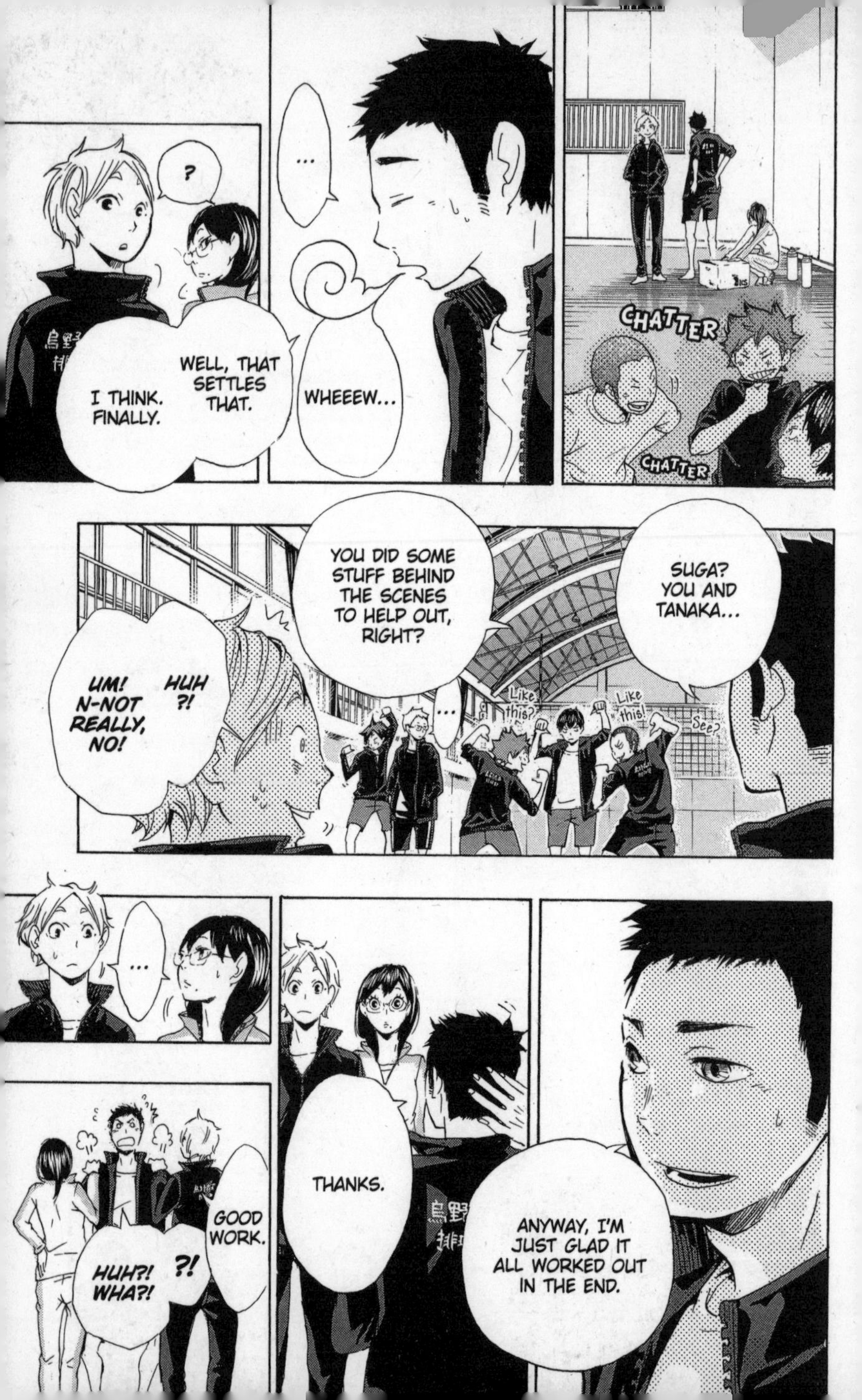
CHATTER
CHATTER
...
WHEEEW...
?
WELL, THAT SETTLES THAT.
I THINK. FINALLY.
SUGA? YOU AND TANAKA...
YOU DID SOME STUFF BEHIND THE SCENES TO HELP OUT, RIGHT?
Like this?
Like this!
See?
...
HUH?!
UM! N-NOT REALLY, NO!
ANYWAY, I'M JUST GLAD IT ALL WORKED OUT IN THE END.
THANKS.
...
GOOD WORK.
?!
HUH?! WHA?!

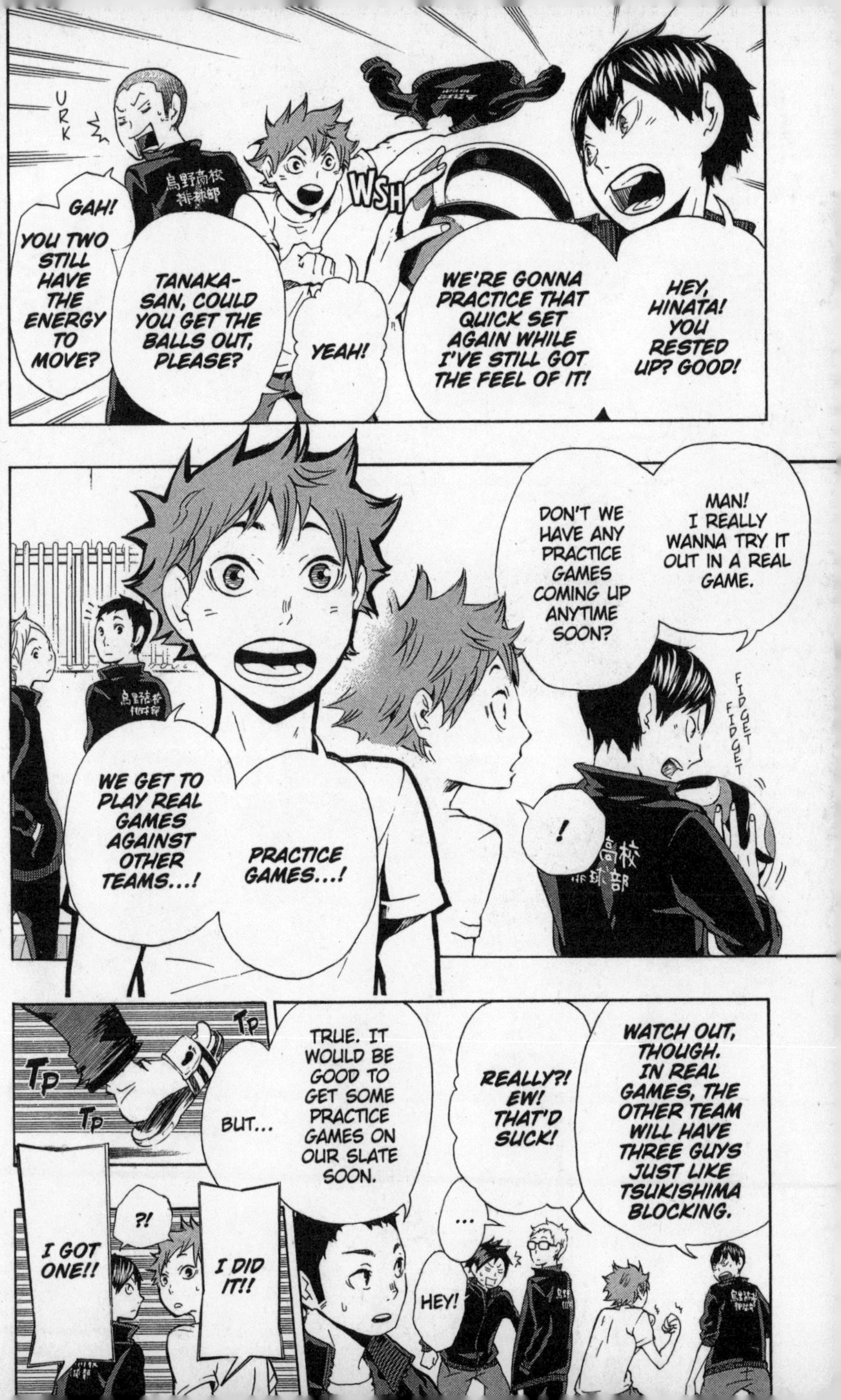
HEY, HINATA! YOU RESTED UP? GOOD!
WE'RE GONNA PRACTICE THAT QUICK SET AGAIN WHILE I'VE STILL GOT THE FEEL OF IT!
WSH
YEAH!
TANAKA-SAN, COULD YOU GET THE BALLS OUT, PLEASE?
URK
烏野高校 排球部
GAH! YOU TWO STILL HAVE THE ENERGY TO MOVE?
MAN! I REALLY WANNA TRY IT OUT IN A REAL GAME.
DON'T WE HAVE ANY PRACTICE GAMES COMING UP ANYTIME SOON?
FIDGET FIDGET
!
PRACTICE GAMES...!
WE GET TO PLAY REAL GAMES AGAINST OTHER TEAMS...!
WATCH OUT, THOUGH. IN REAL GAMES, THE OTHER TEAM WILL HAVE THREE GUYS JUST LIKE TSUKISHIMA BLOCKING.
REALLY?! EW! THAT'D SUCK!
...
HEY!
TRUE. IT WOULD BE GOOD TO GET SOME PRACTICE GAMES ON OUR SLATE SOON.
BUT...
Tp
Tp
Tp
?!
I DID IT!!
I GOT ONE!!

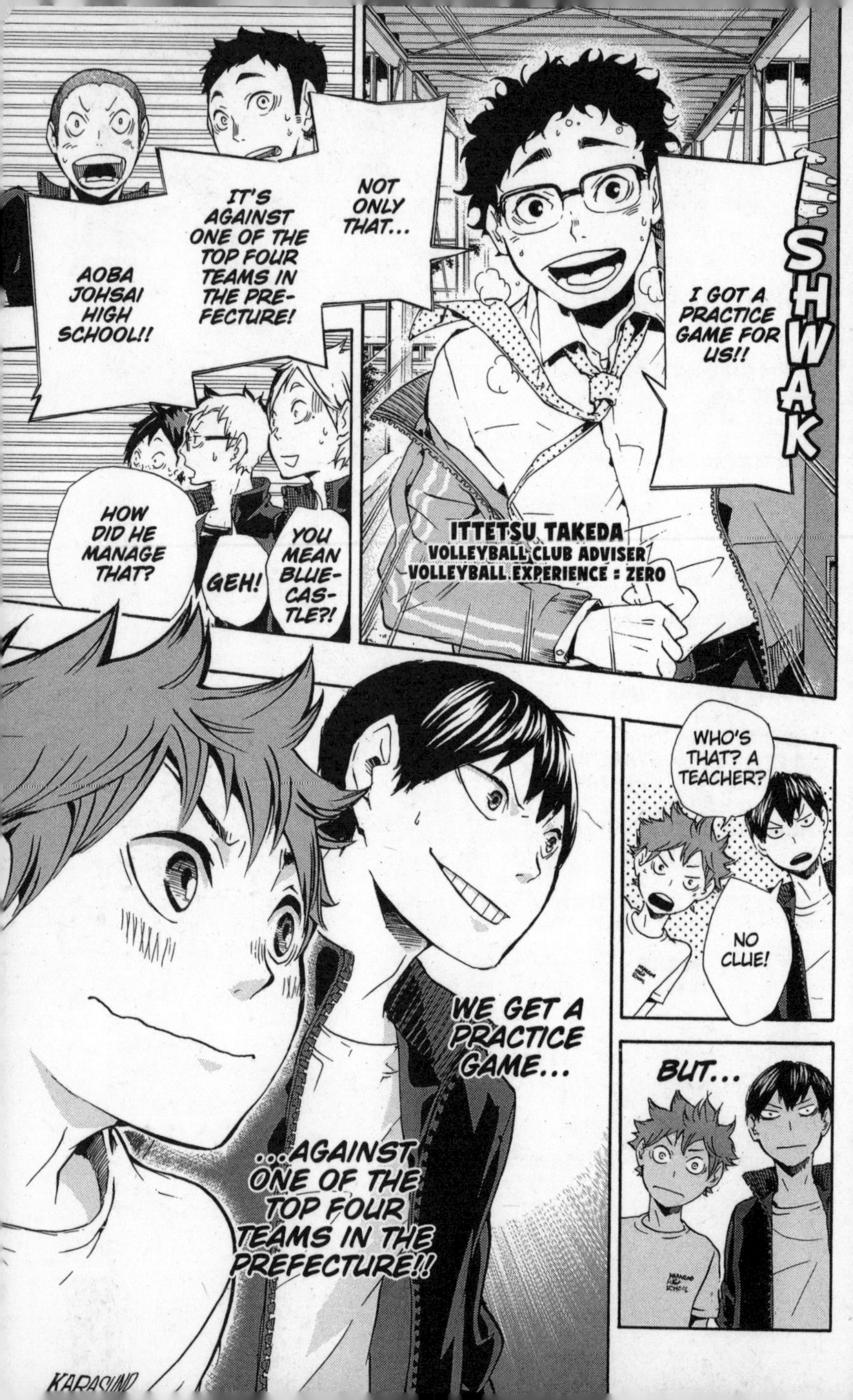
I GOT A PRACTICE GAME FOR US!!
SHWAK
ITTETSU TAKEDA
VOLLEYBALL CLUB ADVISER
VOLLEYBALL EXPERIENCE : ZERO
NOT ONLY THAT...
IT'S AGAINST ONE OF THE TOP FOUR TEAMS IN THE PRE-FECTURE!
AOBA JOHSAI HIGH SCHOOL!!
YOU MEAN BLUE-CASTLE?!
GEH!
HOW DID HE MANAGE THAT?
WHO'S THAT? A TEACHER?
NO CLUE!
BUT...
WE GET A PRACTICE GAME...
...AGAINST ONE OF THE TOP FOUR TEAMS IN THE PREFECTURE!!

TADASHI YAMAGUCHI

KARASUNO HIGH SCHOOL
CLASS 1-4

POSITION:
MIDDLE BLOCKER

HEIGHT: 5'11"
WEIGHT: 139 LBS.
(AS OF APRIL, 1ST YEAR OF HIGH SCHOOL)

BIRTHDAY: NOVEMBER 10

FAVORITE FOOD:
SOGGY FRENCH FRIES

CURRENT WORRY:
A PRETTY GIRL STARTED TALKING TO HIM, BUT ALL SHE WANTED TO TALK TO HIM ABOUT WAS TSUKKI.

ABILITY PARAMETERS
(5-POINT SCALE)

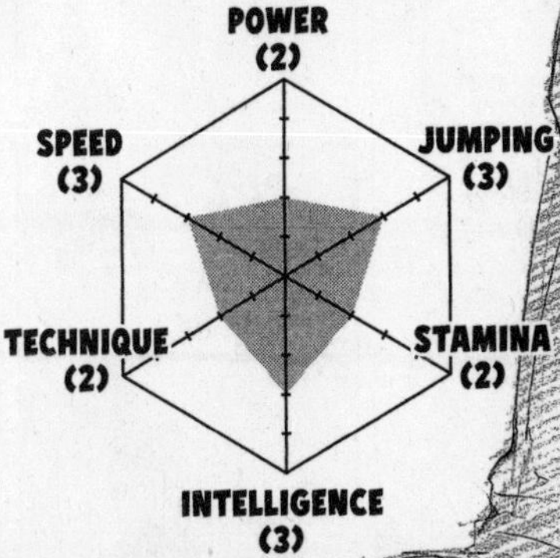
POWER (2)
JUMPING (3)
STAMINA (2)
INTELLIGENCE (3)
TECHNIQUE (2)
SPEED (3)

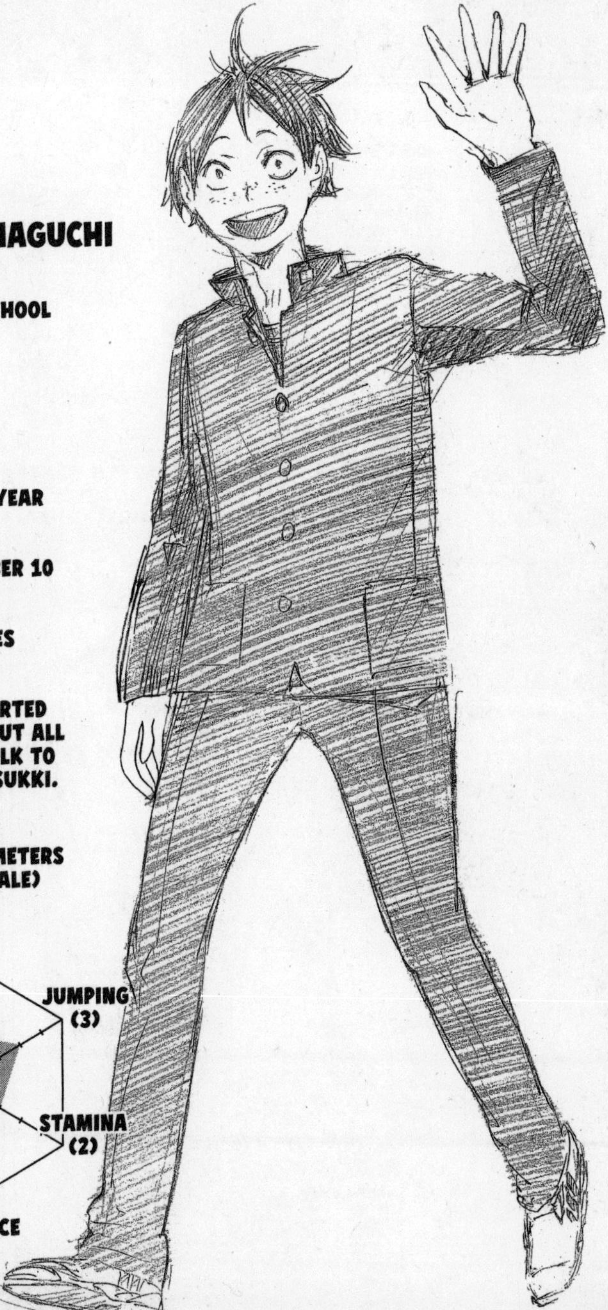

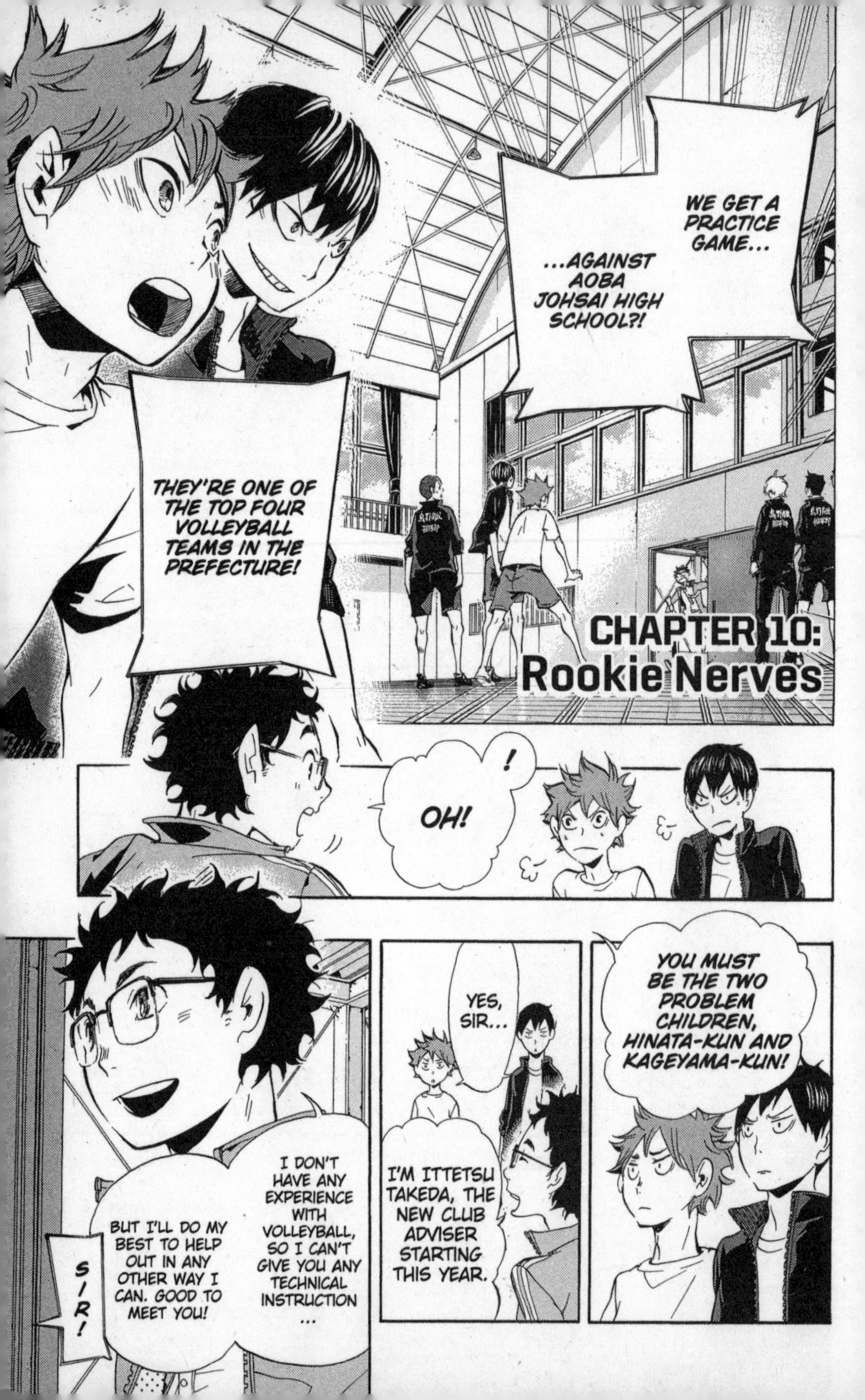
WE GET A PRACTICE GAME...
...AGAINST AOBA JOHSAI HIGH SCHOOL?!
THEY'RE ONE OF THE TOP FOUR VOLLEYBALL TEAMS IN THE PREFECTURE!
CHAPTER 10: Rookie Nerves
!
OH!
YOU MUST BE THE TWO PROBLEM CHILDREN, HINATA-KUN AND KAGEYAMA-KUN!
YES, SIR...
I'M ITTETSU TAKEDA, THE NEW CLUB ADVISER STARTING THIS YEAR.
I DON'T HAVE ANY EXPERIENCE WITH VOLLEYBALL, SO I CAN'T GIVE YOU ANY TECHNICAL INSTRUCTION...
BUT I'LL DO MY BEST TO HELP OUT IN ANY OTHER WAY I CAN. GOOD TO MEET YOU!
SIR!

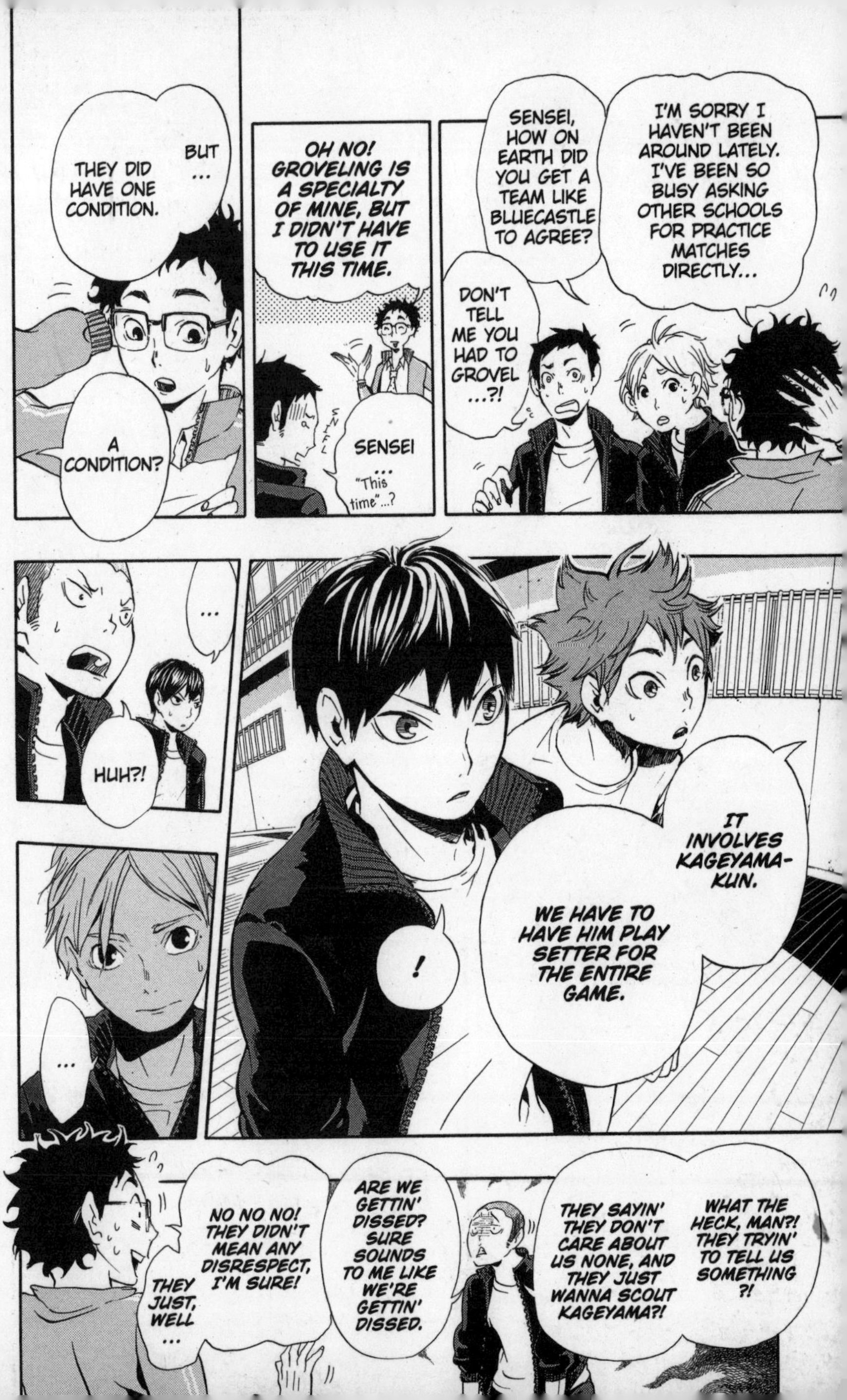
I'M SORRY I HAVEN'T BEEN AROUND LATELY. I'VE BEEN SO BUSY ASKING OTHER SCHOOLS FOR PRACTICE MATCHES DIRECTLY...
SENSEI, HOW ON EARTH DID YOU GET A TEAM LIKE BLUECASTLE TO AGREE?
DON'T TELL ME YOU HAD TO GROVEL ...?!
OH NO! GROVELING IS A SPECIALTY OF MINE, BUT I DIDN'T HAVE TO USE IT THIS TIME.
SNIFL
SENSEI ... "This time"...?
BUT ...
THEY DID HAVE ONE CONDITION.
A CONDITION?
IT INVOLVES KAGEYAMA-KUN.
WE HAVE TO HAVE HIM PLAY SETTER FOR THE ENTIRE GAME.
!
...
HUH?!
...
WHAT THE HECK, MAN?! THEY TRYIN' TO TELL US SOMETHING ?!
THEY SAYIN' THEY DON'T CARE ABOUT US NONE, AND THEY JUST WANNA SCOUT KAGEYAMA?!
ARE WE GETTIN' DISSED? SURE SOUNDS TO ME LIKE WE'RE GETTIN' DISSED.
NO NO NO! THEY DIDN'T MEAN ANY DISRESPECT, I'M SURE!
THEY JUST, WELL ...

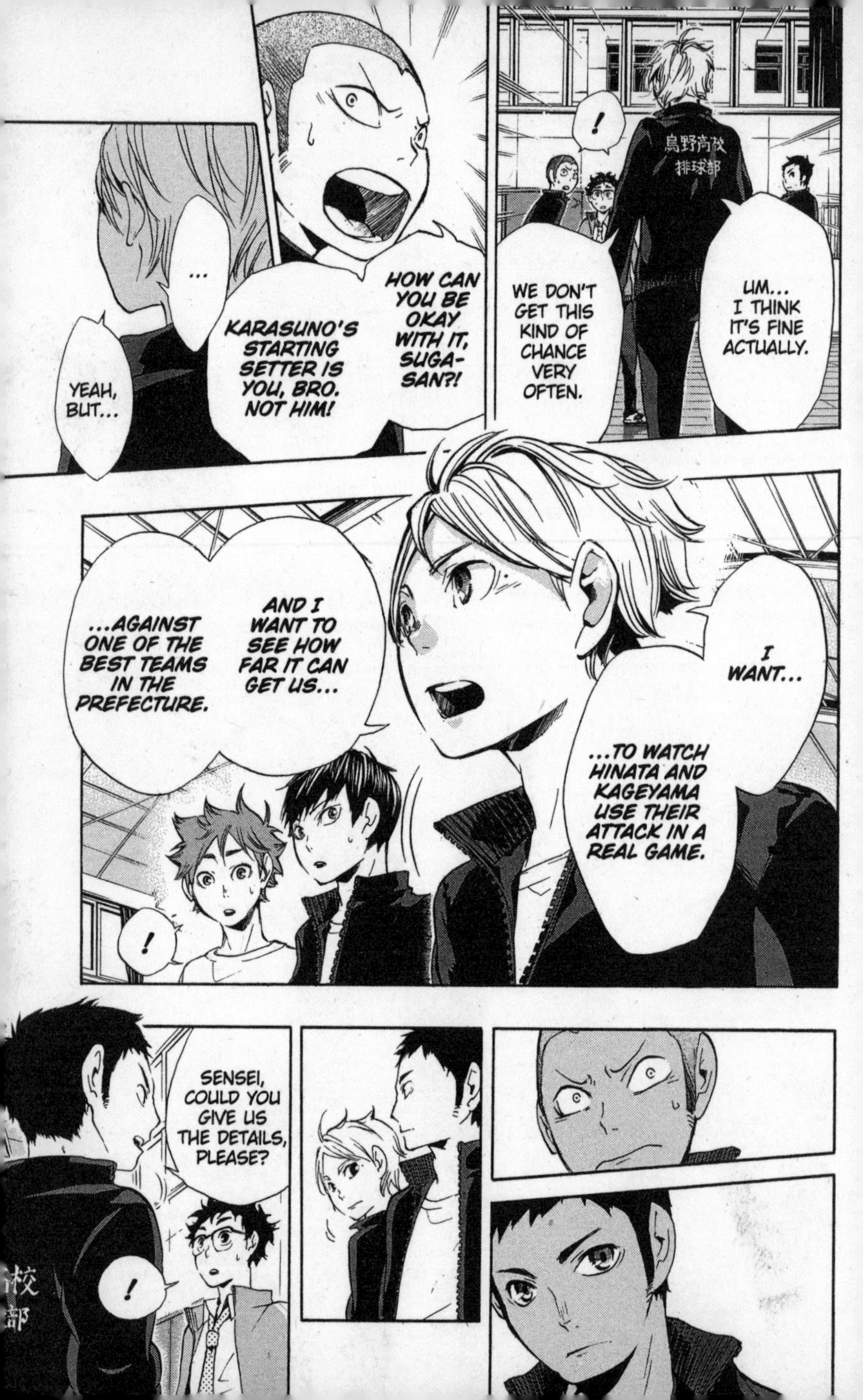
!
烏野高校
排球部
UM... I THINK IT'S FINE ACTUALLY.
WE DON'T GET THIS KIND OF CHANCE VERY OFTEN.
HOW CAN YOU BE OKAY WITH IT, SUGA-SAN?!
KARASUNO'S STARTING SETTER IS YOU, BRO. NOT HIM!
...
YEAH, BUT...
I WANT...
...TO WATCH HINATA AND KAGEYAMA USE THEIR ATTACK IN A REAL GAME.
AND I WANT TO SEE HOW FAR IT CAN GET US...
...AGAINST ONE OF THE BEST TEAMS IN THE PREFECTURE.
!
SENSEI, COULD YOU GIVE US THE DETAILS, PLEASE?
校
部
!

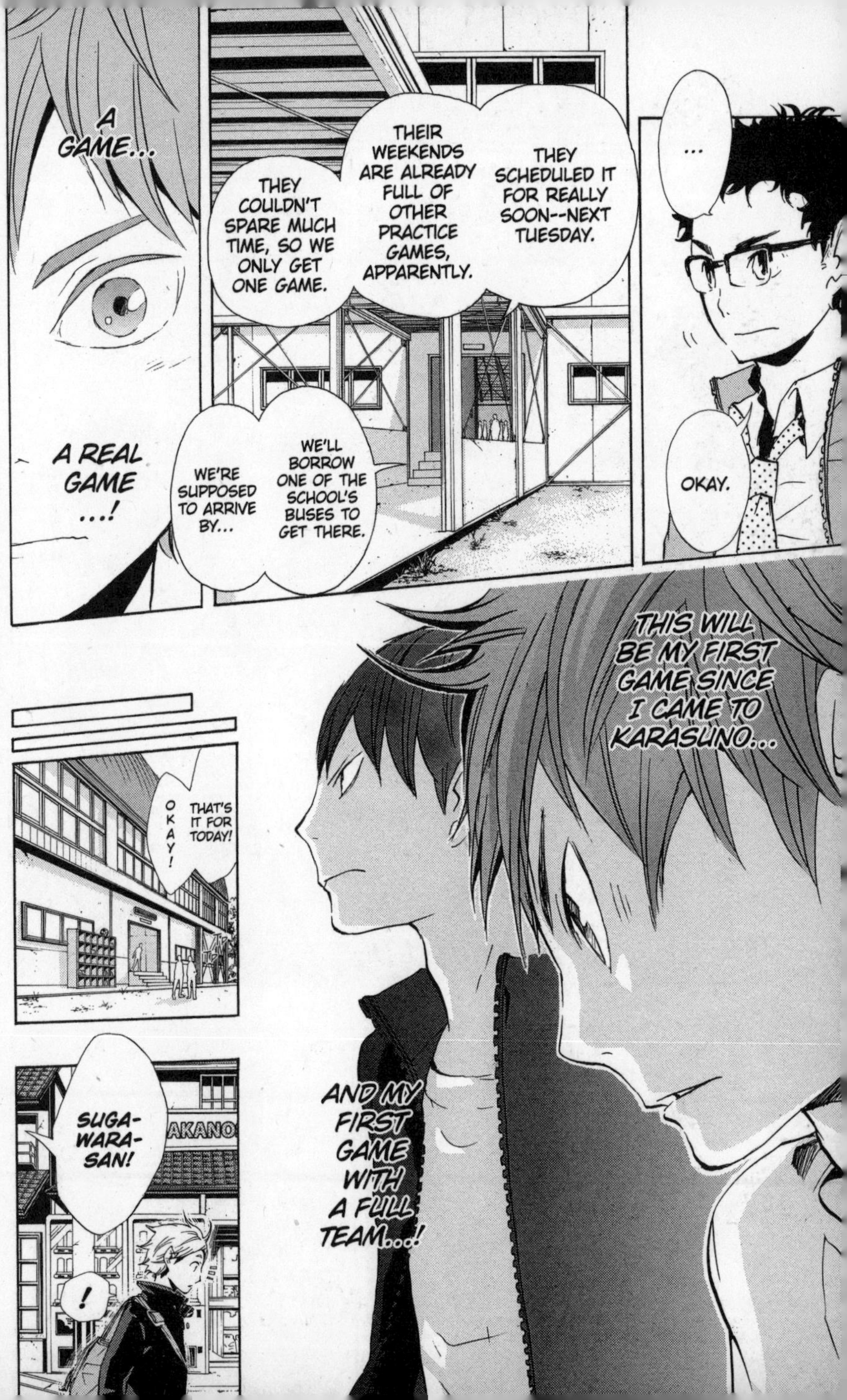
...
OKAY.
THEY SCHEDULED IT FOR REALLY SOON--NEXT TUESDAY.
THEIR WEEKENDS ARE ALREADY FULL OF OTHER PRACTICE GAMES, APPARENTLY.
THEY COULDN'T SPARE MUCH TIME, SO WE ONLY GET ONE GAME.
WE'LL BORROW ONE OF THE SCHOOL'S BUSES TO GET THERE.
WE'RE SUPPOSED TO ARRIVE BY...
A GAME...
A REAL GAME...!
THIS WILL BE MY FIRST GAME SINCE I CAME TO KARASUNO...
AND MY FIRST GAME WITH A FULL TEAM...!
THAT'S IT FOR TODAY!
OKAY!
AKANO
SUGA-WARA-SAN!
!

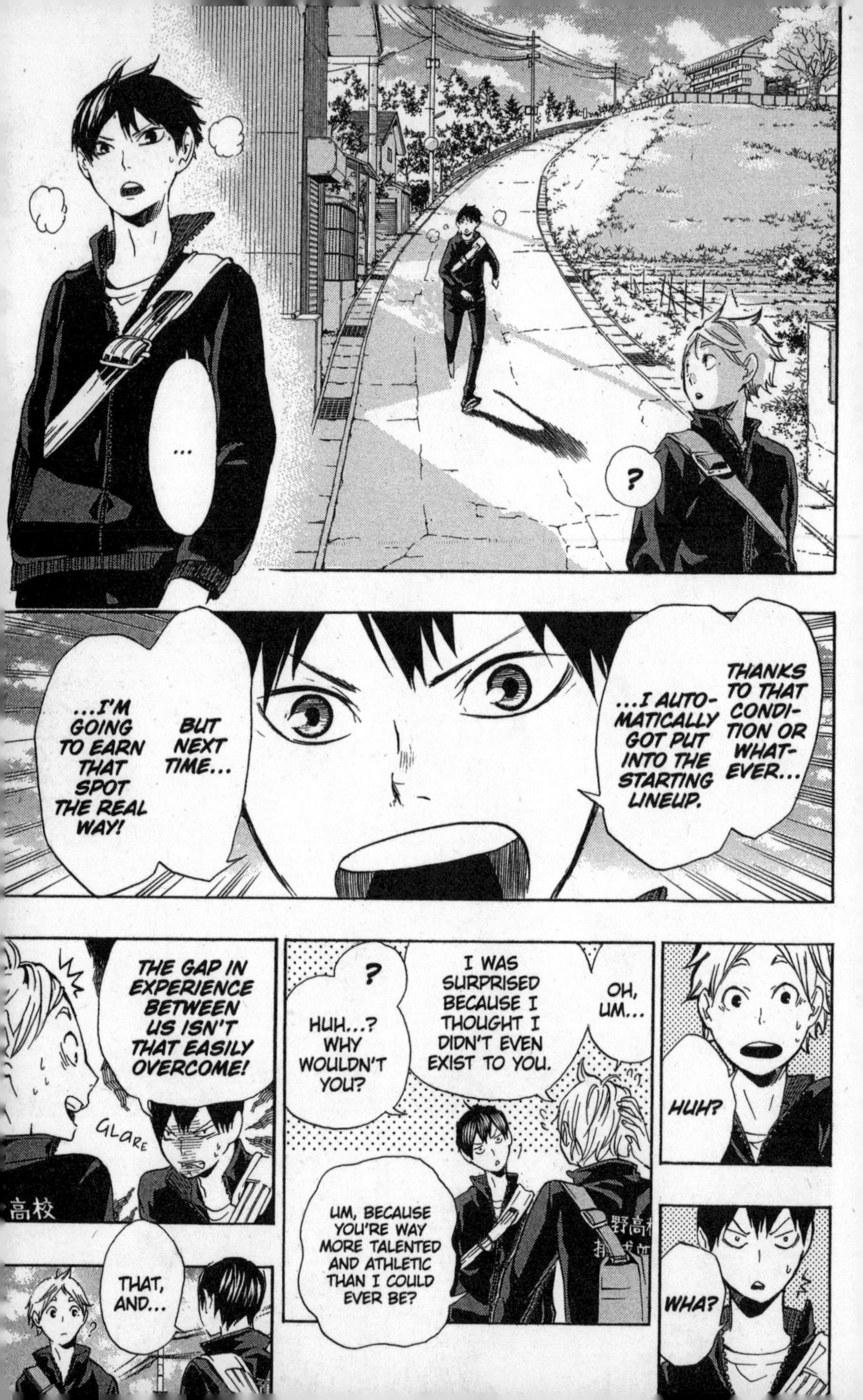
?
...
THANKS TO THAT CONDITION OR WHATEVER...
...I AUTOMATICALLY GOT PUT INTO THE STARTING LINEUP.
BUT NEXT TIME...
...I'M GOING TO EARN THAT SPOT THE REAL WAY!
HUH?
WHA?
OH, UM...
I WAS SURPRISED BECAUSE I THOUGHT I DIDN'T EVEN EXIST TO YOU.
?
HUH...? WHY WOULDN'T YOU?
UM, BECAUSE YOU'RE WAY MORE TALENTED AND ATHLETIC THAN I COULD EVER BE?
THE GAP IN EXPERIENCE BETWEEN US ISN'T THAT EASILY OVERCOME!
GLARE
高校
THAT, AND...

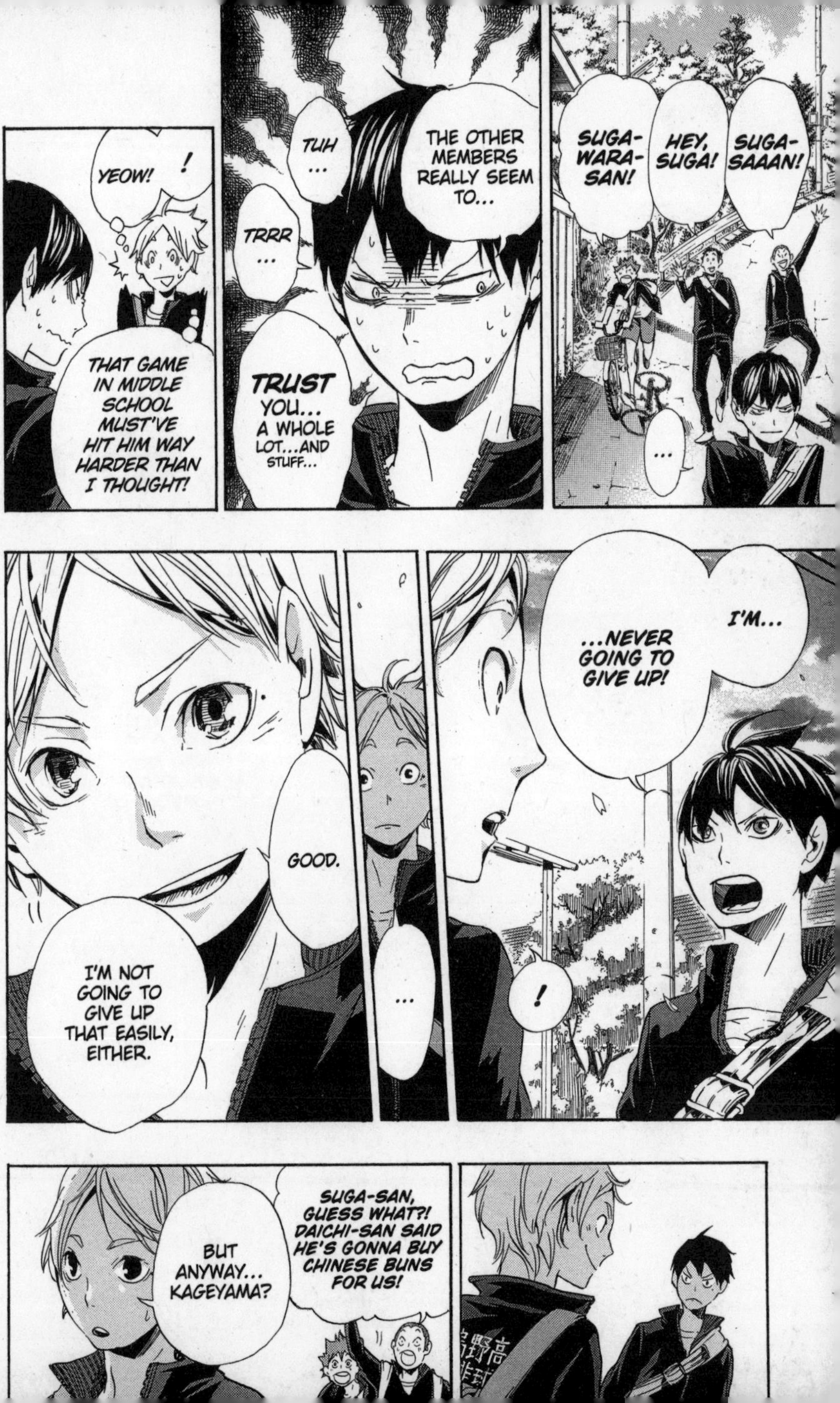
SUGA-SAAAN!
HEY, SUGA!
SUGA-WARA-SAN!
...
THE OTHER MEMBERS REALLY SEEM TO...
TUH ...
TRRR ...
TRUST YOU... A WHOLE LOT...AND STUFF...
!
YEOW!
THAT GAME IN MIDDLE SCHOOL MUST'VE HIT HIM WAY HARDER THAN I THOUGHT!
I'M...
...NEVER GOING TO GIVE UP!
!
...
GOOD.
I'M NOT GOING TO GIVE UP THAT EASILY, EITHER.
SUGA-SAN, GUESS WHAT?! DAICHI-SAN SAID HE'S GONNA BUY CHINESE BUNS FOR US!
BUT ANYWAY... KAGEYAMA?

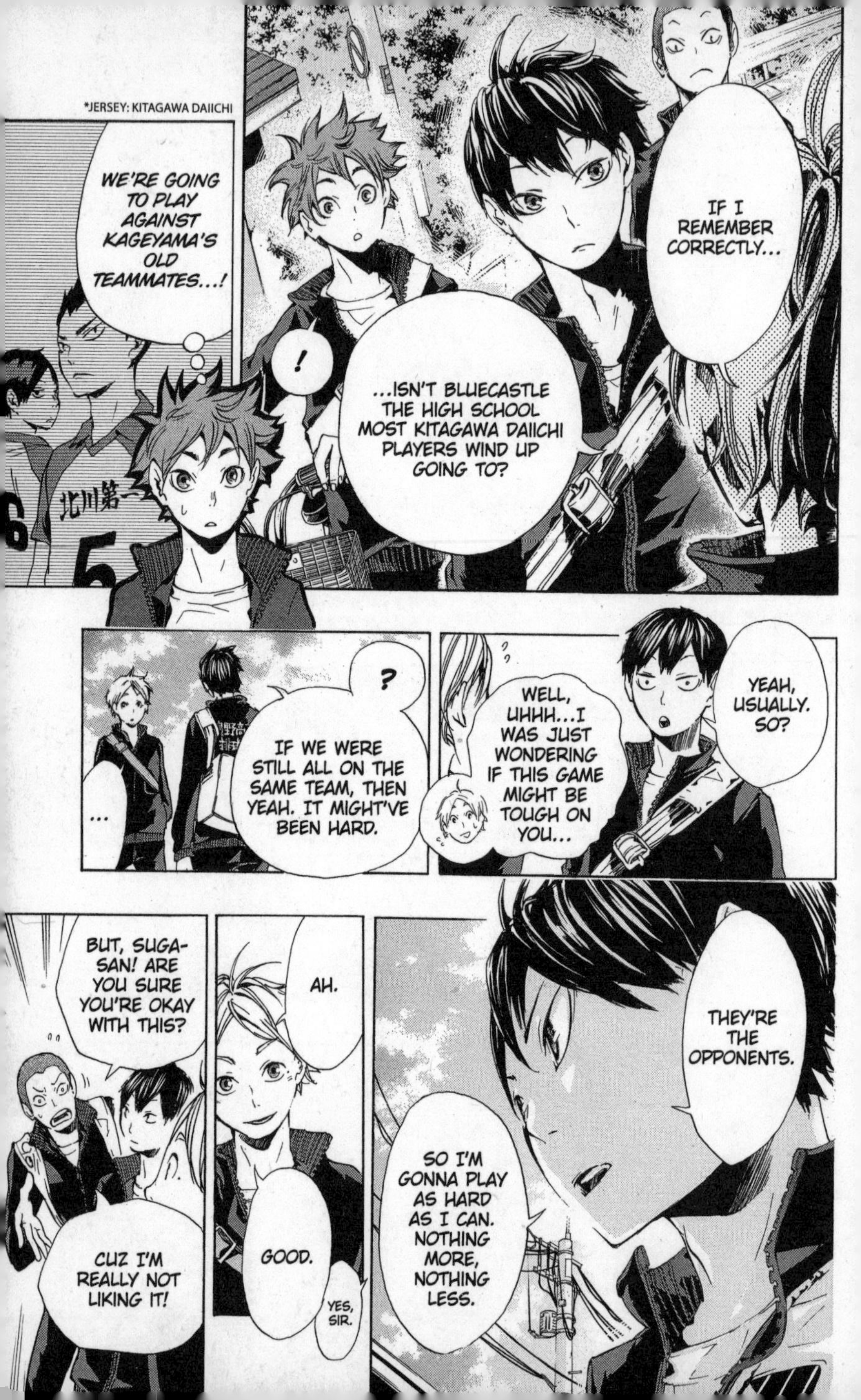
IF I REMEMBER CORRECTLY...
!
...ISN'T BLUECASTLE THE HIGH SCHOOL MOST KITAGAWA DAIICHI PLAYERS WIND UP GOING TO?
*JERSEY: KITAGAWA DAIICHI
WE'RE GOING TO PLAY AGAINST KAGEYAMA'S OLD TEAMMATES...!
北川第一
YEAH, USUALLY. SO?
WELL, UHHH...I WAS JUST WONDERING IF THIS GAME MIGHT BE TOUGH ON YOU...
?
IF WE WERE STILL ALL ON THE SAME TEAM, THEN YEAH. IT MIGHT'VE BEEN HARD.
...
THEY'RE THE OPPONENTS.
SO I'M GONNA PLAY AS HARD AS I CAN. NOTHING MORE, NOTHING LESS.
AH.
GOOD.
YES, SIR.
BUT, SUGA-SAN! ARE YOU SURE YOU'RE OKAY WITH THIS?
CUZ I'M REALLY NOT LIKING IT!

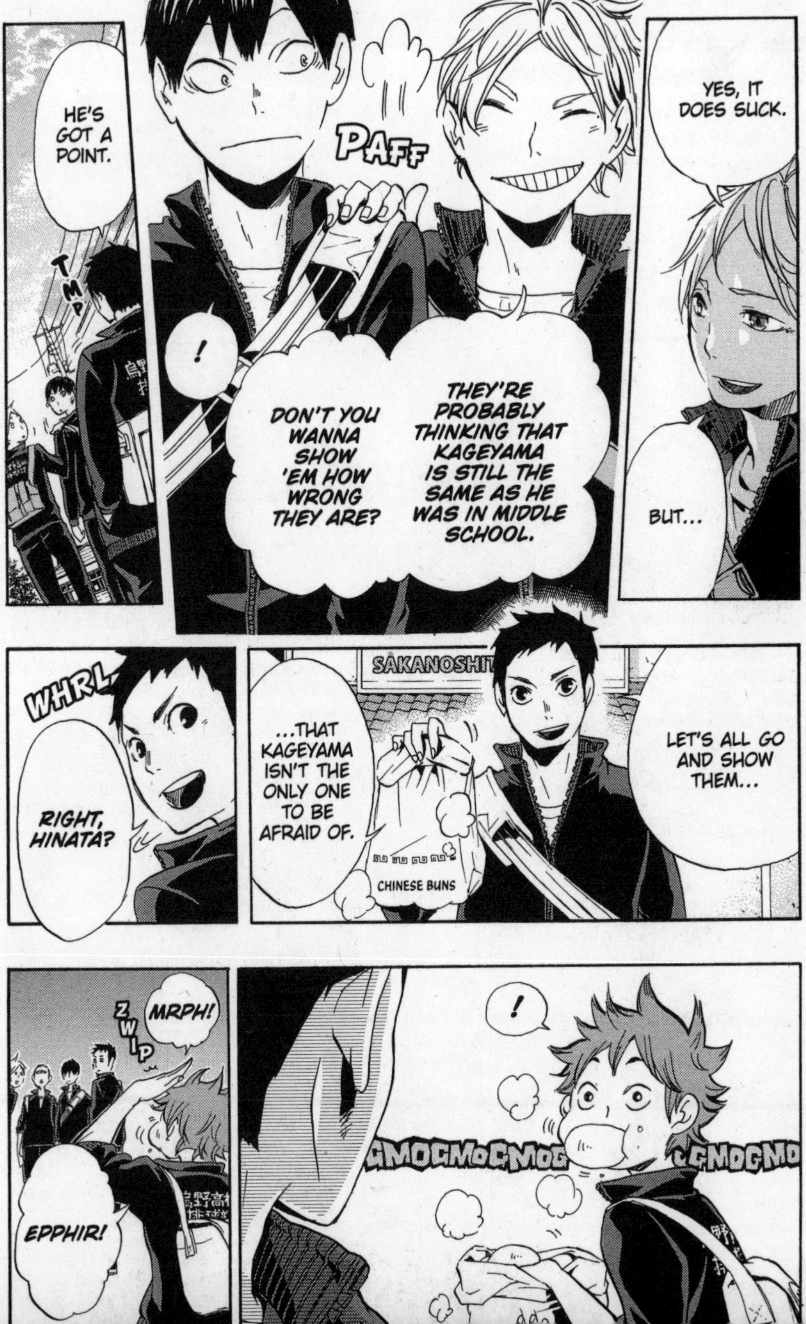
YES, IT DOES SUCK.
BUT...
PAFF
THEY'RE PROBABLY THINKING THAT KAGEYAMA IS STILL THE SAME AS HE WAS IN MIDDLE SCHOOL.
!
DON'T YOU WANNA SHOW 'EM HOW WRONG THEY ARE?
HE'S GOT A POINT.
TMP
LET'S ALL GO AND SHOW THEM...
SAKANOSHIT
...THAT KAGEYAMA ISN'T THE ONLY ONE TO BE AFRAID OF.
CHINESE BUNS
WHRL
RIGHT, HINATA?
!
GMOGMO
GMOGMOGMOG
MRPH!
ZWIP
EPPHIR!

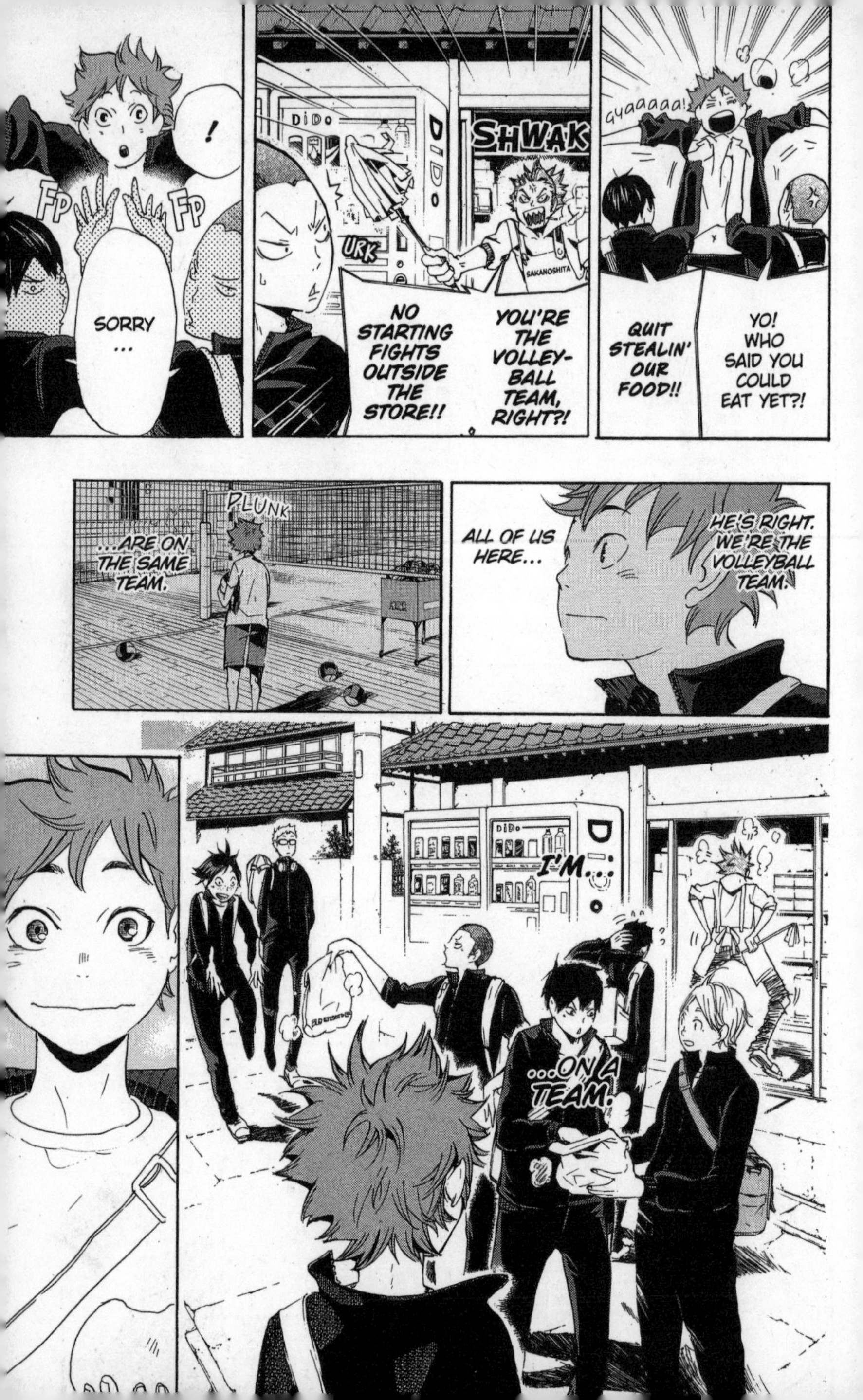
GYAAAAA!
YO! WHO SAID YOU COULD EAT YET?!
QUIT STEALIN' OUR FOOD!!
SHWAK
DiDo
SAKANOSHITA
URK
YOU'RE THE VOLLEYBALL TEAM, RIGHT?!
NO STARTING FIGHTS OUTSIDE THE STORE!!
!
Fp
Fp
SORRY ...
HE'S RIGHT. WE'RE THE VOLLEYBALL TEAM.
ALL OF US HERE...
PLUNK
...ARE ON THE SAME TEAM.
DiDo
I'M...
...ON A TEAM.

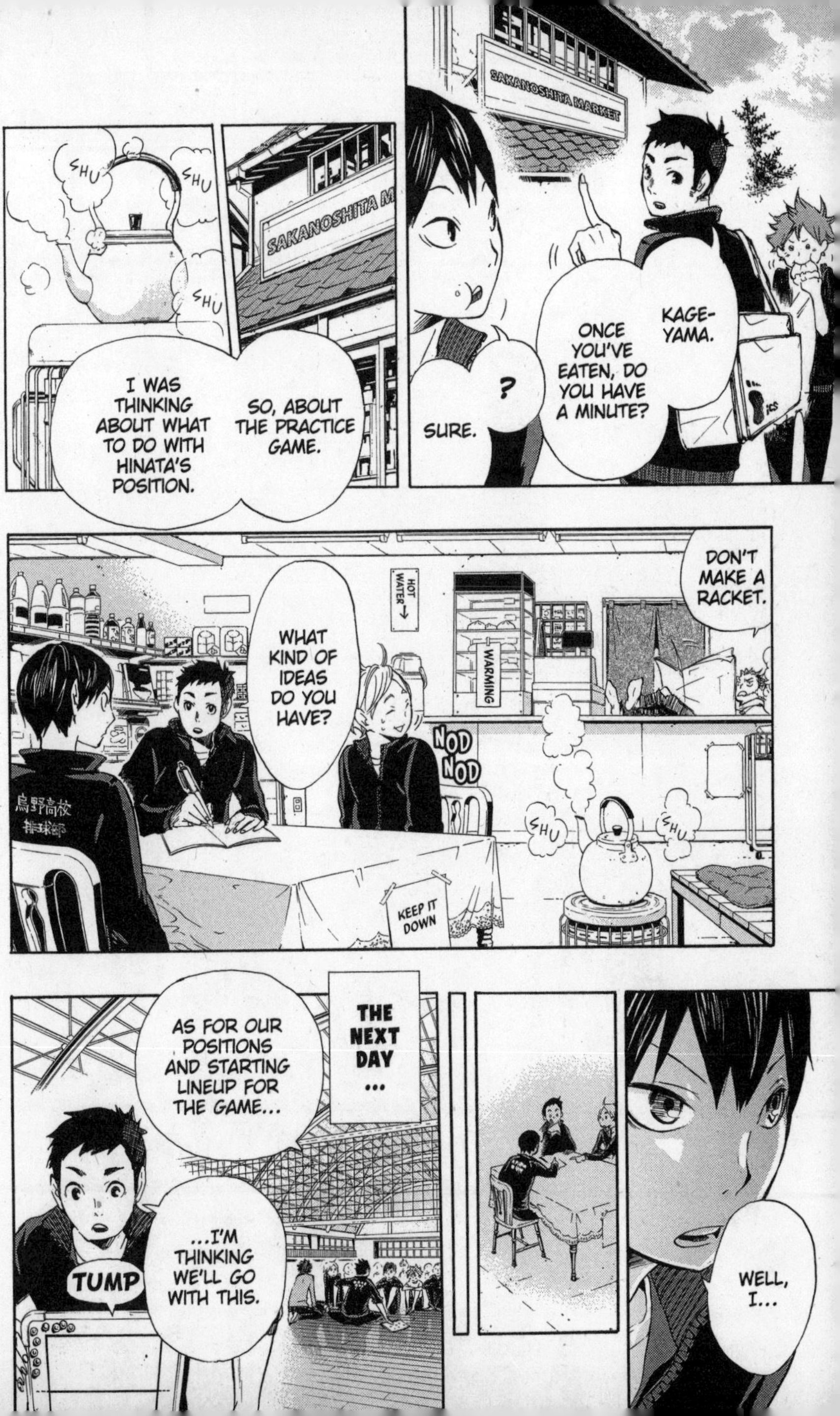
SAKANOSHITA MARKET
KAGE-YAMA.
ONCE YOU'VE EATEN, DO YOU HAVE A MINUTE?
?
SURE.
SAKANOSHITA M
SO, ABOUT THE PRACTICE GAME.
I WAS THINKING ABOUT WHAT TO DO WITH HINATA'S POSITION.
SHU
SHU
SHU
DON'T MAKE A RACKET.
WARMING
HOT WATER
WHAT KIND OF IDEAS DO YOU HAVE?
NOD NOD
SHU
SHU
KEEP IT DOWN
WELL, I...
THE NEXT DAY...
AS FOR OUR POSITIONS AND STARTING LINEUP FOR THE GAME...
...I'M THINKING WE'LL GO WITH THIS.
TUMP

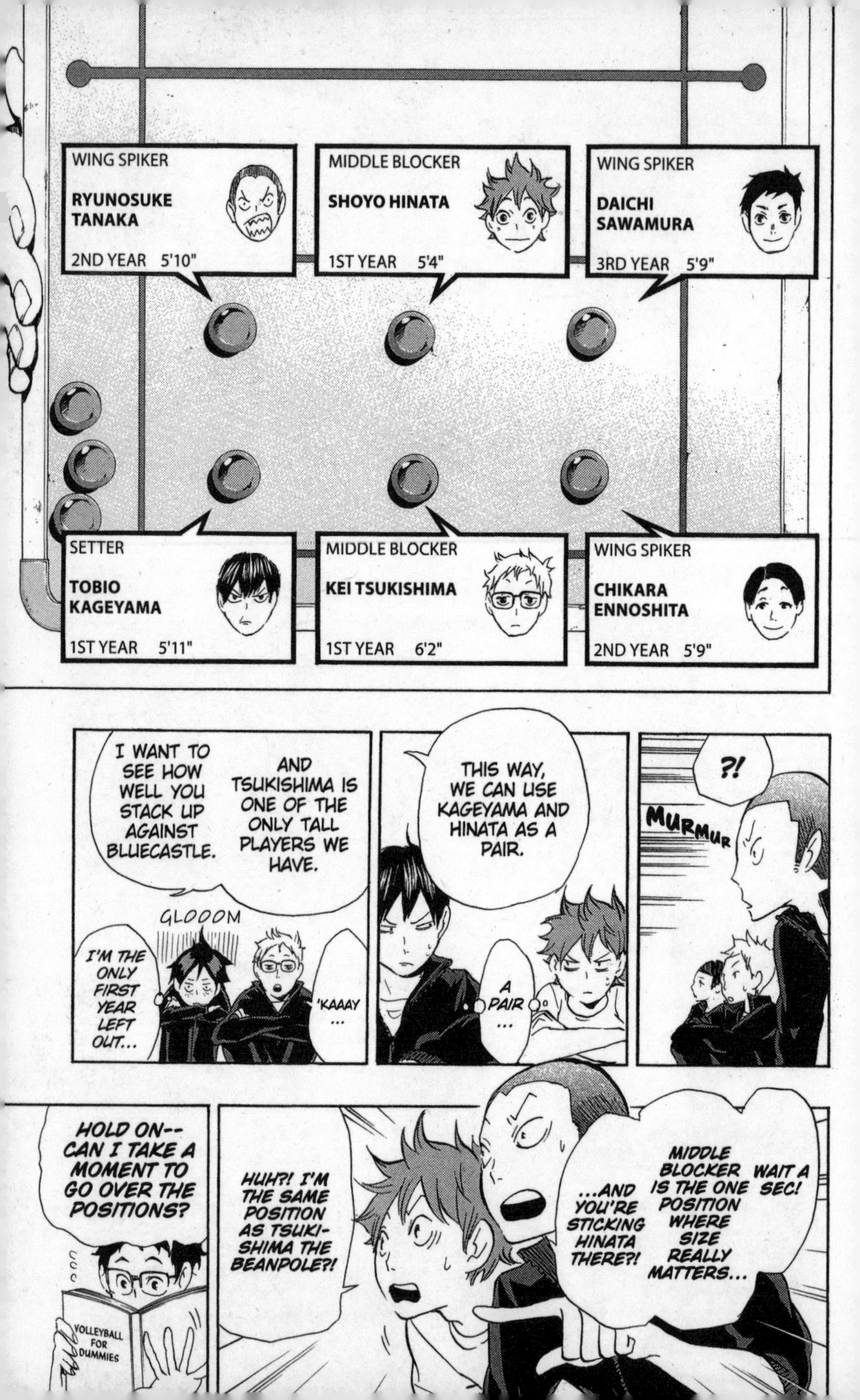
WING SPIKER DAICHI SAWAMURA 3RD YEAR 5'9"
MIDDLE BLOCKER SHOYO HINATA 1ST YEAR 5'4"
WING SPIKER RYUNOSUKE TANAKA 2ND YEAR 5'10"
WING SPIKER CHIKARA ENNOSHITA 2ND YEAR 5'9"
MIDDLE BLOCKER KEI TSUKISHIMA 1ST YEAR 6'2"
SETTER TOBIO KAGEYAMA 1ST YEAR 5'11"
?!
MURMUR
THIS WAY, WE CAN USE KAGEYAMA AND HINATA AS A PAIR.
A PAIR...
AND TSUKISHIMA IS ONE OF THE ONLY TALL PLAYERS WE HAVE.
I WANT TO SEE HOW WELL YOU STACK UP AGAINST BLUECASTLE.
'KAAAY...
GLOOOM
I'M THE ONLY FIRST YEAR LEFT OUT...
WAIT A SEC!
MIDDLE BLOCKER IS THE ONE POSITION WHERE SIZE REALLY MATTERS...
...AND YOU'RE STICKING HINATA THERE?!
HUH?! I'M THE SAME POSITION AS TSUKI-SHIMA THE BEANPOLE?!
HOLD ON-- CAN I TAKE A MOMENT TO GO OVER THE POSITIONS?
VOLLEYBALL FOR DUMMIES

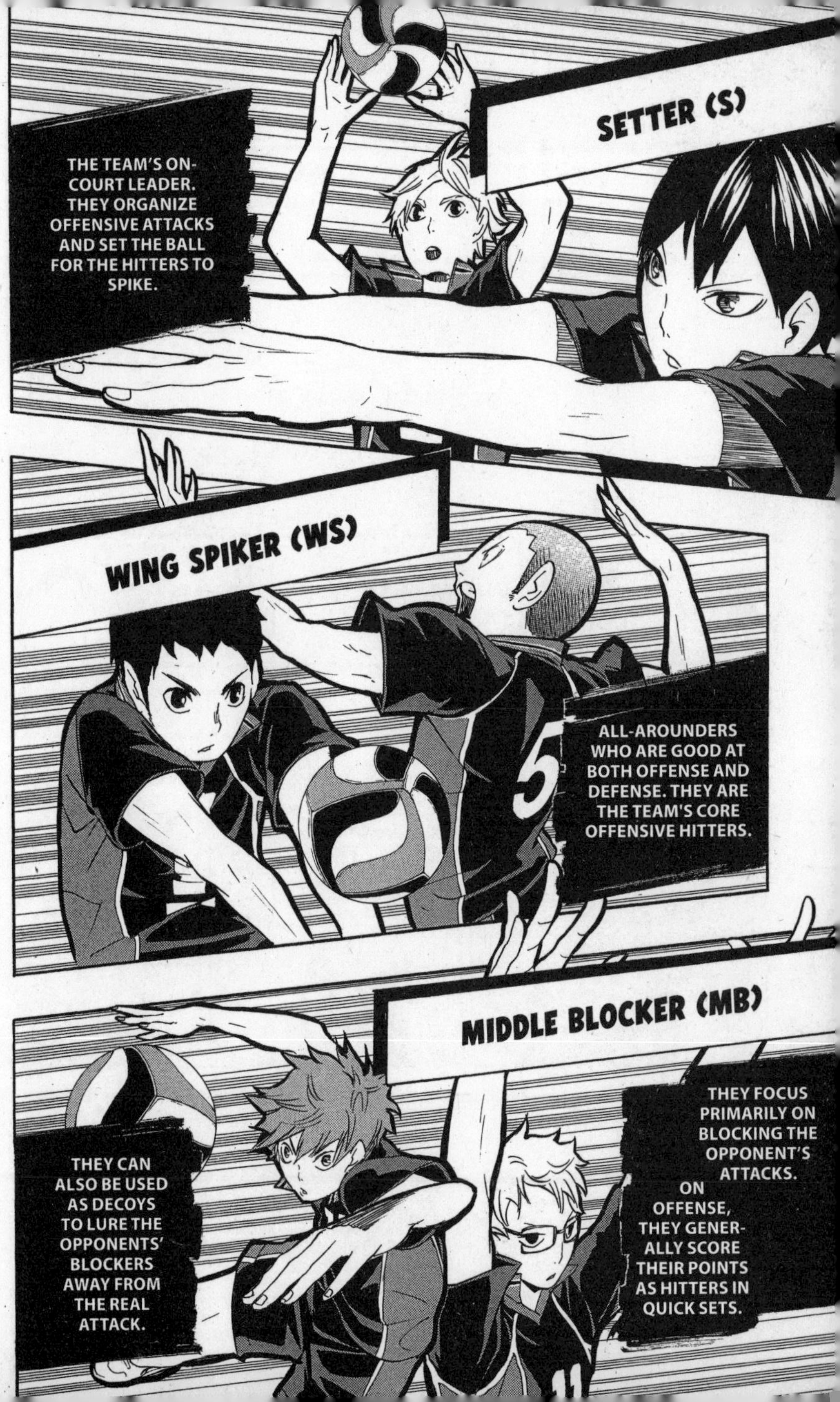
SETTER (S)
THE TEAM'S ON-COURT LEADER. THEY ORGANIZE OFFENSIVE ATTACKS AND SET THE BALL FOR THE HITTERS TO SPIKE.
WING SPIKER (WS)
ALL-AROUNDERS WHO ARE GOOD AT BOTH OFFENSE AND DEFENSE. THEY ARE THE TEAM'S CORE OFFENSIVE HITTERS.
5
MIDDLE BLOCKER (MB)
THEY FOCUS PRIMARILY ON BLOCKING THE OPPONENT'S ATTACKS.
ON OFFENSE, THEY GENER-ALLY SCORE THEIR POINTS AS HITTERS IN QUICK SETS.
THEY CAN ALSO BE USED AS DECOYS TO LURE THE OPPONENTS' BLOCKERS AWAY FROM THE REAL ATTACK.

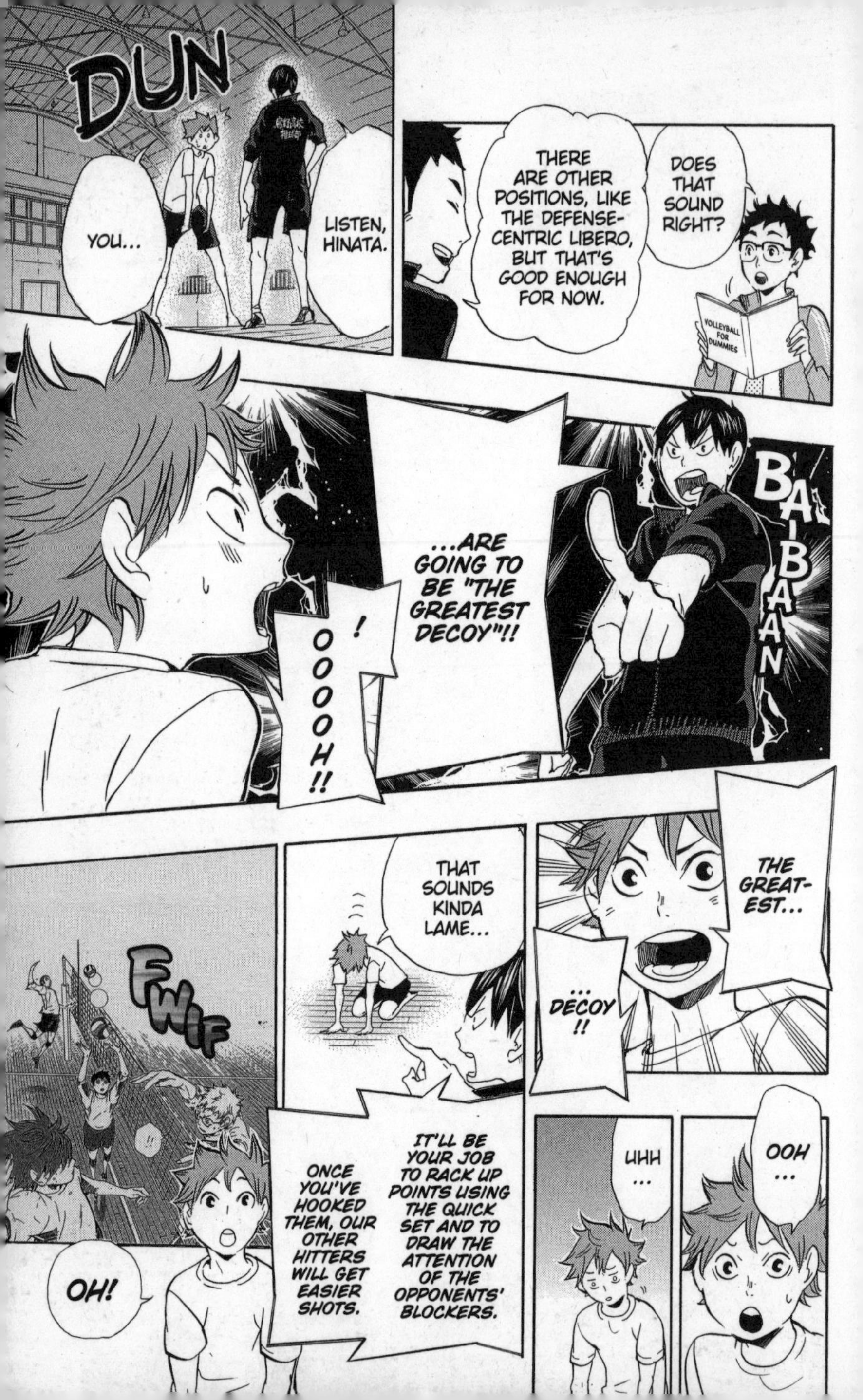
DOES THAT SOUND RIGHT?
THERE ARE OTHER POSITIONS, LIKE THE DEFENSE-CENTRIC LIBERO, BUT THAT'S GOOD ENOUGH FOR NOW.
VOLLEYBALL FOR DUMMIES
DUN
LISTEN, HINATA.
YOU...
BABAAN
...ARE GOING TO BE "THE GREATEST DECOY"!!
!
OOOOOH!!
THE GREAT-EST...
...DECOY !!
THAT SOUNDS KINDA LAME...
OOH...
UHH...
IT'LL BE YOUR JOB TO RACK UP POINTS USING THE QUICK SET AND TO DRAW THE ATTENTION OF THE OPPONENTS' BLOCKERS.
ONCE YOU'VE HOOKED THEM, OUR OTHER HITTERS WILL GET EASIER SHOTS.
FWIF
OH!

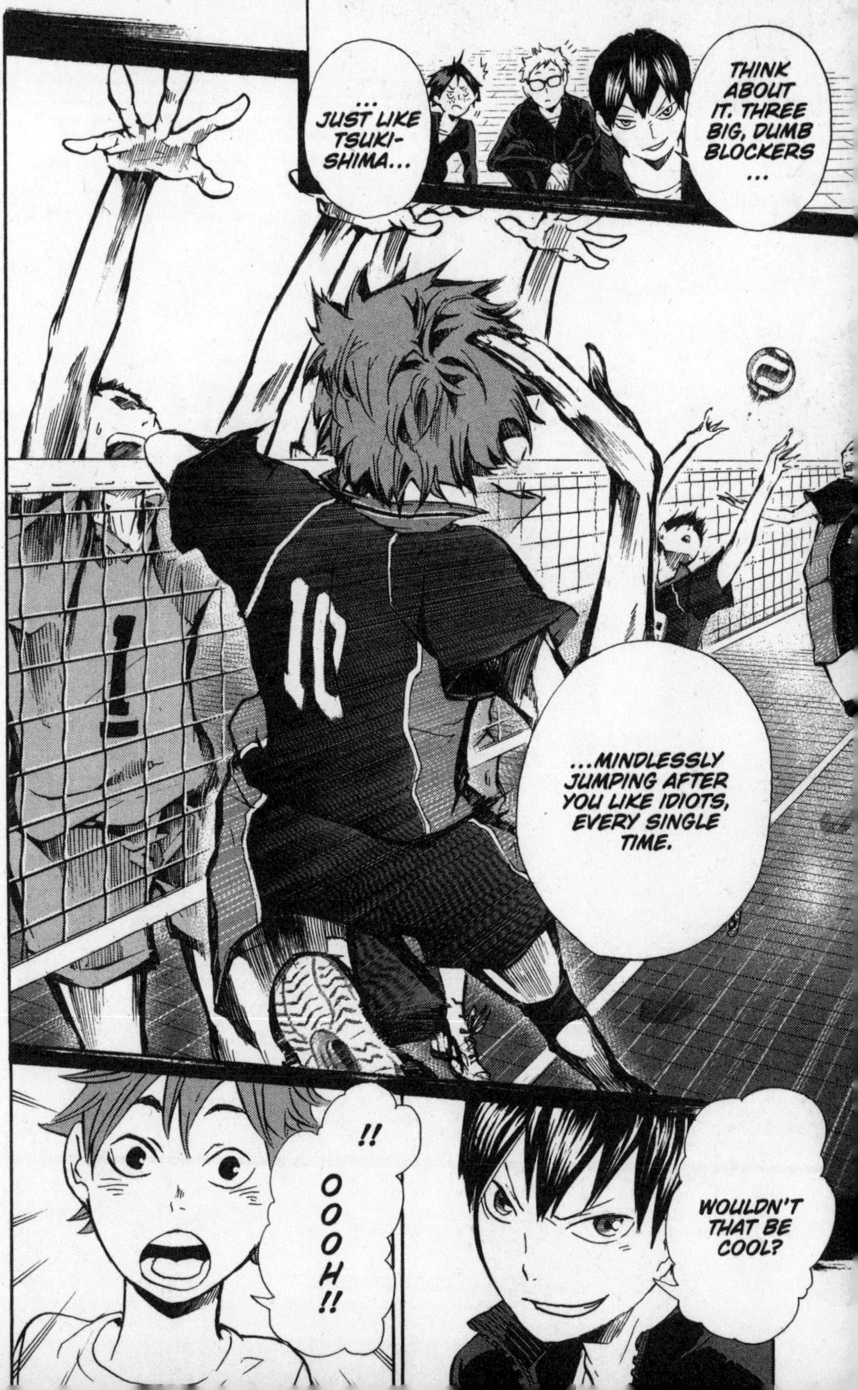
THINK ABOUT IT. THREE BIG, DUMB BLOCKERS...
...JUST LIKE TSUKISHIMA...
...MINDLESSLY JUMPING AFTER YOU LIKE IDIOTS, EVERY SINGLE TIME.
WOULDN'T THAT BE COOL?
!!
OOOOH!!

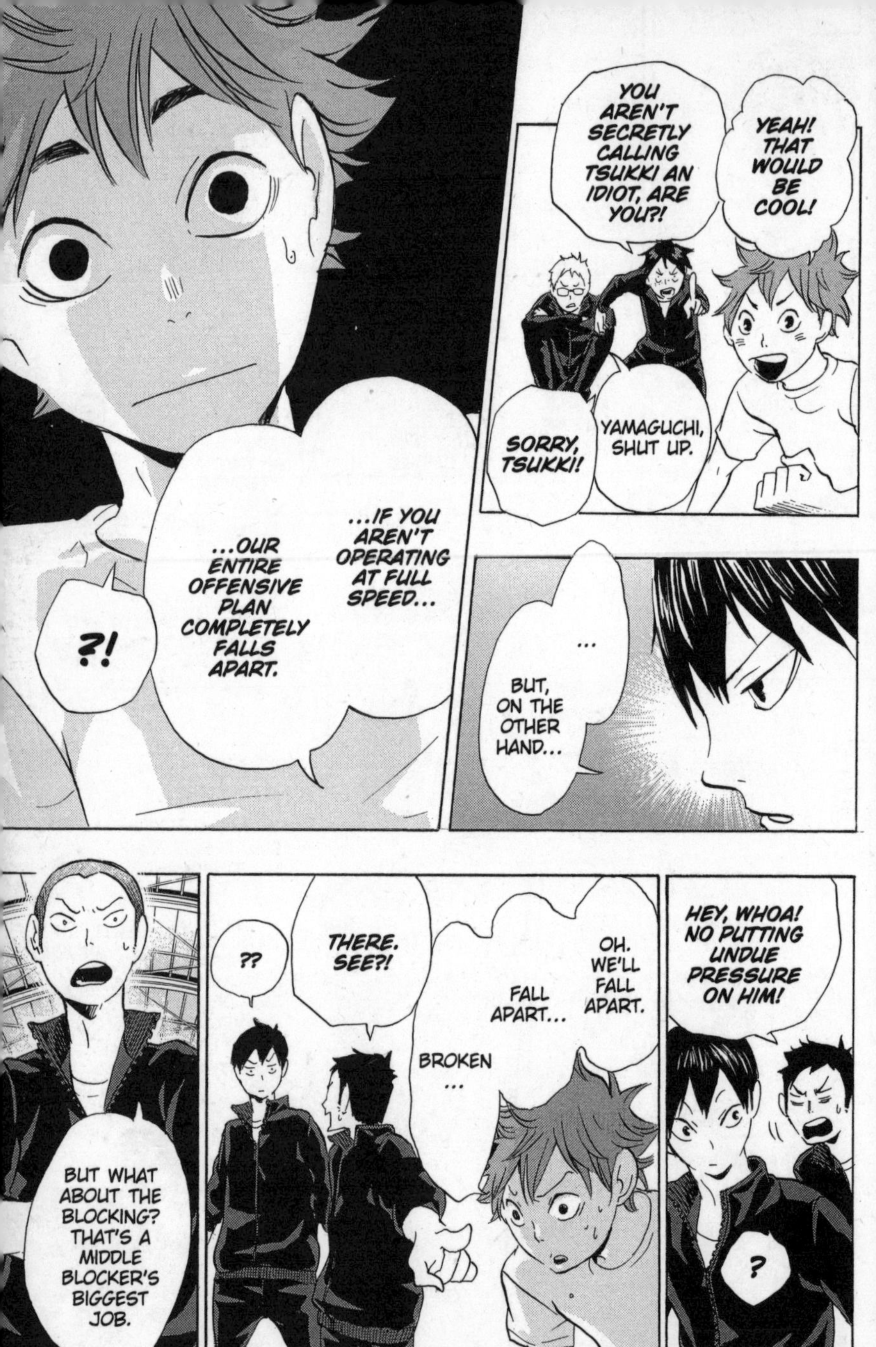
YEAH! THAT WOULD BE COOL!
YOU AREN'T SECRETLY CALLING TSUKKI AN IDIOT, ARE YOU?!
YAMAGUCHI, SHUT UP.
SORRY, TSUKKI!
...
BUT, ON THE OTHER HAND...
...IF YOU AREN'T OPERATING AT FULL SPEED...
...OUR ENTIRE OFFENSIVE PLAN COMPLETELY FALLS APART.
?!
HEY, WHOA! NO PUTTING UNDUE PRESSURE ON HIM!
?
OH. WE'LL FALL APART.
FALL APART...
BROKEN...
THERE. SEE?!
??
BUT WHAT ABOUT THE BLOCKING? THAT'S A MIDDLE BLOCKER'S BIGGEST JOB.

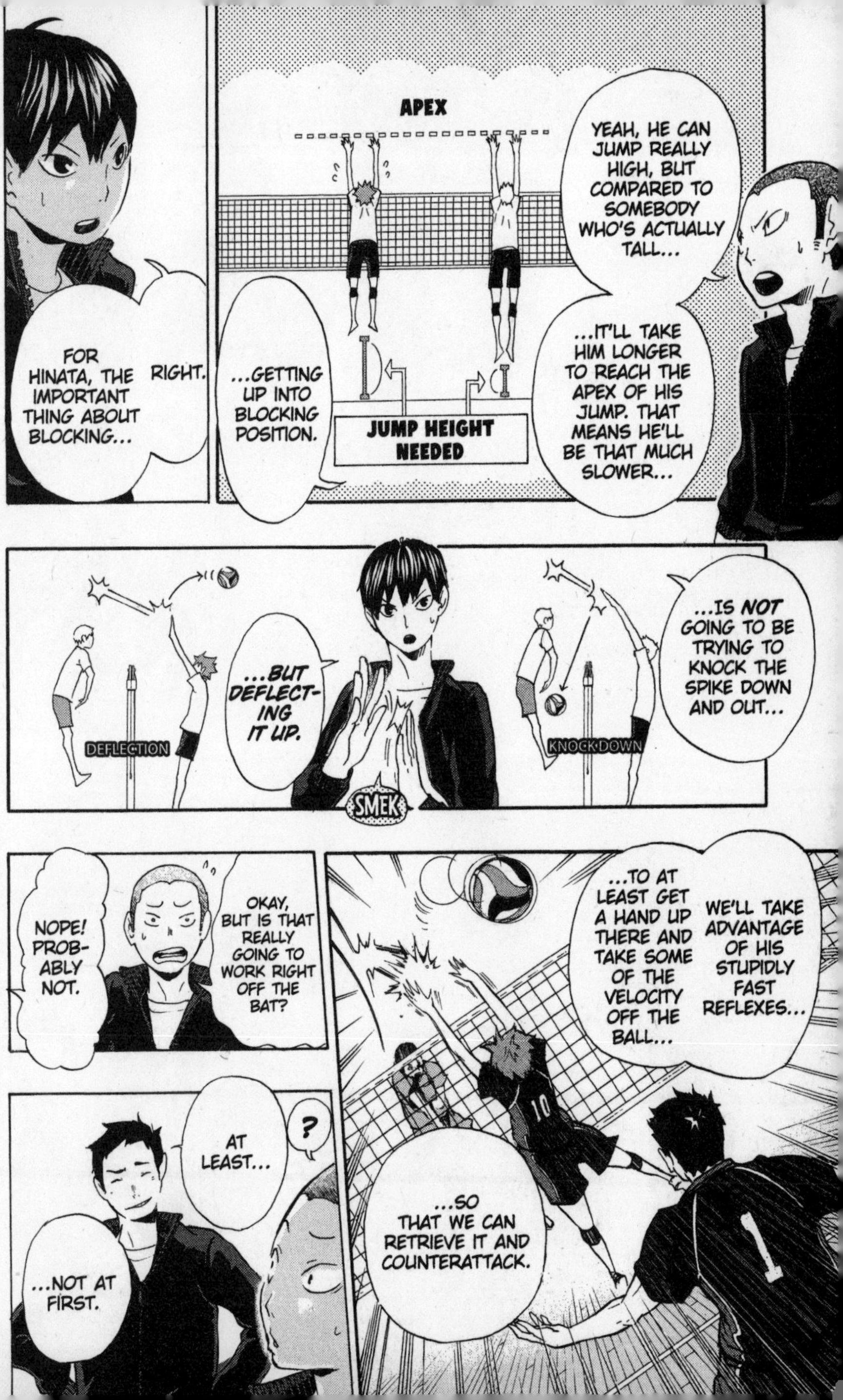
YEAH, HE CAN JUMP REALLY HIGH, BUT COMPARED TO SOMEBODY WHO'S ACTUALLY TALL...
...IT'LL TAKE HIM LONGER TO REACH THE APEX OF HIS JUMP. THAT MEANS HE'LL BE THAT MUCH SLOWER...
APEX
JUMP HEIGHT NEEDED
...GETTING UP INTO BLOCKING POSITION.
RIGHT.
FOR HINATA, THE IMPORTANT THING ABOUT BLOCKING...
KNOCK DOWN
...IS *NOT* GOING TO BE TRYING TO KNOCK THE SPIKE DOWN AND OUT...
...*BUT DEFLECTING IT UP.*
DEFLECTION
SMEK
WE'LL TAKE ADVANTAGE OF HIS STUPIDLY FAST REFLEXES...
...TO AT LEAST GET A HAND UP THERE AND TAKE SOME OF THE VELOCITY OFF THE BALL...
...SO THAT WE CAN RETRIEVE IT AND COUNTERATTACK.
OKAY, BUT IS THAT REALLY GOING TO WORK RIGHT OFF THE BAT?
NOPE! PROBABLY NOT.
?
AT LEAST...
...NOT AT FIRST.

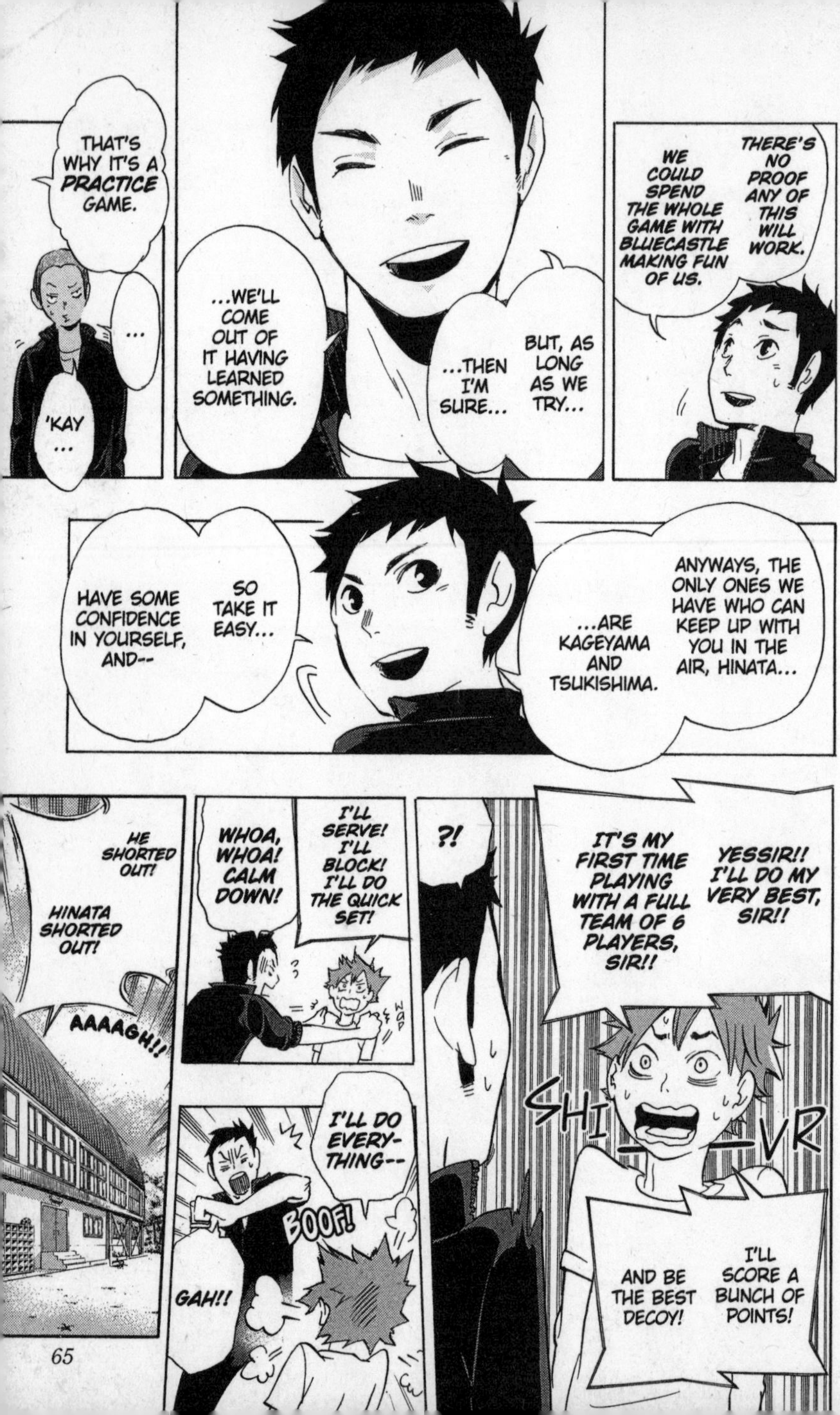
THERE'S NO PROOF ANY OF THIS WILL WORK.
WE COULD SPEND THE WHOLE GAME WITH BLUECASTLE MAKING FUN OF US.
BUT, AS LONG AS WE TRY...
...THEN I'M SURE...
...WE'LL COME OUT OF IT HAVING LEARNED SOMETHING.
THAT'S WHY IT'S A PRACTICE GAME.
...
'KAY ...
ANYWAYS, THE ONLY ONES WE HAVE WHO CAN KEEP UP WITH YOU IN THE AIR, HINATA...
...ARE KAGEYAMA AND TSUKISHIMA.
SO TAKE IT EASY...
HAVE SOME CONFIDENCE IN YOURSELF, AND--
YESSIR!! I'LL DO MY VERY BEST, SIR!!
IT'S MY FIRST TIME PLAYING WITH A FULL TEAM OF 6 PLAYERS, SIR!!
SHI—VR
I'LL SCORE A BUNCH OF POINTS!
AND BE THE BEST DECOY!
?!
I'LL SERVE! I'LL BLOCK! I'LL DO THE QUICK SET!
WHOA, WHOA! CALM DOWN!
WAP
I'LL DO EVERY-THING--
BOOF!
GAH!!
HE SHORTED OUT!
HINATA SHORTED OUT!
AAAAGH!!

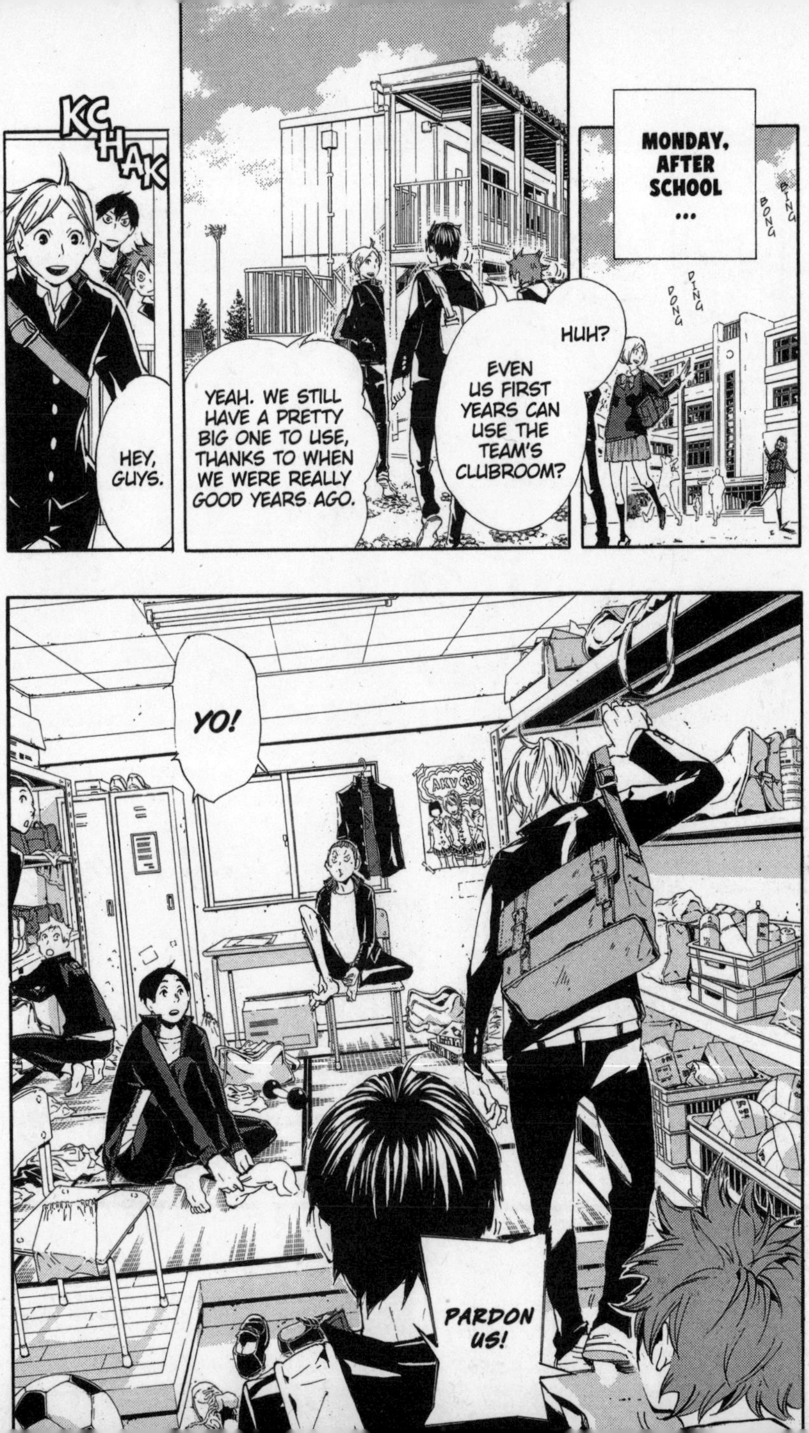
MONDAY, AFTER SCHOOL...
BING BONG
DING DONG
HUH?
EVEN US FIRST YEARS CAN USE THE TEAM'S CLUBROOM?
YEAH. WE STILL HAVE A PRETTY BIG ONE TO USE, THANKS TO WHEN WE WERE REALLY GOOD YEARS AGO.
KCHAK
HEY, GUYS.
YO!
PARDON US!

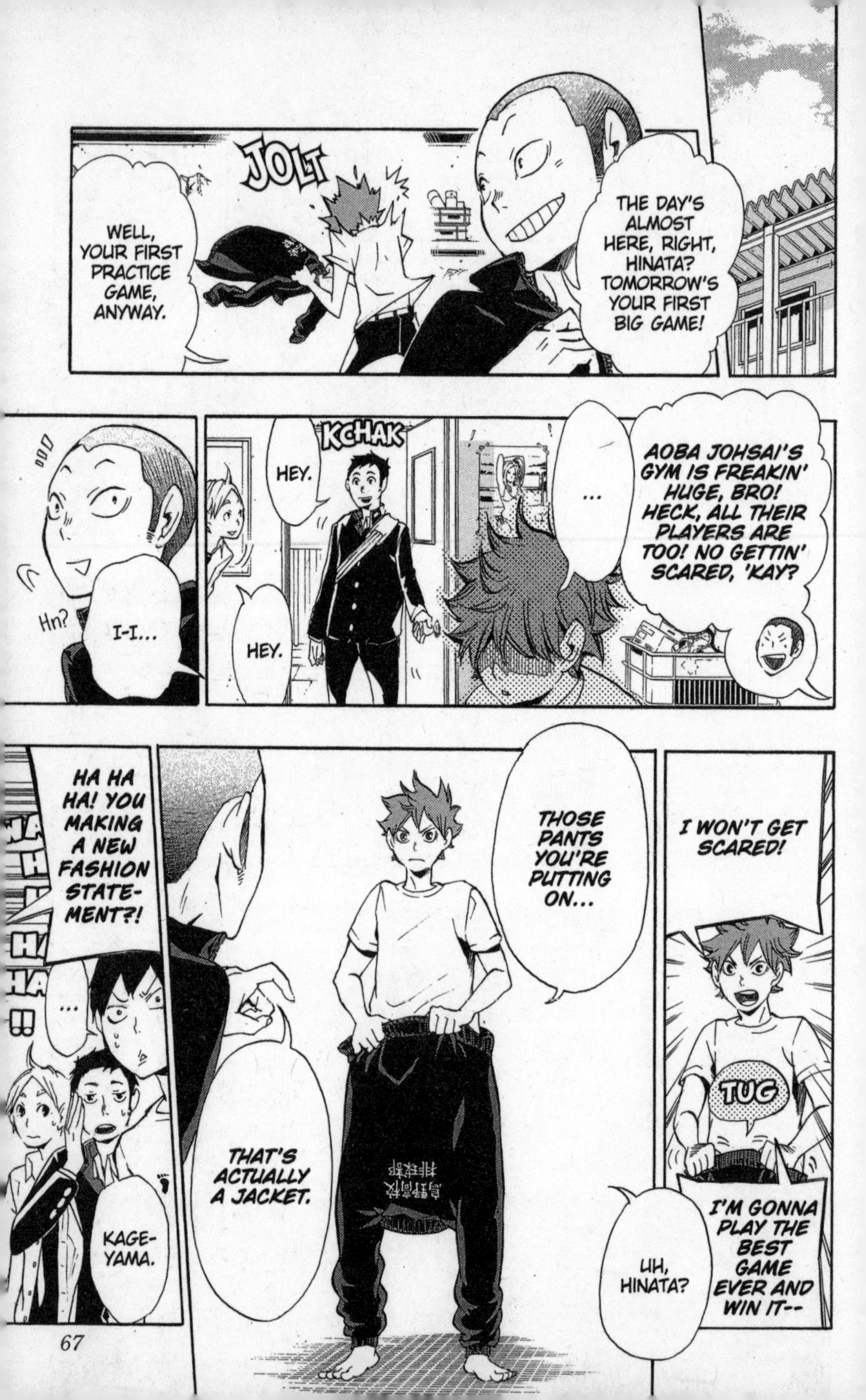
THE DAY'S ALMOST HERE, RIGHT, HINATA? TOMORROW'S YOUR FIRST BIG GAME!
JOLT
WELL, YOUR FIRST PRACTICE GAME, ANYWAY.
AOBA JOHSAI'S GYM IS FREAKIN' HUGE, BRO! HECK, ALL THEIR PLAYERS ARE TOO! NO GETTIN' SCARED, 'KAY?
...
KCHAK
HEY.
HEY.
Hn?
I-I...
I WON'T GET SCARED!
TUG
I'M GONNA PLAY THE BEST GAME EVER AND WIN IT--
UH, HINATA?
THOSE PANTS YOU'RE PUTTING ON...
THAT'S ACTUALLY A JACKET.
HA HA HA! YOU MAKING A NEW FASHION STATEMENT?!
...
KAGE-YAMA.

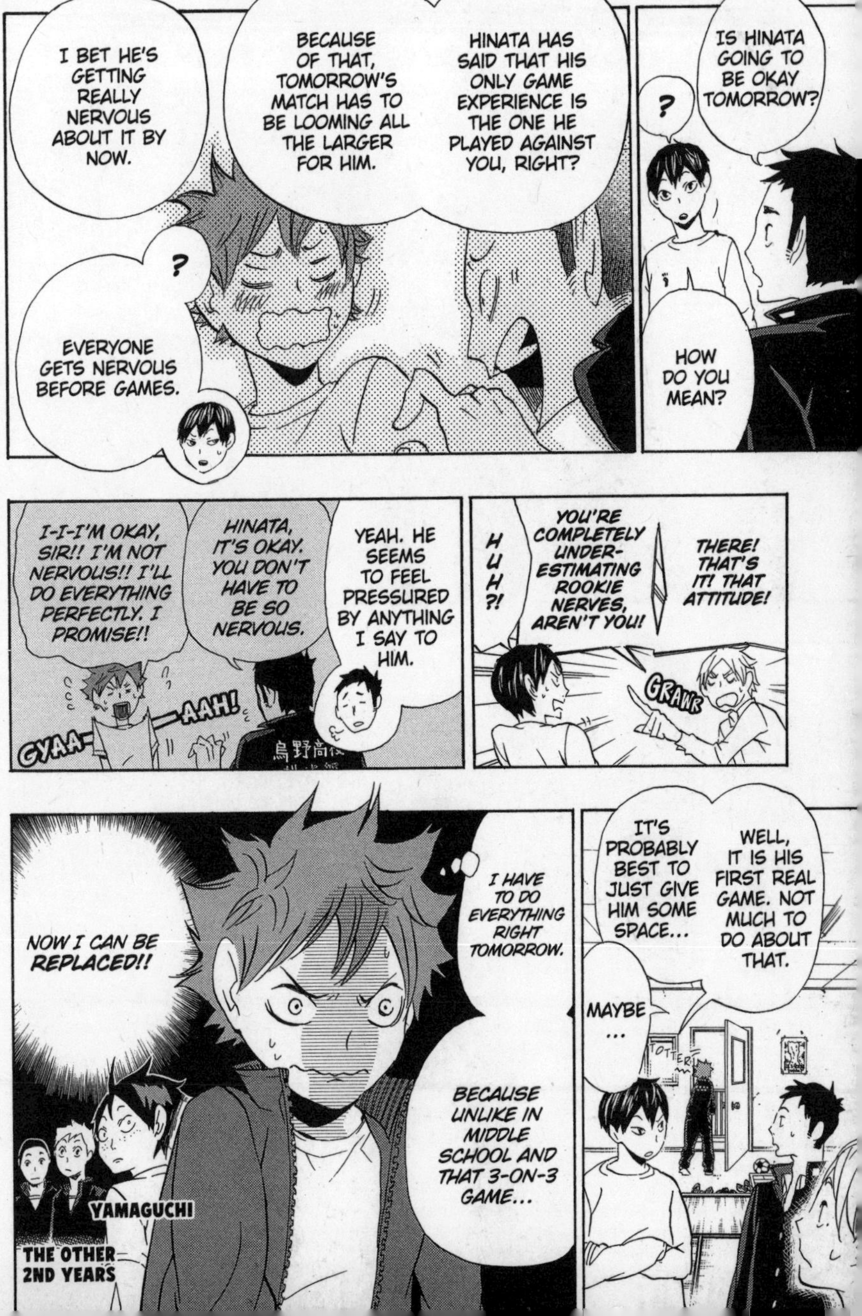
IS HINATA GOING TO BE OKAY TOMORROW?
?
HOW DO YOU MEAN?
HINATA HAS SAID THAT HIS ONLY GAME EXPERIENCE IS THE ONE HE PLAYED AGAINST YOU, RIGHT?
BECAUSE OF THAT, TOMORROW'S MATCH HAS TO BE LOOMING ALL THE LARGER FOR HIM.
I BET HE'S GETTING REALLY NERVOUS ABOUT IT BY NOW.
?
EVERYONE GETS NERVOUS BEFORE GAMES.
THERE! THAT'S IT! THAT ATTITUDE!
YOU'RE COMPLETELY UNDER-ESTIMATING ROOKIE NERVES, AREN'T YOU!
HUH?!
GRAWR
YEAH. HE SEEMS TO FEEL PRESSURED BY ANYTHING I SAY TO HIM.
HINATA, IT'S OKAY. YOU DON'T HAVE TO BE SO NERVOUS.
I-I-I'M OKAY, SIR!! I'M NOT NERVOUS!! I'LL DO EVERYTHING PERFECTLY. I PROMISE!!
GYAA—AAH!
WELL, IT IS HIS FIRST REAL GAME. NOT MUCH TO DO ABOUT THAT.
IT'S PROBABLY BEST TO JUST GIVE HIM SOME SPACE...
MAYBE...
TOTTER
I HAVE TO DO EVERYTHING RIGHT TOMORROW.
BECAUSE UNLIKE IN MIDDLE SCHOOL AND THAT 3-ON-3 GAME...
NOW I CAN BE REPLACED!!
YAMAGUCHI
THE OTHER 2ND YEARS

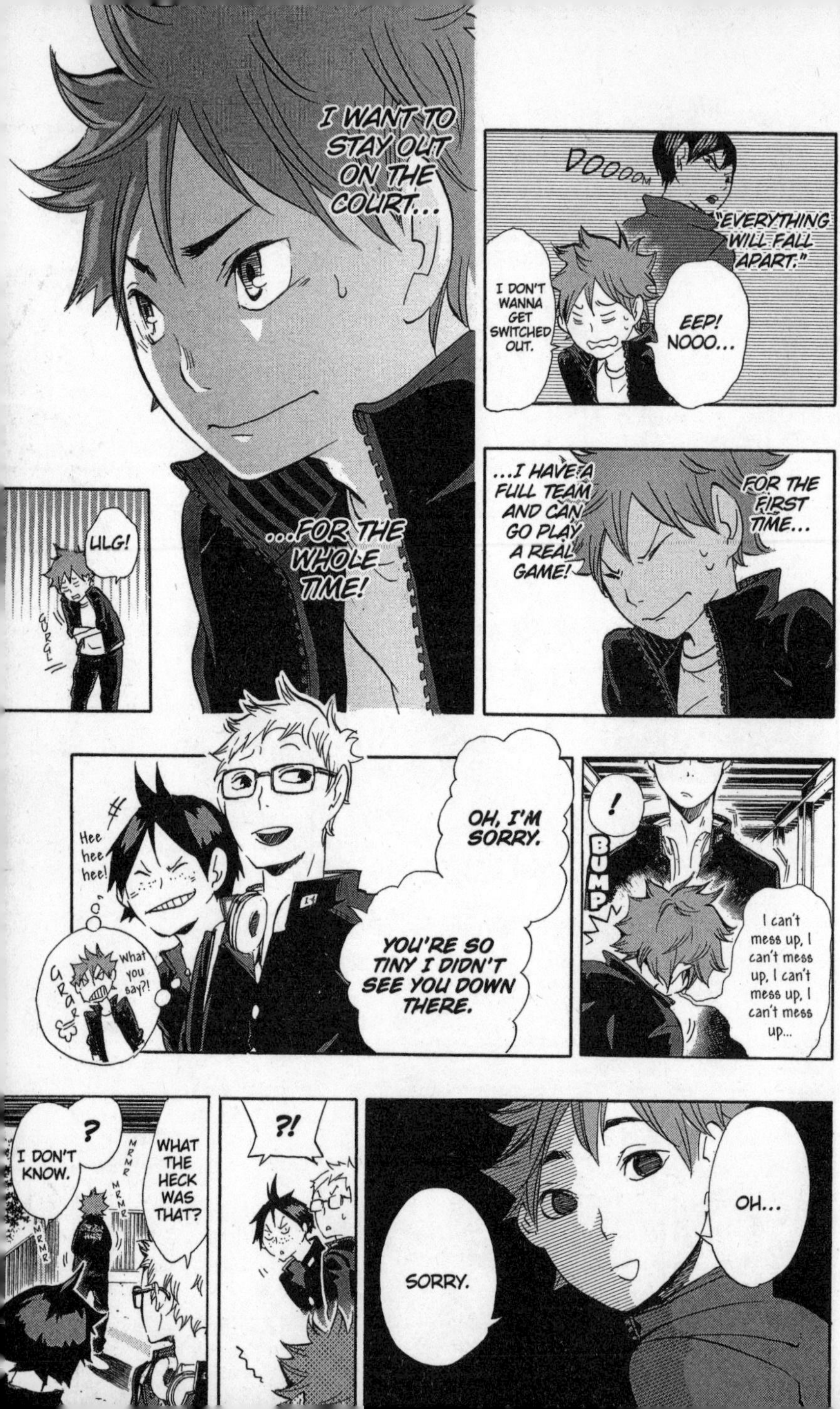
DOOOOOM
"EVERYTHING WILL FALL APART."
EEP! NOOO...
I DON'T WANNA GET SWITCHED OUT.
FOR THE FIRST TIME...
...I HAVE A FULL TEAM AND CAN GO PLAY A REAL GAME!
I WANT TO STAY OUT ON THE COURT...
...FOR THE WHOLE TIME!
ULG!
GURGL
!
BUMP
I can't mess up, I can't mess up, I can't mess up, I can't mess up...
OH, I'M SORRY.
YOU'RE SO TINY I DIDN'T SEE YOU DOWN THERE.
Hee hee hee!
What you say?!
GRAR
OH...
SORRY.
?!
WHAT THE HECK WAS THAT?
?
I DON'T KNOW.
MRMR
MRMR
MRMR

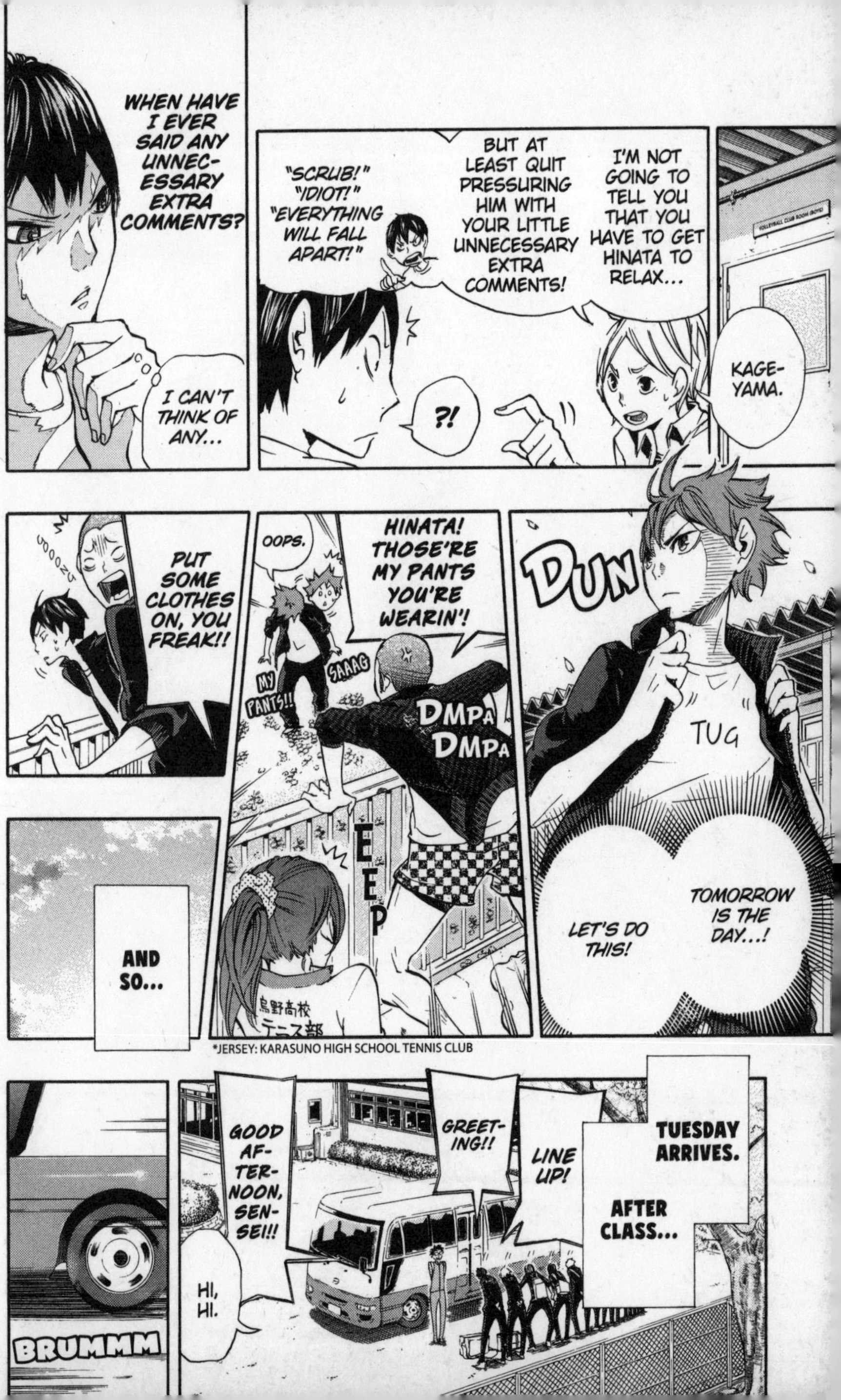
KAGE-YAMA.
I'M NOT GOING TO TELL YOU THAT YOU HAVE TO GET HINATA TO RELAX...
BUT AT LEAST QUIT PRESSURING HIM WITH YOUR LITTLE UNNECESSARY EXTRA COMMENTS!
"SCRUB!" "IDIOT!" "EVERYTHING WILL FALL APART!"
?!
WHEN HAVE I EVER SAID ANY UNNEC-ESSARY EXTRA COMMENTS?
I CAN'T THINK OF ANY...
DUN
TUG
TOMORROW IS THE DAY...!
LET'S DO THIS!
HINATA! THOSE'RE MY PANTS YOU'RE WEARIN'!
OOPS.
SAAAG
MY PANTS!!
DMPA DMPA
EEP
烏野高校
テニス部
PUT SOME CLOTHES ON, YOU FREAK!!
AND SO...
TUESDAY ARRIVES.
AFTER CLASS...
LINE UP!
GREET-ING!!
GOOD AF-TER-NOON, SEN-SEI!!!
HI, HI.
BRUMMMM

*JERSEY: KARASUNO HIGH SCHOOL TENNIS CLUB

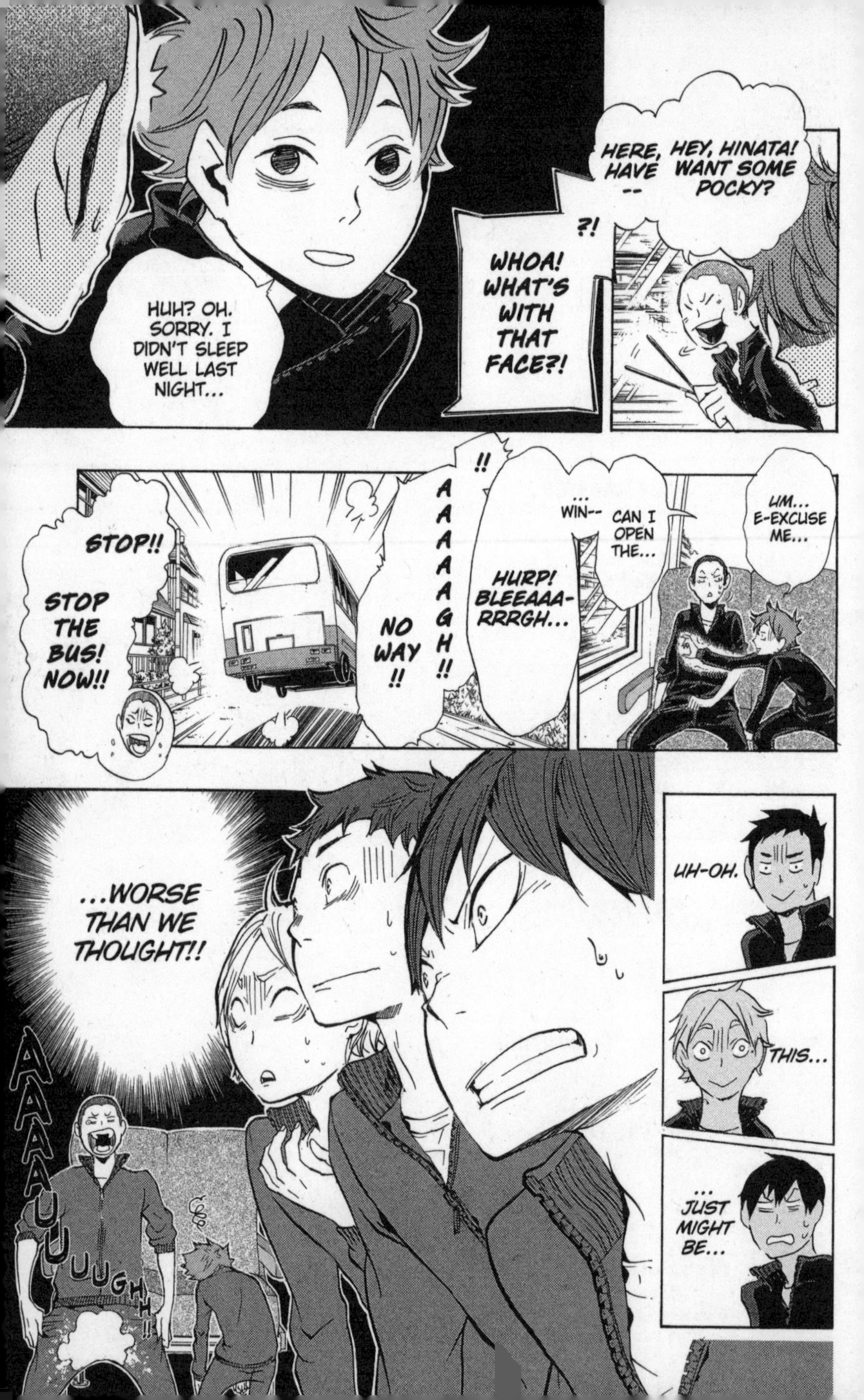
HEY, HINATA! WANT SOME POCKY?
HERE, HAVE --
?!
WHOA! WHAT'S WITH THAT FACE?!
HUH? OH. SORRY. I DIDN'T SLEEP WELL LAST NIGHT...
UM... E-EXCUSE ME...
CAN I OPEN THE...
... WIN--
HURP! BLEEAAA-RRRGH...
!!
AAAAAAAGH!!
NO WAY!!
STOP!!
STOP THE BUS! NOW!!
UH-OH.
THIS...
... JUST MIGHT BE...
...WORSE THAN WE THOUGHT!!
AAAAUUUUUGHH!!

KIYOKO SHIMIZU

KARASUNO HIGH SCHOOL
CLASS 3-2

POSITION:
VOLLEYBALL CLUB MANAGER

HEIGHT: 5'5"
WEIGHT: 113 LBS.
(AS OF APRIL, 3RD YEAR
OF HIGH SCHOOL)

BIRTHDAY: JANUARY 6

FAVORITE FOOD:
TEMPURA SHRIMP RICE BALLS

CURRENT WORRY:
WHETHER TO HAVE JAGARIKO
OR JAGABEE POTATO STICKS
FOR A SNACK.

ABILITY PARAMETERS
(5-POINT SCALE)

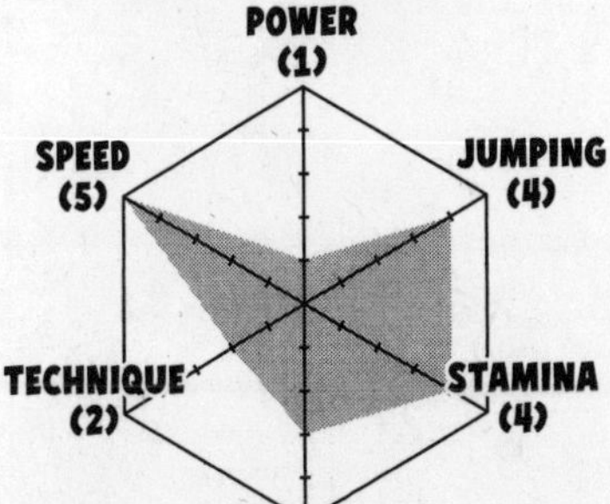
POWER
(1)
JUMPING
(4)
STAMINA
(4)
INTELLIGENCE
(3)
TECHNIQUE
(2)
SPEED
(5)

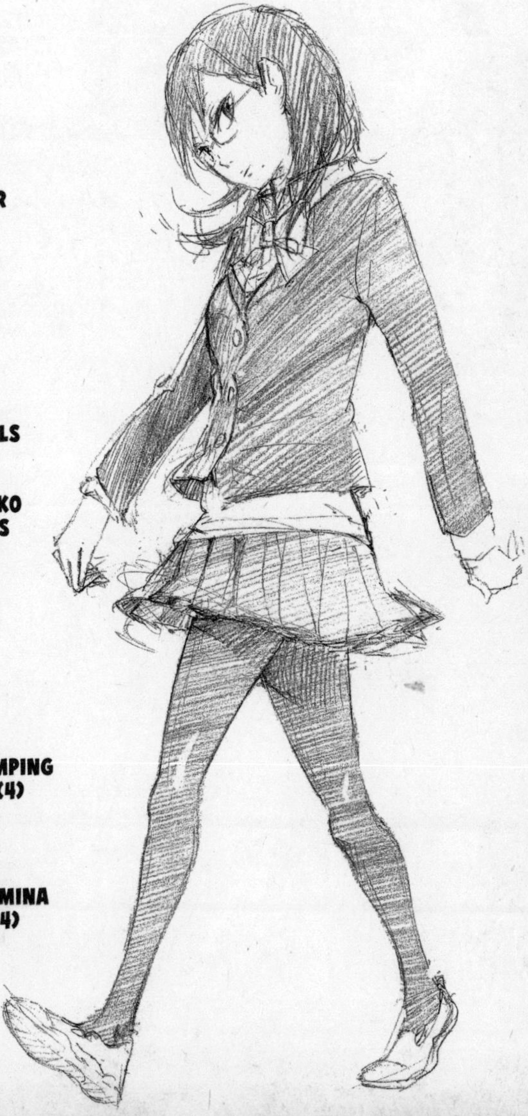

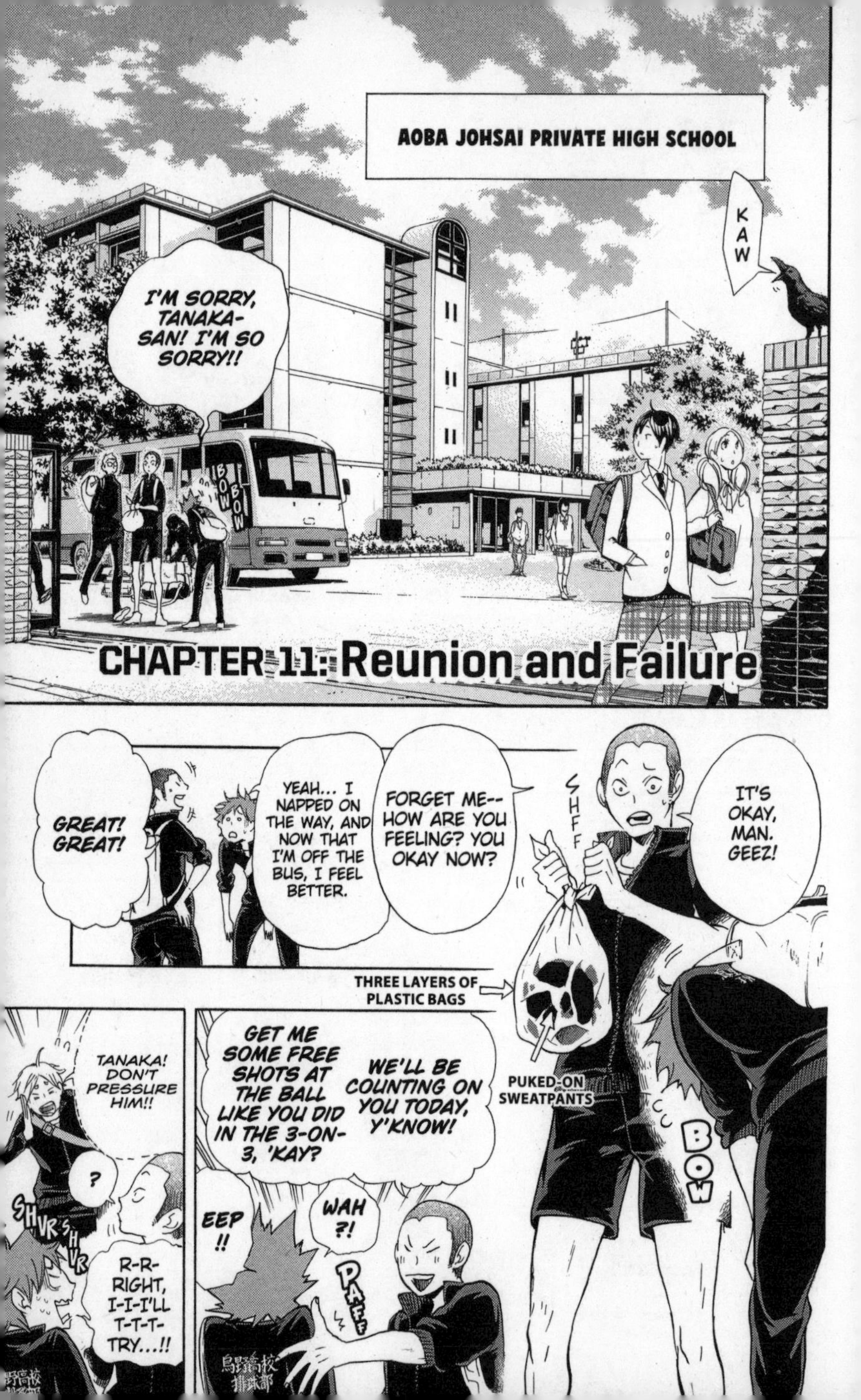
AOBA JOHSAI PRIVATE HIGH SCHOOL
KAW
I'M SORRY, TANAKA-SAN! I'M SO SORRY!!
BOW BOW
CHAPTER 11: Reunion and Failure
IT'S OKAY, MAN. GEEZ!
SHFF
THREE LAYERS OF PLASTIC BAGS
PUKED-ON SWEATPANTS
BOW
FORGET ME-- HOW ARE YOU FEELING? YOU OKAY NOW?
YEAH... I NAPPED ON THE WAY, AND NOW THAT I'M OFF THE BUS, I FEEL BETTER.
GREAT! GREAT!
WE'LL BE COUNTING ON YOU TODAY, Y'KNOW!
GET ME SOME FREE SHOTS AT THE BALL LIKE YOU DID IN THE 3-ON-3, 'KAY?
PAFF
WAH?!
EEP!!
TANAKA! DON'T PRESSURE HIM!!
?
SHVR SHVR
R-R-RIGHT, I-I-I'LL T-T-T-TRY...!!

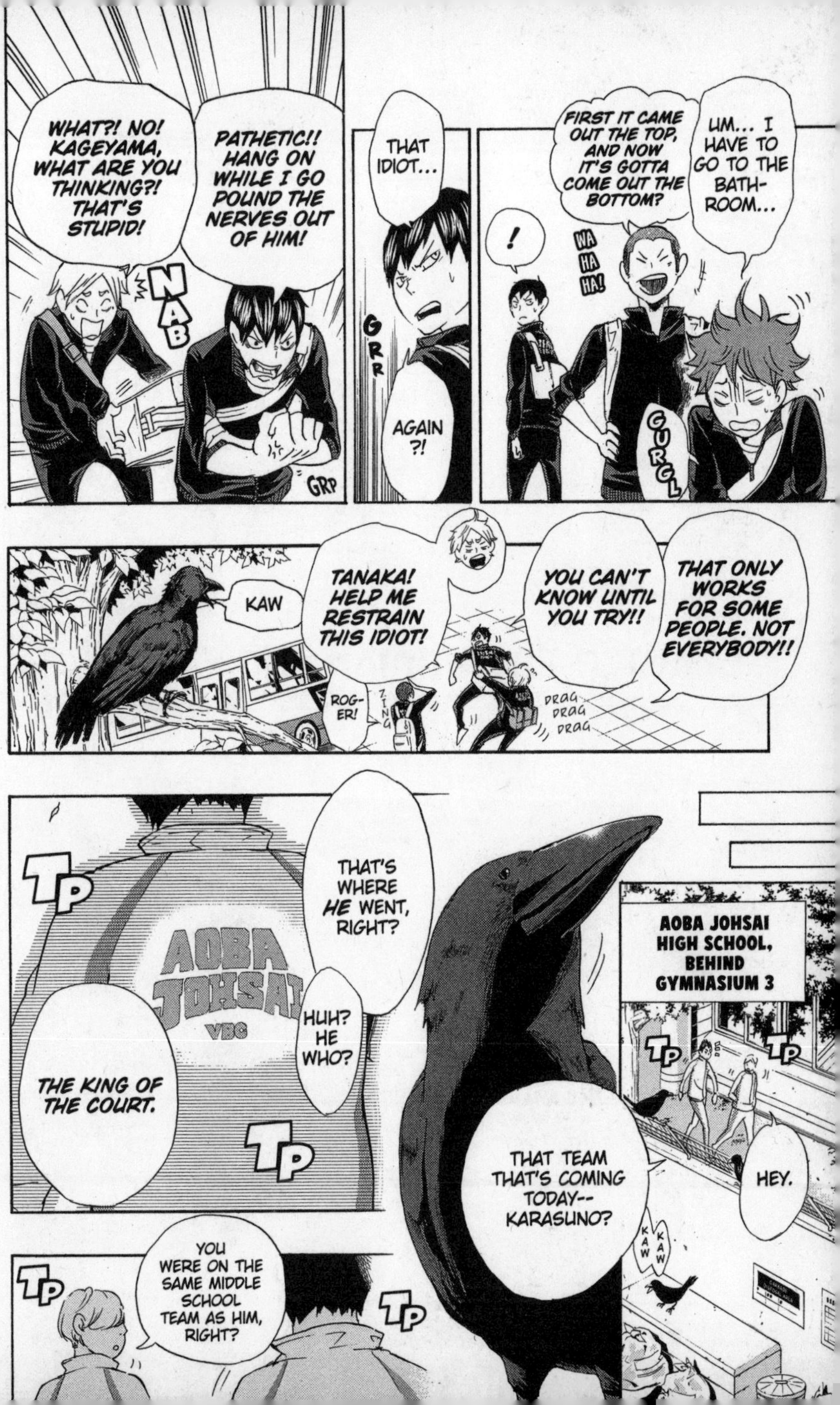

UM... I HAVE TO GO TO THE BATH-ROOM...
FIRST IT CAME OUT THE TOP, AND NOW IT'S GOTTA COME OUT THE BOTTOM?
WA HA HA!
!
GURGL
THAT IDIOT...
GRR
AGAIN?!
PATHETIC!! HANG ON WHILE I GO POUND THE NERVES OUT OF HIM!
WHAT?! NO! KAGEYAMA, WHAT ARE YOU THINKING?! THAT'S STUPID!
NAB
GRP
THAT ONLY WORKS FOR SOME PEOPLE. NOT EVERYBODY!!
YOU CAN'T KNOW UNTIL YOU TRY!!
TANAKA! HELP ME RESTRAIN THIS IDIOT!
DRAG DRAG DRAG
ZING
ROG-ER!
KAW
AOBA JOHSAI HIGH SCHOOL, BEHIND GYMNASIUM 3
TP
TP
HEY.
KAW KAW
THAT TEAM THAT'S COMING TODAY-- KARASUNO?
THAT'S WHERE HE WENT, RIGHT?
TP
AOBA JOHSAI VBC
HUH? HE WHO?
THE KING OF THE COURT.
TP
TP
YOU WERE ON THE SAME MIDDLE SCHOOL TEAM AS HIM, RIGHT?
TP

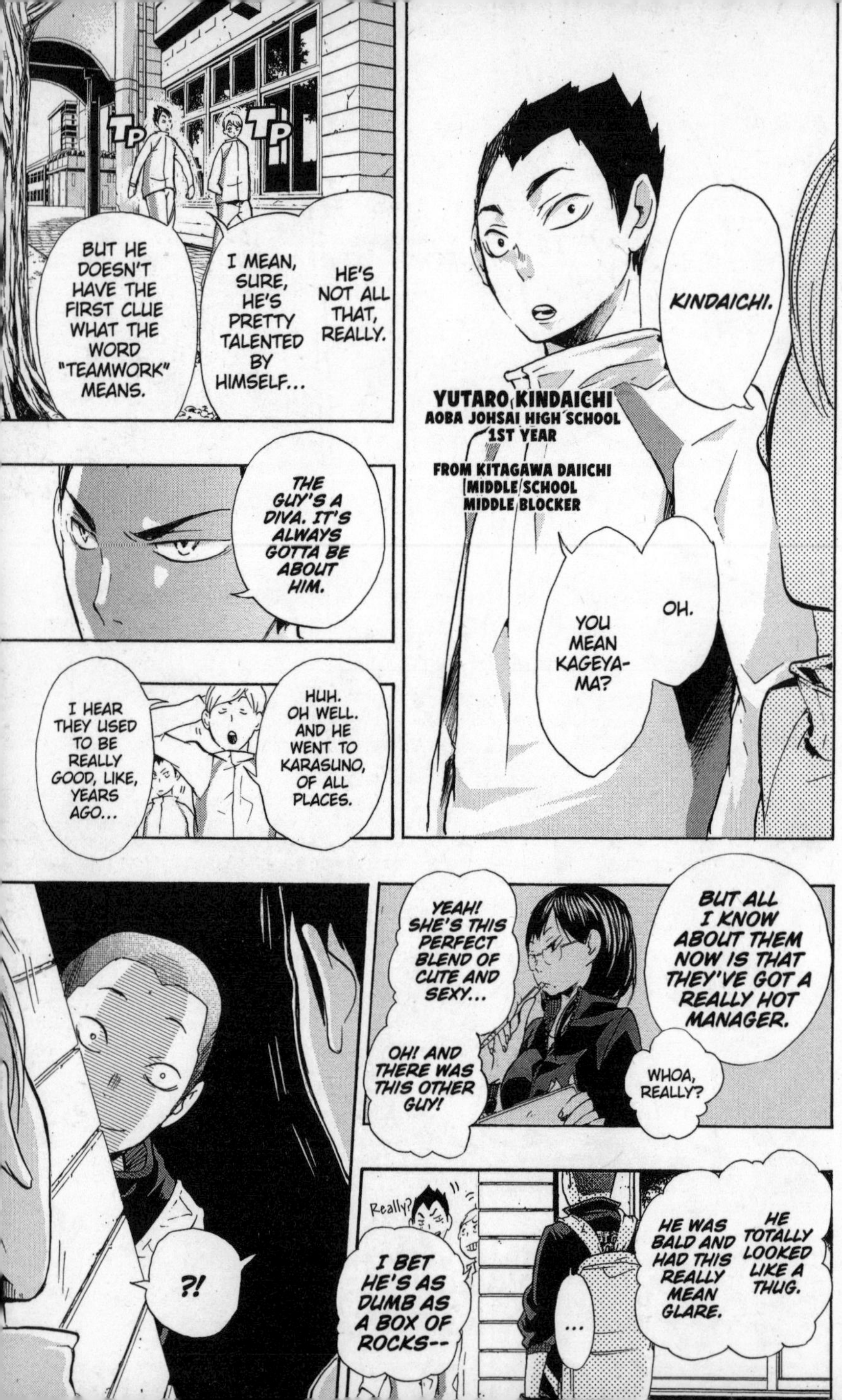
KINDAICHI.
YUTARO KINDAICHI
AOBA JOHSAI HIGH SCHOOL
1ST YEAR
FROM KITAGAWA DAIICHI
MIDDLE SCHOOL
MIDDLE BLOCKER
OH.
YOU MEAN KAGEYAMA?
TP
TP
HE'S NOT ALL THAT, REALLY.
I MEAN, SURE, HE'S PRETTY TALENTED BY HIMSELF...
BUT HE DOESN'T HAVE THE FIRST CLUE WHAT THE WORD "TEAMWORK" MEANS.
THE GUY'S A DIVA. IT'S ALWAYS GOTTA BE ABOUT HIM.
HUH. OH WELL. AND HE WENT TO KARASUNO, OF ALL PLACES.
I HEAR THEY USED TO BE REALLY GOOD, LIKE, YEARS AGO...
BUT ALL I KNOW ABOUT THEM NOW IS THAT THEY'VE GOT A REALLY HOT MANAGER.
WHOA, REALLY?
YEAH! SHE'S THIS PERFECT BLEND OF CUTE AND SEXY...
OH! AND THERE WAS THIS OTHER GUY!
HE TOTALLY LOOKED LIKE A THUG.
HE WAS BALD AND HAD THIS REALLY MEAN GLARE.
...
Really?
I BET HE'S AS DUMB AS A BOX OF ROCKS--
?!

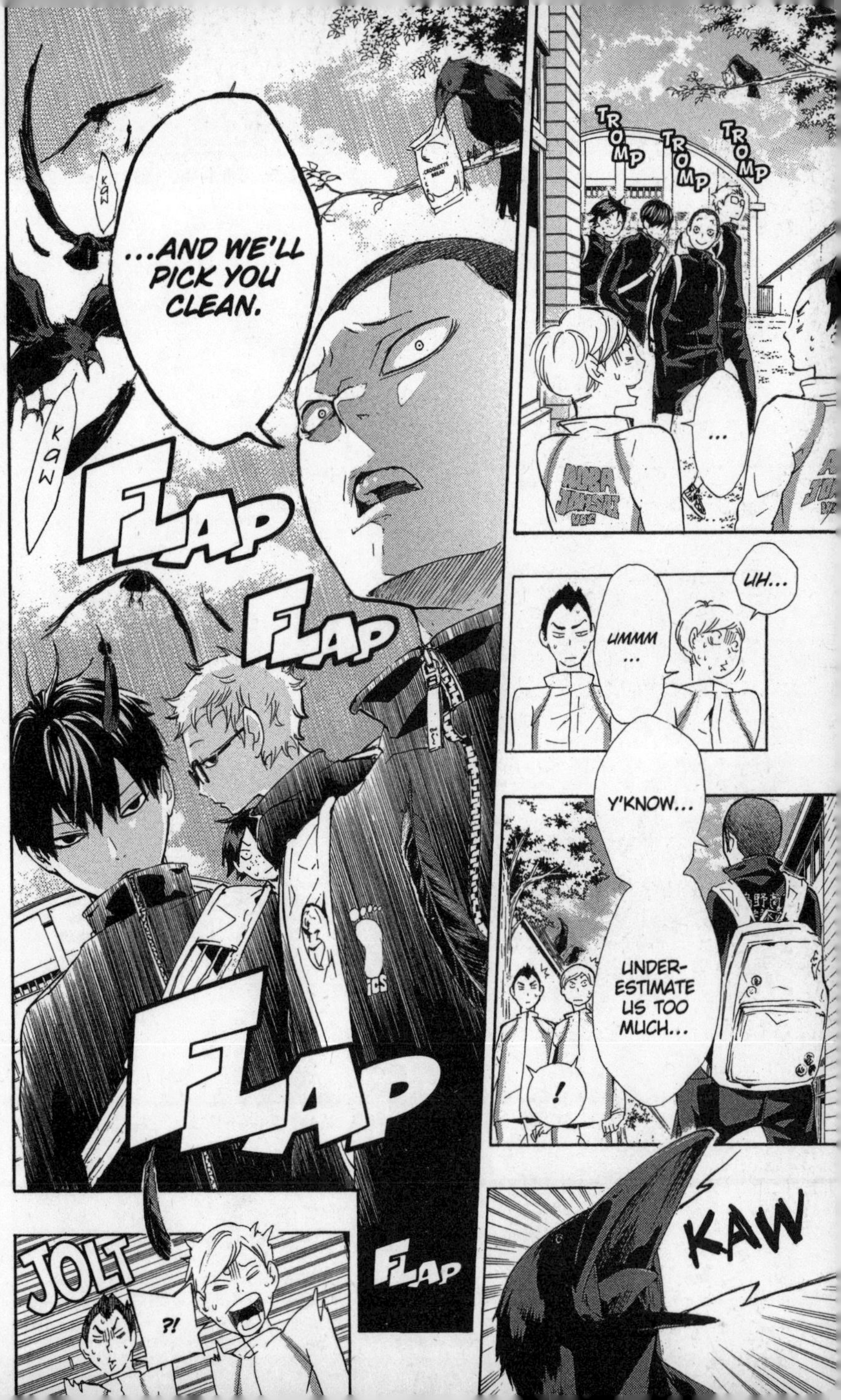
TROMP
TROMP
TROMP
...
UH...
UMMM...
Y'KNOW...
UNDER-ESTIMATE US TOO MUCH...
!
KAW
KAW
...AND WE'LL PICK YOU CLEAN.
FLAP
FLAP
FLAP
CROQUETTE BREAD
KAW
FLAP
JOLT
?!

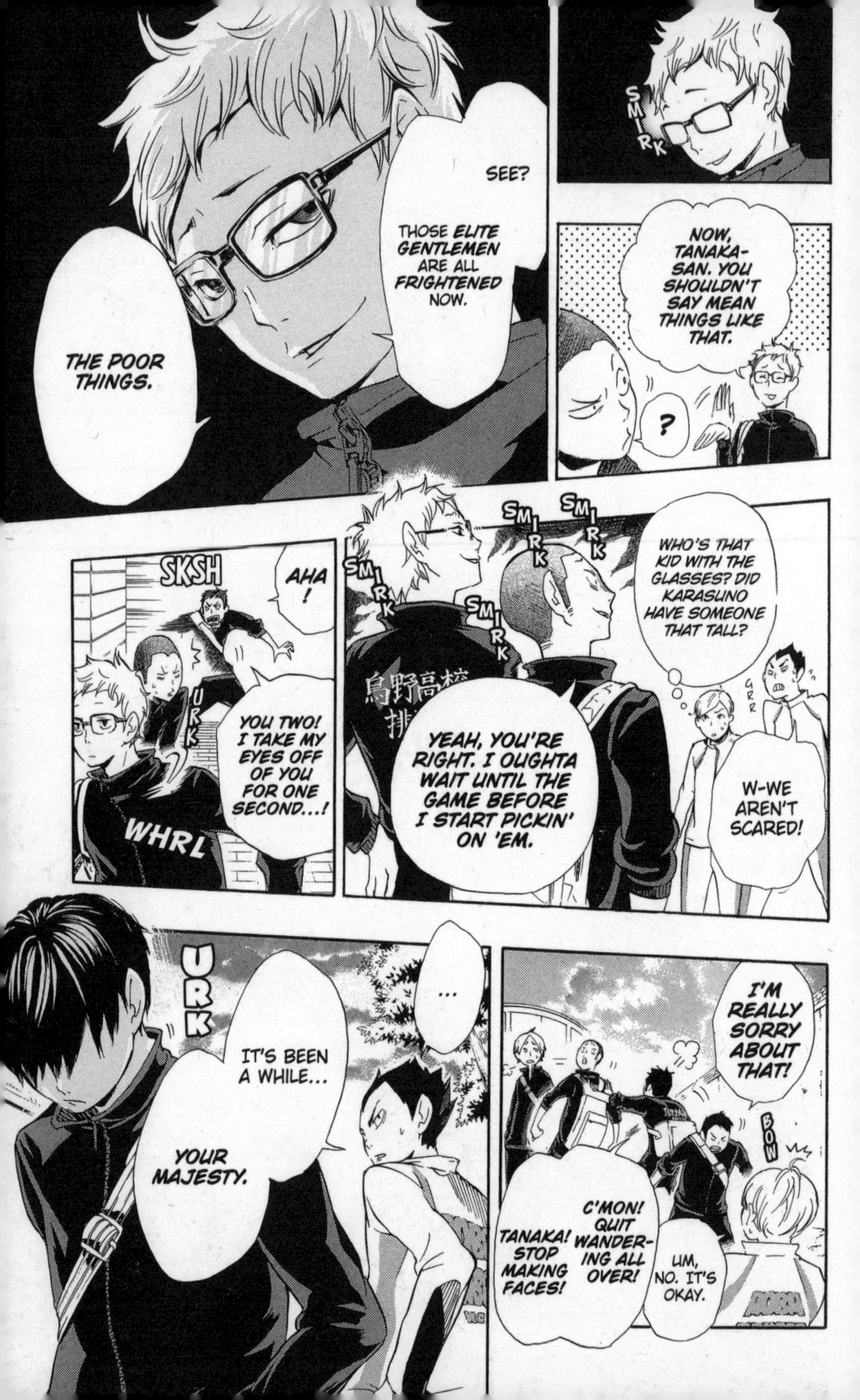

SMIRK
NOW, TANAKA-SAN. YOU SHOULDN'T SAY MEAN THINGS LIKE THAT.
?
SEE?
THOSE ELITE GENTLEMEN ARE ALL FRIGHTENED NOW.
THE POOR THINGS.
WHO'S THAT KID WITH THE GLASSES? DID KARASUNO HAVE SOMEONE THAT TALL?
SMIRK
SMIRK
SMIRK
SMIRK
YEAH, YOU'RE RIGHT. I OUGHTA WAIT UNTIL THE GAME BEFORE I START PICKIN' ON 'EM.
烏野高校
GRR
W-WE AREN'T SCARED!
AHA!
SKSH
URK
YOU TWO! I TAKE MY EYES OFF OF YOU FOR ONE SECOND...!
WHRL
I'M REALLY SORRY ABOUT THAT!
BOW
C'MON! QUIT WANDERING ALL OVER!
UM, NO. IT'S OKAY.
TANAKA! STOP MAKING FACES!
...
URK
IT'S BEEN A WHILE...
YOUR MAJESTY.

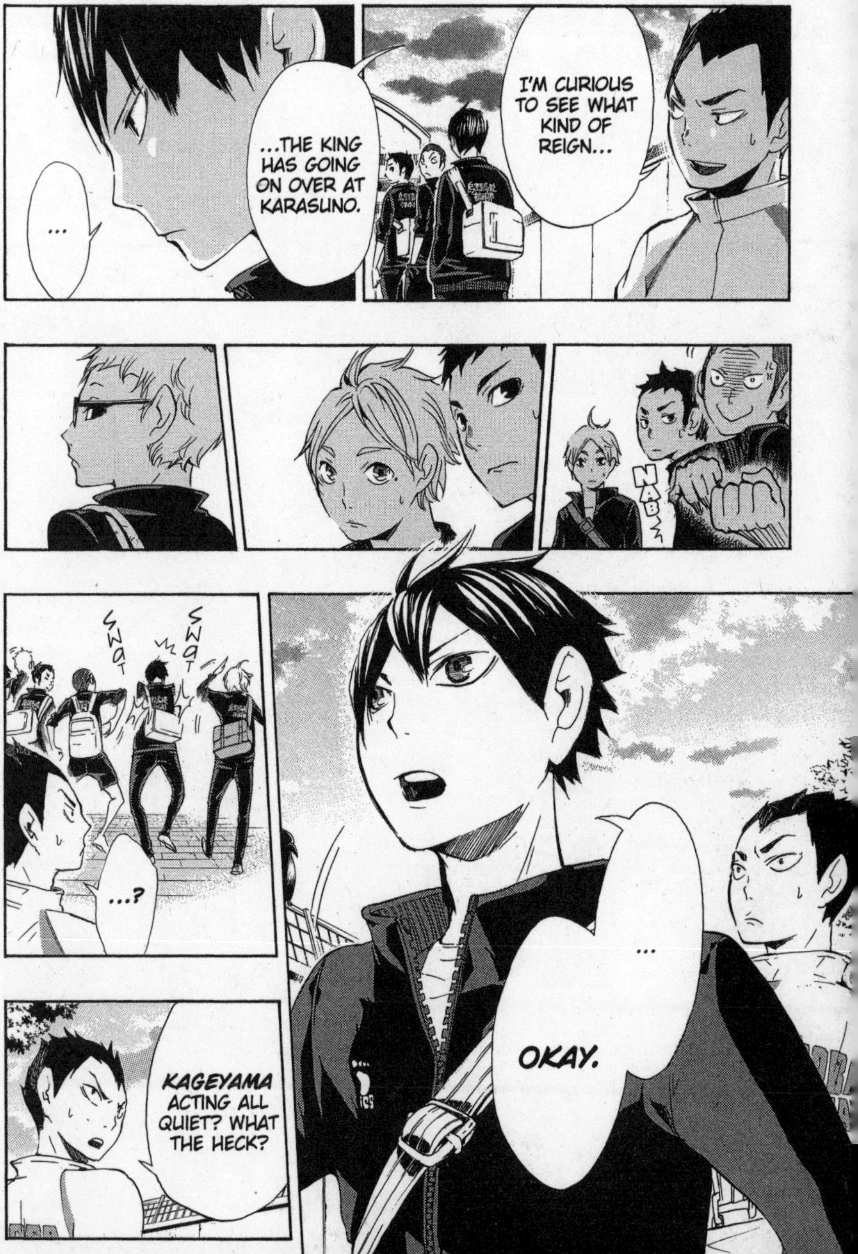
I'M CURIOUS TO SEE WHAT KIND OF REIGN...
...THE KING HAS GOING ON OVER AT KARASUNO.
...
NAB
...
OKAY.
SWAT
SWAT
...?
KAGEYAMA ACTING ALL QUIET? WHAT THE HECK?

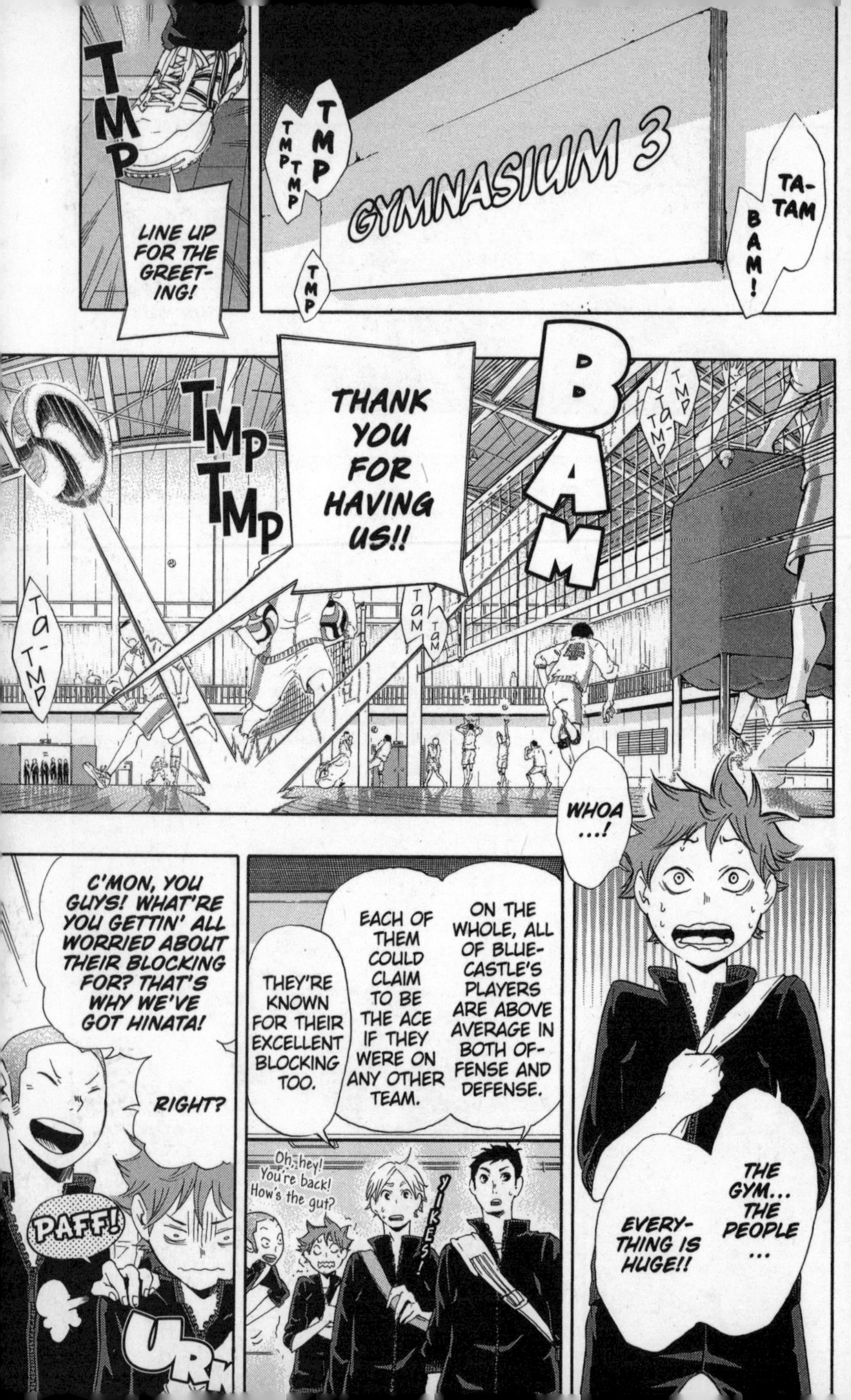
TMP TMP
TMP TMP
TMP
GYMNASIUM 3
TA-TAM
BAM!
TMP
LINE UP FOR THE GREET-ING!
BAM
TA-TAM TMP
THANK YOU FOR HAVING US!!
TMP TMP
TA-TMP
TAM TAM
WHOA ...!
THE GYM... THE PEOPLE ...
EVERY-THING IS HUGE!!
ON THE WHOLE, ALL OF BLUE-CASTLE'S PLAYERS ARE ABOVE AVERAGE IN BOTH OF-FENSE AND DEFENSE.
EACH OF THEM COULD CLAIM TO BE THE ACE IF THEY WERE ON ANY OTHER TEAM.
THEY'RE KNOWN FOR THEIR EXCELLENT BLOCKING TOO.
YIKES!
Oh, hey! You're back! How's the gut?
C'MON, YOU GUYS! WHAT'RE YOU GETTIN' ALL WORRIED ABOUT THEIR BLOCKING FOR? THAT'S WHY WE'VE GOT HINATA!
RIGHT?
PAFF!
URK

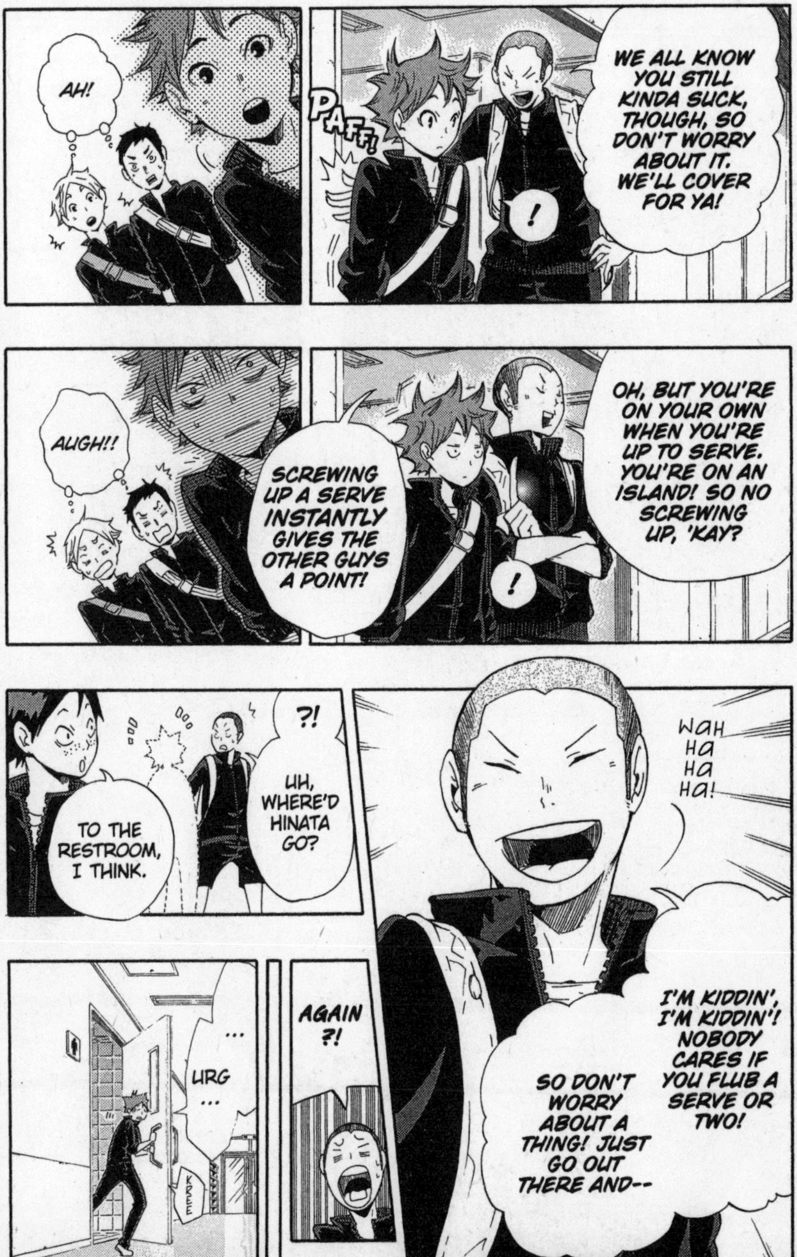
WE ALL KNOW YOU STILL KINDA SUCK, THOUGH, SO DON'T WORRY ABOUT IT. WE'LL COVER FOR YA!
!
PAFF!
AH!
OH, BUT YOU'RE ON YOUR OWN WHEN YOU'RE UP TO SERVE. YOU'RE ON AN ISLAND! SO NO SCREWING UP, 'KAY?
!
SCREWING UP A SERVE INSTANTLY GIVES THE OTHER GUYS A POINT!
AUGH!!
WAH HA HA HA!
I'M KIDDIN', I'M KIDDIN'! NOBODY CARES IF YOU FLUB A SERVE OR TWO!
SO DON'T WORRY ABOUT A THING! JUST GO OUT THERE AND--
?!
UH, WHERE'D HINATA GO?
TO THE RESTROOM, I THINK.
AGAIN ?!
...
URG ...
KREE

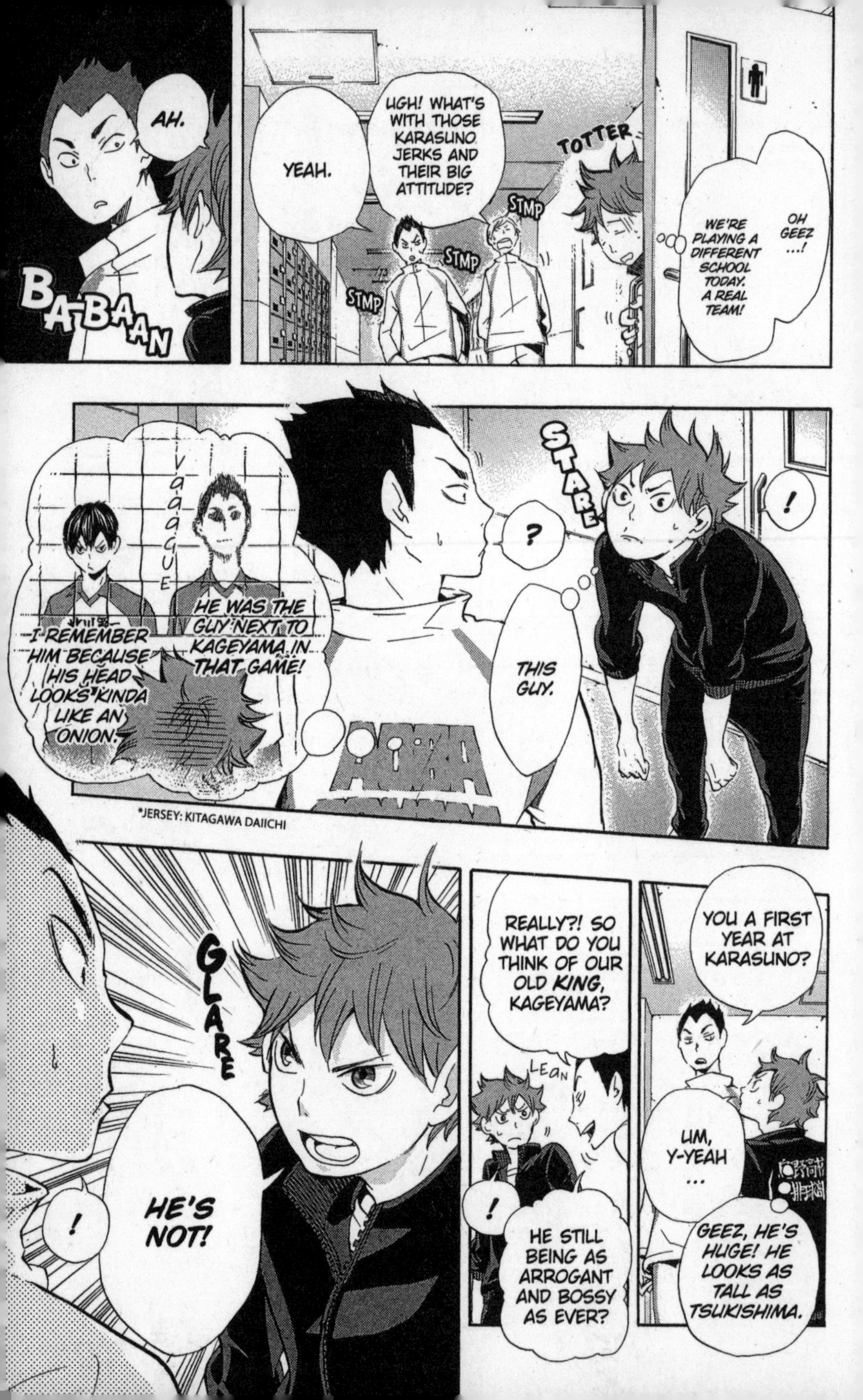
TOTTER
OH GEEZ ...!
WE'RE PLAYING A DIFFERENT SCHOOL TODAY. A REAL TEAM!
UGH! WHAT'S WITH THOSE KARASUNO JERKS AND THEIR BIG ATTITUDE?
YEAH.
STMP
STMP
STMP
AH.
BA-BAAAN
STARE
!
?
THIS GUY.
HE WAS THE GUY NEXT TO KAGEYAMA IN THAT GAME!
I REMEMBER HIM BECAUSE HIS HEAD LOOKS KINDA LIKE AN ONION.
VaaaGUE
YOU A FIRST YEAR AT KARASUNO?
UM, Y-YEAH ...
GEEZ, HE'S HUGE! HE LOOKS AS TALL AS TSUKISHIMA.
REALLY?! SO WHAT DO YOU THINK OF OUR OLD KING, KAGEYAMA?
LEan
!
HE STILL BEING AS ARROGANT AND BOSSY AS EVER?
GLARE
HE'S NOT!
!
*JERSEY: KITAGAWA DAIICHI

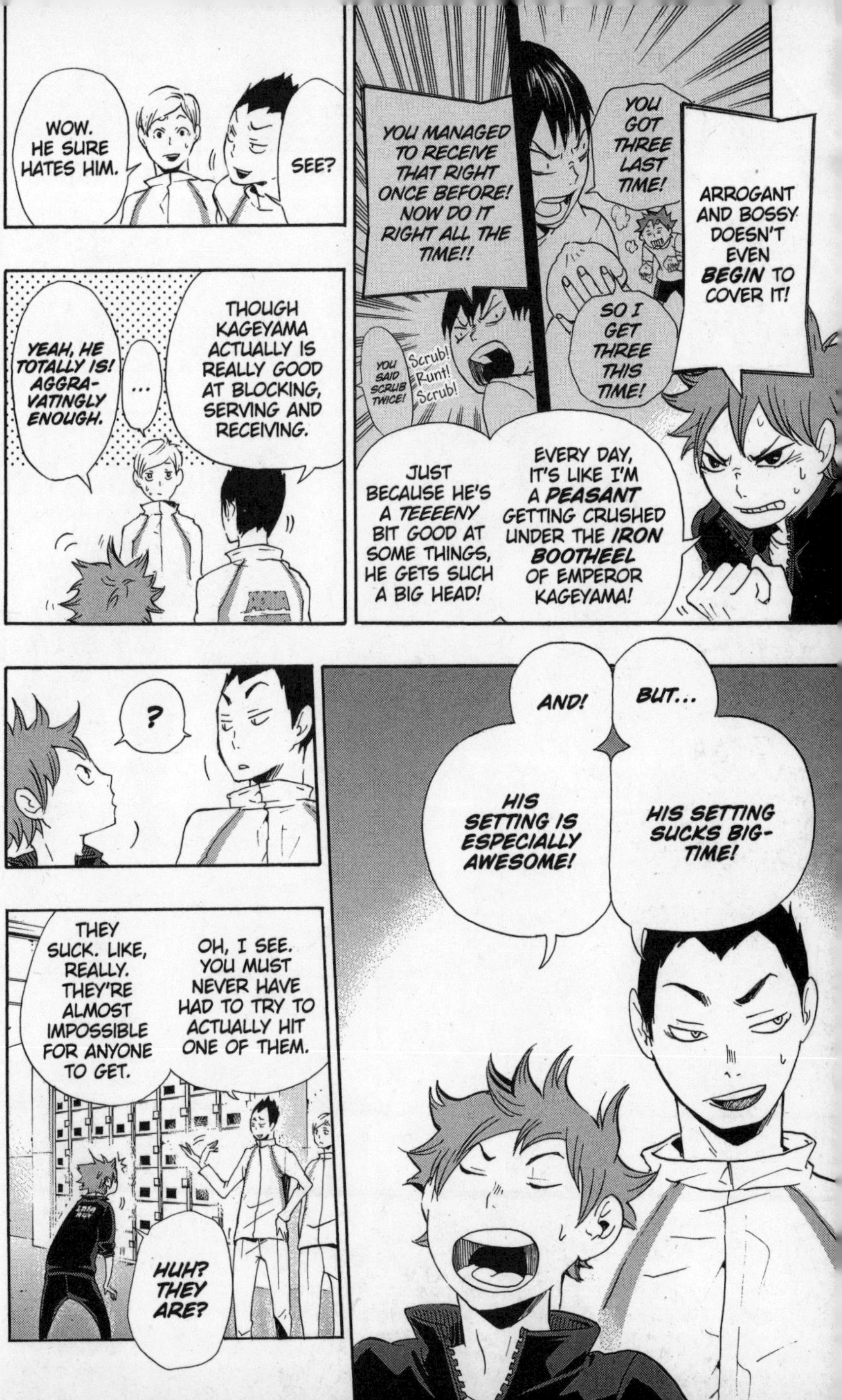
ARROGANT AND BOSSY DOESN'T EVEN BEGIN TO COVER IT!
YOU GOT THREE LAST TIME!
YOU MANAGED TO RECEIVE THAT RIGHT ONCE BEFORE! NOW DO IT RIGHT ALL THE TIME!!
SO I GET THREE THIS TIME!
Scrub! Runt! Scrub!
YOU SAID SCRUB TWICE!
EVERY DAY, IT'S LIKE I'M A PEASANT GETTING CRUSHED UNDER THE IRON BOOTHEEL OF EMPEROR KAGEYAMA!
JUST BECAUSE HE'S A TEEEENY BIT GOOD AT SOME THINGS, HE GETS SUCH A BIG HEAD!
SEE?
WOW. HE SURE HATES HIM.
THOUGH KAGEYAMA ACTUALLY IS REALLY GOOD AT BLOCKING, SERVING AND RECEIVING.
...
YEAH, HE TOTALLY IS! AGGRA-VATINGLY ENOUGH.
BUT...
HIS SETTING SUCKS BIG-TIME!
AND!
HIS SETTING IS ESPECIALLY AWESOME!
?
OH, I SEE. YOU MUST NEVER HAVE HAD TO TRY TO ACTUALLY HIT ONE OF THEM.
THEY SUCK. LIKE, REALLY. THEY'RE ALMOST IMPOSSIBLE FOR ANYONE TO GET.
HUH? THEY ARE?

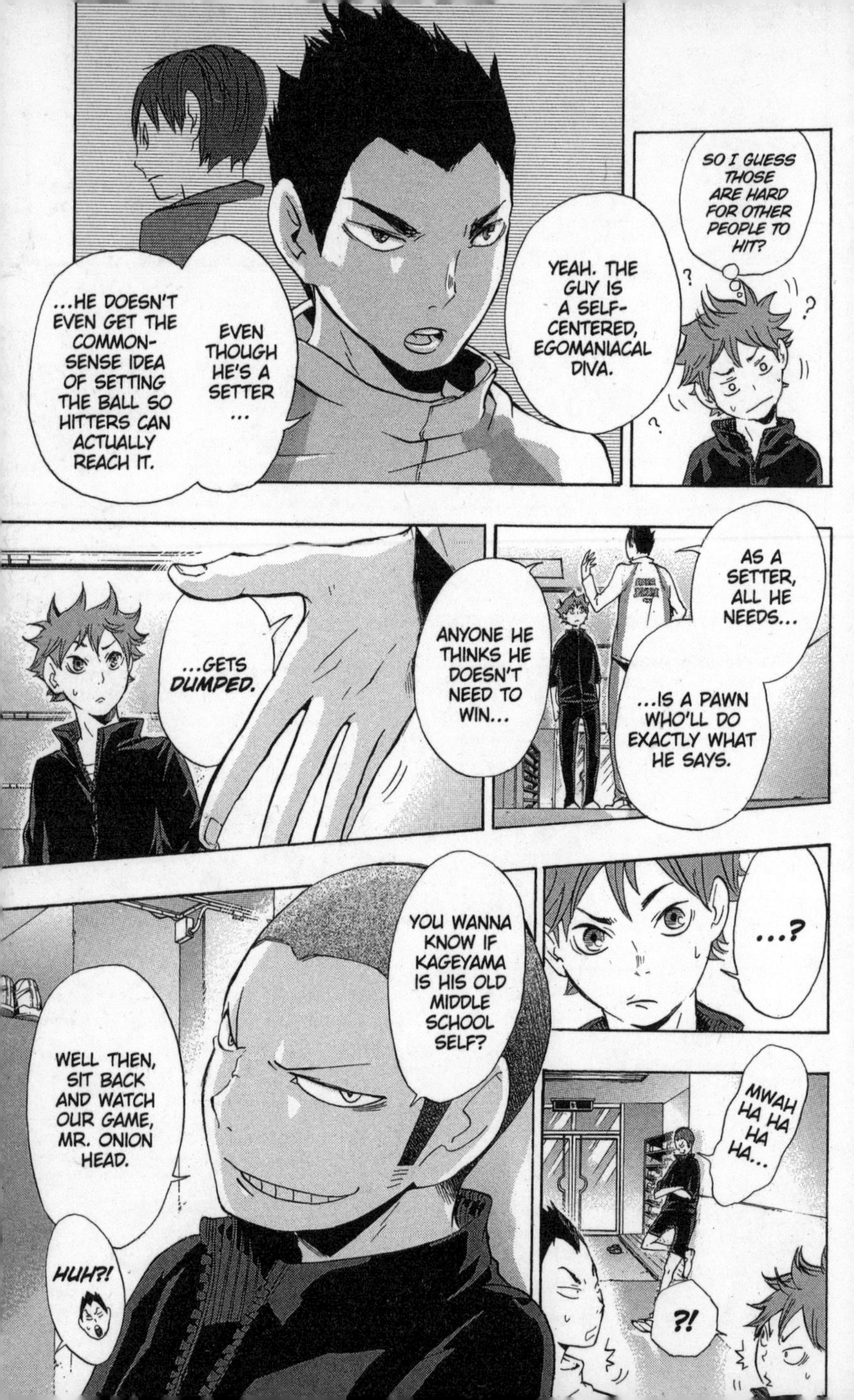
SO I GUESS THOSE ARE HARD FOR OTHER PEOPLE TO HIT?
YEAH. THE GUY IS A SELF-CENTERED, EGOMANIACAL DIVA.
EVEN THOUGH HE'S A SETTER...
...HE DOESN'T EVEN GET THE COMMON-SENSE IDEA OF SETTING THE BALL SO HITTERS CAN ACTUALLY REACH IT.
AS A SETTER, ALL HE NEEDS...
...IS A PAWN WHO'LL DO EXACTLY WHAT HE SAYS.
ANYONE HE THINKS HE DOESN'T NEED TO WIN...
...GETS DUMPED.
...?
MWAH HA HA HA HA...
?!
YOU WANNA KNOW IF KAGEYAMA IS HIS OLD MIDDLE SCHOOL SELF?
WELL THEN, SIT BACK AND WATCH OUR GAME, MR. ONION HEAD.
HUH?!

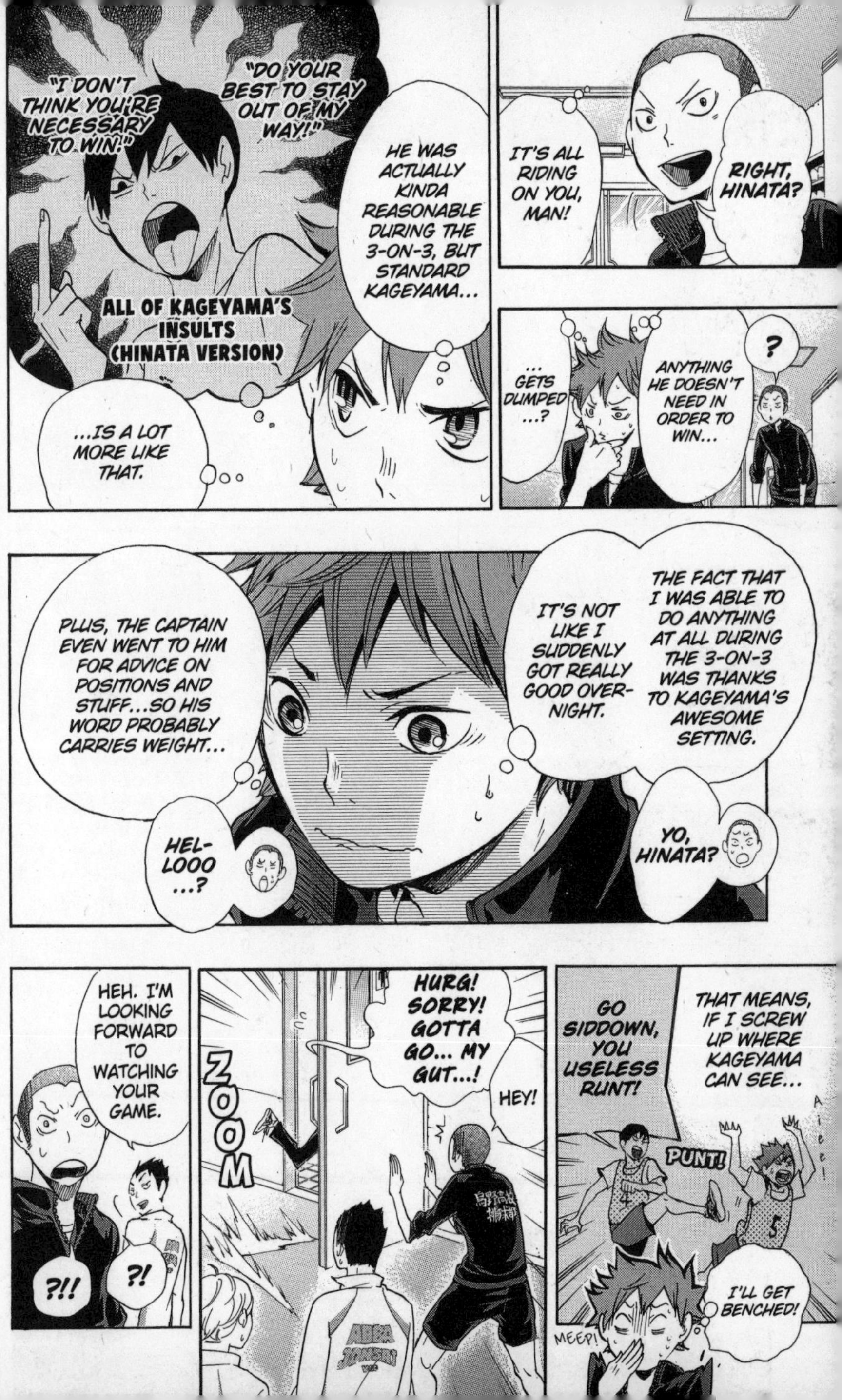
RIGHT, HINATA?
IT'S ALL RIDING ON YOU, MAN!
?
ANYTHING HE DOESN'T NEED IN ORDER TO WIN...
...GETS DUMPED...?
HE WAS ACTUALLY KINDA REASONABLE DURING THE 3-ON-3, BUT STANDARD KAGEYAMA...
"DO YOUR BEST TO STAY OUT OF MY WAY!"
"I DON'T THINK YOU'RE NECESSARY TO WIN."
ALL OF KAGEYAMA'S INSULTS (HINATA VERSION)
...IS A LOT MORE LIKE THAT.
THE FACT THAT I WAS ABLE TO DO ANYTHING AT ALL DURING THE 3-ON-3 WAS THANKS TO KAGEYAMA'S AWESOME SETTING.
IT'S NOT LIKE I SUDDENLY GOT REALLY GOOD OVER-NIGHT.
YO, HINATA?
PLUS, THE CAPTAIN EVEN WENT TO HIM FOR ADVICE ON POSITIONS AND STUFF...SO HIS WORD PROBABLY CARRIES WEIGHT...
HEL-LOOO ...?
THAT MEANS, IF I SCREW UP WHERE KAGEYAMA CAN SEE...
GO SIDDOWN, YOU USELESS RUNT!
PUNT!
Aiee!
I'LL GET BENCHED!
MEEP!
HURG! SORRY! GOTTA GO... MY GUT...!
HEY!
ZOOM
HEH. I'M LOOKING FORWARD TO WATCHING YOUR GAME.
?!
?!!

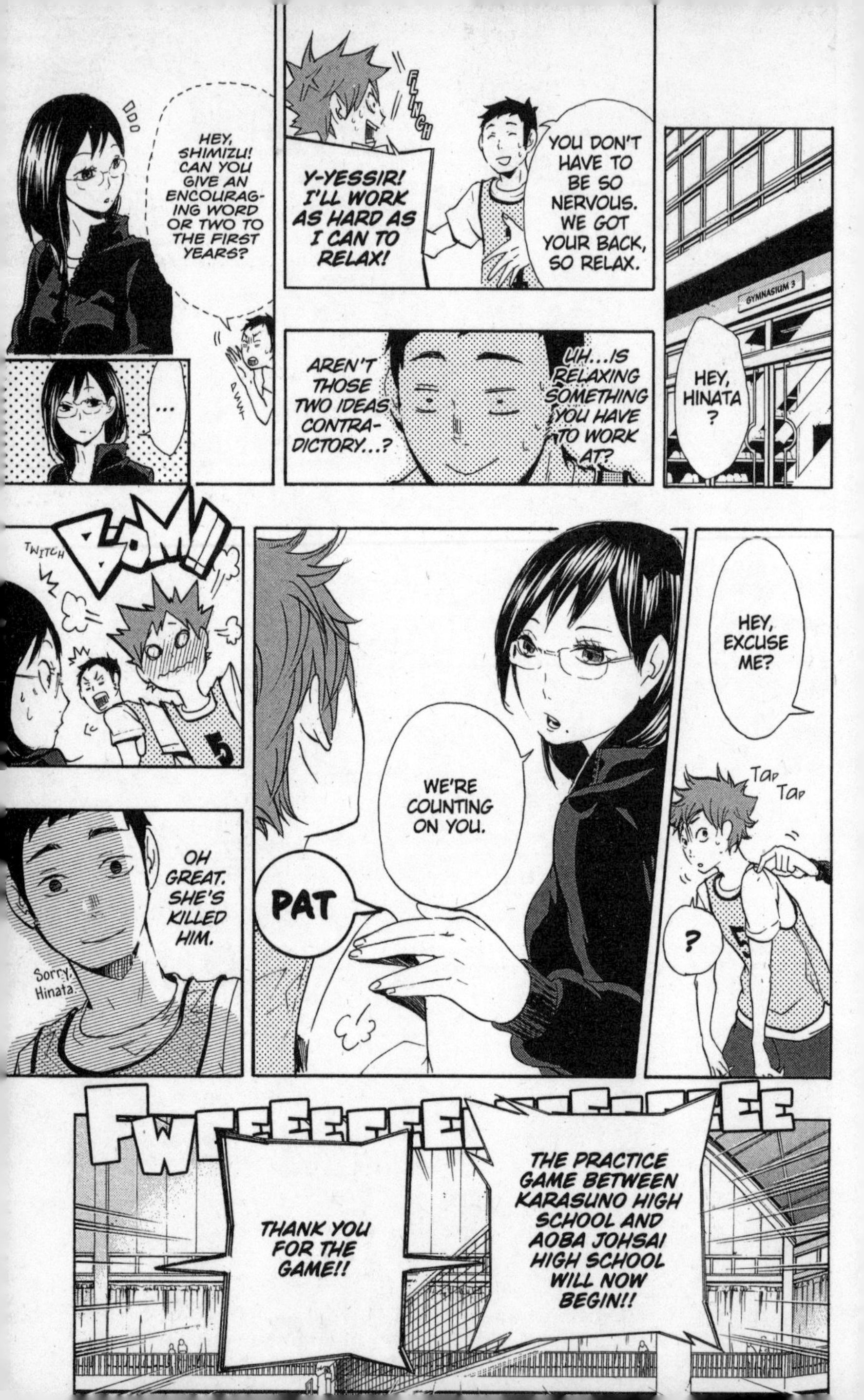
GYMNASIUM 3
HEY, HINATA?
YOU DON'T HAVE TO BE SO NERVOUS. WE GOT YOUR BACK, SO RELAX.
FLINCH
Y-YESSIR! I'LL WORK AS HARD AS I CAN TO RELAX!
UH...IS RELAXING SOMETHING YOU HAVE TO WORK AT?
AREN'T THOSE TWO IDEAS CONTRADICTORY...?
HEY, SHIMIZU! CAN YOU GIVE AN ENCOURAGING WORD OR TWO TO THE FIRST YEARS?
...
HEY, EXCUSE ME?
Tap Tap
?
WE'RE COUNTING ON YOU.
PAT
BOOM!!
TWITCH
OH GREAT. SHE'S KILLED HIM.
Sorry, Hinata.
THE PRACTICE GAME BETWEEN KARASUNO HIGH SCHOOL AND AOBA JOHSAI HIGH SCHOOL WILL NOW BEGIN!!
THANK YOU FOR THE GAME!!

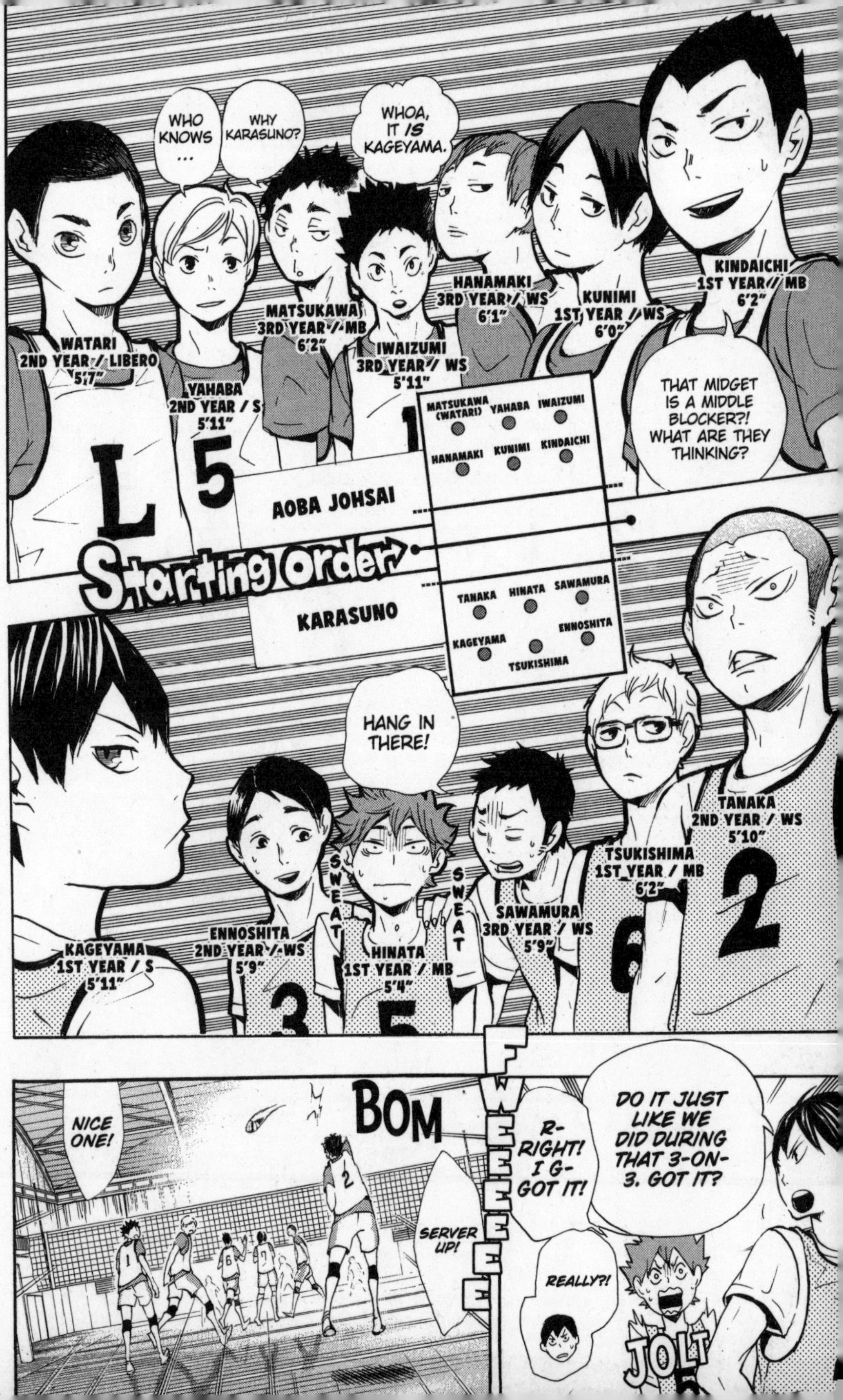
WHOA, IT IS KAGEYAMA.
WHY KARASUNO?
WHO KNOWS...
KINDAICHI 1ST YEAR / MB 6'2"
KUNIMI 1ST YEAR / WS 6'0"
HANAMAKI 3RD YEAR / WS 6'1"
IWAIZUMI 3RD YEAR / WS 5'11"
MATSUKAWA 3RD YEAR / MB 6'2"
YAHABA 2ND YEAR / S 5'11"
WATARI 2ND YEAR / LIBERO 5'7"
THAT MIDGET IS A MIDDLE BLOCKER?! WHAT ARE THEY THINKING?
Starting order
AOBA JOHSAI
MATSUKAWA (WATARI)
YAHABA
IWAIZUMI
HANAMAKI
KUNIMI
KINDAICHI
KARASUNO
TANAKA
HINATA
SAWAMURA
KAGEYAMA
TSUKISHIMA
ENNOSHITA
HANG IN THERE!
TANAKA 2ND YEAR / WS 5'10"
TSUKISHIMA 1ST YEAR / MB 6'2"
SAWAMURA 3RD YEAR / WS 5'9"
SWEAT
SWEAT
HINATA 1ST YEAR / MB 5'4"
ENNOSHITA 2ND YEAR / WS 5'9"
KAGEYAMA 1ST YEAR / S 5'11"
DO IT JUST LIKE WE DID DURING THAT 3-ON-3. GOT IT?
R-RIGHT! I G-GOT IT!
REALLY?!
JOLT
FWEEEEEE
SERVER UP!
BOM
NICE ONE!

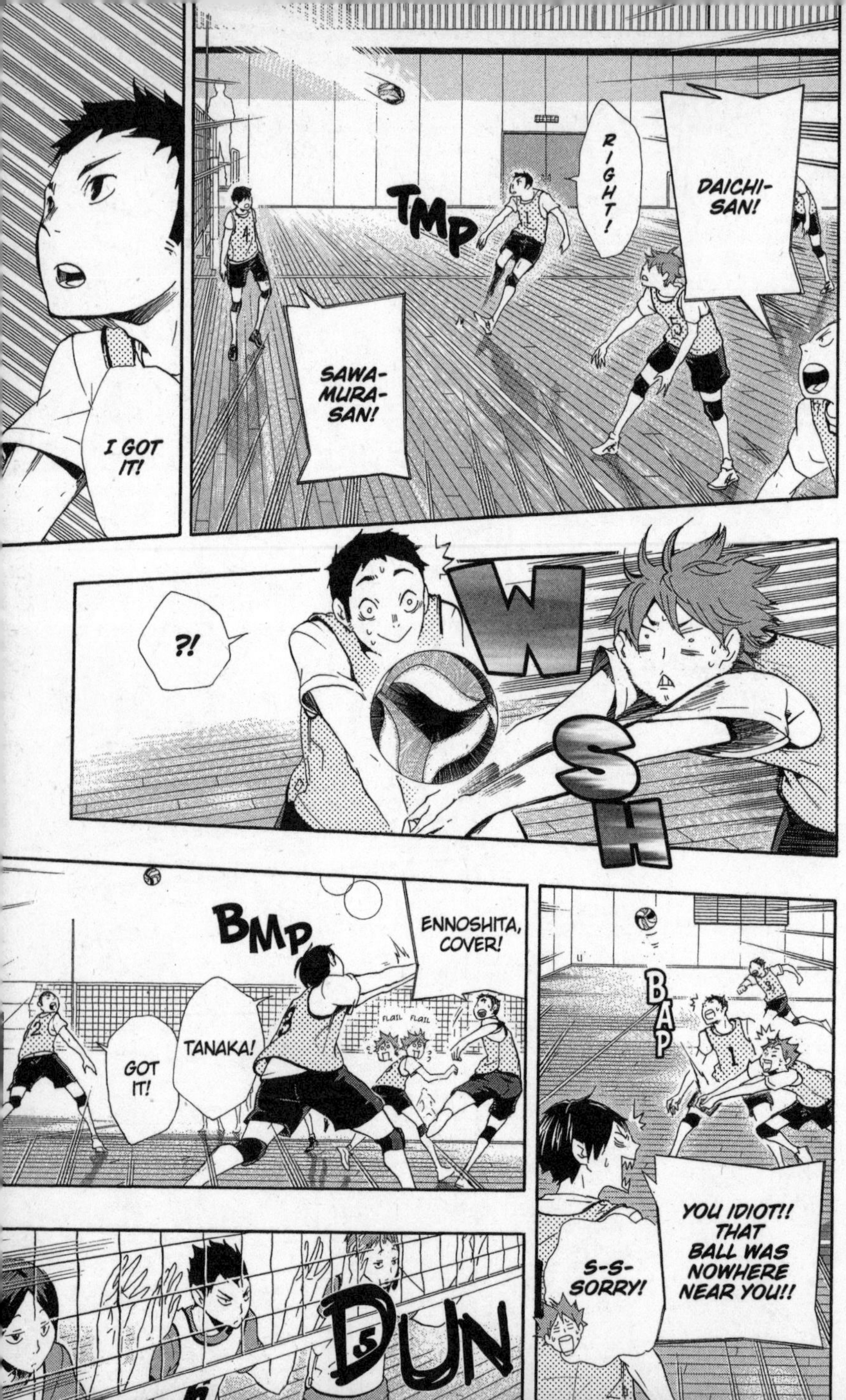
DAICHI-SAN!
RIGHT!
TMP
SAWAMURA-SAN!
I GOT IT!
WSH
?!
BAP
YOU IDIOT!! THAT BALL WAS NOWHERE NEAR YOU!!
S-S-SORRY!
ENNOSHITA, COVER!
BMP
TANAKA!
FLAIL FLAIL
GOT IT!
DUN

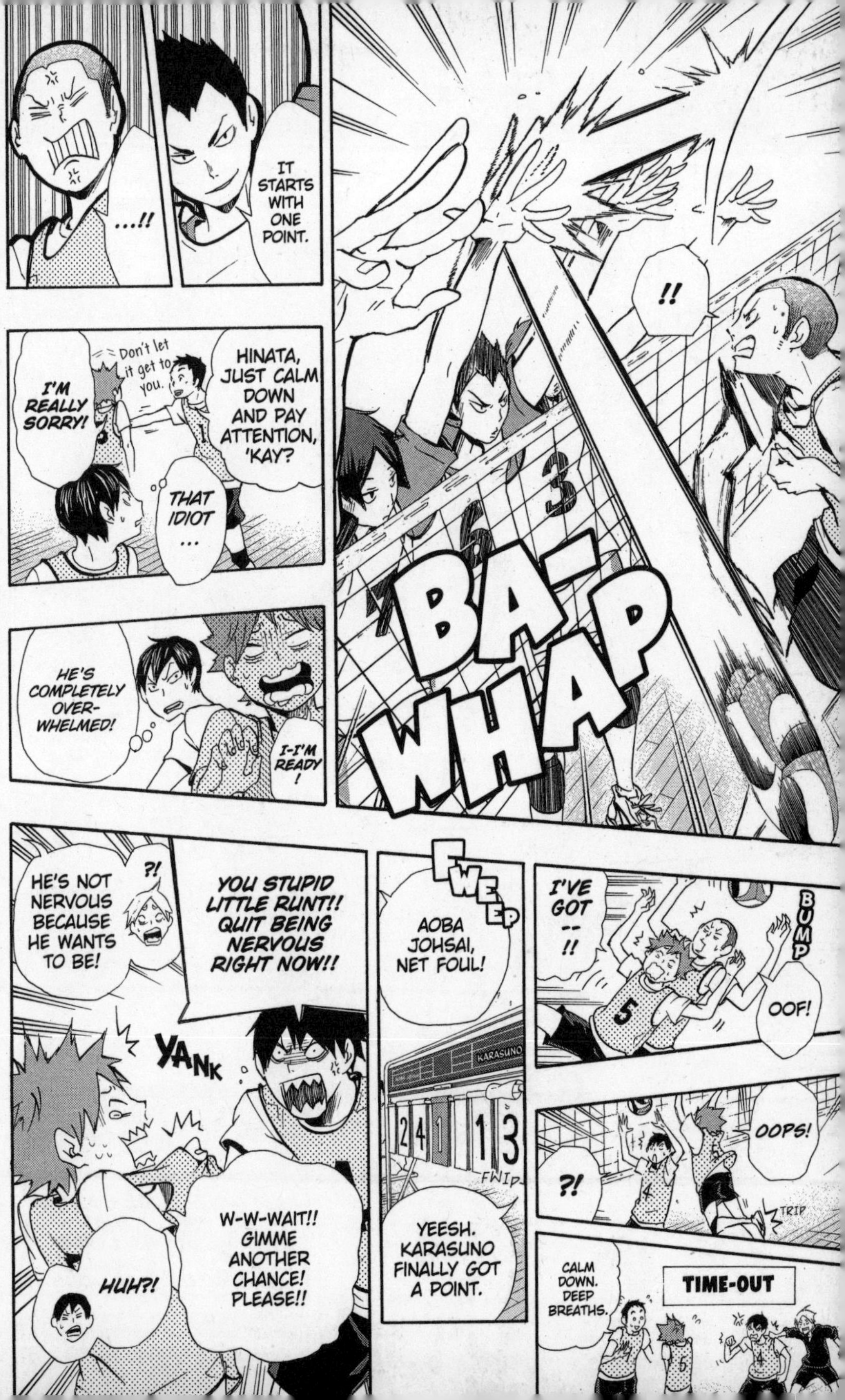
!!
BA-WHAP
IT STARTS WITH ONE POINT.
...!!
HINATA, JUST CALM DOWN AND PAY ATTENTION, 'KAY?
Don't let it get to you.
I'M REALLY SORRY!
THAT IDIOT...
HE'S COMPLETELY OVER-WHELMED!
I-I'M READY!
I'VE GOT--!!
BUMP
OOF!
OOPS!
?!
TRIP
TIME-OUT
CALM DOWN. DEEP BREATHS.
FWEEP
AOBA JOHSAI, NET FOUL!
KARASUNO
FWIP
YEESH. KARASUNO FINALLY GOT A POINT.
YOU STUPID LITTLE RUNT!! QUIT BEING NERVOUS RIGHT NOW!!
?!
HE'S NOT NERVOUS BECAUSE HE WANTS TO BE!
YANK
W-W-WAIT!! GIMME ANOTHER CHANCE! PLEASE!!
HUH?!

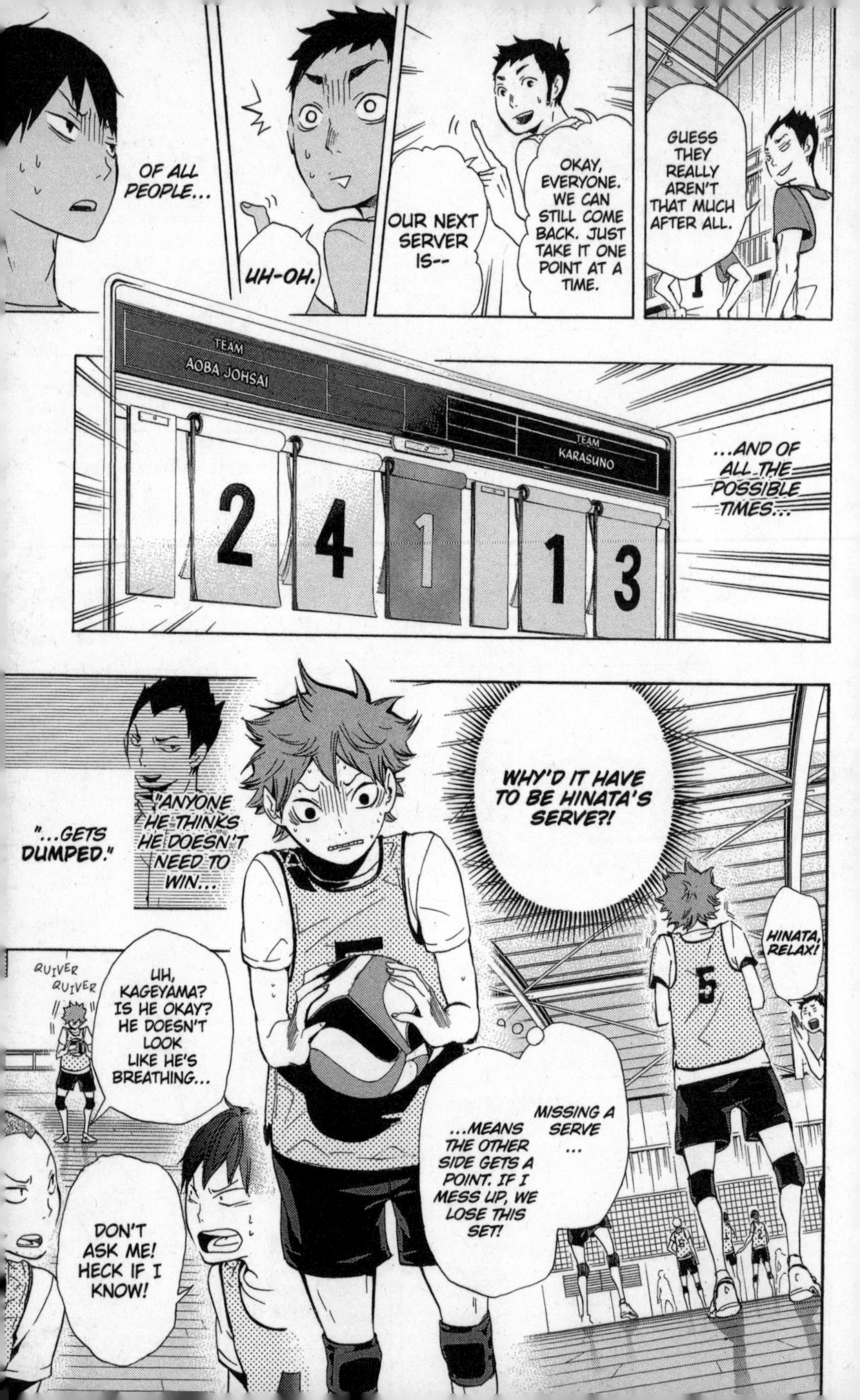
GUESS THEY REALLY AREN'T THAT MUCH AFTER ALL.
OKAY, EVERYONE. WE CAN STILL COME BACK. JUST TAKE IT ONE POINT AT A TIME.
OUR NEXT SERVER IS--
UH-OH.
OF ALL PEOPLE...
TEAM AOBA JOHSAI
TEAM KARASUNO
2 4 1 1 3
...AND OF ALL THE POSSIBLE TIMES...
WHY'D IT HAVE TO BE HINATA'S SERVE?!
"ANYONE HE THINKS HE DOESN'T NEED TO WIN...
"...GETS DUMPED."
HINATA, RELAX!
MISSING A SERVE...
...MEANS THE OTHER SIDE GETS A POINT. IF I MESS UP, WE LOSE THIS SET!
UH, KAGEYAMA? IS HE OKAY? HE DOESN'T LOOK LIKE HE'S BREATHING...
QUIVER QUIVER
DON'T ASK ME! HECK IF I KNOW!

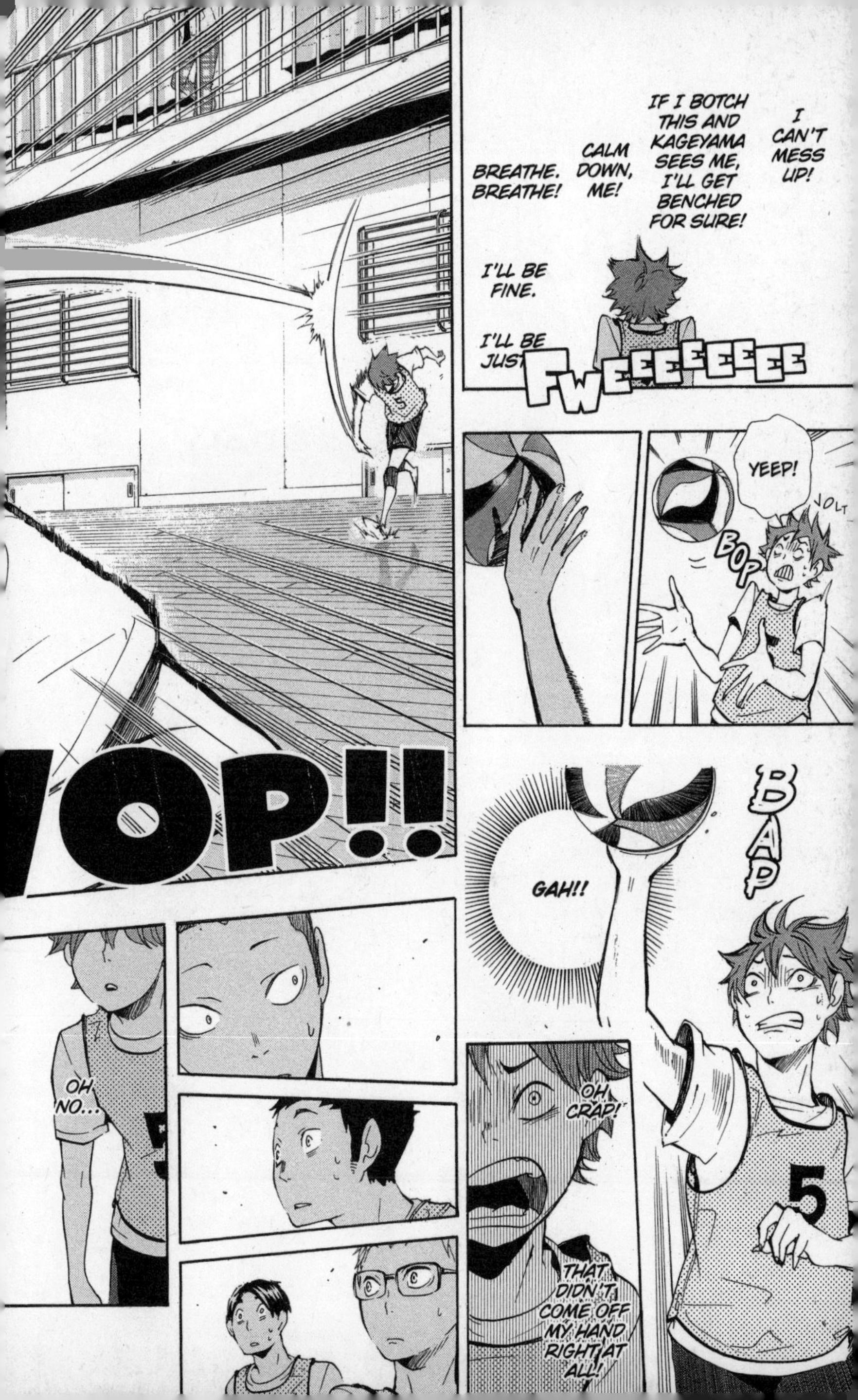
I CAN'T MESS UP!
IF I BOTCH THIS AND KAGEYAMA SEES ME, I'LL GET BENCHED FOR SURE!
CALM DOWN, ME!
BREATHE. BREATHE!
I'LL BE FINE.
I'LL BE JUST
FWEEEEEEEE
YEEP!
JOLT
BOP
BAP
GAH!!
OH CRAP!
THAT DIDN'T COME OFF MY HAND RIGHT AT ALL!
OP!!
OH NO...

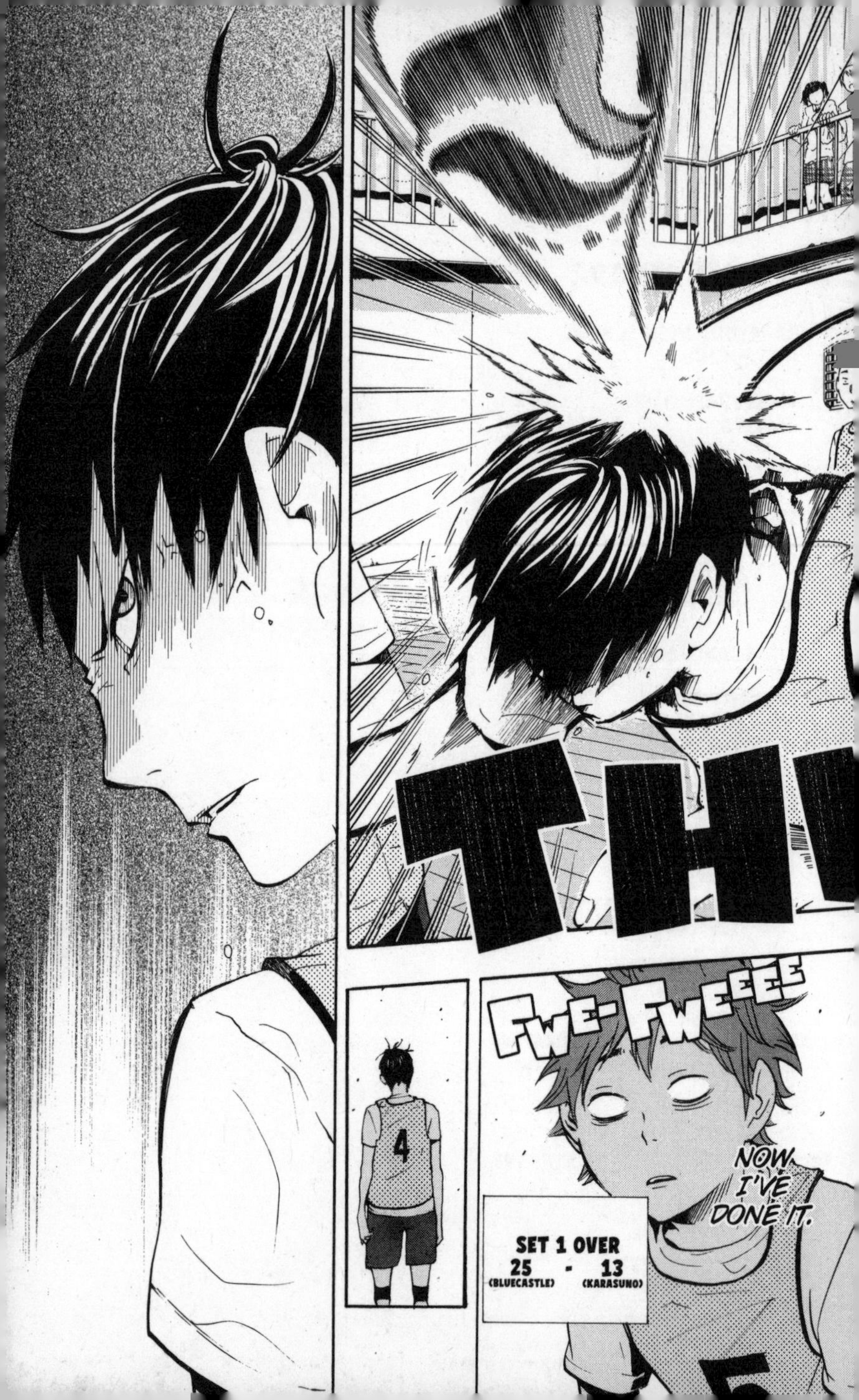
THU
FWE-FWEEEE
NOW I'VE DONE IT.
SET 1 OVER
25 - 13
(BLUECASTLE) (KARASUNO)
4

ITTETSU TAKEDA

KARASUNO HIGH SCHOOL INSTRUCTOR

VOLLEYBALL CLUB ADVISER

AGE: 29
TEACHES MODERN LITERATURE

HEIGHT: 5'6"

WEIGHT: 131 LBS.

BIRTHDAY: JANUARY 10

FAVORITE FOOD:
***NIKUJAGA* BEEF AND POTATO STEW**

CURRENT WORRY:
ONE OF HIS STUDENTS TOLD HIM HIS GLASSES LOOKED DORKY.

ABILITY PARAMETERS (5-POINT SCALE)

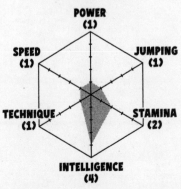

POWER
(1)

JUMPING
(1)

SPEED
(1)

STAMINA
(2)

TECHNIQUE
(1)

INTELLIGENCE
(4)

*NOTE: THE SPEED STAT LISTED ABOVE IS FOR NORMAL SITUATIONS ONLY. HIS BOWING SPEED IS TOO FAST TO BE MEASURED BY THIS SCALE.

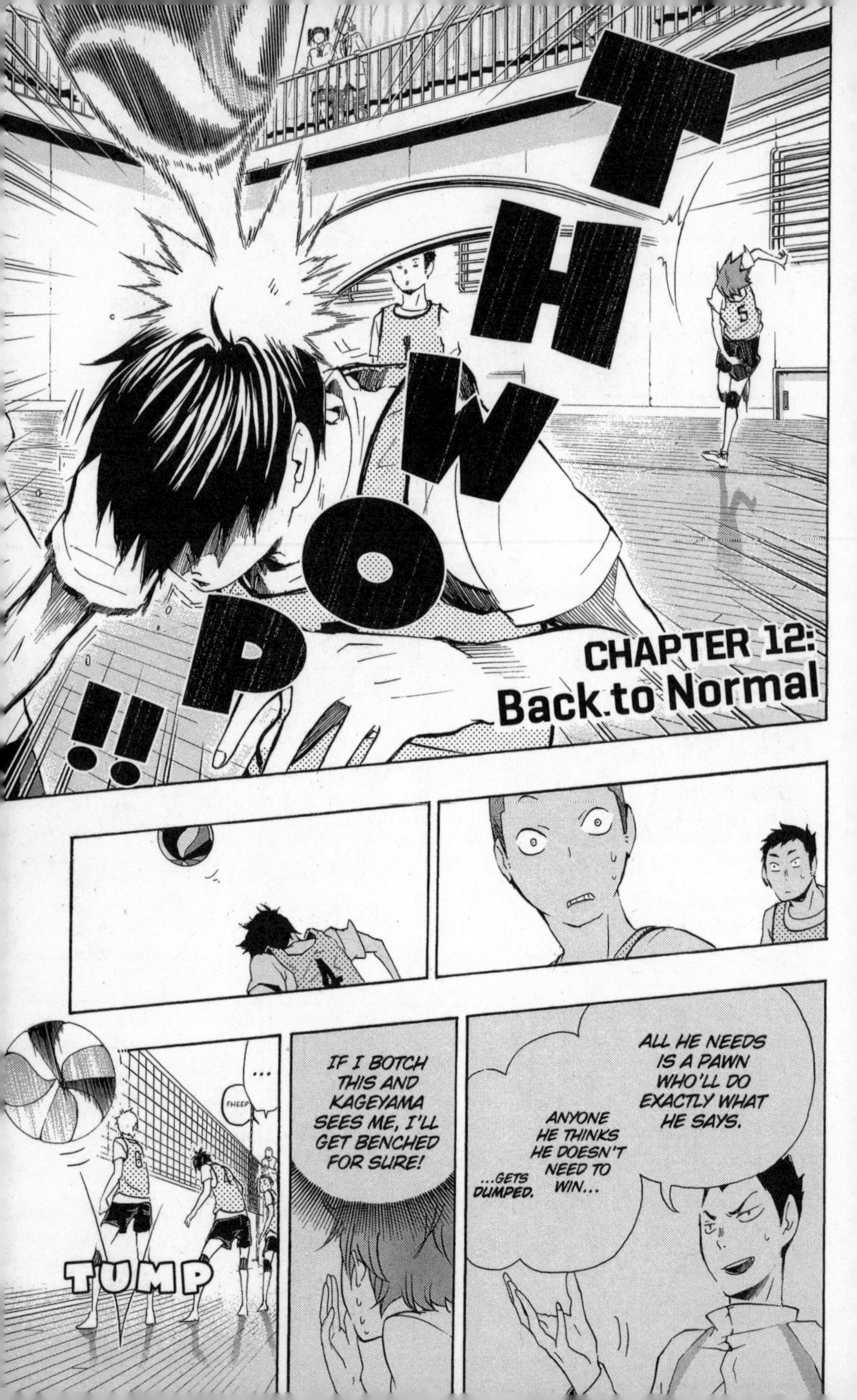
THWOMP!!
CHAPTER 12: Back to Normal
ALL HE NEEDS IS A PAWN WHO'LL DO EXACTLY WHAT HE SAYS.
ANYONE HE THINKS HE DOESN'T NEED TO WIN...
...GETS DUMPED.
IF I BOTCH THIS AND KAGEYAMA SEES ME, I'LL GET BENCHED FOR SURE!
...
FWEEP
TUMP

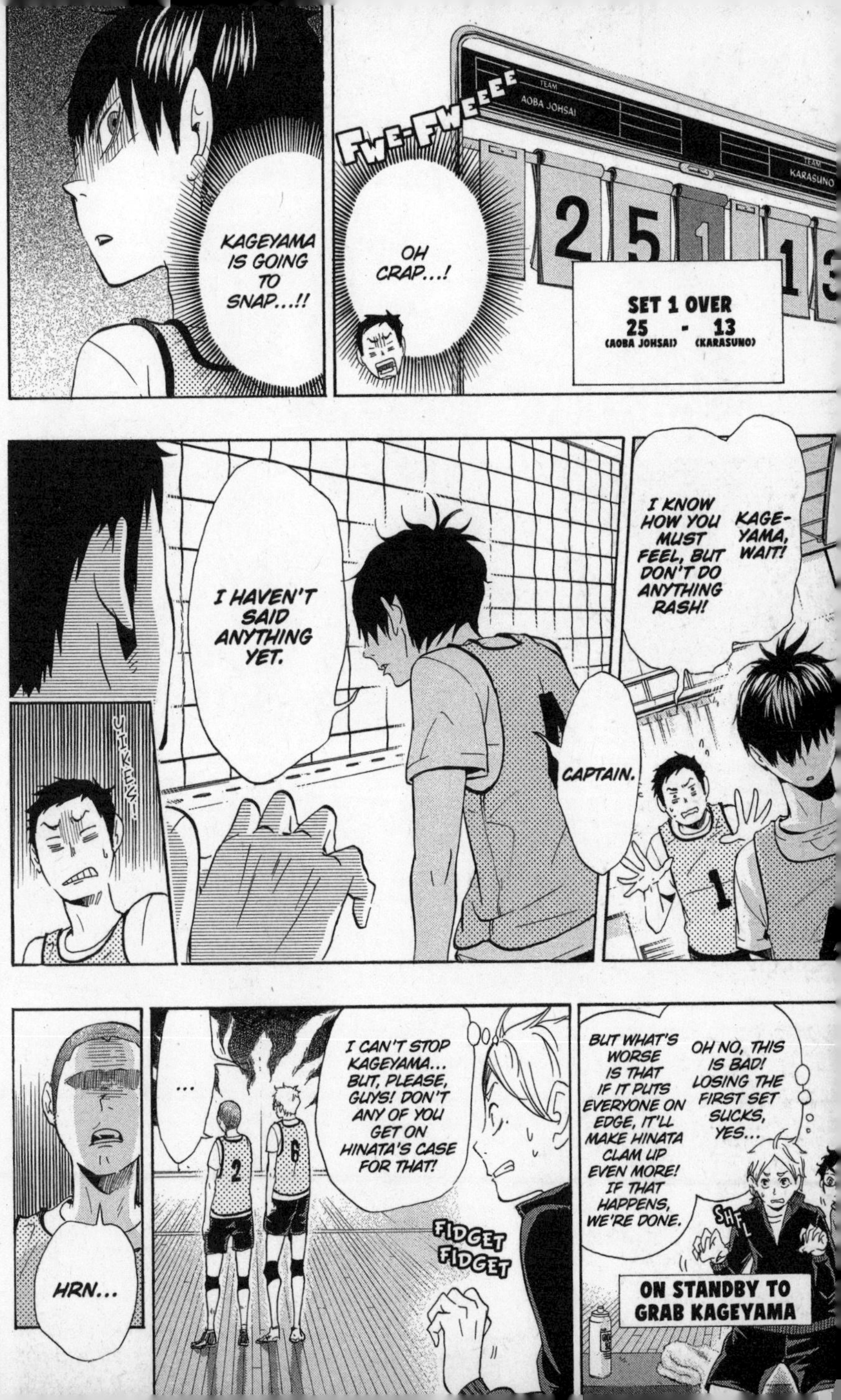
FWE-FWEEEE
TEAM
AOBA JOHSAI
TEAM
KARASUNO
25 1 13
OH CRAP...!
SET 1 OVER
25 - 13
(AOBA JOHSAI) (KARASUNO)
KAGEYAMA IS GOING TO SNAP...!!
KAGE-YAMA, WAIT!
I KNOW HOW YOU MUST FEEL, BUT DON'T DO ANYTHING RASH!
CAPTAIN.
I HAVEN'T SAID ANYTHING YET.
OH NO, THIS IS BAD! LOSING THE FIRST SET SUCKS, YES...
BUT WHAT'S WORSE IS THAT IF IT PUTS EVERYONE ON EDGE, IT'LL MAKE HINATA CLAM UP EVEN MORE! IF THAT HAPPENS, WE'RE DONE.
SHF
ON STANDBY TO GRAB KAGEYAMA
I CAN'T STOP KAGEYAMA... BUT, PLEASE, GUYS! DON'T ANY OF YOU GET ON HINATA'S CASE FOR THAT!
FIDGET FIDGET
...
HRN...

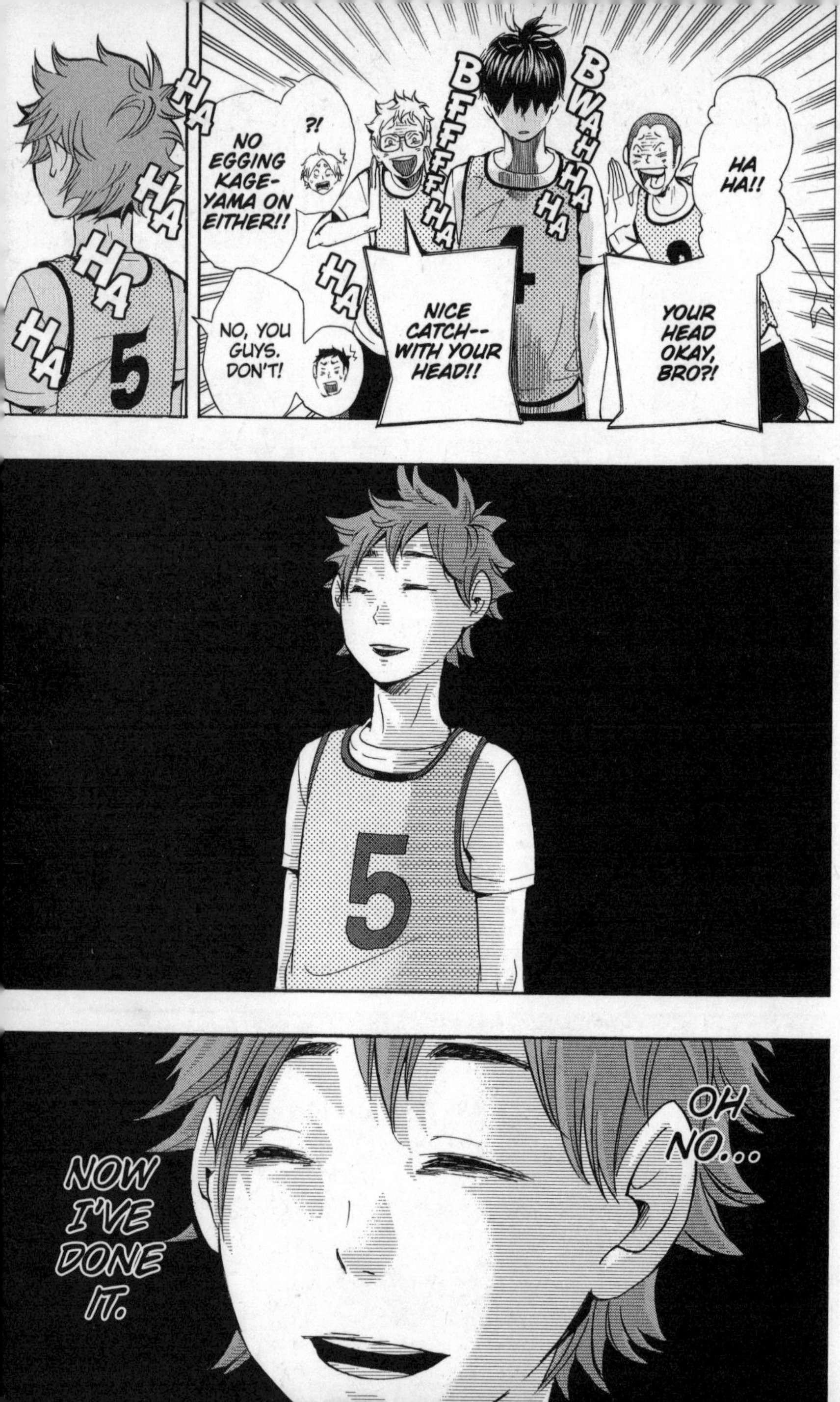
HA HA!!
YOUR HEAD OKAY, BRO?!
BWAHHAHA
BFFFFHA
NICE CATCH-- WITH YOUR HEAD!!
?!
NO EGGING KAGE-YAMA ON EITHER!!
HA
NO, YOU GUYS. DON'T!
HA HA HA HA
OH NO...
NOW I'VE DONE IT.

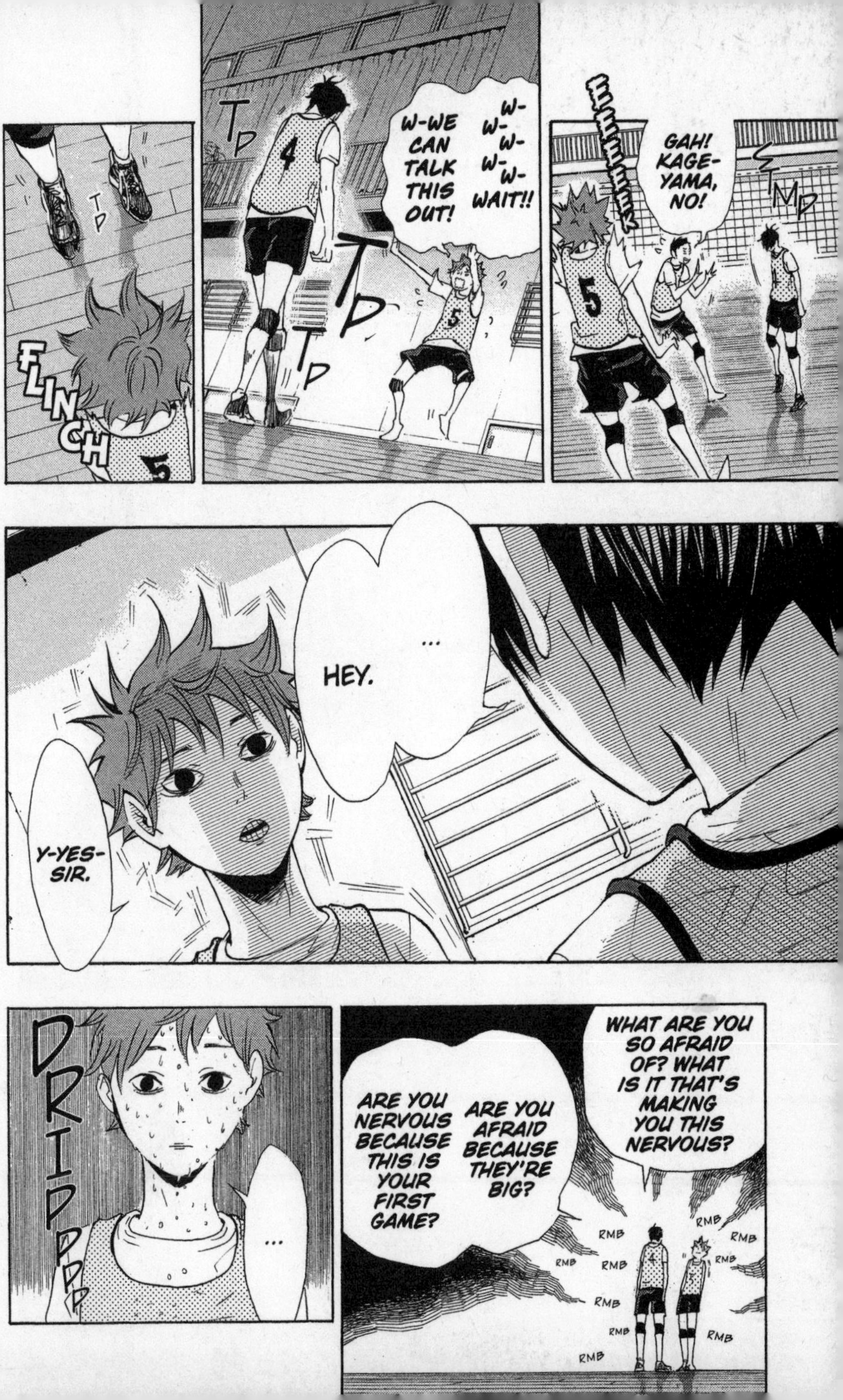
GAH! KAGE-YAMA, NO!
STMP
W-W-W-W-W-WAIT!!
W-WE CAN TALK THIS OUT!
TP
TP
TP
TP
FLINCH
...
HEY.
Y-YES-SIR.
WHAT ARE YOU SO AFRAID OF? WHAT IS IT THAT'S MAKING YOU THIS NERVOUS?
ARE YOU AFRAID BECAUSE THEY'RE BIG?
ARE YOU NERVOUS BECAUSE THIS IS YOUR FIRST GAME?
RMB
RMB
RMB
RMB
RMB
RMB
RMB
RMB
RMB
RMB
RMB
...
DRIPPPP

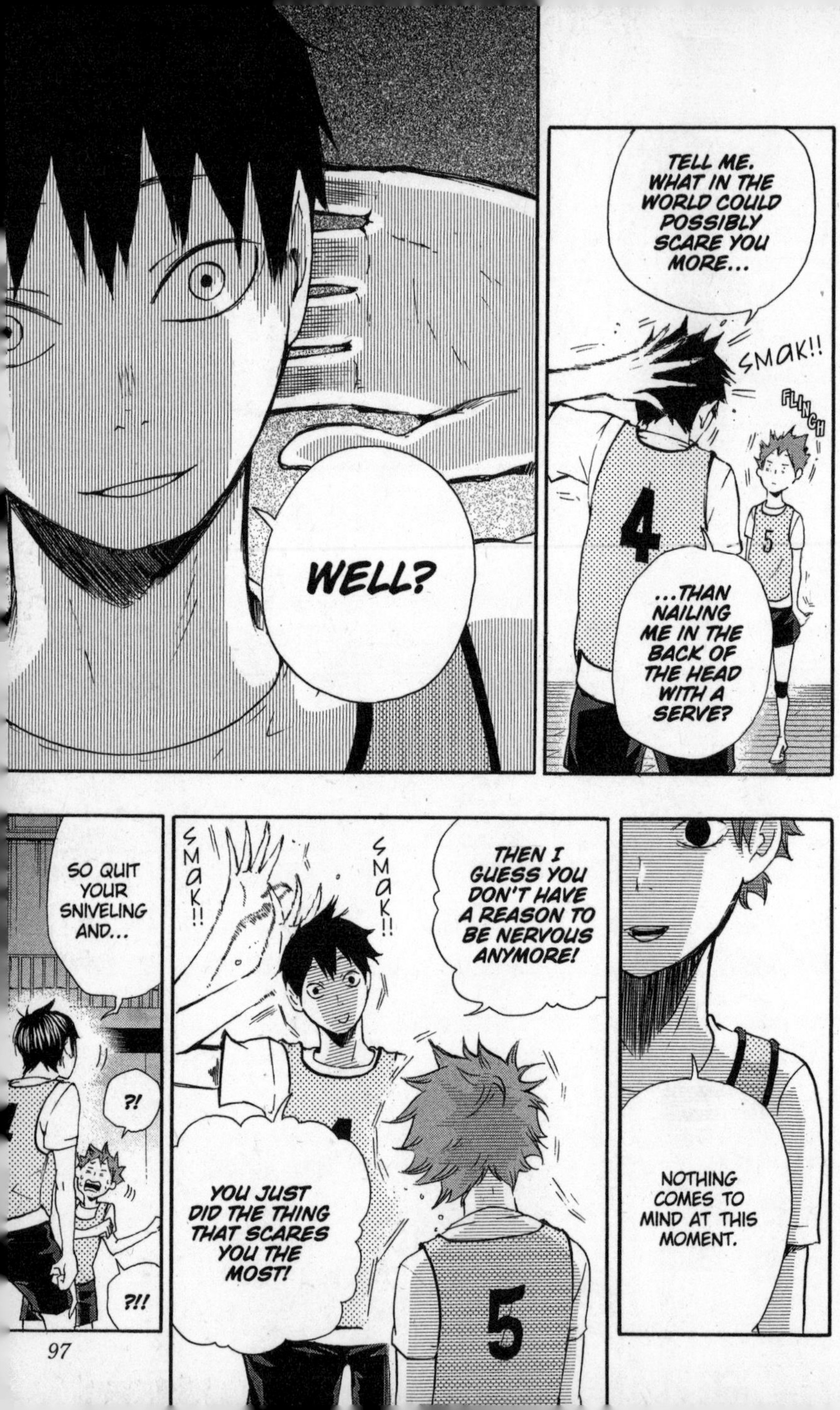
TELL ME. WHAT IN THE WORLD COULD POSSIBLY SCARE YOU MORE...
SMAK!!
FLINCH
...THAN NAILING ME IN THE BACK OF THE HEAD WITH A SERVE?
WELL?
NOTHING COMES TO MIND AT THIS MOMENT.
THEN I GUESS YOU DON'T HAVE A REASON TO BE NERVOUS ANYMORE!
SMAK!!
SMAK!!
YOU JUST DID THE THING THAT SCARES YOU THE MOST!
SO QUIT YOUR SNIVELING AND...
?!
?!!

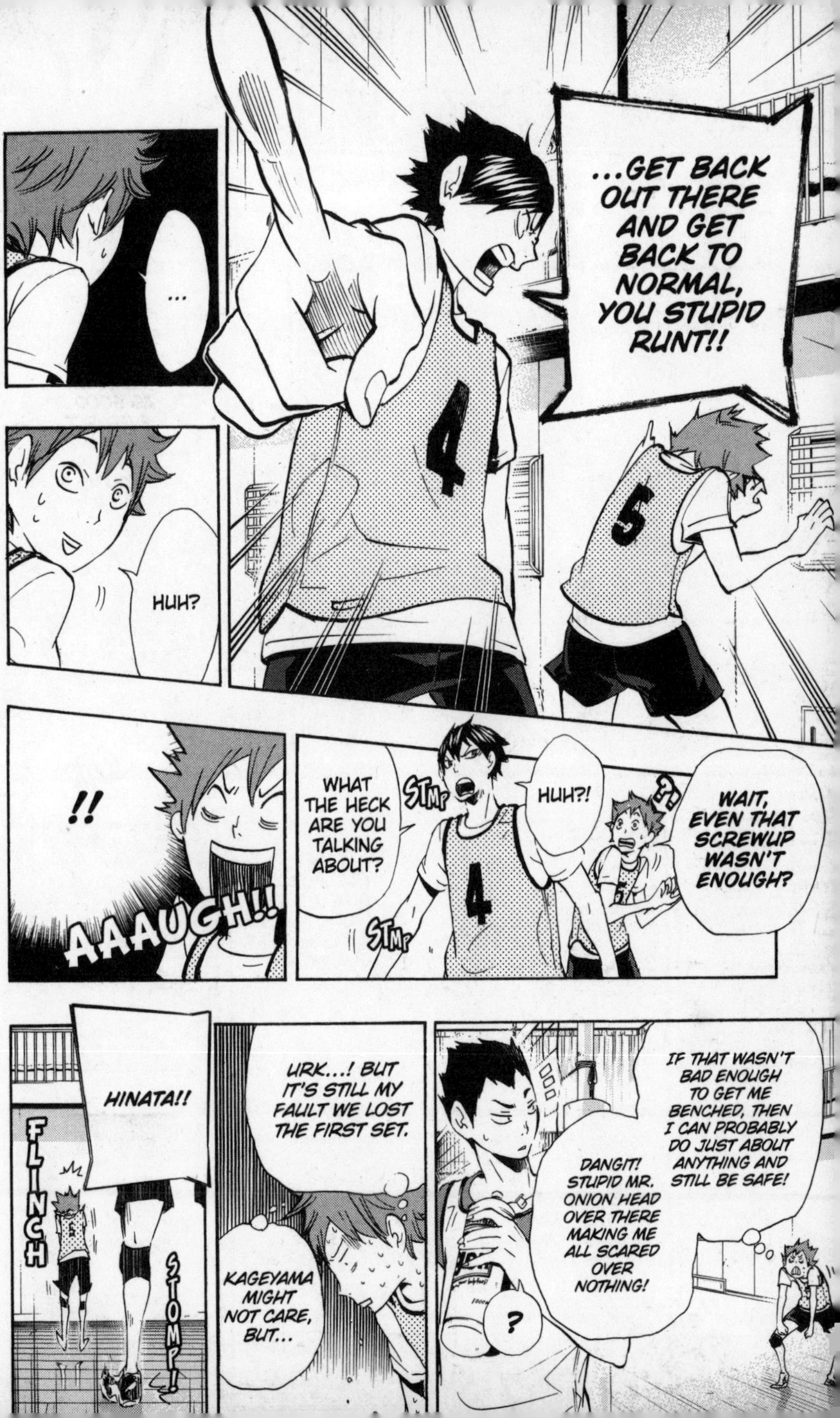
...GET BACK OUT THERE AND GET BACK TO NORMAL, YOU STUPID RUNT!!
...
HUH?
WAIT, EVEN THAT SCREWUP WASN'T ENOUGH?
HUH?!
WHAT THE HECK ARE YOU TALKING ABOUT?
STMP
STMP
!!
AAAUGH!!
IF THAT WASN'T BAD ENOUGH TO GET ME BENCHED, THEN I CAN PROBABLY DO JUST ABOUT ANYTHING AND STILL BE SAFE!
DANGIT! STUPID MR. ONION HEAD OVER THERE MAKING ME ALL SCARED OVER NOTHING!
?
URK...! BUT IT'S STILL MY FAULT WE LOST THE FIRST SET.
KAGEYAMA MIGHT NOT CARE, BUT...
HINATA!!
FLINCH
STOMP!

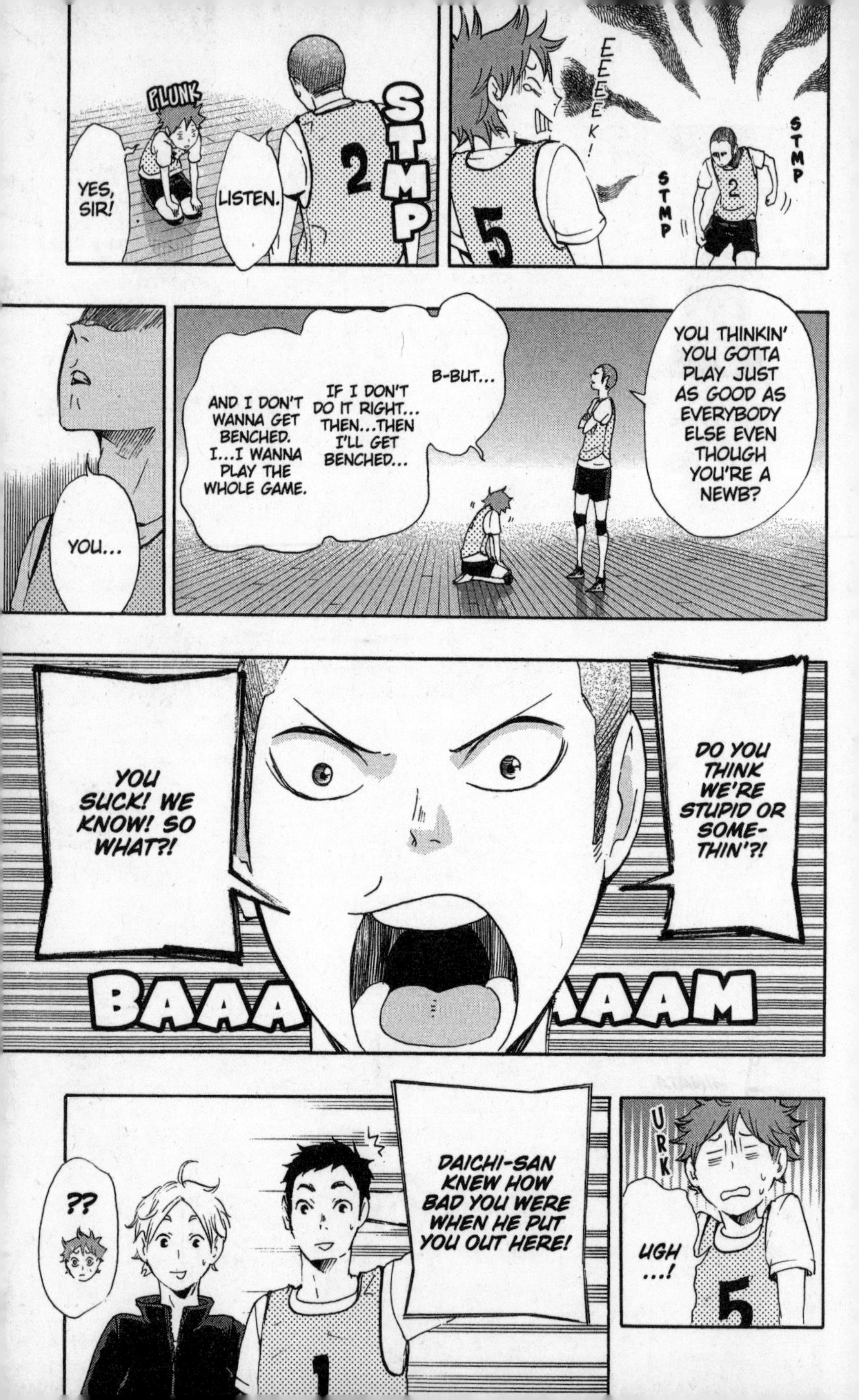
EEEEEK!
STMP
STMP
STMP
STMP
LISTEN.
PLUNK
YES, SIR!
YOU THINKIN' YOU GOTTA PLAY JUST AS GOOD AS EVERYBODY ELSE EVEN THOUGH YOU'RE A NEWB?
B-BUT...
IF I DON'T DO IT RIGHT... THEN...THEN I'LL GET BENCHED...
AND I DON'T WANNA GET BENCHED. I...I WANNA PLAY THE WHOLE GAME.
YOU...
DO YOU THINK WE'RE STUPID OR SOME-THIN'?!
YOU SUCK! WE KNOW! SO WHAT?!
BAAA AAAM
URK
UGH...!
DAICHI-SAN KNEW HOW BAD YOU WERE WHEN HE PUT YOU OUT HERE!
??

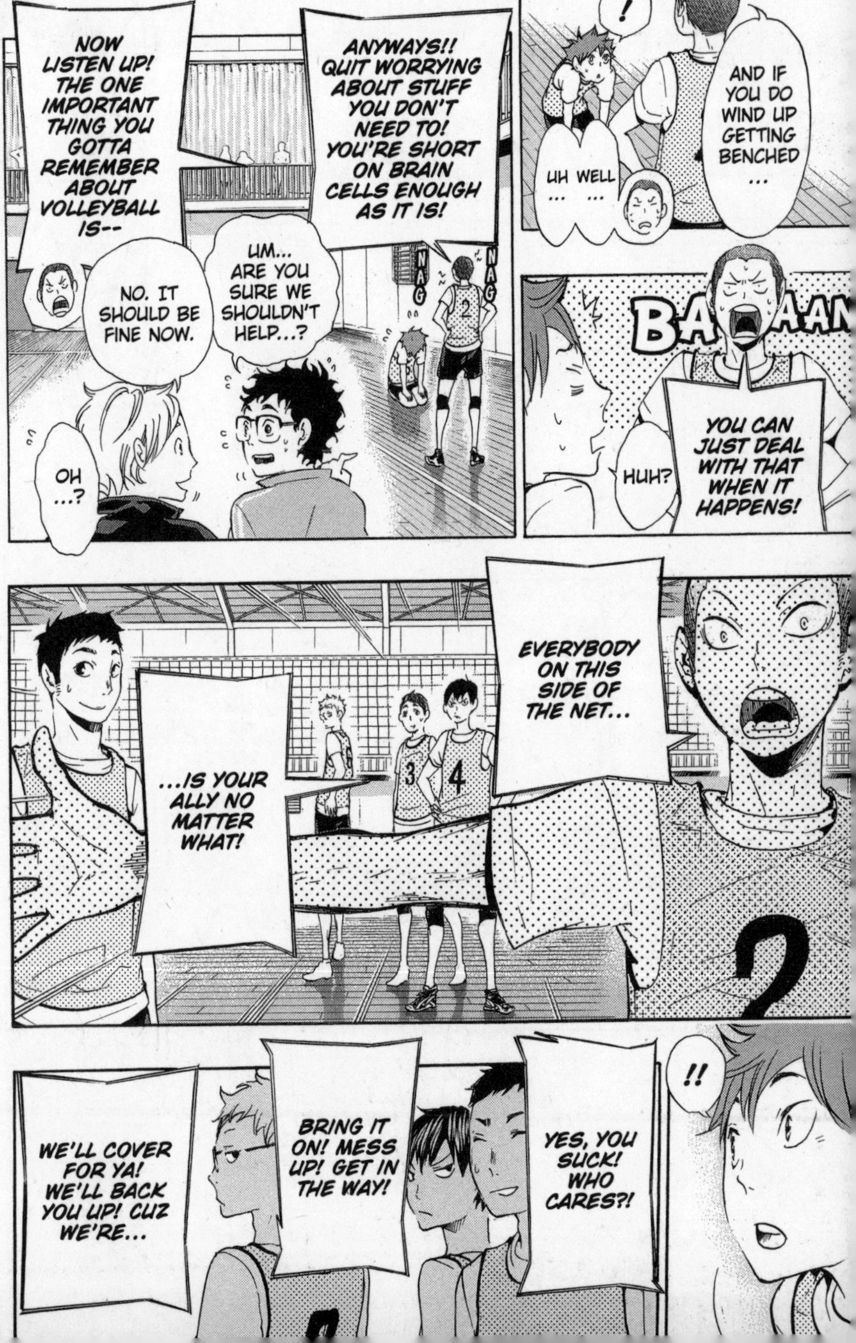
!
AND IF YOU DO WIND UP GETTING BENCHED ...
UH WELL ... ...
BA AAN
YOU CAN JUST DEAL WITH THAT WHEN IT HAPPENS!
HUH?
ANYWAYS!! QUIT WORRYING ABOUT STUFF YOU DON'T NEED TO! YOU'RE SHORT ON BRAIN CELLS ENOUGH AS IT IS!
NOW LISTEN UP! THE ONE IMPORTANT THING YOU GOTTA REMEMBER ABOUT VOLLEYBALL IS--
NAG
NAG
UM... ARE YOU SURE WE SHOULDN'T HELP...?
NO. IT SHOULD BE FINE NOW.
OH ...?
EVERYBODY ON THIS SIDE OF THE NET...
...IS YOUR ALLY NO MATTER WHAT!
?
!!
YES, YOU SUCK! WHO CARES?!
BRING IT ON! MESS UP! GET IN THE WAY!
WE'LL COVER FOR YA! WE'LL BACK YOU UP! CUZ WE'RE...

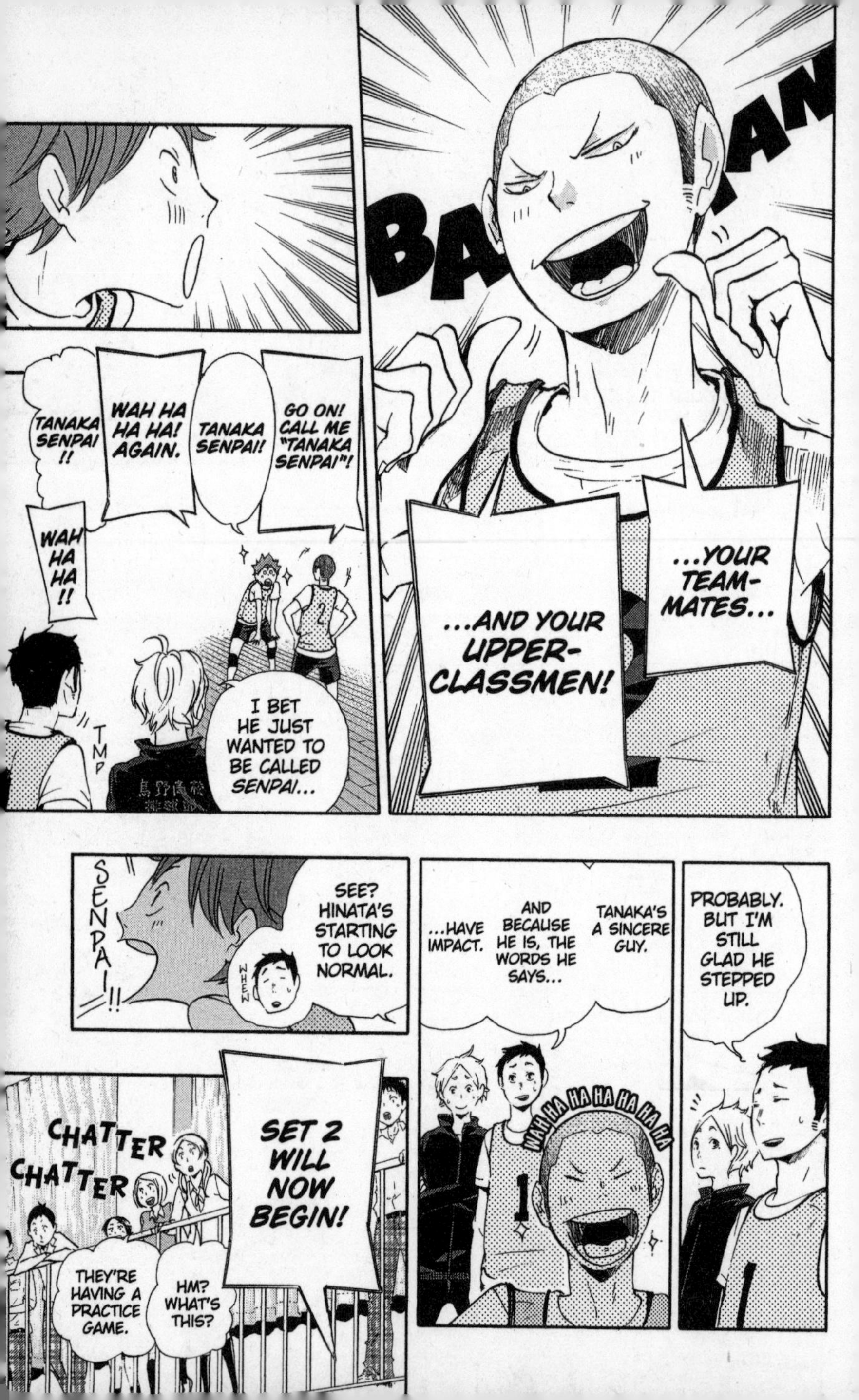
BA
AN
...YOUR TEAMMATES...
...AND YOUR UPPERCLASSMEN!
GO ON! CALL ME "TANAKA SENPAI"!
TANAKA SENPAI!
WAH HA HA HA! AGAIN.
TANAKA SENPAI !!
WAH HA HA HA !!
I BET HE JUST WANTED TO BE CALLED SENPAI...
TMP
PROBABLY. BUT I'M STILL GLAD HE STEPPED UP.
TANAKA'S A SINCERE GUY.
AND BECAUSE HE IS, THE WORDS HE SAYS...
...HAVE IMPACT.
WAH HA HA HA HA HA HA
SEE? HINATA'S STARTING TO LOOK NORMAL.
WHEW
SENPAI!!
SET 2 WILL NOW BEGIN!
HM? WHAT'S THIS?
THEY'RE HAVING A PRACTICE GAME.
CHATTER
CHATTER

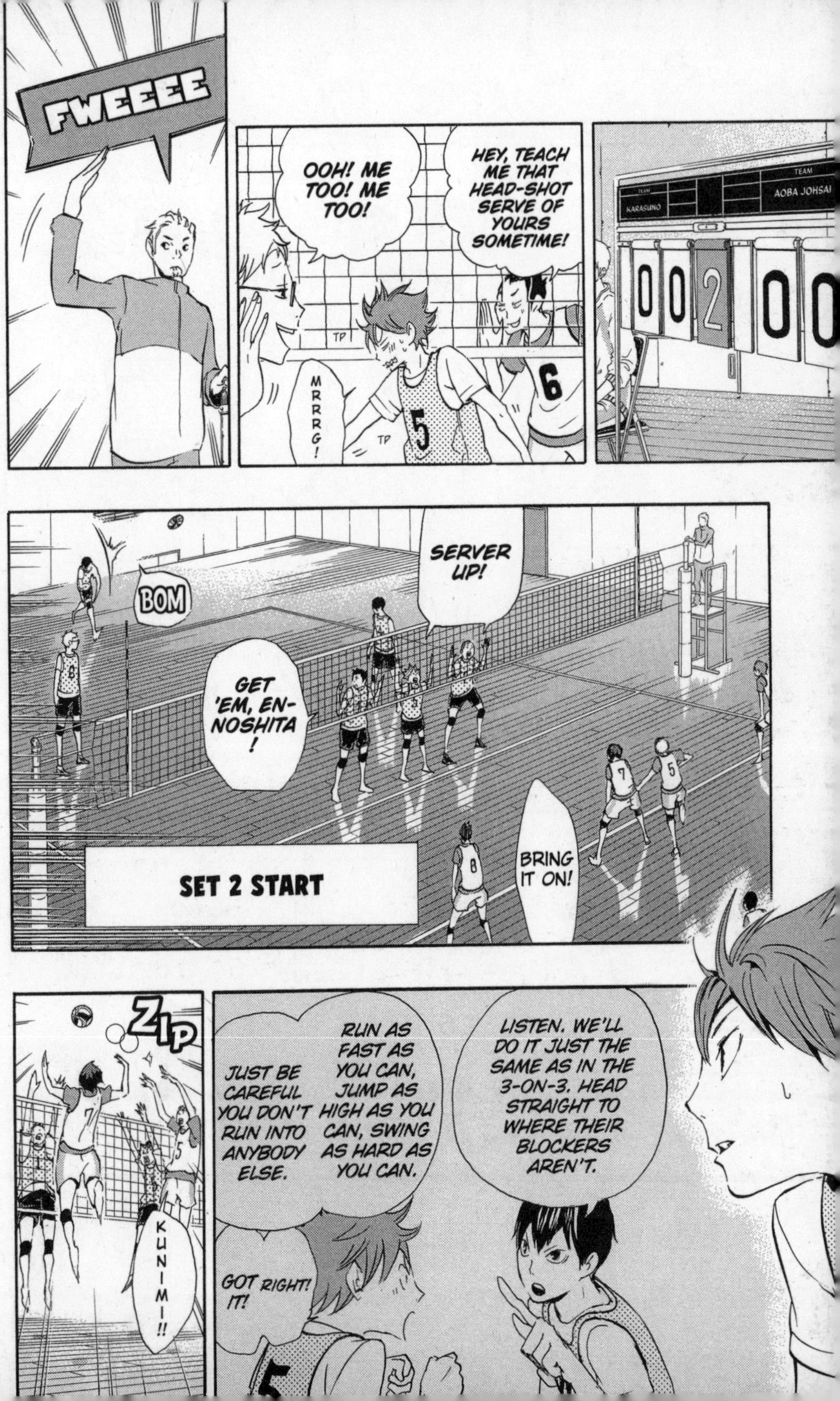
TEAM KARASUNO
TEAM AOBA JOHSAI
HEY, TEACH ME THAT HEAD-SHOT SERVE OF YOURS SOMETIME!
OOH! ME TOO! ME TOO!
TP
MRRRG!
TP
FWEEEE
SERVER UP!
GET 'EM, ENNOSHITA!
BOM
BRING IT ON!
SET 2 START
LISTEN. WE'LL DO IT JUST THE SAME AS IN THE 3-ON-3. HEAD STRAIGHT TO WHERE THEIR BLOCKERS AREN'T.
RUN AS FAST AS YOU CAN, JUMP AS HIGH AS YOU CAN, SWING AS HARD AS YOU CAN.
JUST BE CAREFUL YOU DON'T RUN INTO ANYBODY ELSE.
RIGHT!
GOT IT!
ZIP
KUNIMI!!

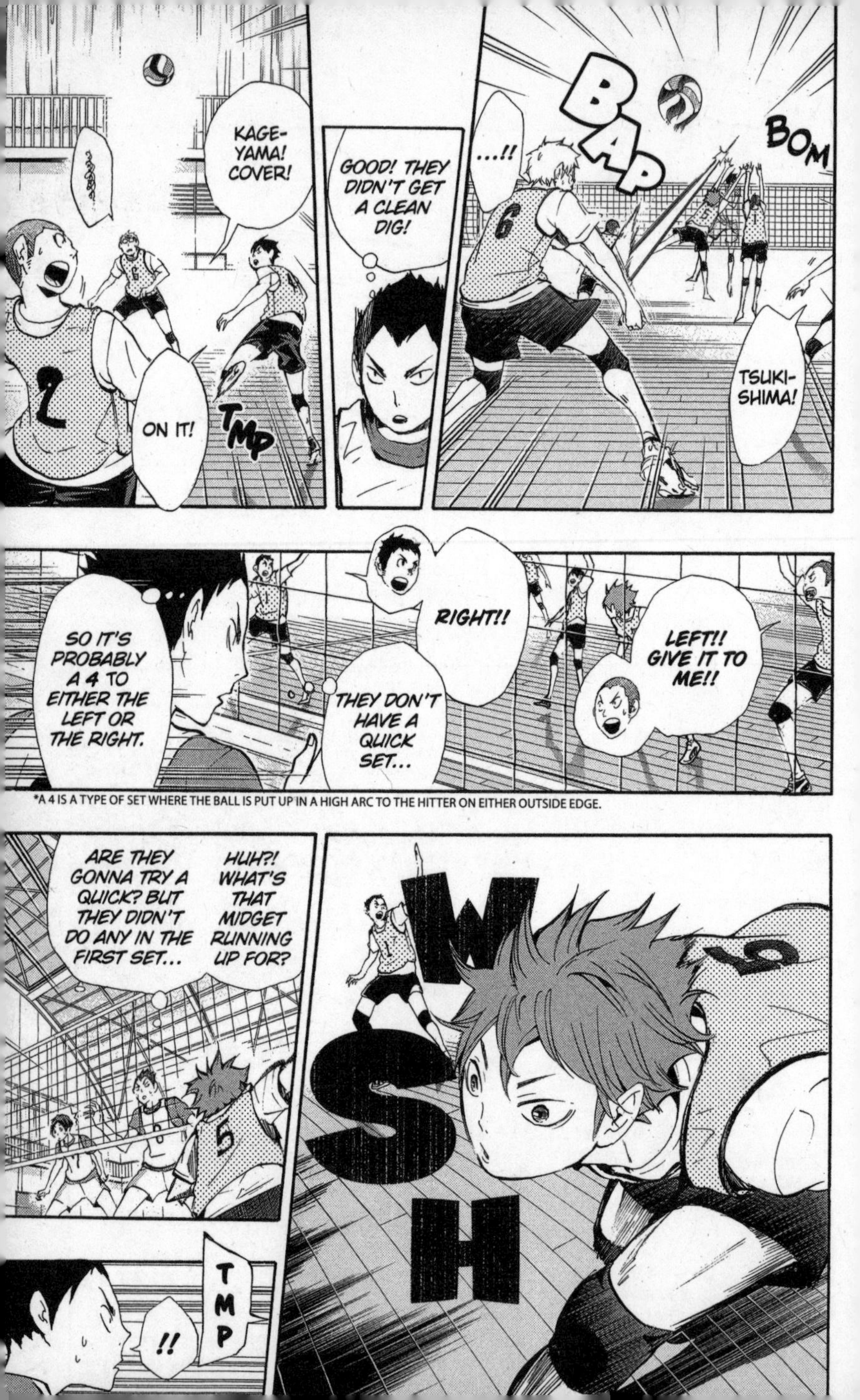
BOM
BAP
...!!
TSUKI-SHIMA!
GOOD! THEY DIDN'T GET A CLEAN DIG!
KAGE-YAMA! COVER!
ON IT!
TMP
LEFT!! GIVE IT TO ME!!
RIGHT!!
THEY DON'T HAVE A QUICK SET...
SO IT'S PROBABLY A 4 TO EITHER THE LEFT OR THE RIGHT.
WSH
HUH?! WHAT'S THAT MIDGET RUNNING UP FOR?
ARE THEY GONNA TRY A QUICK? BUT THEY DIDN'T DO ANY IN THE FIRST SET...
TMP
!!

*A 4 IS A TYPE OF SET WHERE THE BALL IS PUT UP IN A HIGH ARC TO THE HITTER ON EITHER OUTSIDE EDGE.

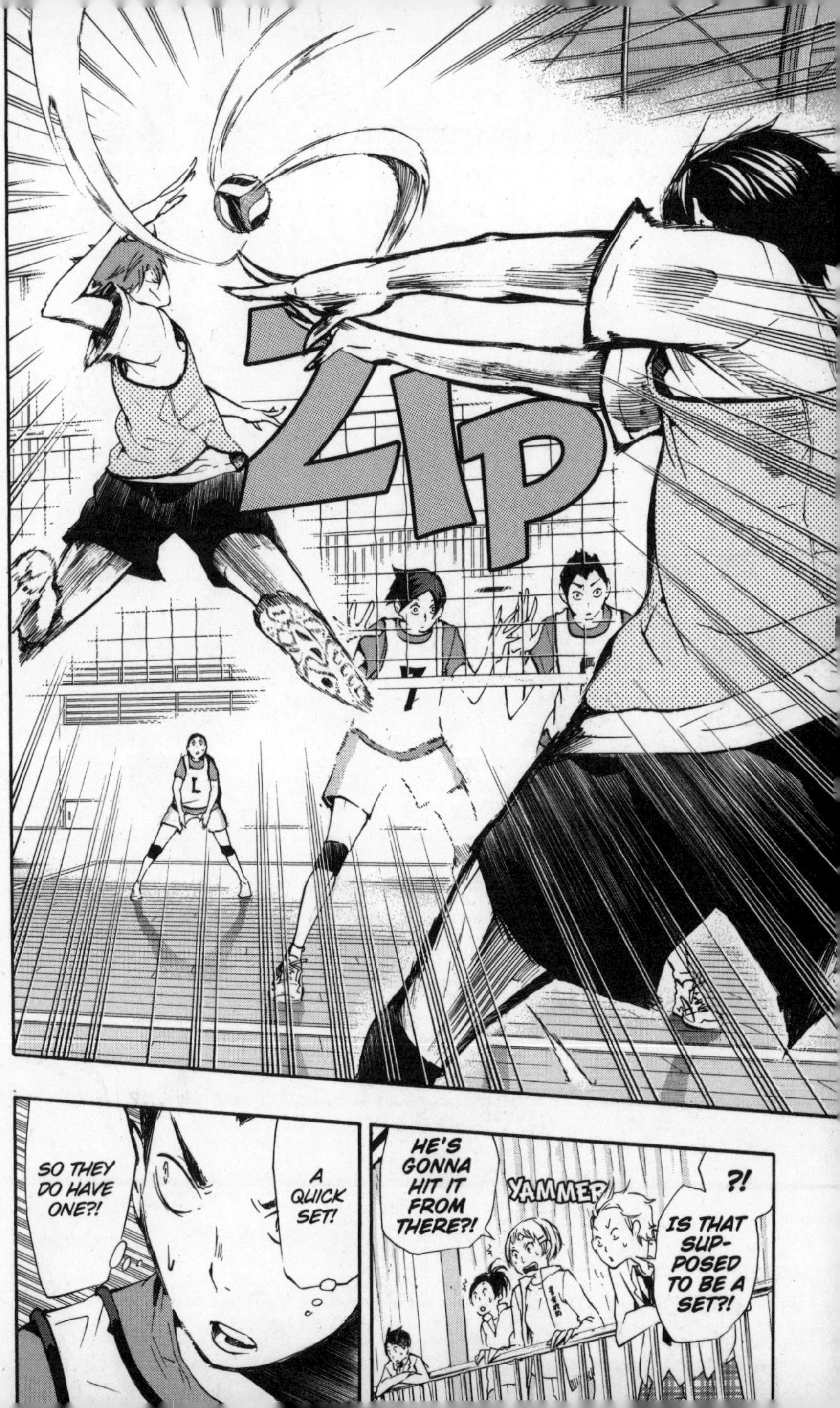
ZIP
?!
IS THAT SUP-POSED TO BE A SET?!
YAMMER
HE'S GONNA HIT IT FROM THERE?!
A QUICK SET!
SO THEY DO HAVE ONE?!

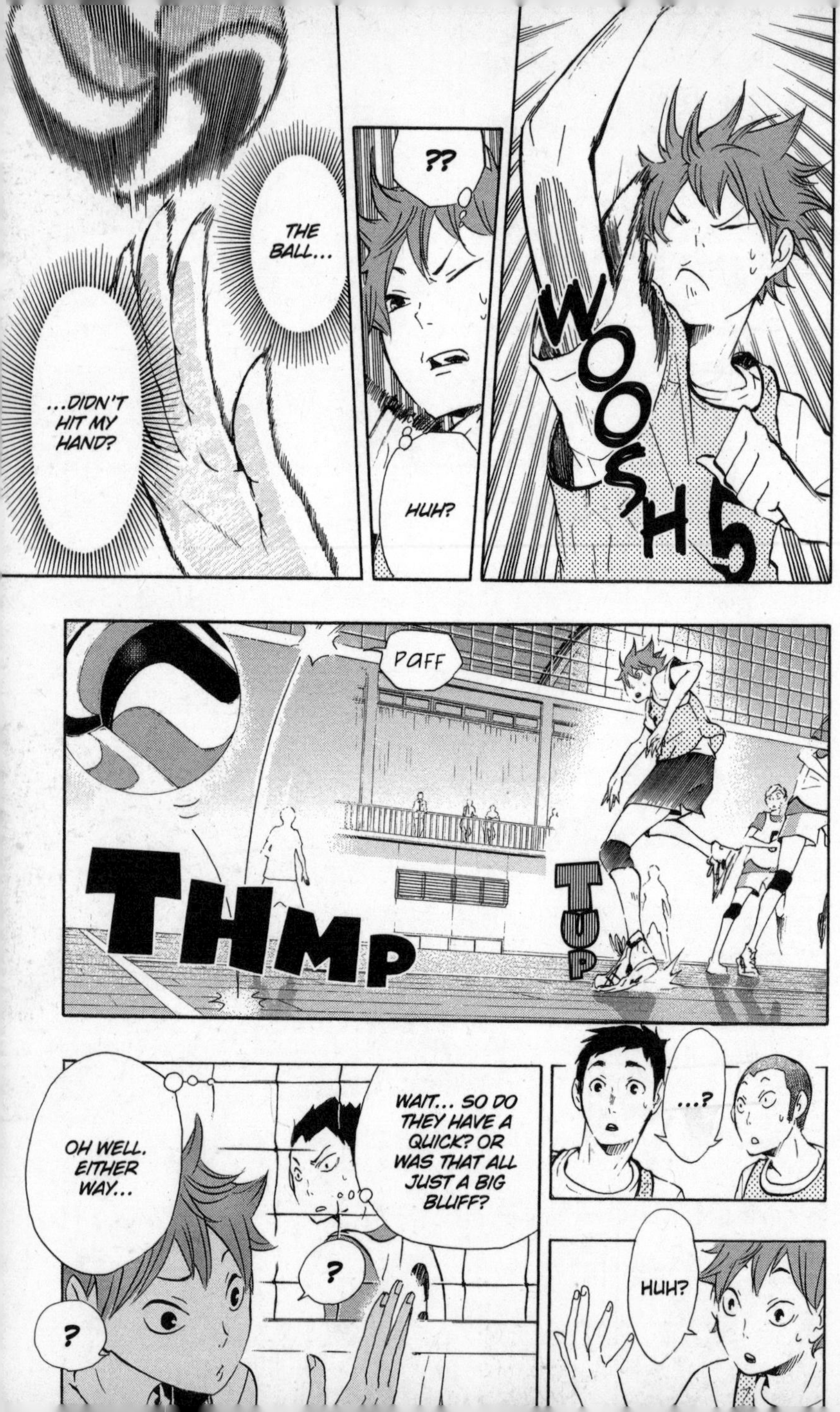
WOOSH
??
HUH?
THE BALL...
...DIDN'T HIT MY HAND?
PAFF
TUP
THMP
...?
HUH?
WAIT... SO DO THEY HAVE A QUICK? OR WAS THAT ALL JUST A BIG BLUFF?
?
OH WELL. EITHER WAY...
?

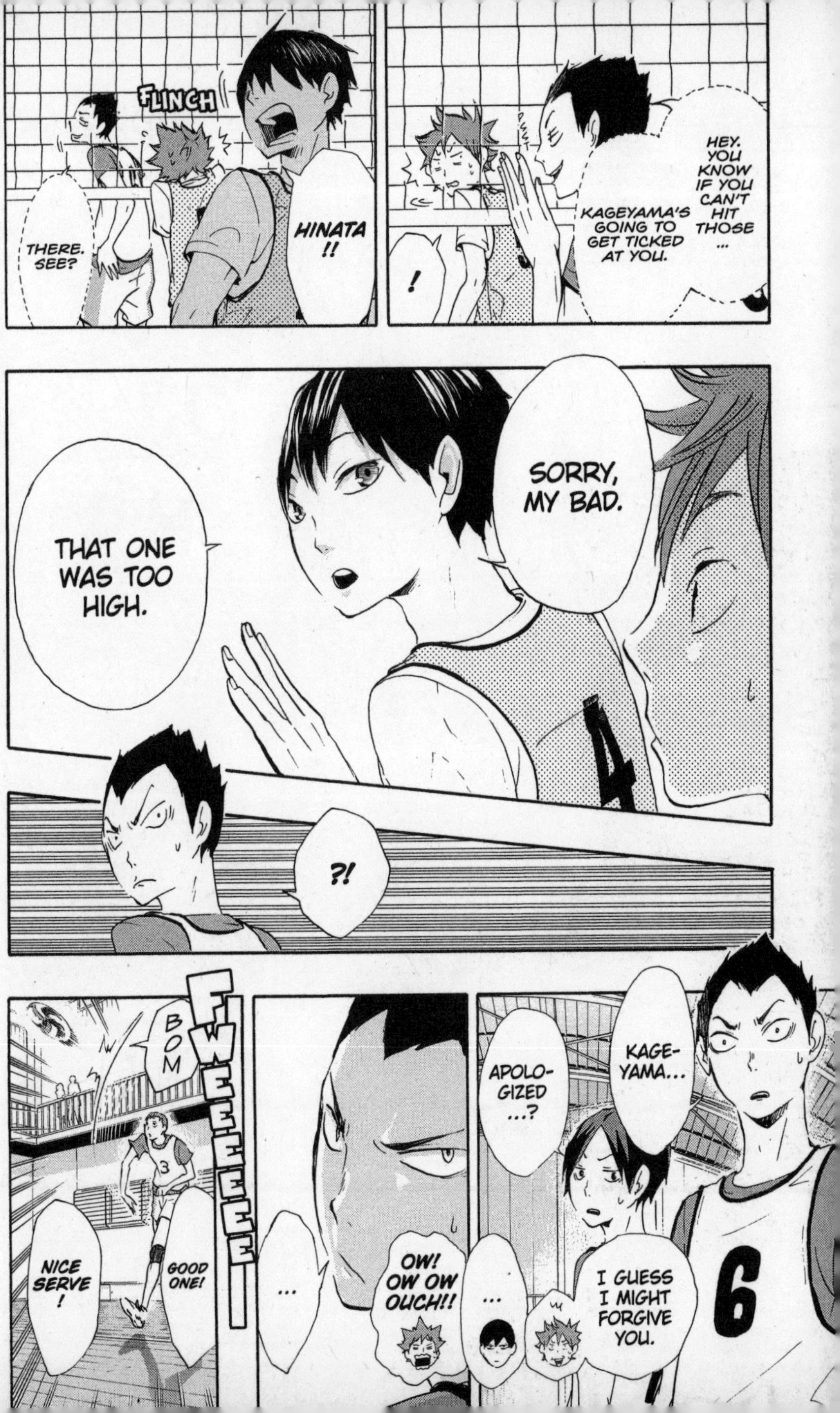
HEY. YOU KNOW IF YOU CAN'T HIT THOSE ...
KAGEYAMA'S GOING TO GET TICKED AT YOU.
!
FLINCH
HINATA !!
THERE. SEE?
SORRY, MY BAD.
THAT ONE WAS TOO HIGH.
?!
KAGE-YAMA...
APOLO-GIZED ...?
I GUESS I MIGHT FORGIVE YOU.
...
OW! OW OW OUCH!!
...
FWEEEEEEE
BOM
GOOD ONE!
NICE SERVE !

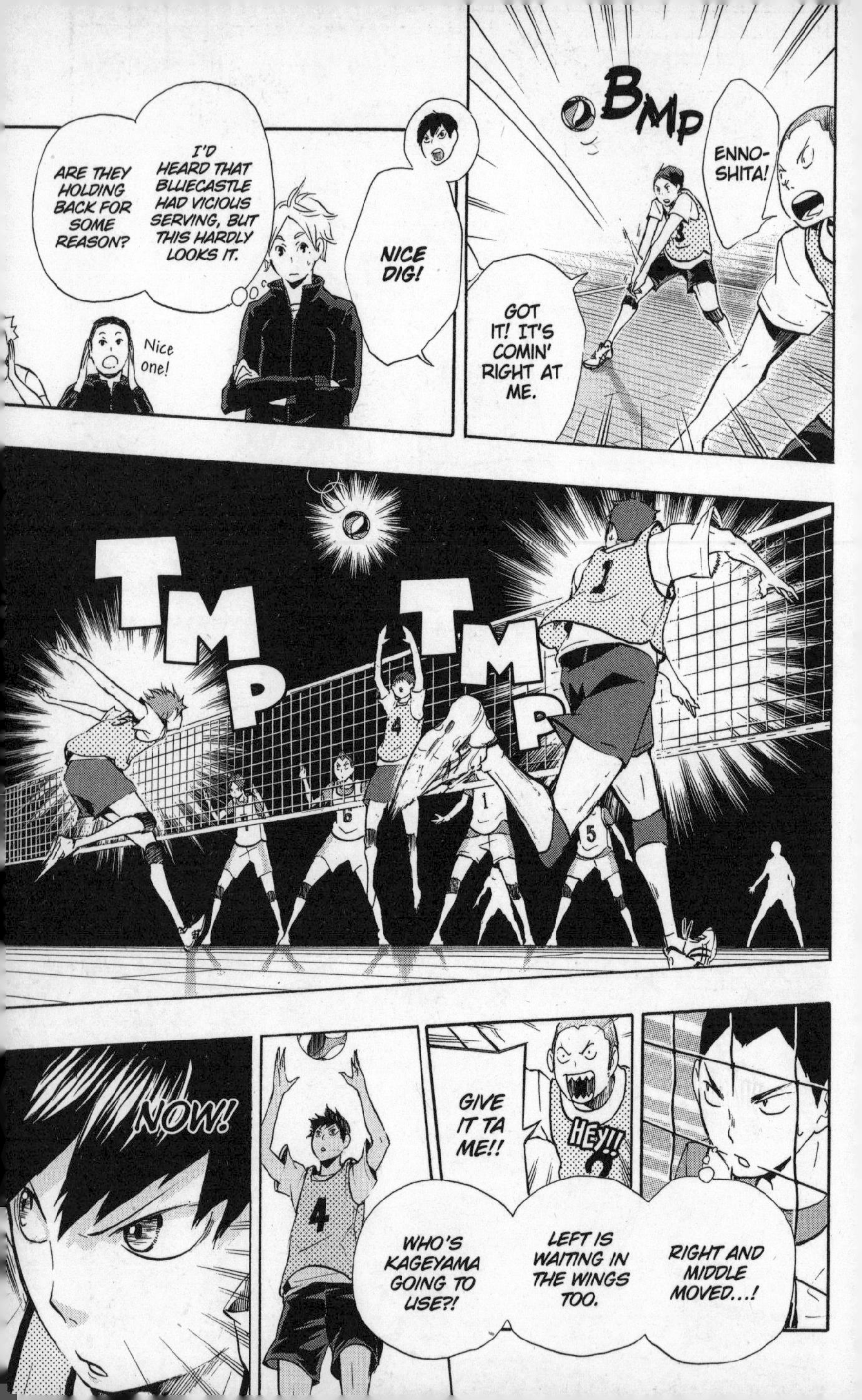
BMP
ENNO-SHITA!
GOT IT! IT'S COMIN' RIGHT AT ME.
NICE DIG!
I'D HEARD THAT BLUECASTLE HAD VICIOUS SERVING, BUT THIS HARDLY LOOKS IT.
ARE THEY HOLDING BACK FOR SOME REASON?
Nice one!
TMP
TMP
RIGHT AND MIDDLE MOVED...!
GIVE IT TA ME!!
HEY!!
LEFT IS WAITING IN THE WINGS TOO.
WHO'S KAGEYAMA GOING TO USE?!
NOW!

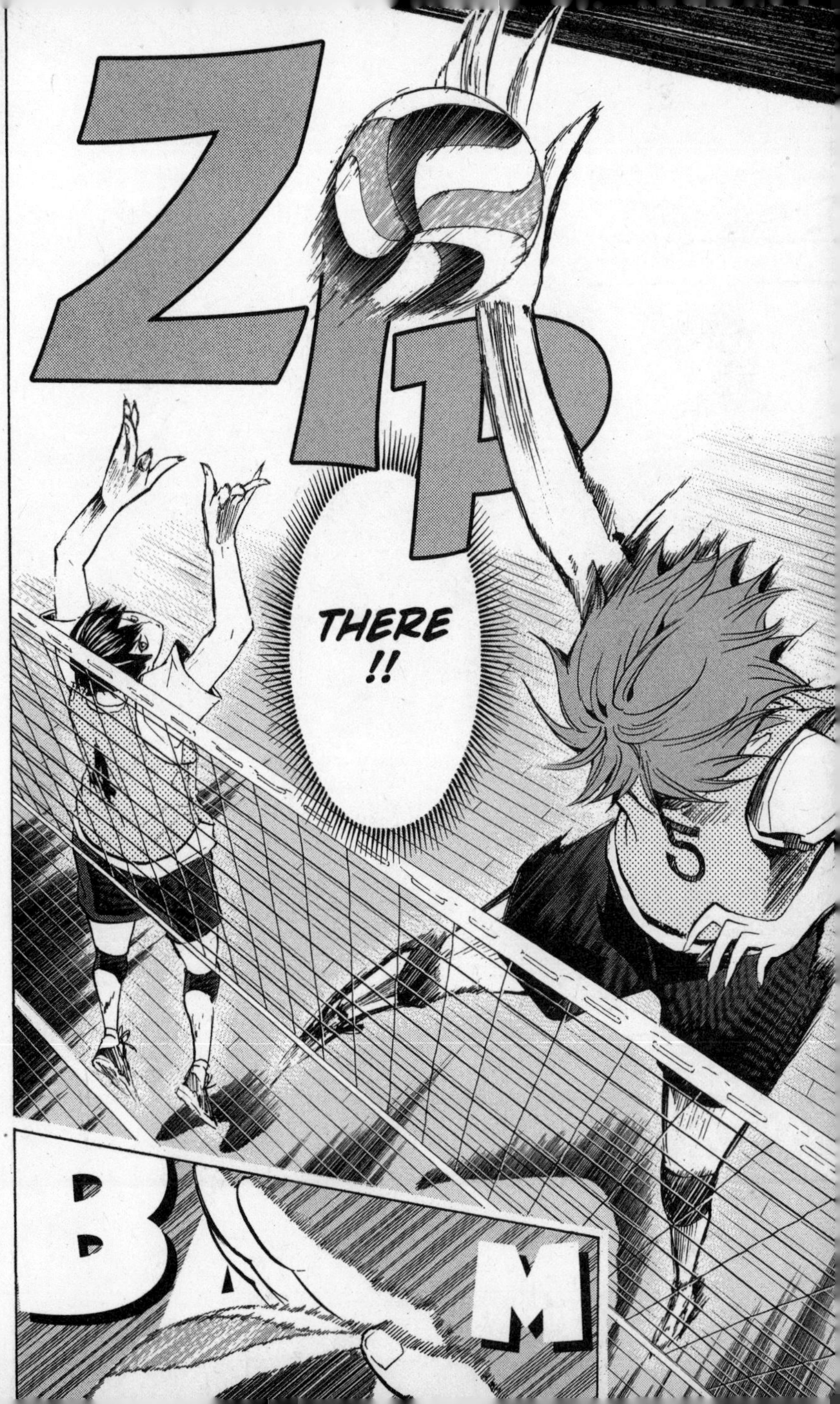
ZIP
THERE !!
BAM

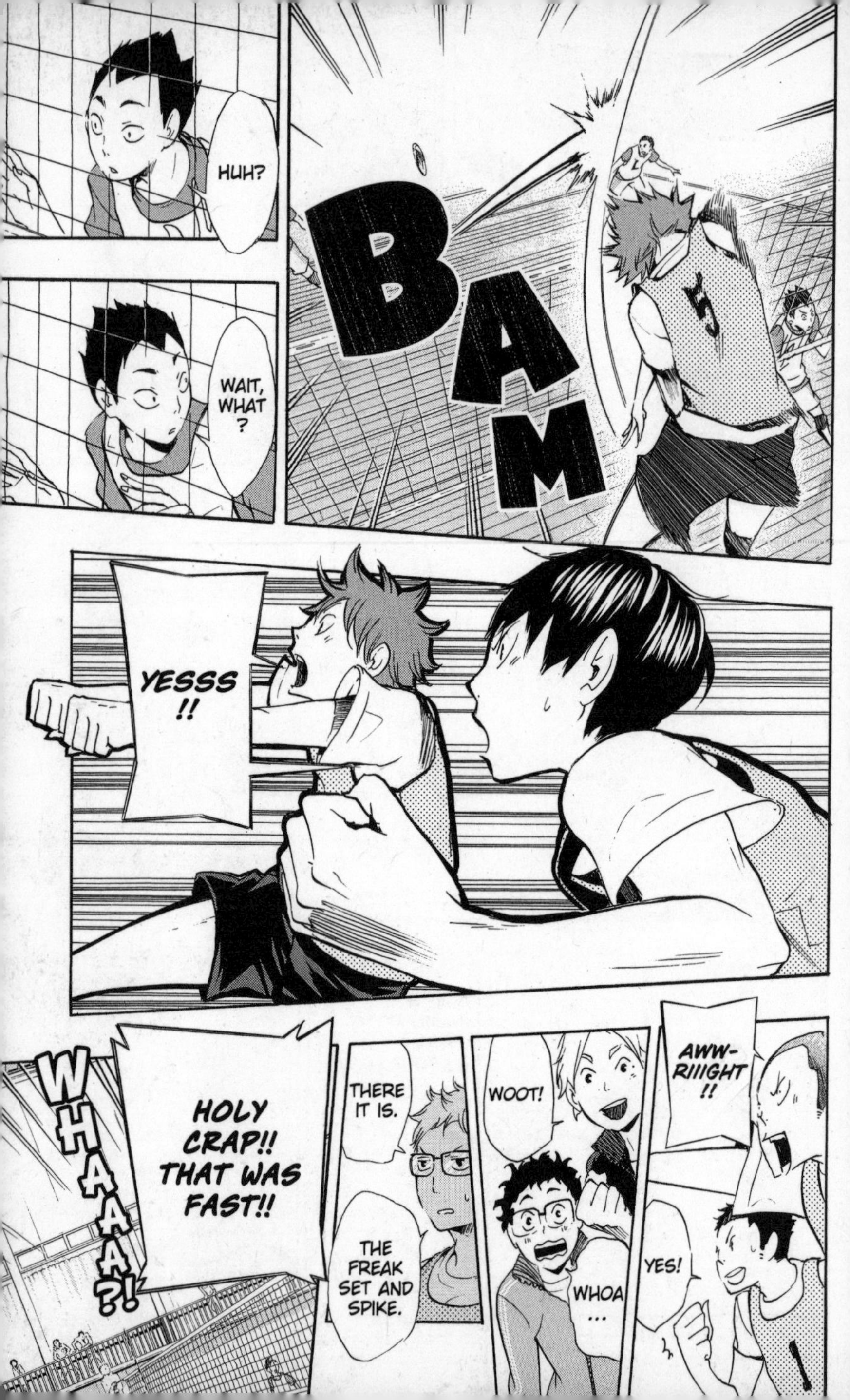
BAM
HUH?
WAIT, WHAT ?
YESSS !!
AWW-RIIIGHT !!
YES!
WOOT!
WHOA ...
THERE IT IS.
THE FREAK SET AND SPIKE.
HOLY CRAP!! THAT WAS FAST!!
WHAAAA?!

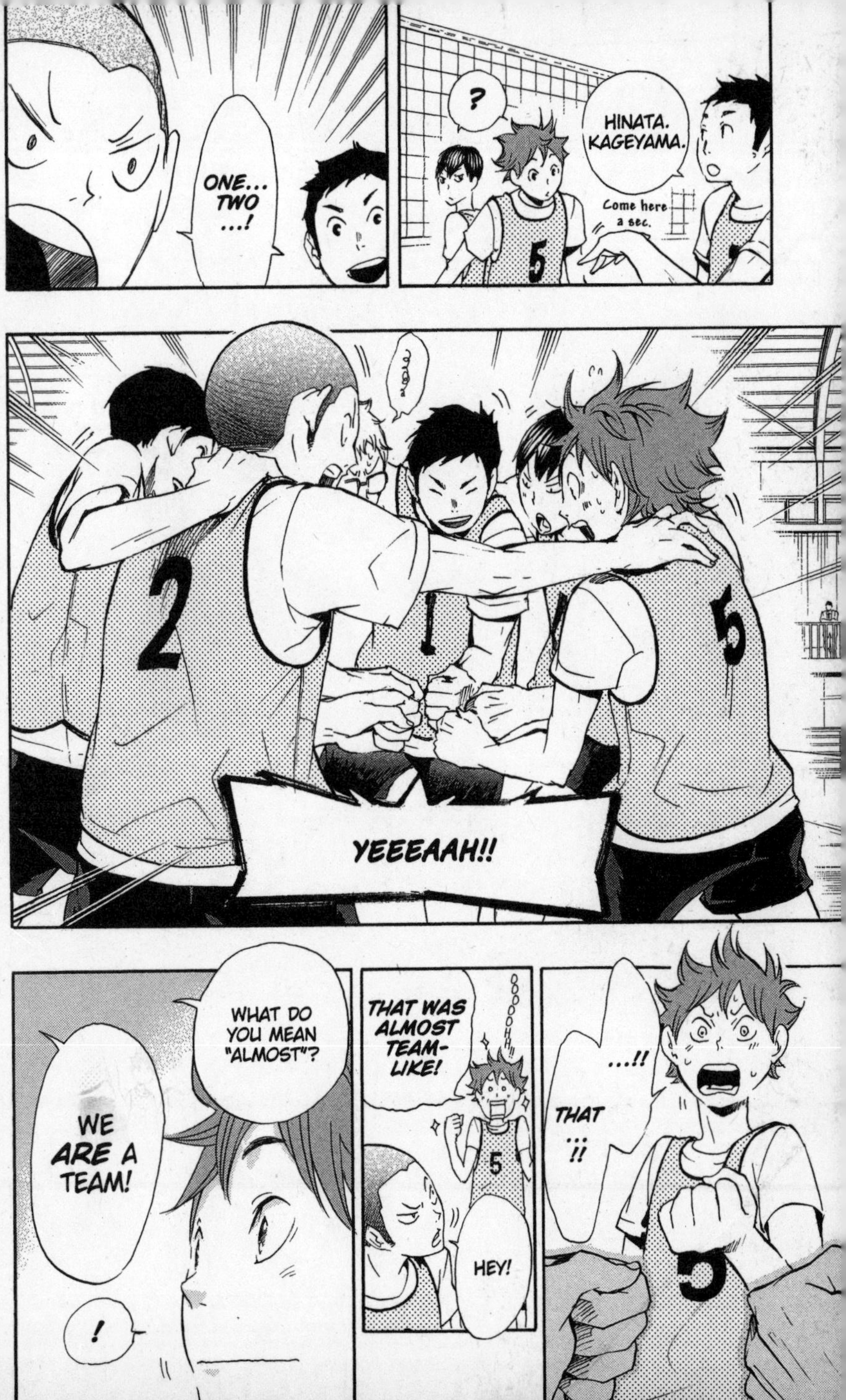
HINATA. KAGEYAMA.
Come here a sec.
?
ONE... TWO ...!
YEEEAAH!!
...!!
THAT...!!
OOOOOHH!!
THAT WAS ALMOST TEAM-LIKE!
HEY!
WHAT DO YOU MEAN "ALMOST"?
WE ARE A TEAM!
!

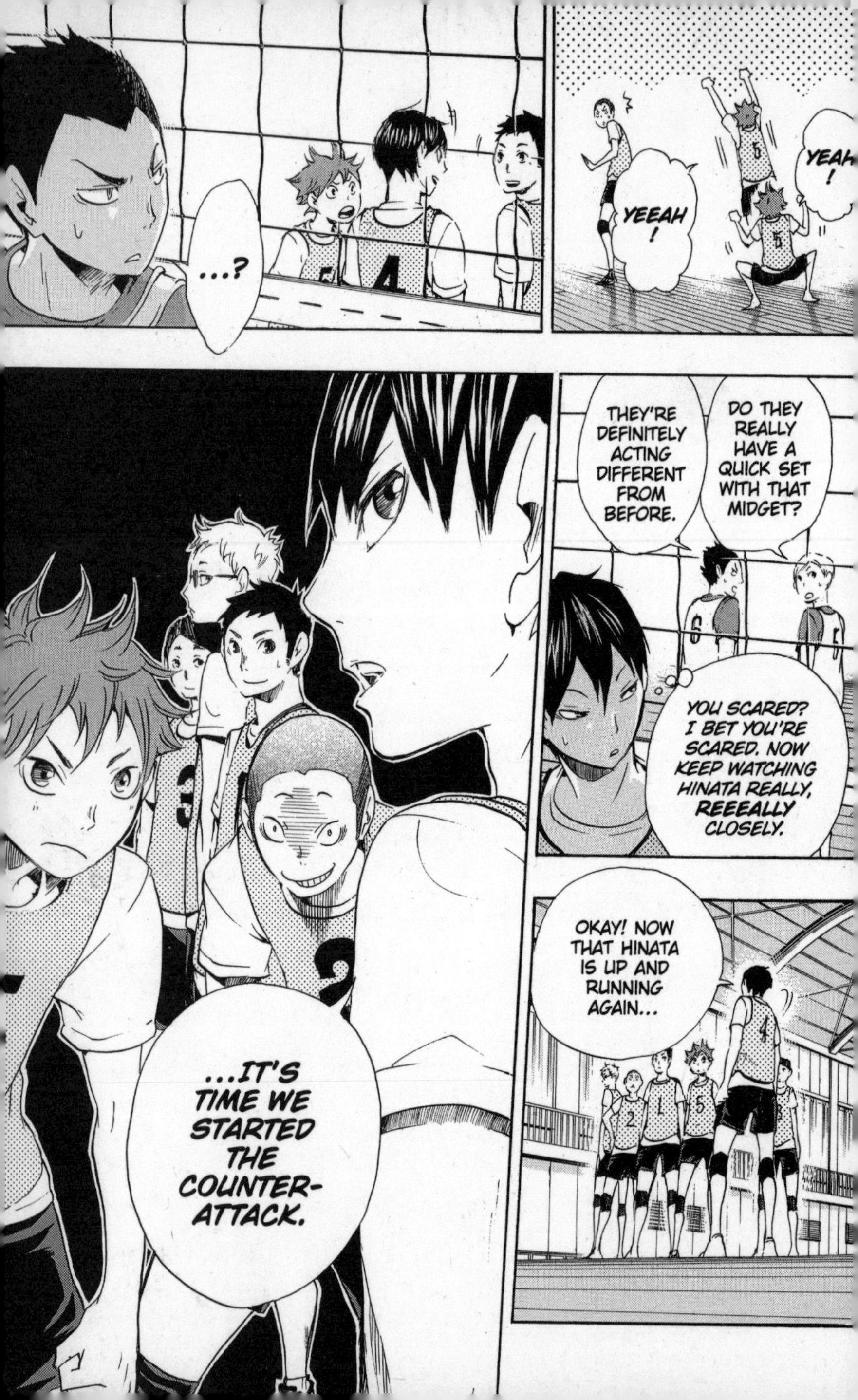
YEAH!
YEEAH!
...?
DO THEY REALLY HAVE A QUICK SET WITH THAT MIDGET?
THEY'RE DEFINITELY ACTING DIFFERENT FROM BEFORE.
YOU SCARED? I BET YOU'RE SCARED. NOW KEEP WATCHING HINATA REALLY, REEEALLY CLOSELY.
OKAY! NOW THAT HINATA IS UP AND RUNNING AGAIN...
...IT'S TIME WE STARTED THE COUNTER-ATTACK.

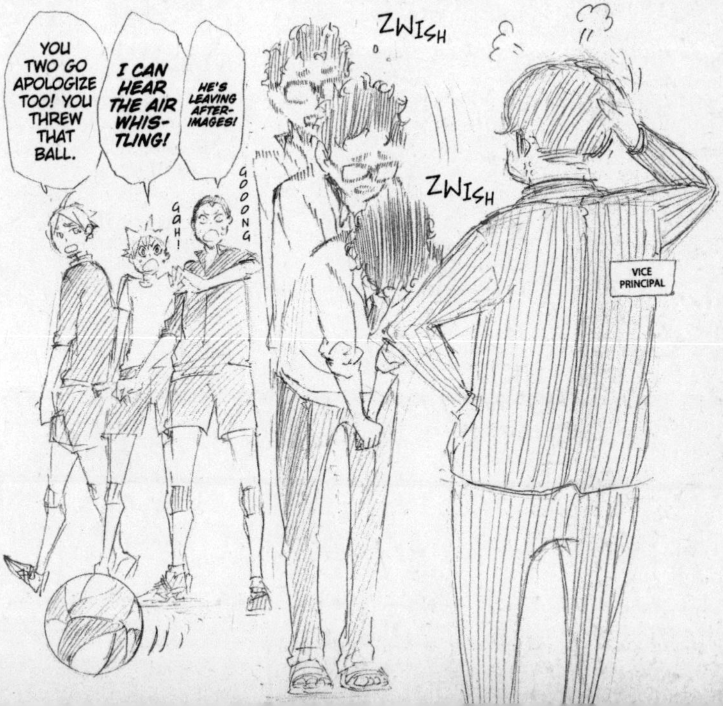
ZWISH
ZWISH
VICE PRINCIPAL
HE'S LEAVING AFTER-IMAGES!
GOOOONG
I CAN HEAR THE AIR WHISTLING!
GAH!
YOU TWO GO APOLOGIZE TOO! YOU THREW THAT BALL.

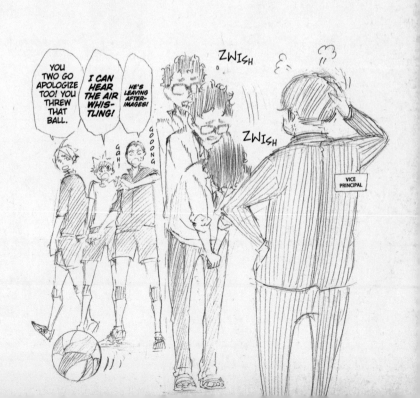

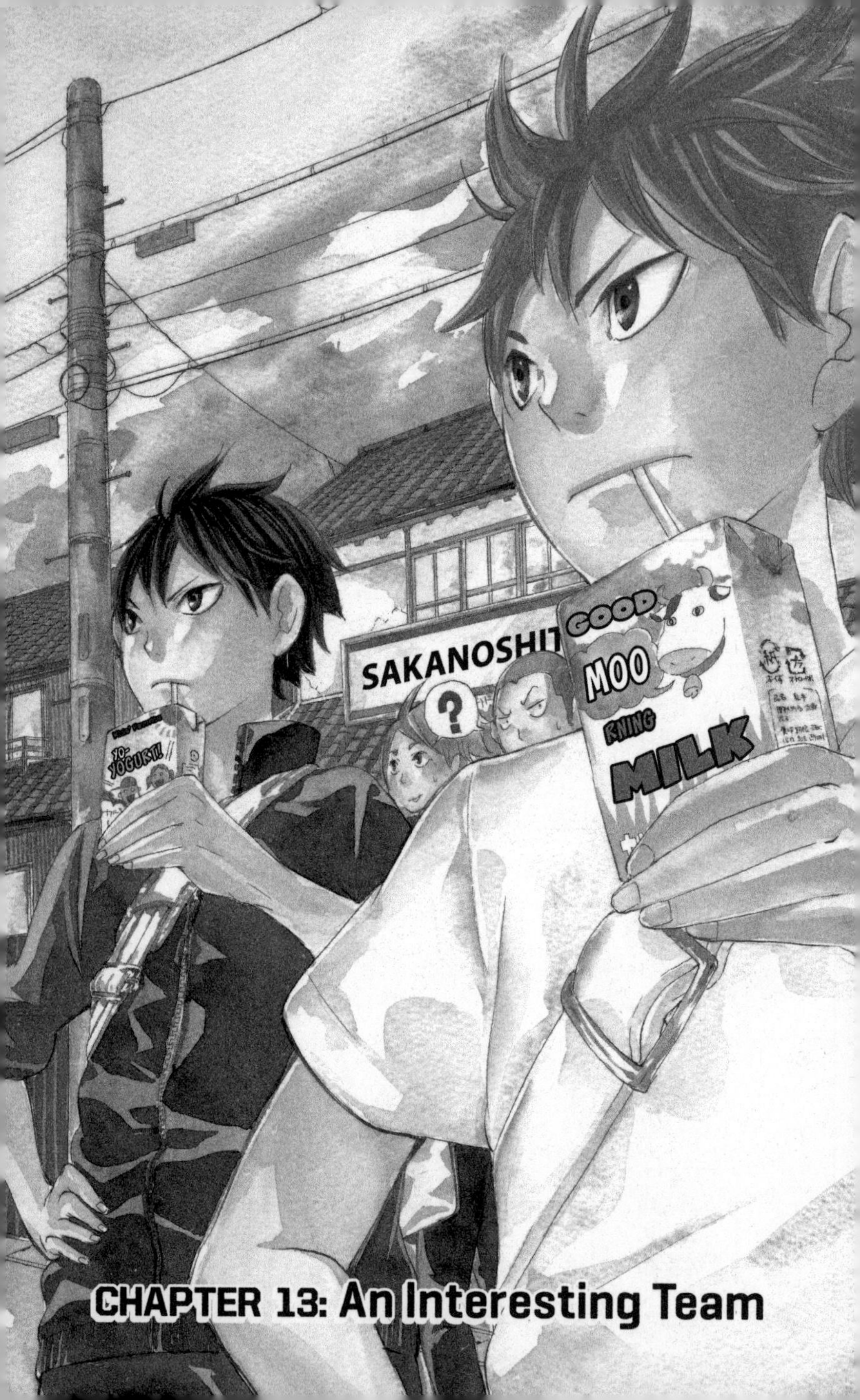
SAKANOSHIT
?
GOOD MOO RNING MILK

CHAPTER 13: An Interesting Team

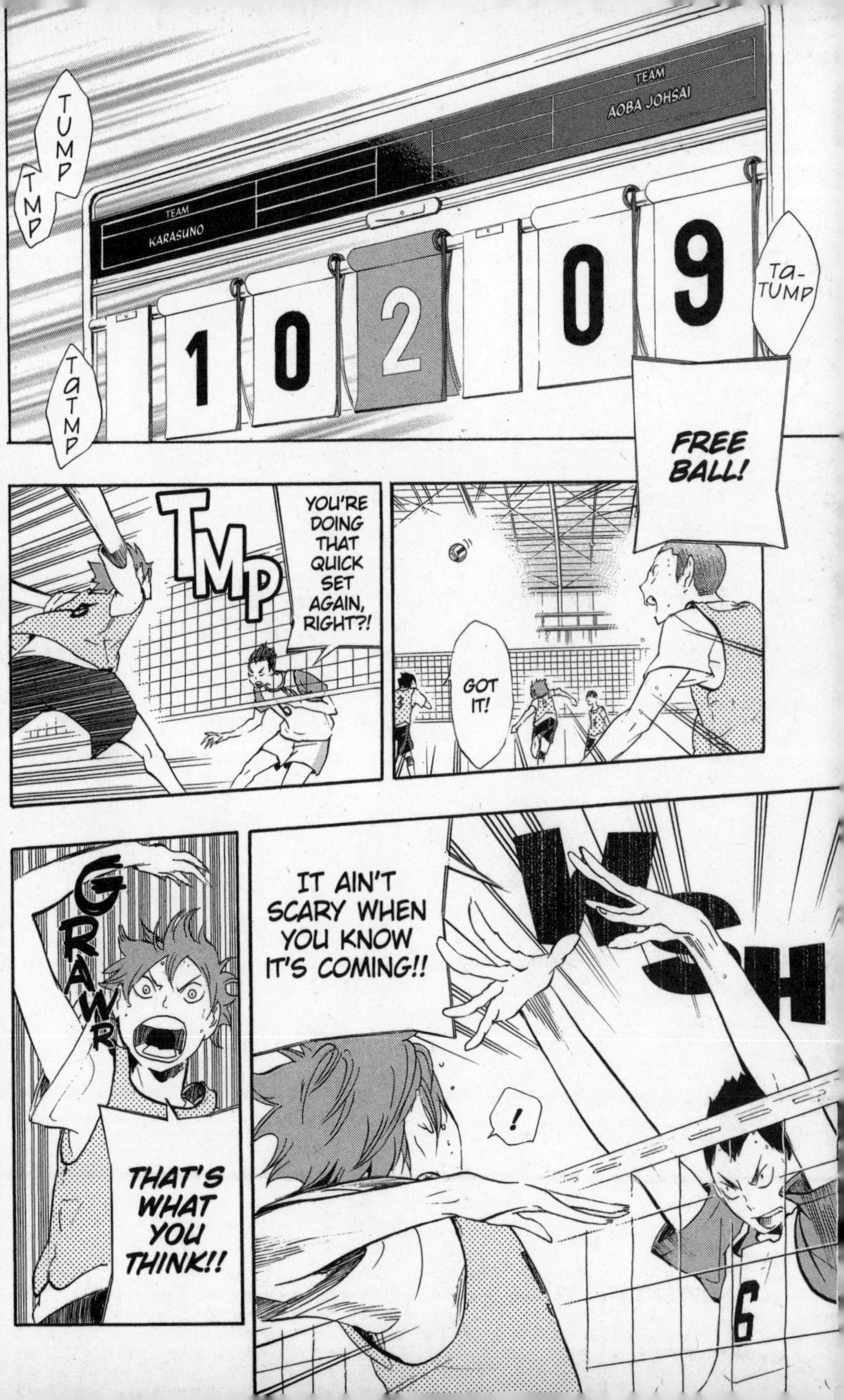
TEAM
AOBA JOHSAI
TEAM
KARASUNO
10 2 09
Ta-TUMP
TUMP
TMP
TaTMP
FREE BALL!
GOT IT!
YOU'RE DOING THAT QUICK SET AGAIN, RIGHT?!
TMP
IT AIN'T SCARY WHEN YOU KNOW IT'S COMING!!
!
GRAWR
THAT'S WHAT YOU THINK!!

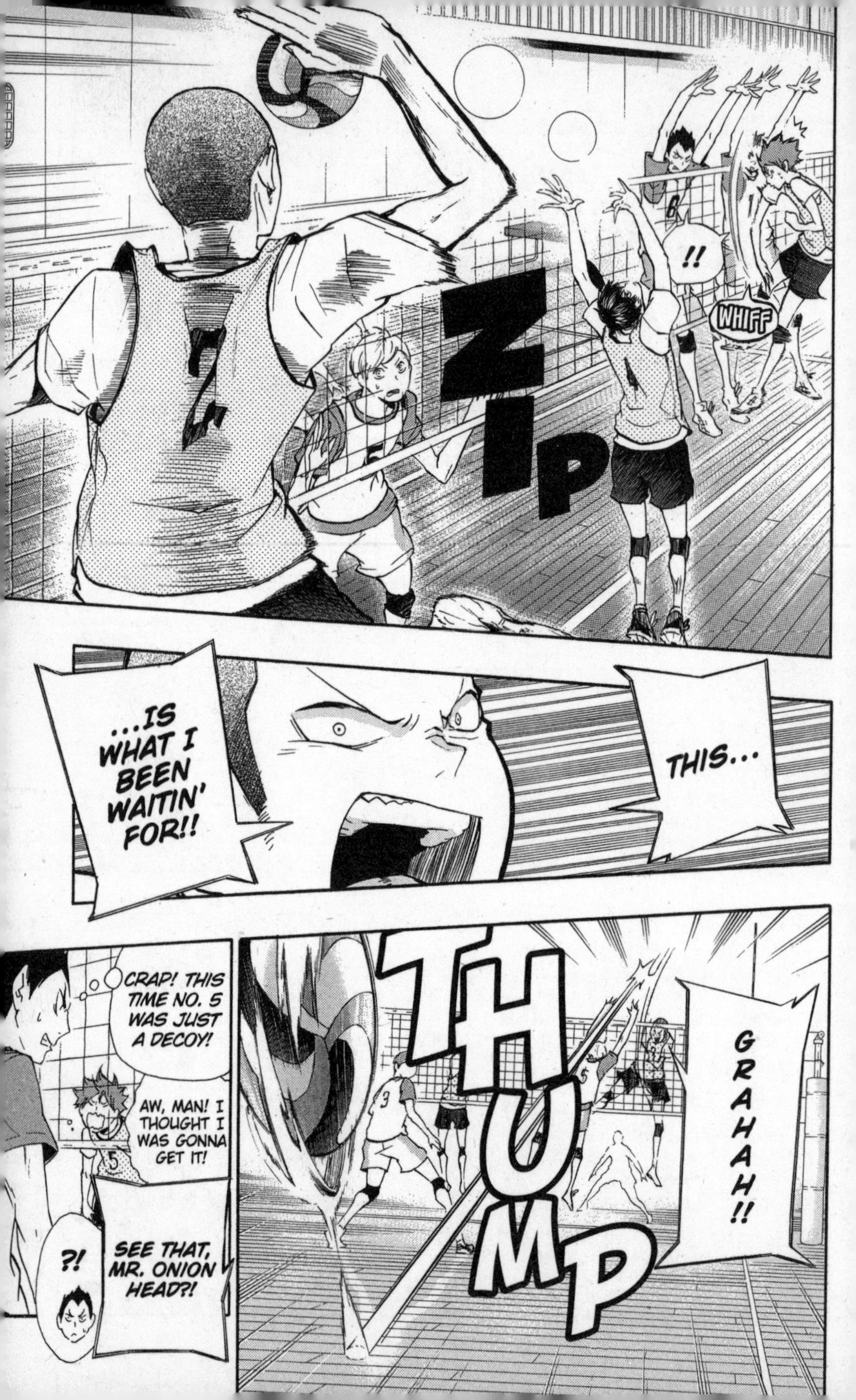
!!
WHIFF
ZIP
THIS...
...IS WHAT I BEEN WAITIN' FOR!!
GRAHAH!!
THUMP
CRAP! THIS TIME NO. 5 WAS JUST A DECOY!
AW, MAN! I THOUGHT I WAS GONNA GET IT!
SEE THAT, MR. ONION HEAD?!
?!

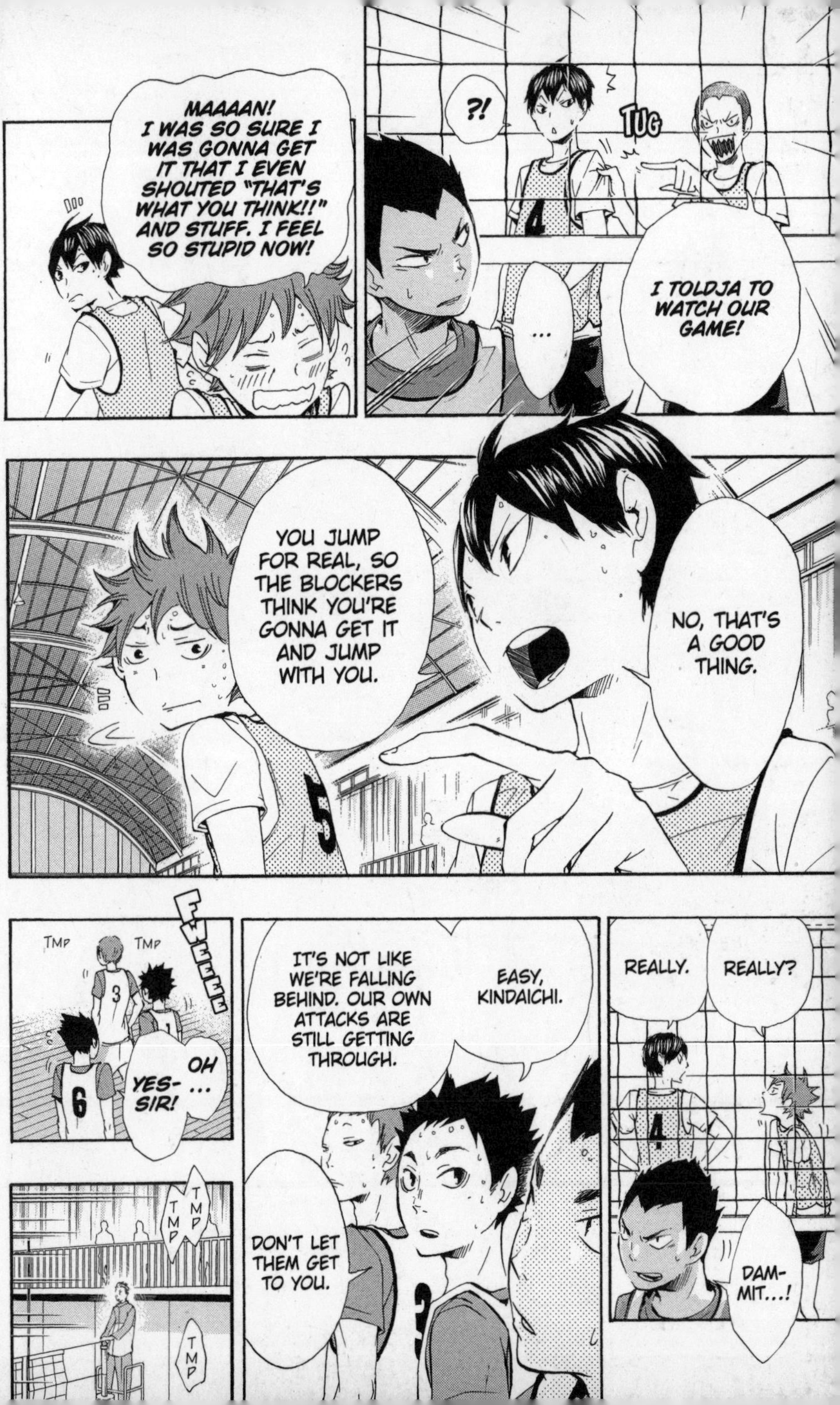

?!
TUG
I TOLDJA TO WATCH OUR GAME!
...
MAAAAN! I WAS SO SURE I WAS GONNA GET IT THAT I EVEN SHOUTED "THAT'S WHAT YOU THINK!!" AND STUFF. I FEEL SO STUPID NOW!
NO, THAT'S A GOOD THING.
YOU JUMP FOR REAL, SO THE BLOCKERS THINK YOU'RE GONNA GET IT AND JUMP WITH YOU.
REALLY?
REALLY.
DAM-MIT...!
EASY, KINDAICHI.
IT'S NOT LIKE WE'RE FALLING BEHIND. OUR OWN ATTACKS ARE STILL GETTING THROUGH.
DON'T LET THEM GET TO YOU.
FWEEEE
TMP
TMP
OH ... YES-SIR!
TMP
TMP
TMP

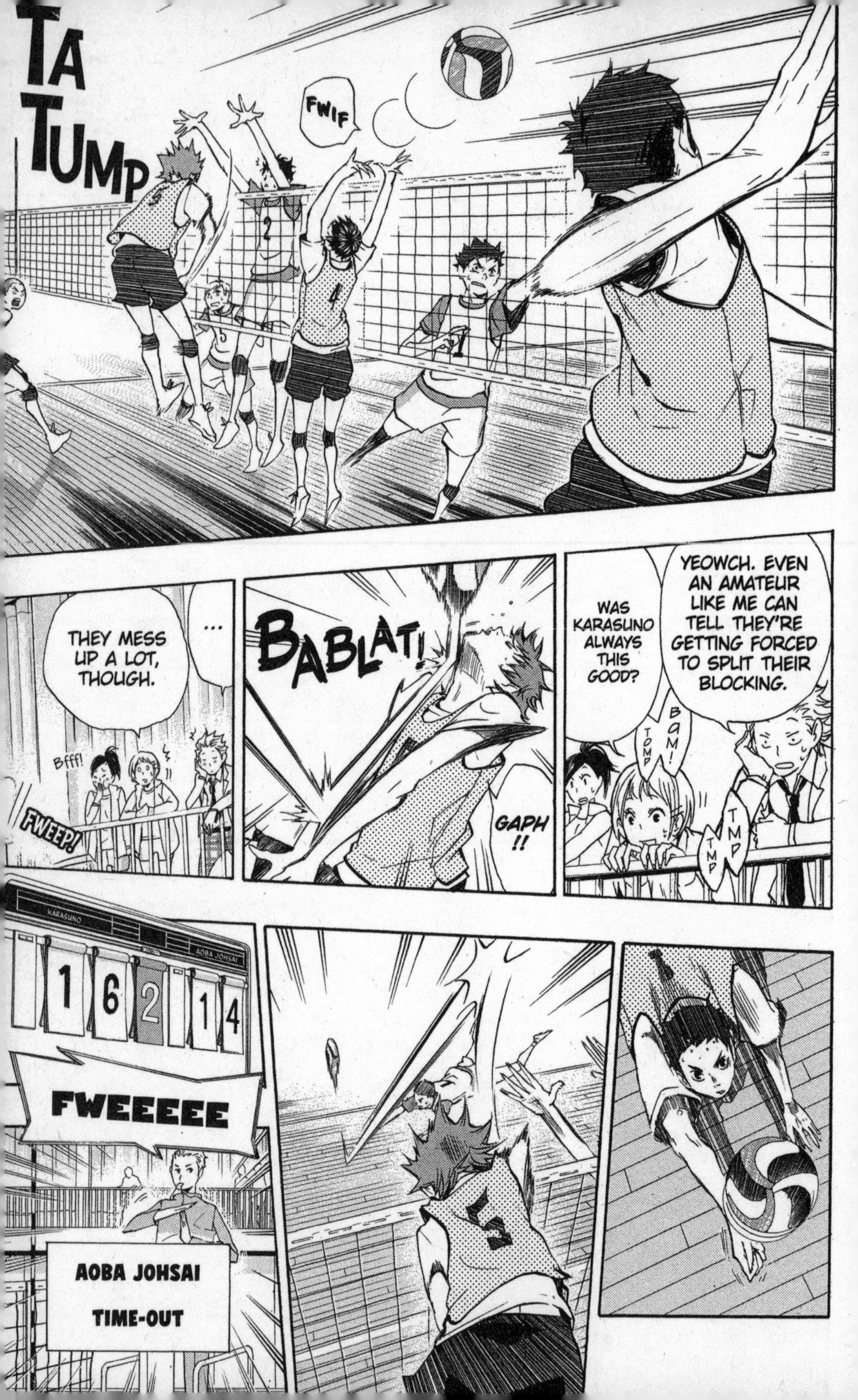
TA TUMP
FWIF
YEOWCH. EVEN AN AMATEUR LIKE ME CAN TELL THEY'RE GETTING FORCED TO SPLIT THEIR BLOCKING.
WAS KARASUNO ALWAYS THIS GOOD?
BAM!
TOMP
TMP TMP TMP
BABLAT!
GAPH!!
...
THEY MESS UP A LOT, THOUGH.
Bfff!
FWEEP!
KARASUNO
AOBA JOHSAI
1 6 2 1 4
FWEEEEE
AOBA JOHSAI TIME-OUT

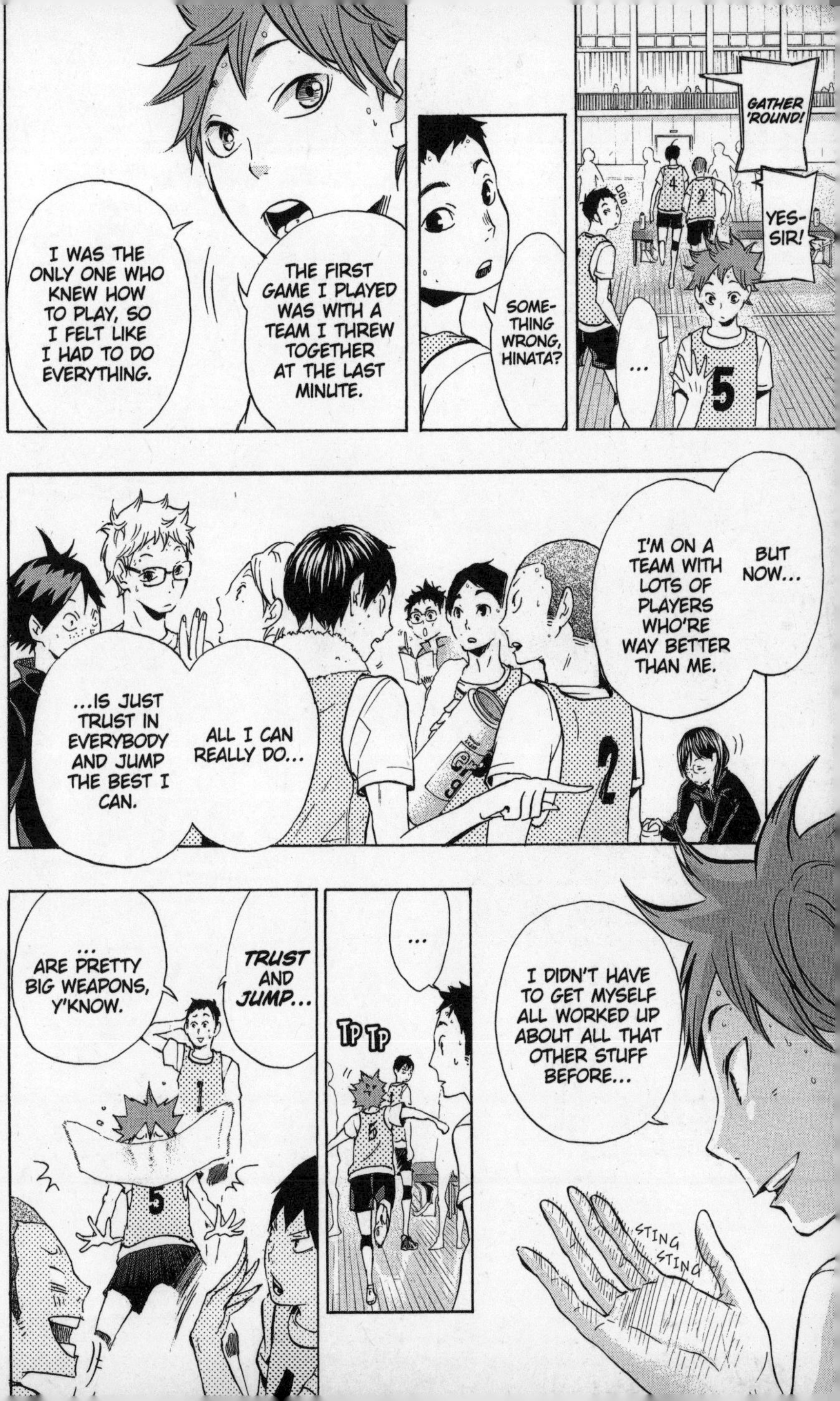
GATHER 'ROUND!
YES-SIR!
...
SOME-THING WRONG, HINATA?
THE FIRST GAME I PLAYED WAS WITH A TEAM I THREW TOGETHER AT THE LAST MINUTE.
I WAS THE ONLY ONE WHO KNEW HOW TO PLAY, SO I FELT LIKE I HAD TO DO EVERYTHING.
BUT NOW...
I'M ON A TEAM WITH LOTS OF PLAYERS WHO'RE WAY BETTER THAN ME.
ALL I CAN REALLY DO...
...IS JUST TRUST IN EVERYBODY AND JUMP THE BEST I CAN.
I DIDN'T HAVE TO GET MYSELF ALL WORKED UP ABOUT ALL THAT OTHER STUFF BEFORE...
STING STING
...
TP TP
TRUST AND *JUMP*...
... ARE PRETTY BIG WEAPONS, Y'KNOW.

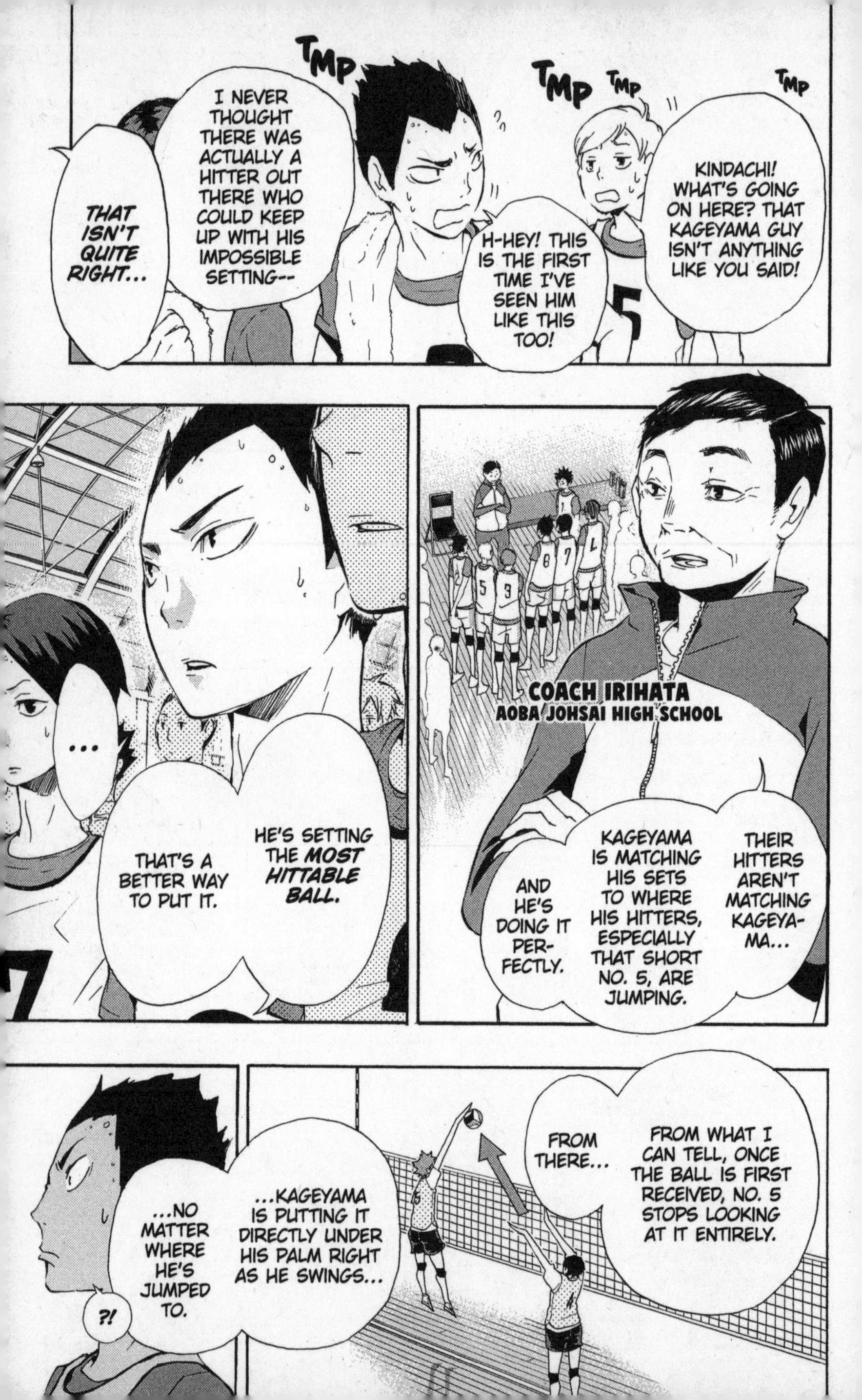
TMP
TMP
TMP
TMP
KINDACHI! WHAT'S GOING ON HERE? THAT KAGEYAMA GUY ISN'T ANYTHING LIKE YOU SAID!
H-HEY! THIS IS THE FIRST TIME I'VE SEEN HIM LIKE THIS TOO!
I NEVER THOUGHT THERE WAS ACTUALLY A HITTER OUT THERE WHO COULD KEEP UP WITH HIS IMPOSSIBLE SETTING--
THAT ISN'T QUITE RIGHT...
COACH IRIHATA
AOBA JOHSAI HIGH SCHOOL
THEIR HITTERS AREN'T MATCHING KAGEYA-MA...
KAGEYAMA IS MATCHING HIS SETS TO WHERE HIS HITTERS, ESPECIALLY THAT SHORT NO. 5, ARE JUMPING.
AND HE'S DOING IT PER-FECTLY.
HE'S SETTING THE MOST HITTABLE BALL.
THAT'S A BETTER WAY TO PUT IT.
...
FROM WHAT I CAN TELL, ONCE THE BALL IS FIRST RECEIVED, NO. 5 STOPS LOOKING AT IT ENTIRELY.
FROM THERE...
...KAGEYAMA IS PUTTING IT DIRECTLY UNDER HIS PALM RIGHT AS HE SWINGS...
...NO MATTER WHERE HE'S JUMPED TO.
?!

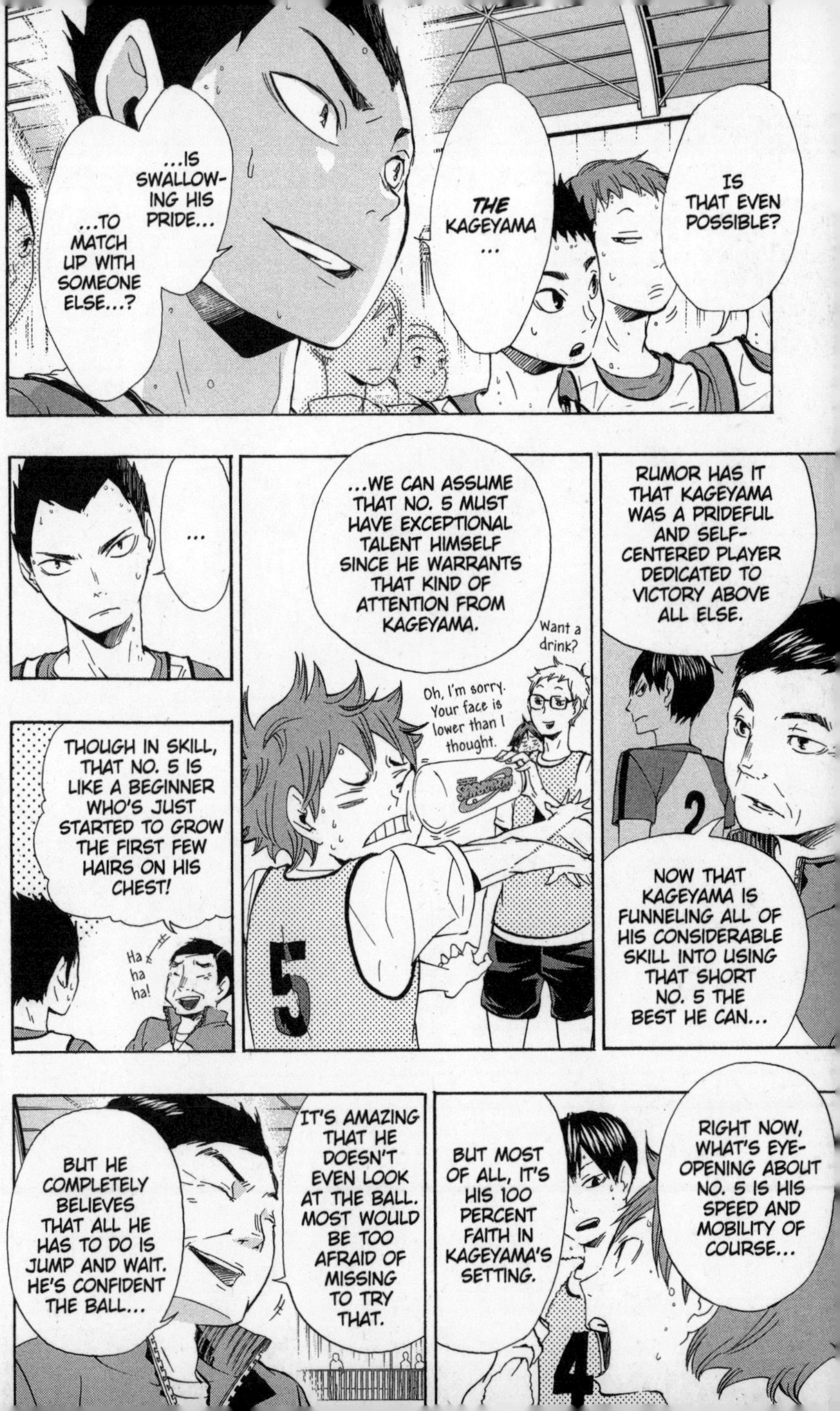
IS THAT EVEN POSSIBLE?
THE KAGEYAMA...
...IS SWALLOWING HIS PRIDE...
...TO MATCH UP WITH SOMEONE ELSE...?
RUMOR HAS IT THAT KAGEYAMA WAS A PRIDEFUL AND SELF-CENTERED PLAYER DEDICATED TO VICTORY ABOVE ALL ELSE.
NOW THAT KAGEYAMA IS FUNNELING ALL OF HIS CONSIDERABLE SKILL INTO USING THAT SHORT NO. 5 THE BEST HE CAN...
...WE CAN ASSUME THAT NO. 5 MUST HAVE EXCEPTIONAL TALENT HIMSELF SINCE HE WARRANTS THAT KIND OF ATTENTION FROM KAGEYAMA.
Want a drink?
Oh, I'm sorry. Your face is lower than I thought.
...
THOUGH IN SKILL, THAT NO. 5 IS LIKE A BEGINNER WHO'S JUST STARTED TO GROW THE FIRST FEW HAIRS ON HIS CHEST!
Ha ha ha!
RIGHT NOW, WHAT'S EYE-OPENING ABOUT NO. 5 IS HIS SPEED AND MOBILITY OF COURSE...
BUT MOST OF ALL, IT'S HIS 100 PERCENT FAITH IN KAGEYAMA'S SETTING.
IT'S AMAZING THAT HE DOESN'T EVEN LOOK AT THE BALL. MOST WOULD BE TOO AFRAID OF MISSING TO TRY THAT.
BUT HE COMPLETELY BELIEVES THAT ALL HE HAS TO DO IS JUMP AND WAIT. HE'S CONFIDENT THE BALL...

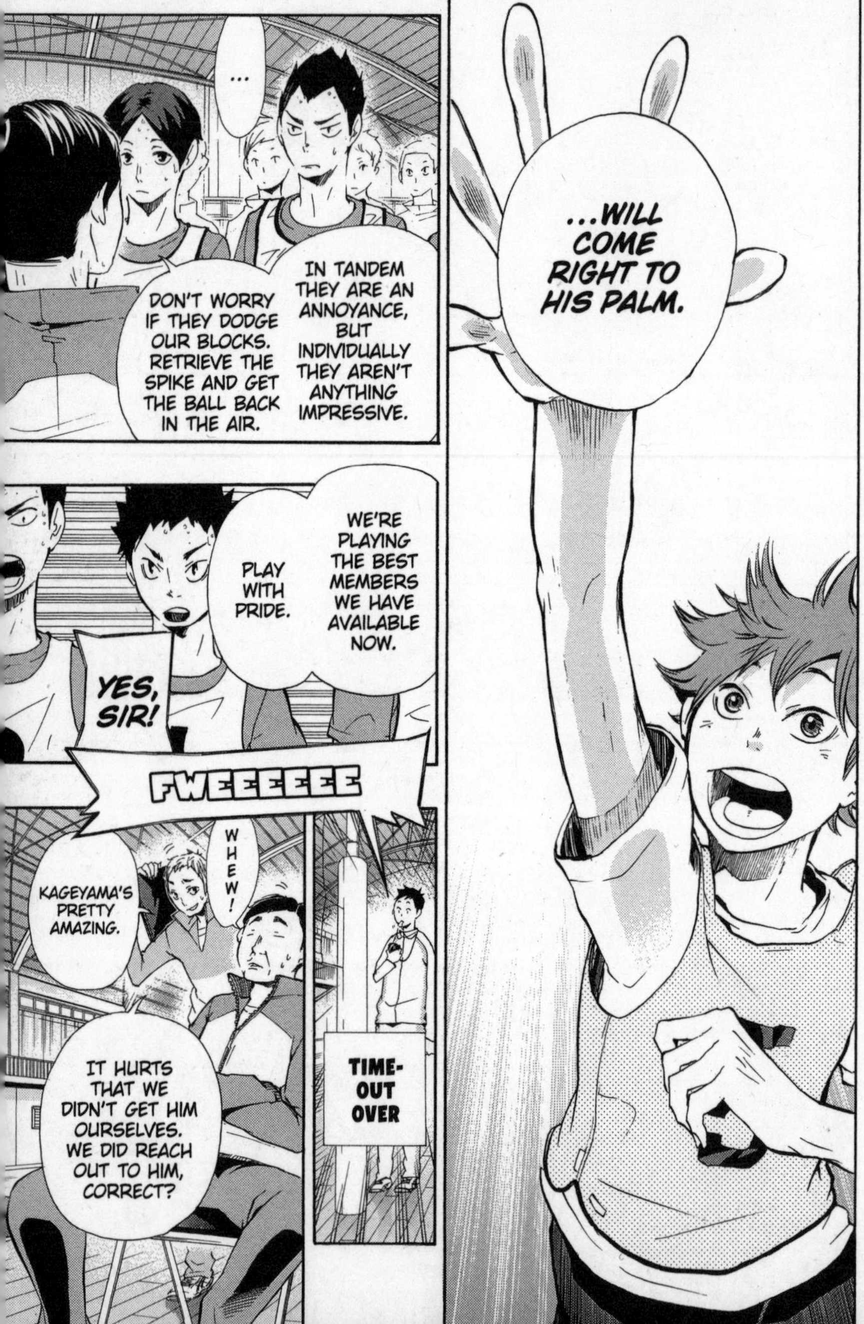
...WILL COME RIGHT TO HIS PALM.
...
IN TANDEM THEY ARE AN ANNOYANCE, BUT INDIVIDUALLY THEY AREN'T ANYTHING IMPRESSIVE.
DON'T WORRY IF THEY DODGE OUR BLOCKS. RETRIEVE THE SPIKE AND GET THE BALL BACK IN THE AIR.
WE'RE PLAYING THE BEST MEMBERS WE HAVE AVAILABLE NOW.
PLAY WITH PRIDE.
YES, SIR!
FWEEEEEE
TIME-OUT OVER
WHEW!
KAGEYAMA'S PRETTY AMAZING.
IT HURTS THAT WE DIDN'T GET HIM OURSELVES. WE DID REACH OUT TO HIM, CORRECT?

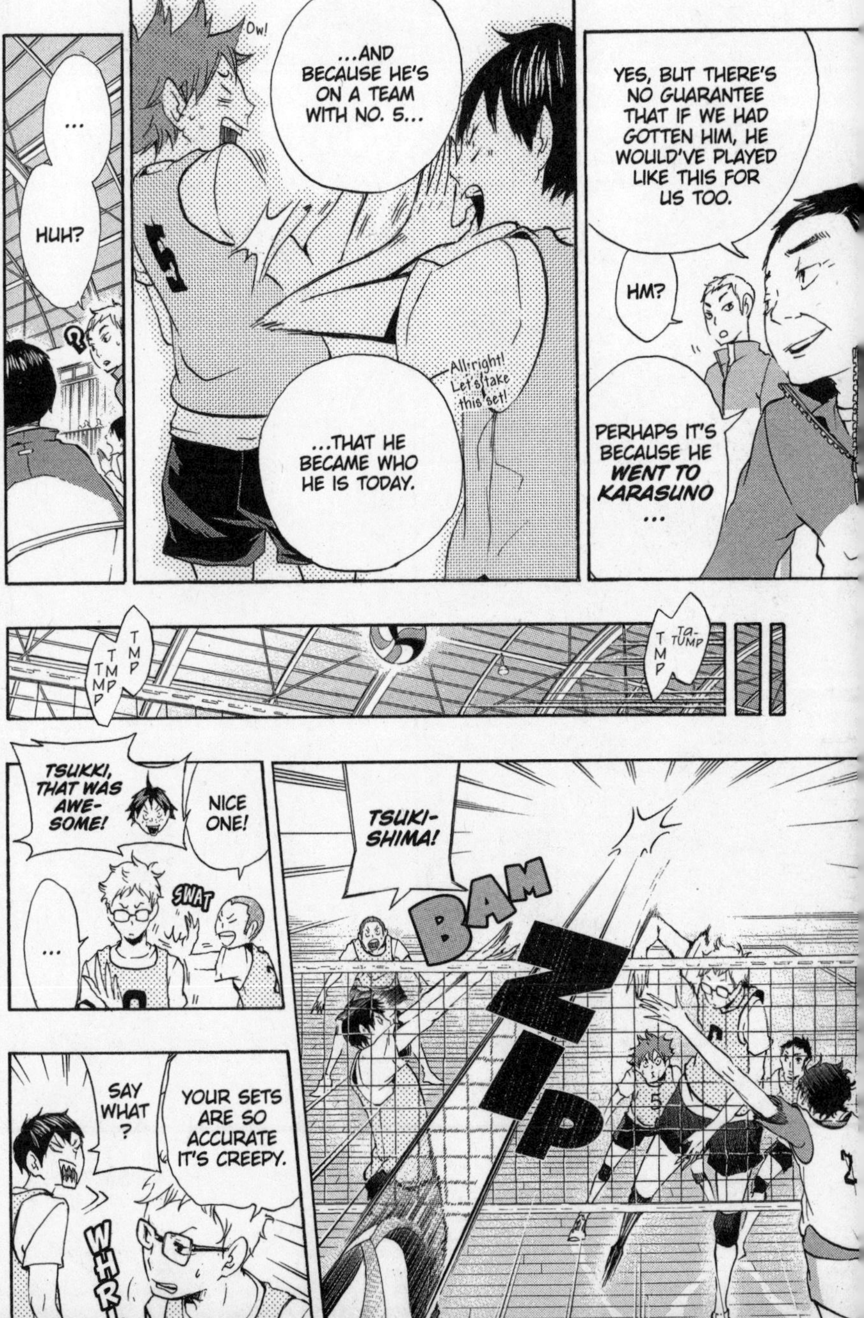
YES, BUT THERE'S NO GUARANTEE THAT IF WE HAD GOTTEN HIM, HE WOULD'VE PLAYED LIKE THIS FOR US TOO.
HM?
PERHAPS IT'S BECAUSE HE *WENT TO KARASUNO* ...
...AND BECAUSE HE'S ON A TEAM WITH NO. 5...
Ow!
All right! Let's take this set!
...THAT HE BECAME WHO HE IS TODAY.
...
HUH?
TA-TUMP
TMP
TMP
TMP
TMP
TSUKI-SHIMA!
BAM
ZIP
NICE ONE!
TSUKKI, THAT WAS AWE-SOME!
SWAT
...
YOUR SETS ARE SO ACCURATE IT'S CREEPY.
SAY WHAT?
WHRL

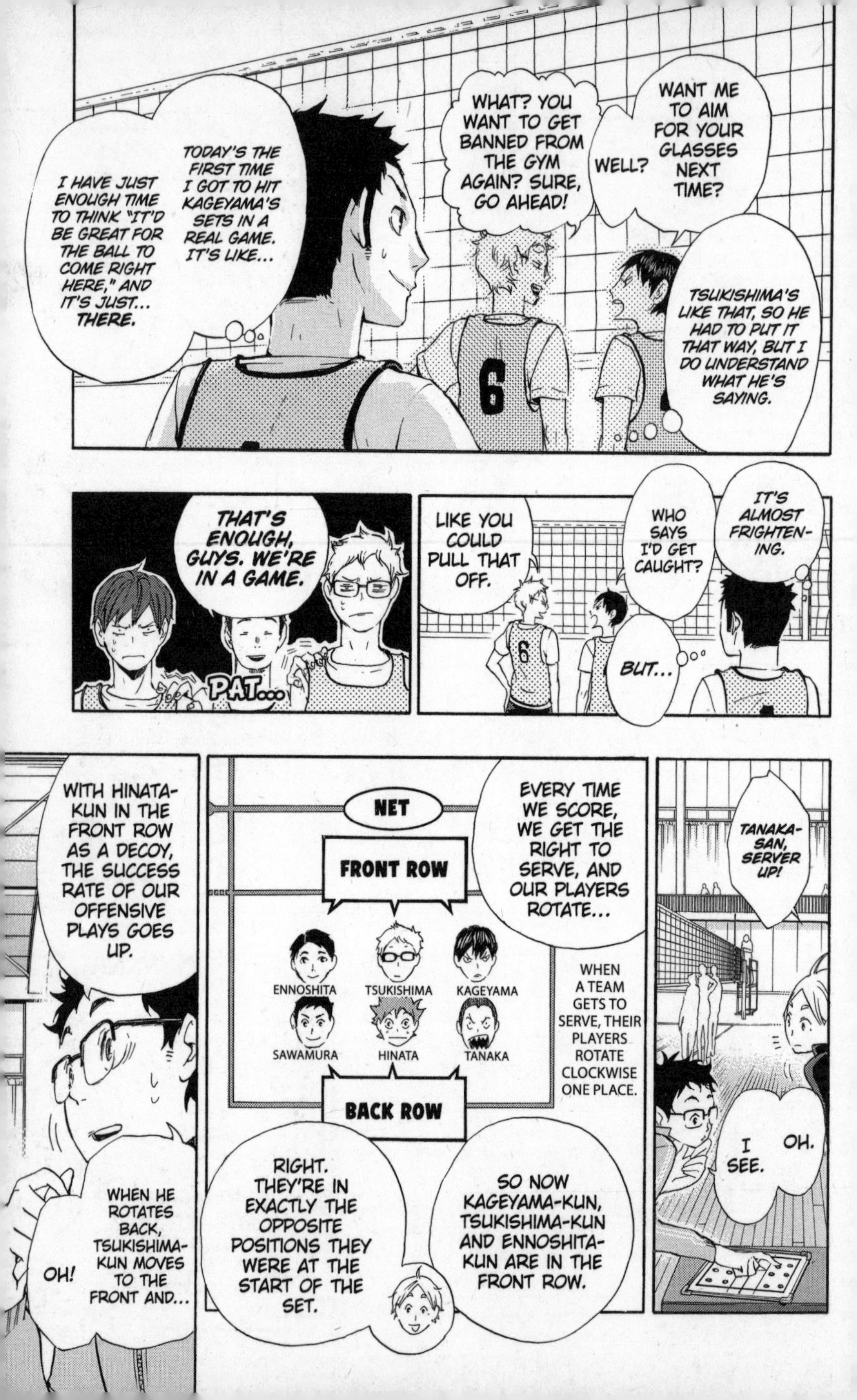

WANT ME TO AIM FOR YOUR GLASSES NEXT TIME?
WELL?
WHAT? YOU WANT TO GET BANNED FROM THE GYM AGAIN? SURE, GO AHEAD!
TSUKISHIMA'S LIKE THAT, SO HE HAD TO PUT IT THAT WAY, BUT I DO UNDERSTAND WHAT HE'S SAYING.
TODAY'S THE FIRST TIME I GOT TO HIT KAGEYAMA'S SETS IN A REAL GAME. IT'S LIKE...
I HAVE JUST ENOUGH TIME TO THINK "IT'D BE GREAT FOR THE BALL TO COME RIGHT HERE," AND IT'S JUST... THERE.
IT'S ALMOST FRIGHTENING.
WHO SAYS I'D GET CAUGHT?
LIKE YOU COULD PULL THAT OFF.
BUT...
THAT'S ENOUGH, GUYS. WE'RE IN A GAME.
PAT...
TANAKA-SAN, SERVER UP!
OH.
I SEE.
EVERY TIME WE SCORE, WE GET THE RIGHT TO SERVE, AND OUR PLAYERS ROTATE...
NET
FRONT ROW
ENNOSHITA
TSUKISHIMA
KAGEYAMA
SAWAMURA
HINATA
TANAKA
BACK ROW
WHEN A TEAM GETS TO SERVE, THEIR PLAYERS ROTATE CLOCKWISE ONE PLACE.
SO NOW KAGEYAMA-KUN, TSUKISHIMA-KUN AND ENNOSHITA-KUN ARE IN THE FRONT ROW.
RIGHT. THEY'RE IN EXACTLY THE OPPOSITE POSITIONS THEY WERE AT THE START OF THE SET.
WITH HINATA-KUN IN THE FRONT ROW AS A DECOY, THE SUCCESS RATE OF OUR OFFENSIVE PLAYS GOES UP.
WHEN HE ROTATES BACK, TSUKISHIMA-KUN MOVES TO THE FRONT AND...
OH!

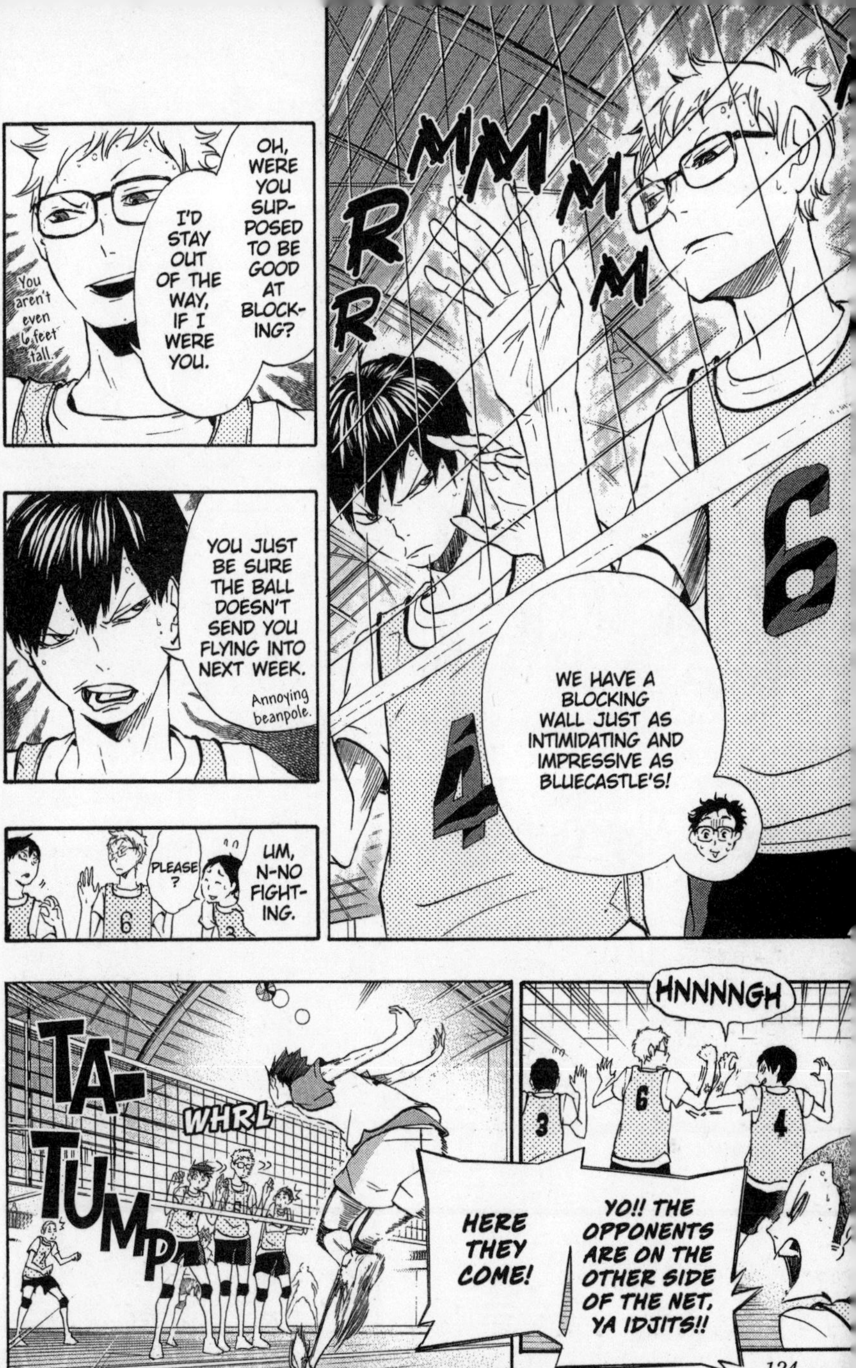
RRMMMMMM
WE HAVE A BLOCKING WALL JUST AS INTIMIDATING AND IMPRESSIVE AS BLUECASTLE'S!
OH, WERE YOU SUP-POSED TO BE GOOD AT BLOCK-ING?
I'D STAY OUT OF THE WAY, IF I WERE YOU.
You aren't even 6 feet tall.
YOU JUST BE SURE THE BALL DOESN'T SEND YOU FLYING INTO NEXT WEEK.
Annoying beanpole.
UM, N-NO FIGHT-ING.
PLEASE?
HNNNNGH
YO!! THE OPPONENTS ARE ON THE OTHER SIDE OF THE NET, YA IDJITS!!
HERE THEY COME!
TA-TUMP
WHRL

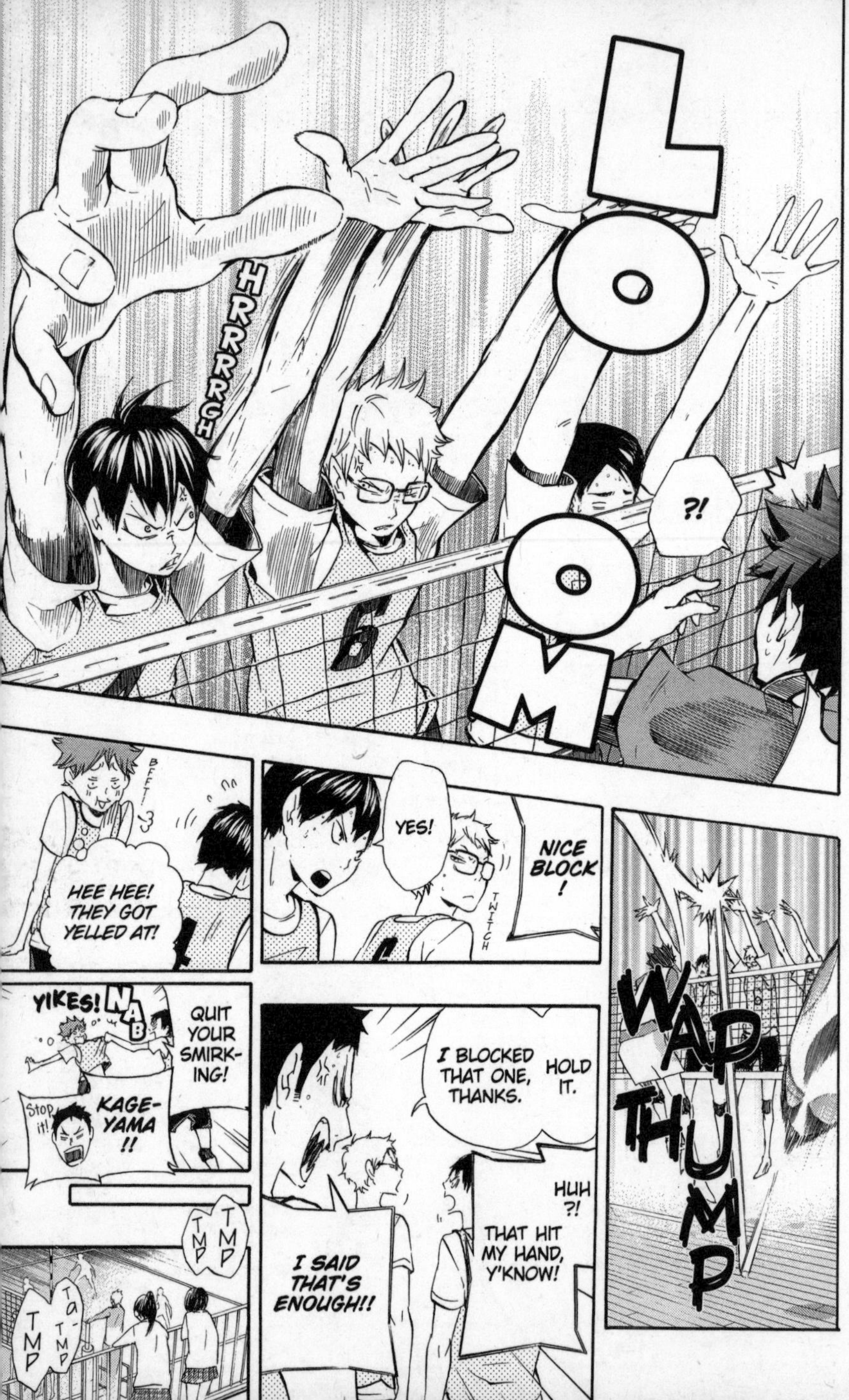
LOOM
?!
HRRRRGH
WAP
THUMP
NICE BLOCK!
YES!
TWITCH
BFFT!
HEE HEE! THEY GOT YELLED AT!
HOLD IT.
I BLOCKED THAT ONE, THANKS.
HUH?!
THAT HIT MY HAND, Y'KNOW!
I SAID THAT'S ENOUGH!!
QUIT YOUR SMIRK-ING!
NAB
YIKES!
KAGE-YAMA!!
Stop it!
TMP TMP
TA-TMP TMP

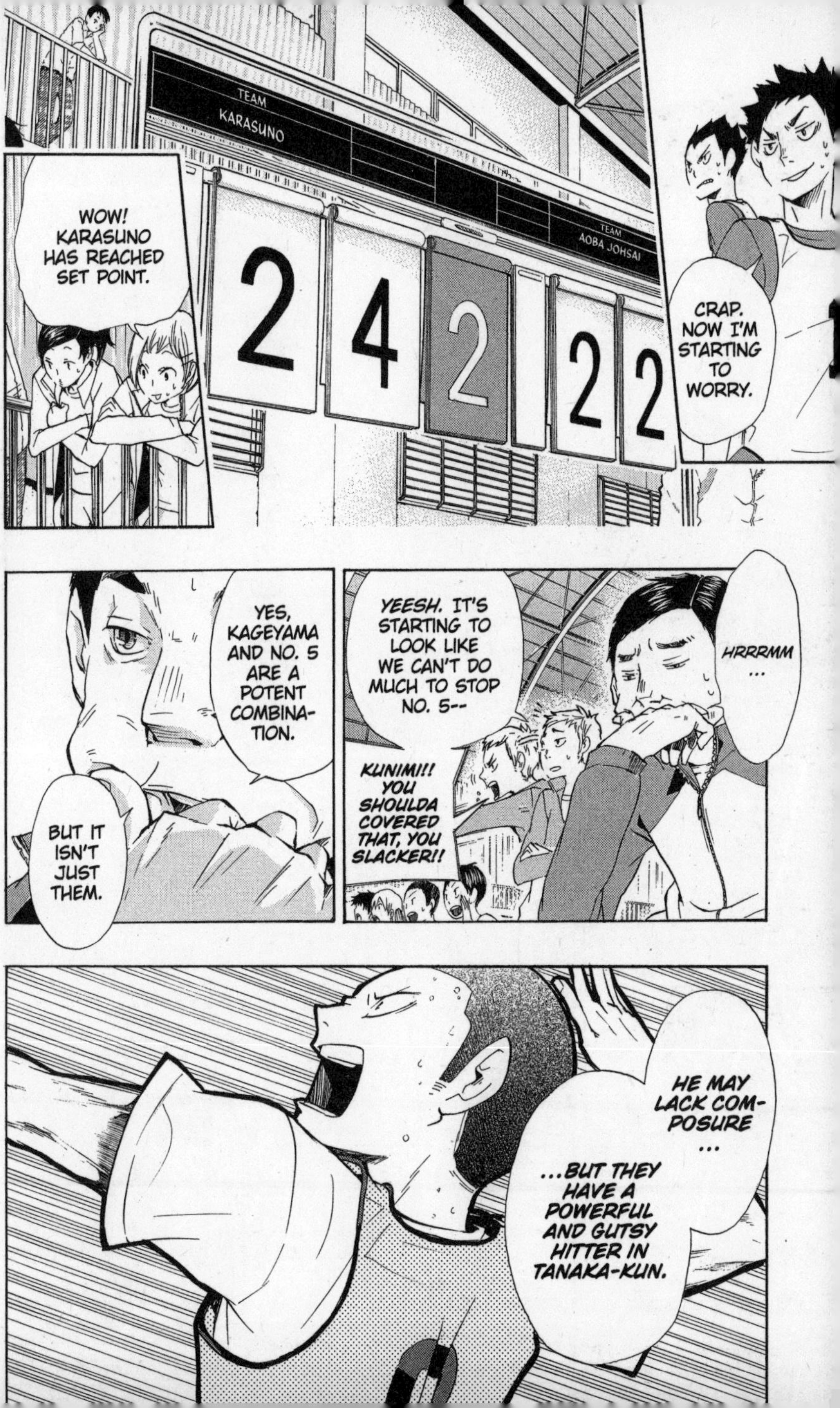
CRAP. NOW I'M STARTING TO WORRY.
TEAM
KARASUNO
TEAM
AOBA JOHSAI
2 4 2 22
WOW! KARASUNO HAS REACHED SET POINT.
HRRRMM ...
YEESH. IT'S STARTING TO LOOK LIKE WE CAN'T DO MUCH TO STOP NO. 5--
KUNIMI!! YOU SHOULDA COVERED THAT, YOU SLACKER!!
YES, KAGEYAMA AND NO. 5 ARE A POTENT COMBINATION.
BUT IT ISN'T JUST THEM.
HE MAY LACK COMPOSURE ...
...BUT THEY HAVE A POWERFUL AND GUTSY HITTER IN TANAKA-KUN.

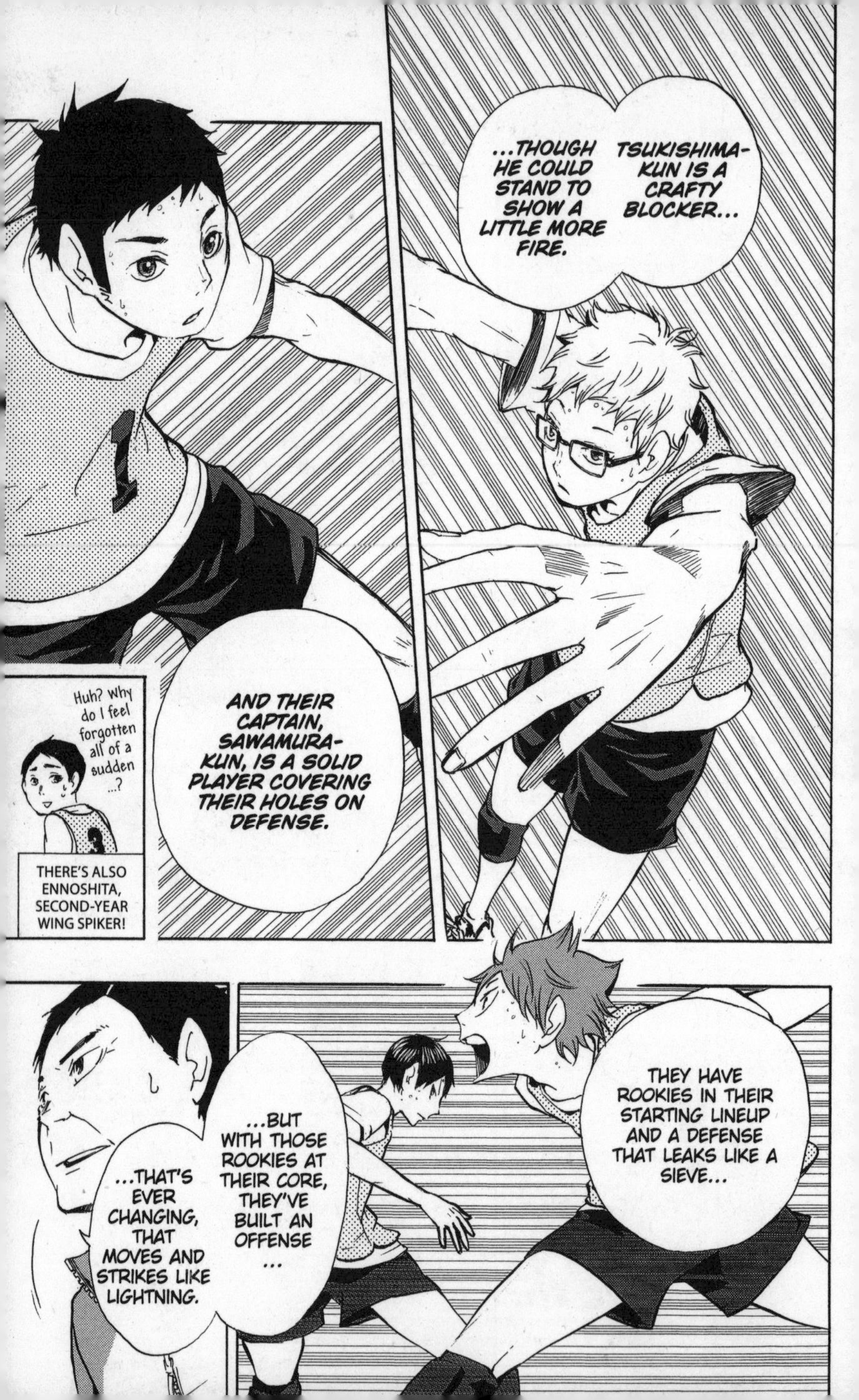
TSUKISHIMA-KUN IS A CRAFTY BLOCKER...
...THOUGH HE COULD STAND TO SHOW A LITTLE MORE FIRE.
AND THEIR CAPTAIN, SAWAMURA-KUN, IS A SOLID PLAYER COVERING THEIR HOLES ON DEFENSE.
Huh? Why do I feel forgotten all of a sudden ...?
THERE'S ALSO ENNOSHITA, SECOND-YEAR WING SPIKER!
THEY HAVE ROOKIES IN THEIR STARTING LINEUP AND A DEFENSE THAT LEAKS LIKE A SIEVE...
...BUT WITH THOSE ROOKIES AT THEIR CORE, THEY'VE BUILT AN OFFENSE ...
...THAT'S EVER CHANGING, THAT MOVES AND STRIKES LIKE LIGHTNING.

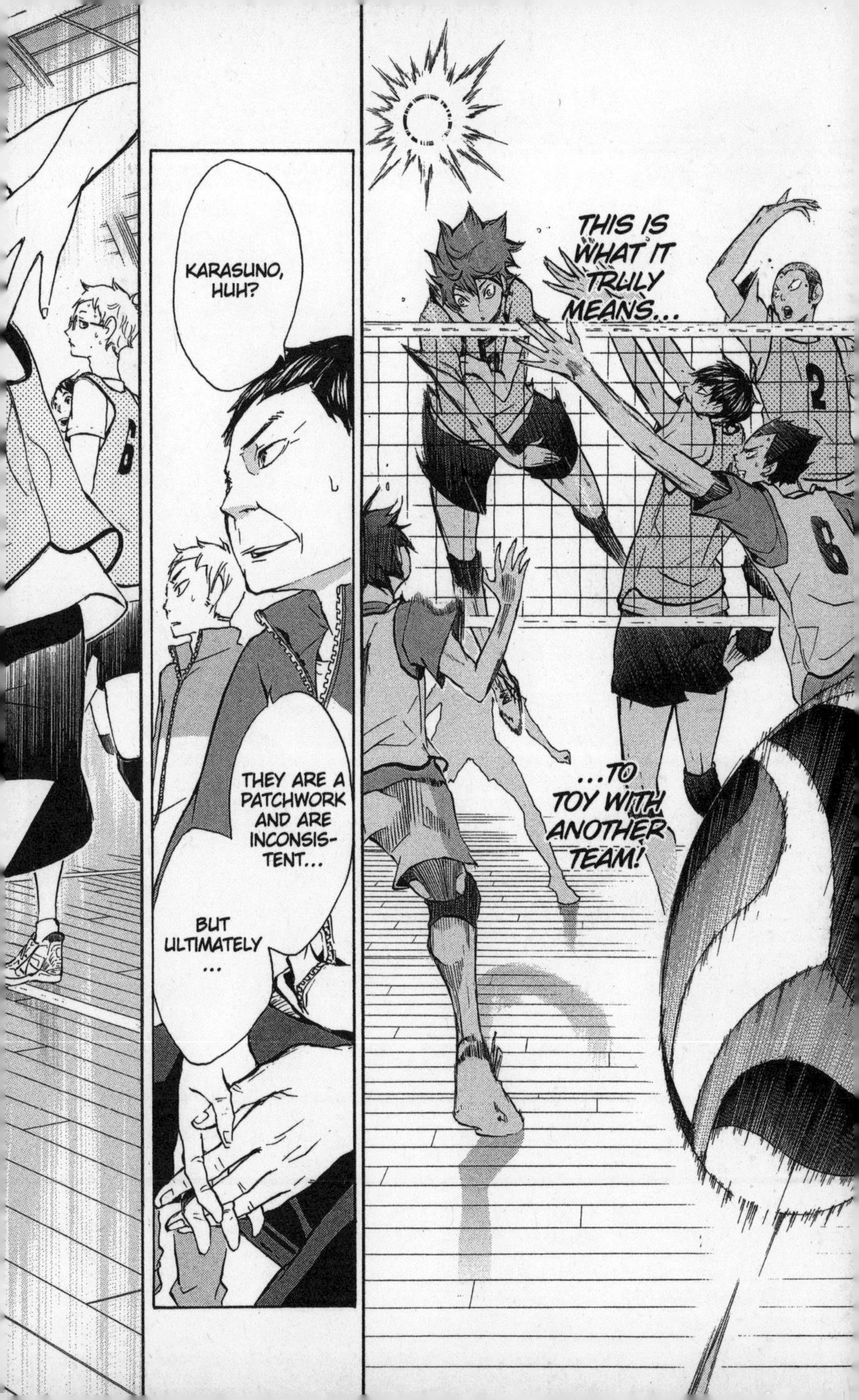
THIS IS WHAT IT TRULY MEANS...
...TO TOY WITH ANOTHER TEAM!
KARASUNO, HUH?
THEY ARE A PATCHWORK AND ARE INCONSIS- TENT...
BUT ULTIMATELY ...

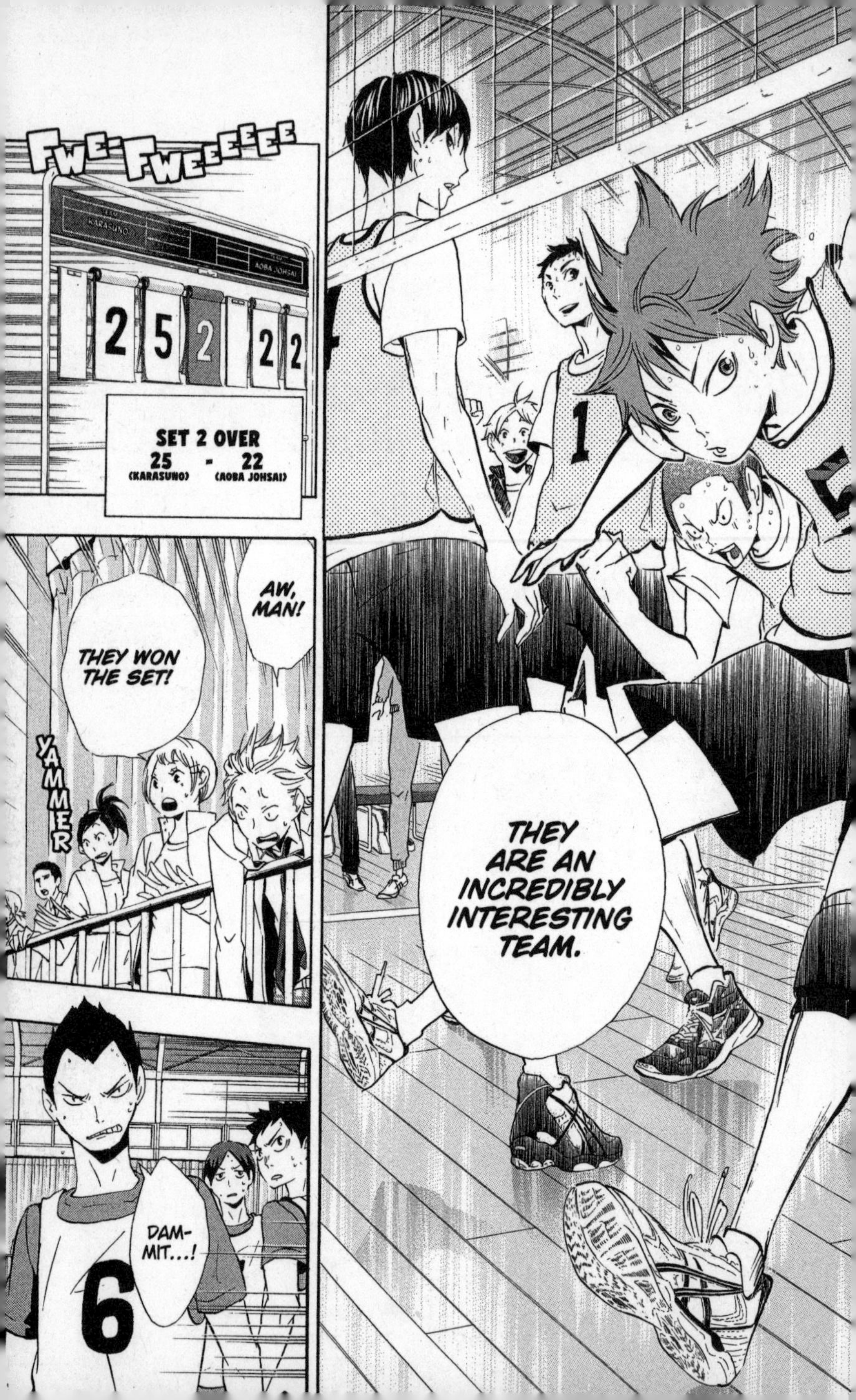
THEY ARE AN INCREDIBLY INTERESTING TEAM.
FWE-FWEEEEEE
KARASUNO
AOBA JOHSAI
SET 2 OVER
25 - 22
(KARASUNO) (AOBA JOHSAI)
AW, MAN!
THEY WON THE SET!
YAMMER
DAM-MIT...!

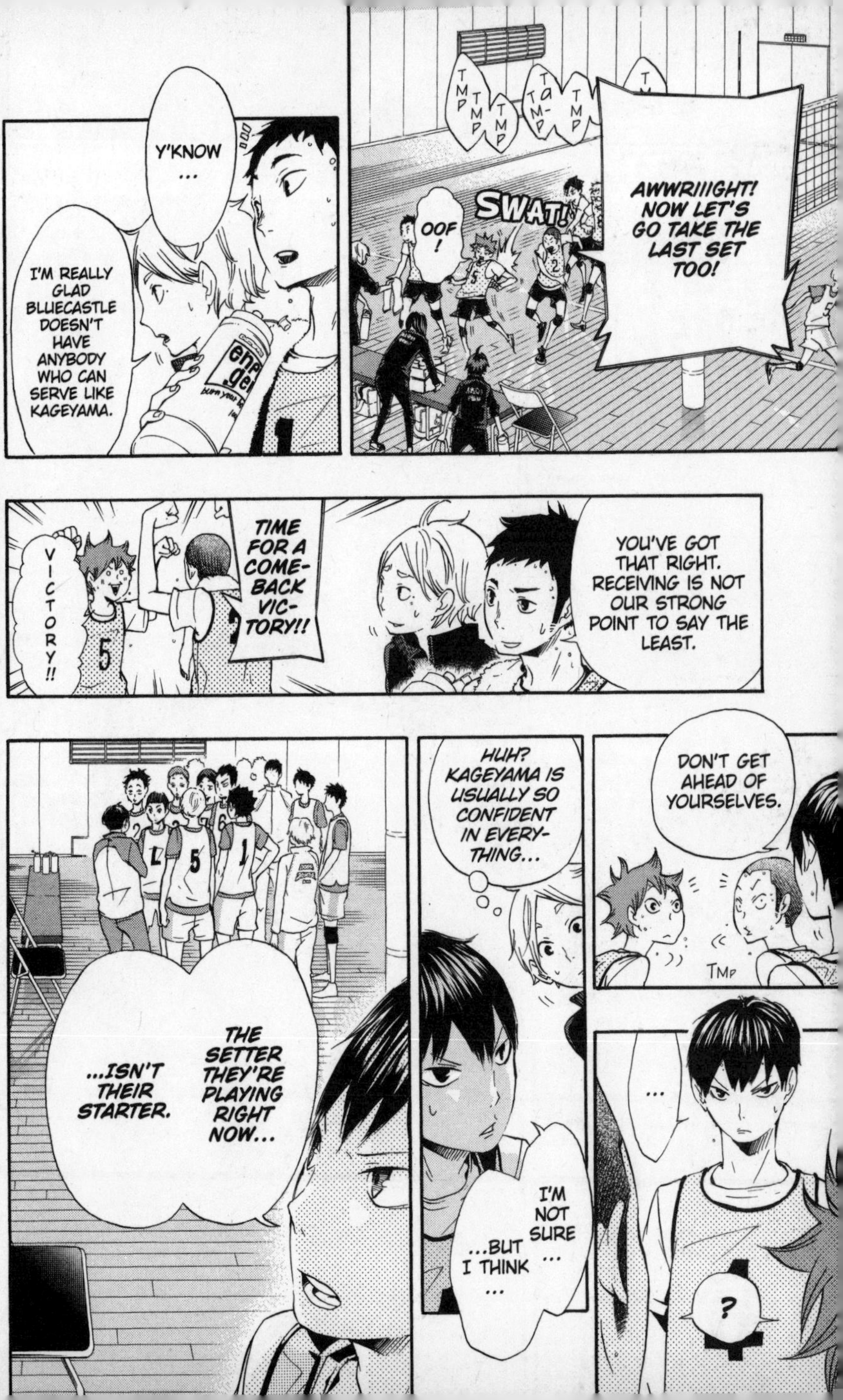

TMP TMP TMP TMP TAMP TMP
AWWRIIIGHT! NOW LET'S GO TAKE THE LAST SET TOO!
SWAT!
OOF!
Y'KNOW ...
I'M REALLY GLAD BLUECASTLE DOESN'T HAVE ANYBODY WHO CAN SERVE LIKE KAGEYAMA.
YOU'VE GOT THAT RIGHT. RECEIVING IS NOT OUR STRONG POINT TO SAY THE LEAST.
TIME FOR A COME-BACK VIC-TORY!!
VICTORY!!
DON'T GET AHEAD OF YOURSELVES.
TMP
...
?
HUH? KAGEYAMA IS USUALLY SO CONFIDENT IN EVERY-THING...
I'M NOT SURE ...
...BUT I THINK ...
THE SETTER THEY'RE PLAYING RIGHT NOW...
...ISN'T THEIR STARTER.

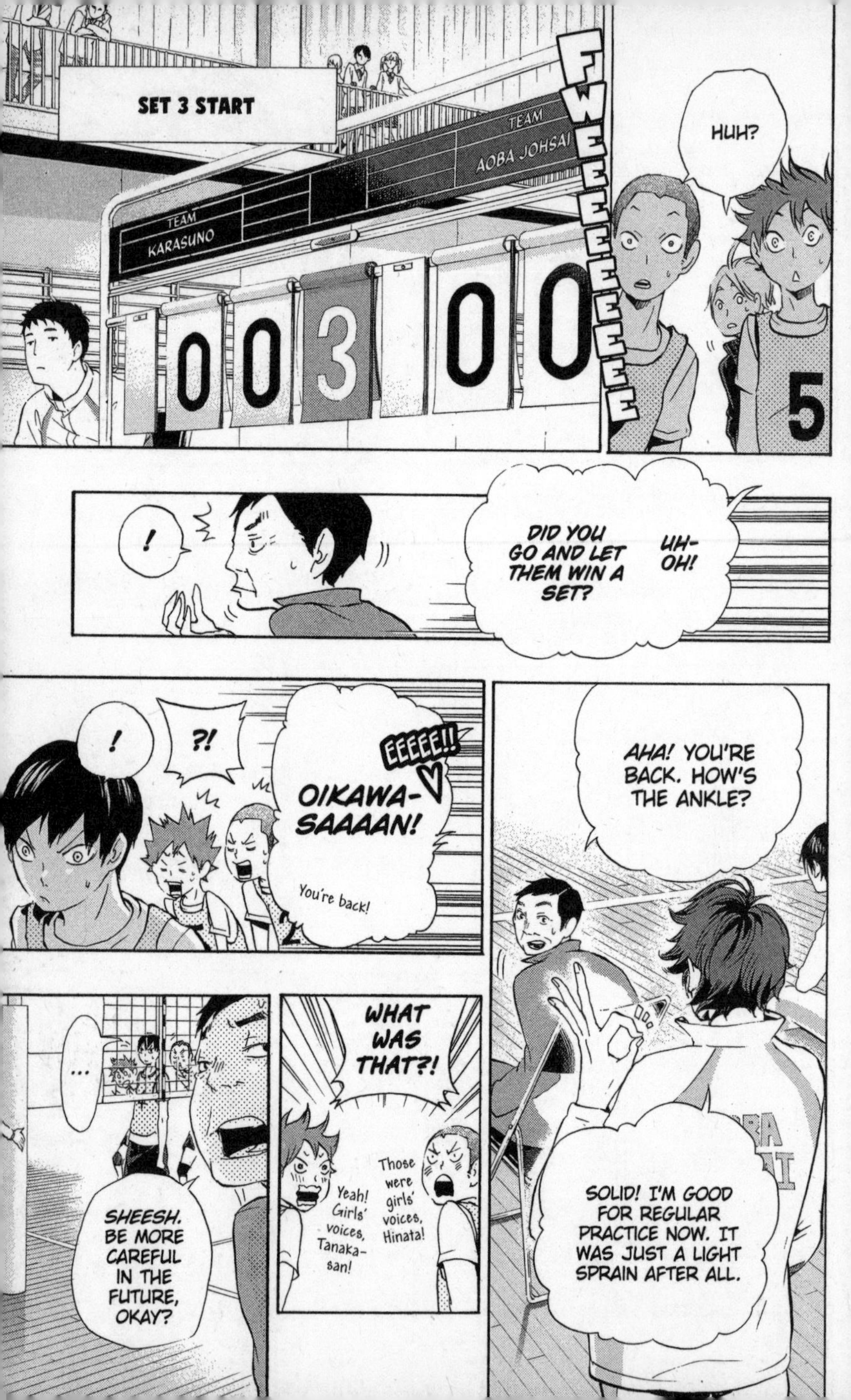
HUH?
FWEEEEEEEE
SET 3 START
TEAM AOBA JOHSAI
TEAM KARASUNO
0 0 3 0 0
5
UH-OH!
DID YOU GO AND LET THEM WIN A SET?
!
AHA! YOU'RE BACK. HOW'S THE ANKLE?
SOLID! I'M GOOD FOR REGULAR PRACTICE NOW. IT WAS JUST A LIGHT SPRAIN AFTER ALL.
EEEEE!! ♥
OIKAWA-SAAAAN!
You're back!
?!
!
WHAT WAS THAT?!
Those were girls' voices, Hinata!
Yeah! Girls' voices, Tanaka-san!
...
SHEESH. BE MORE CAREFUL IN THE FUTURE, OKAY?

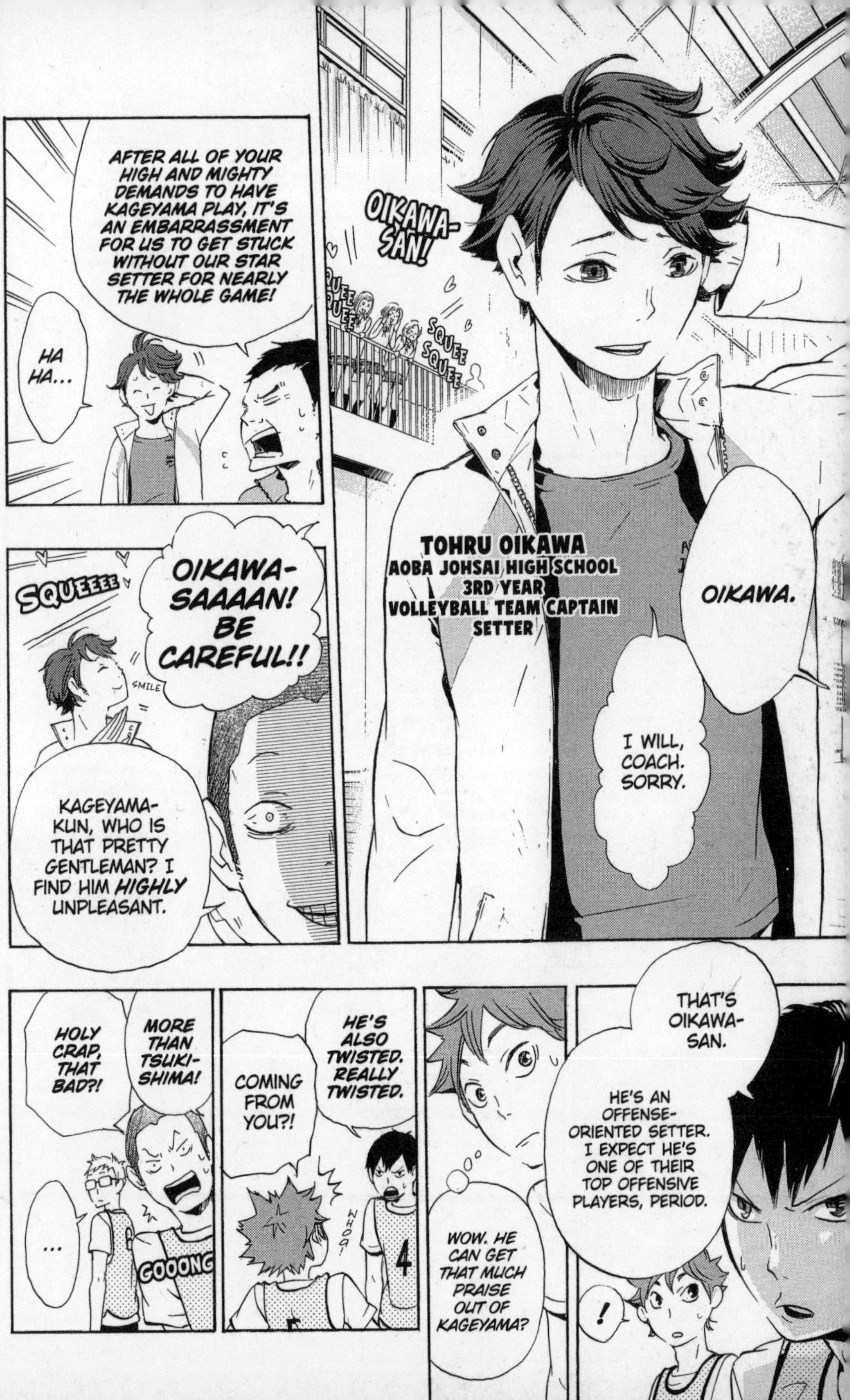
OIKAWA-SAN!
SQUEE SQUEE
SQUEE SQUEE
TOHRU OIKAWA
AOBA JOHSAI HIGH SCHOOL
3RD YEAR
VOLLEYBALL TEAM CAPTAIN
SETTER
OIKAWA.
I WILL, COACH. SORRY.
AFTER ALL OF YOUR HIGH AND MIGHTY DEMANDS TO HAVE KAGEYAMA PLAY, IT'S AN EMBARRASSMENT FOR US TO GET STUCK WITHOUT OUR STAR SETTER FOR NEARLY THE WHOLE GAME!
HA HA...
OIKAWA-SAAAAN! BE CAREFUL!!
SQUEEEE
SMILE
KAGEYAMA-KUN, WHO IS THAT PRETTY GENTLEMAN? I FIND HIM *HIGHLY* UNPLEASANT.
THAT'S OIKAWA-SAN.
HE'S AN OFFENSE-ORIENTED SETTER. I EXPECT HE'S ONE OF THEIR TOP OFFENSIVE PLAYERS, PERIOD.
!
WOW. HE CAN GET THAT MUCH PRAISE OUT OF KAGEYAMA?
HE'S ALSO TWISTED. REALLY TWISTED.
COMING FROM YOU?!
MORE THAN TSUKISHIMA!
HOLY CRAP, THAT BAD?!
GOOONG
...

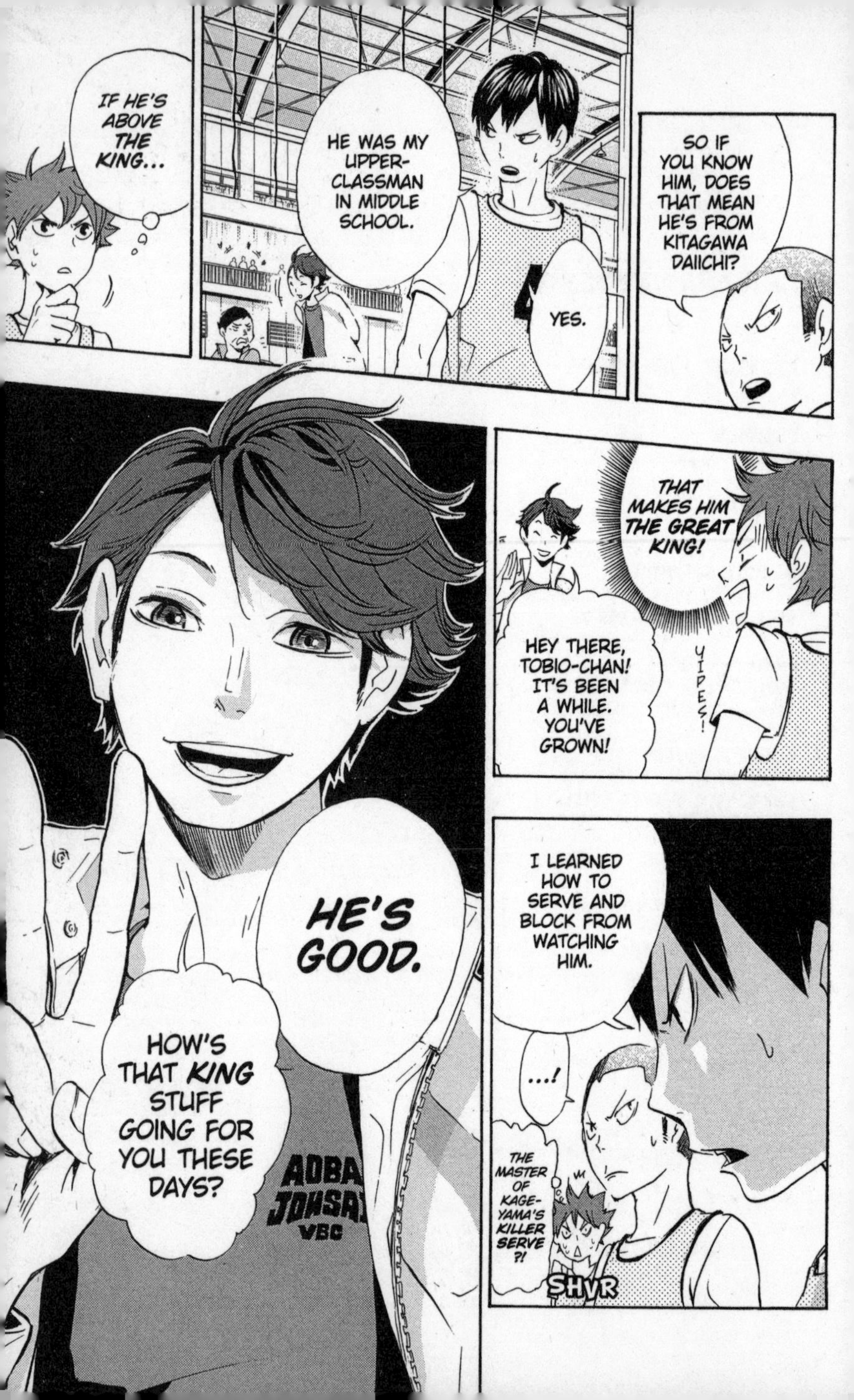
SO IF YOU KNOW HIM, DOES THAT MEAN HE'S FROM KITAGAWA DAIICHI?
YES.
HE WAS MY UPPER-CLASSMAN IN MIDDLE SCHOOL.
IF HE'S ABOVE THE KING...
THAT MAKES HIM THE GREAT KING!
YIPES!
HEY THERE, TOBIO-CHAN! IT'S BEEN A WHILE. YOU'VE GROWN!
I LEARNED HOW TO SERVE AND BLOCK FROM WATCHING HIM.
...!
THE MASTER OF KAGE-YAMA'S KILLER SERVE?!
SHVR
HE'S GOOD.
HOW'S THAT KING STUFF GOING FOR YOU THESE DAYS?
AOBA JOHSAI
VBC

CHIKARA ENNOSHITA

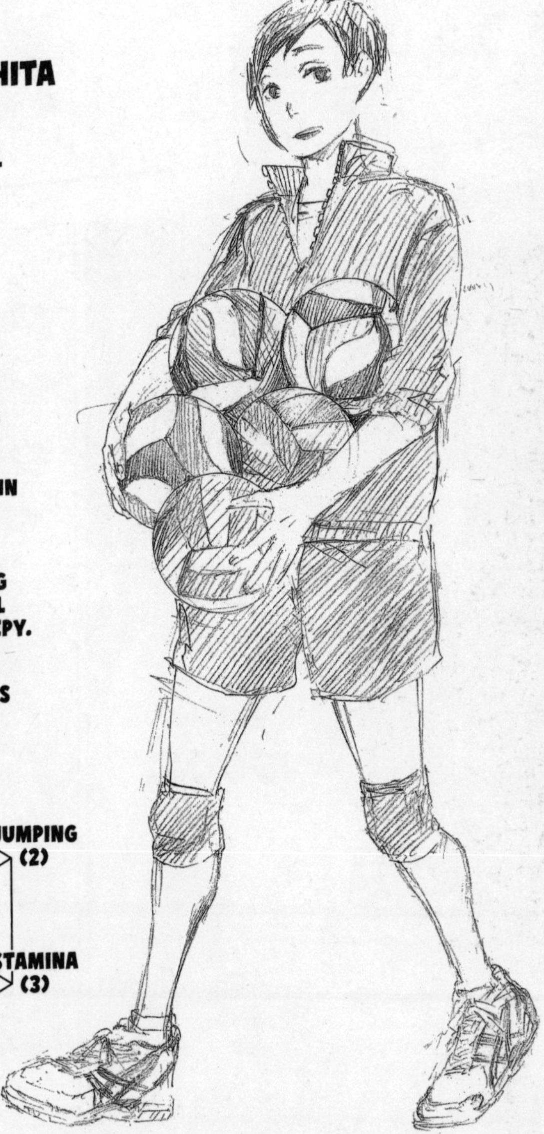

KARASUNO HIGH SCHOOL
CLASS 2-4

POSITION:
WING SPIKER

HEIGHT: 5'9"
WEIGHT: 146 LBS.
(AS OF APRIL, 2ND YEAR OF HIGH SCHOOL)

BIRTHDAY: DECEMBER 26

FAVORITE FOOD:
HOYASU SEA PINEAPPLE IN VINEGARED SOY SAUCE

CURRENT WORRY:
EVEN WHEN HE'S FEELING ENERGETIC, PEOPLE STILL TELL HIM HE LOOKS SLEEPY.

ABILITY PARAMETERS
(5-POINT SCALE)

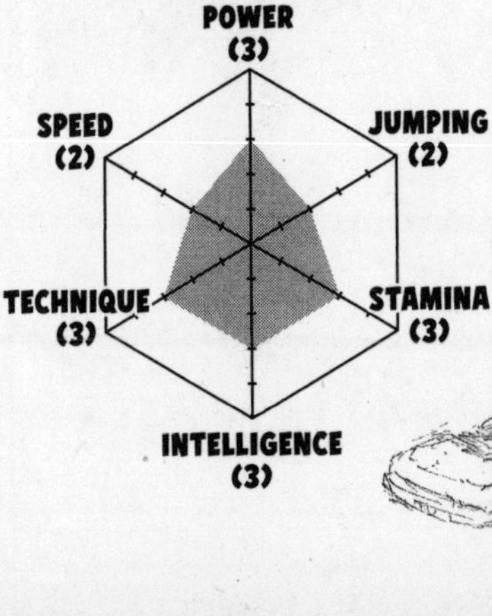
POWER (3)
JUMPING (2)
STAMINA (3)
INTELLIGENCE (3)
TECHNIQUE (3)
SPEED (2)

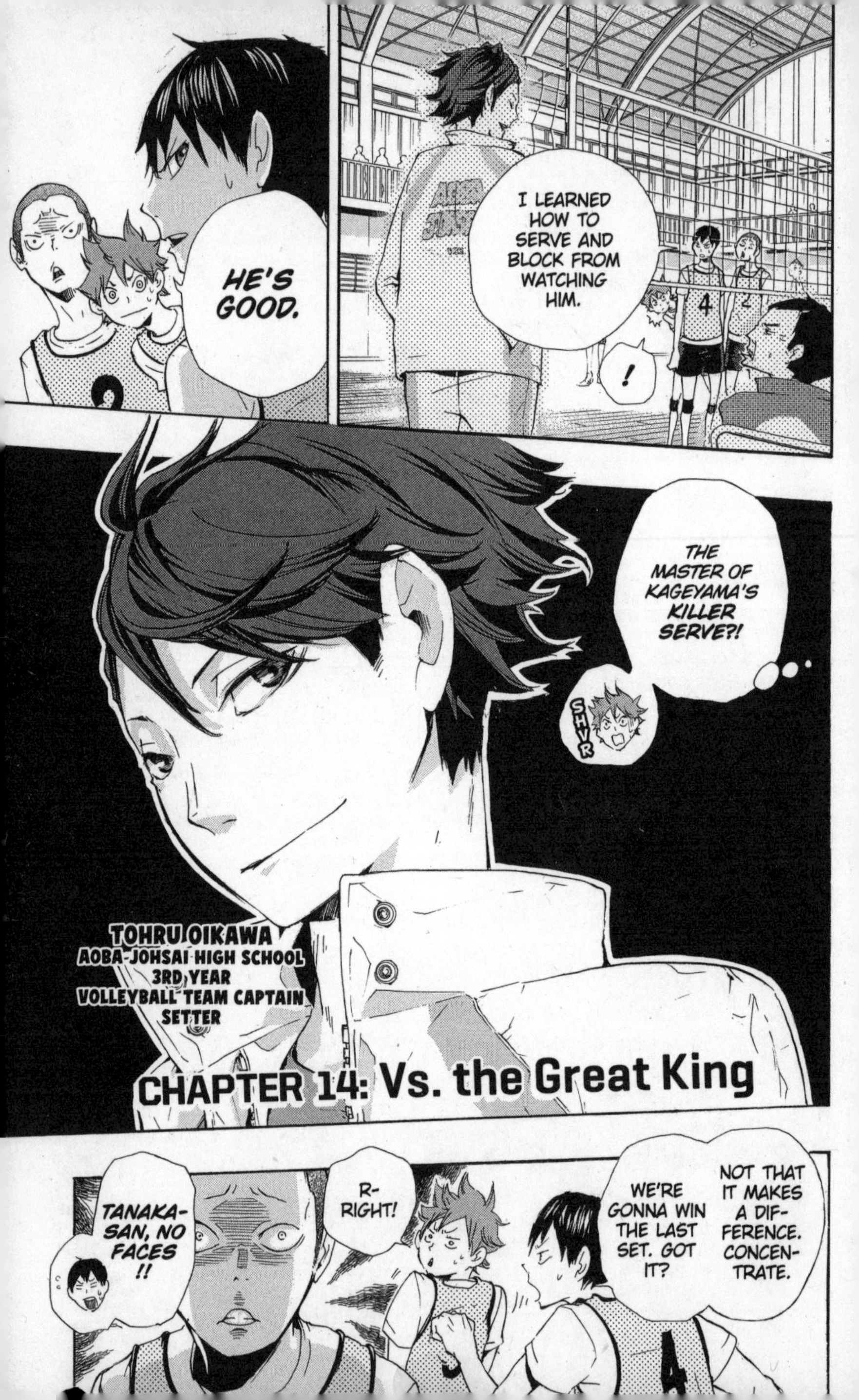
I LEARNED HOW TO SERVE AND BLOCK FROM WATCHING HIM.
!
HE'S GOOD.
THE MASTER OF KAGEYAMA'S KILLER SERVE?!
SHVR
TOHRU OIKAWA
AOBA-JOHSAI HIGH SCHOOL
3RD YEAR
VOLLEYBALL TEAM CAPTAIN
SETTER
CHAPTER 14: Vs. the Great King
NOT THAT IT MAKES A DIF-FERENCE. CONCEN-TRATE.
WE'RE GONNA WIN THE LAST SET. GOT IT?
R-RIGHT!
TANAKA-SAN, NO FACES!!

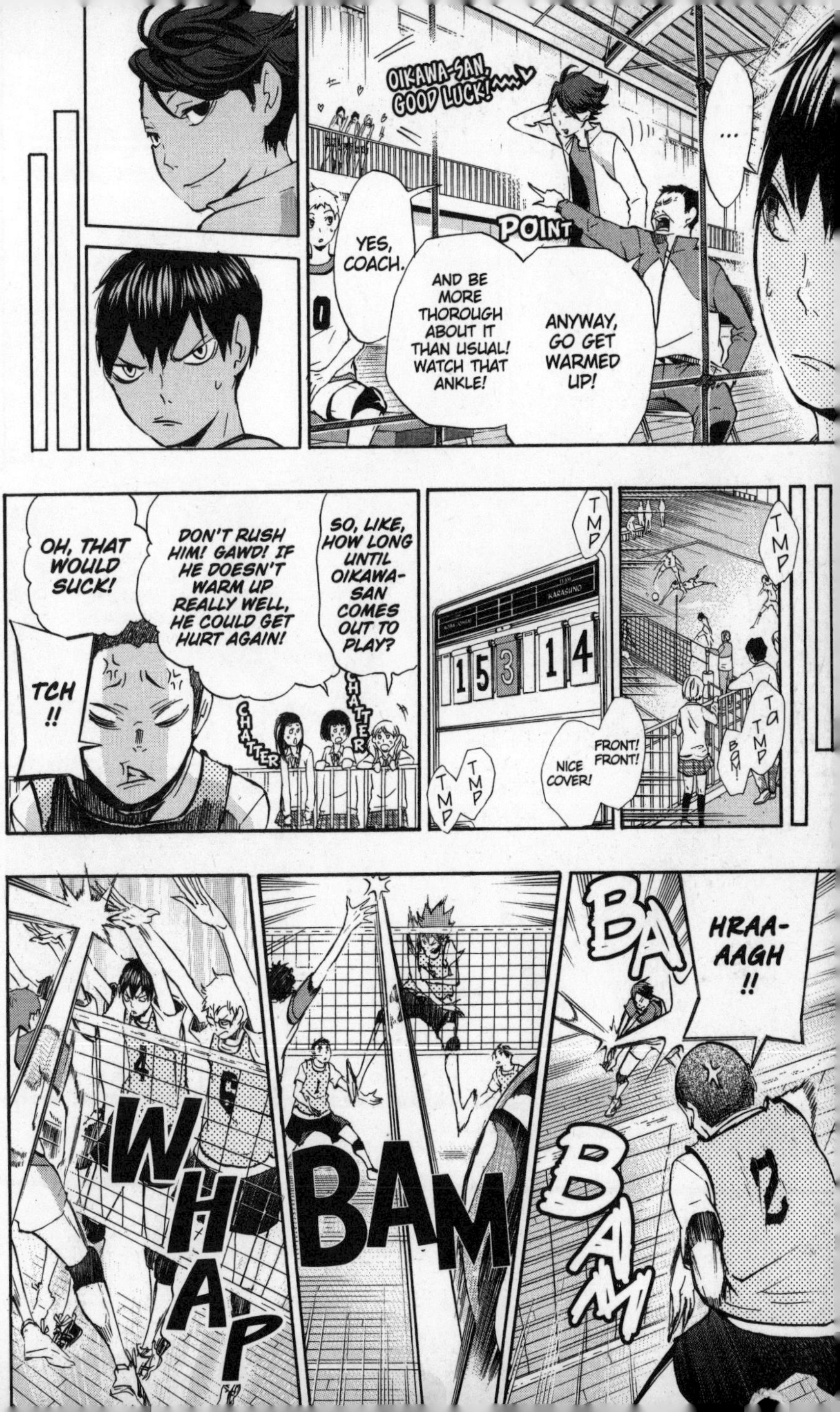
...
OIKAWA-SAN, GOOD LUCK!~~~♥
POINT
ANYWAY, GO GET WARMED UP!
AND BE MORE THOROUGH ABOUT IT THAN USUAL! WATCH THAT ANKLE!
YES, COACH.
TMP
TA TMP
BAM!
FRONT! FRONT!
NICE COVER!
TMP
KARASUNO
15 3 14
TMP TMP
SO, LIKE, HOW LONG UNTIL OIKAWA-SAN COMES OUT TO PLAY?
CHATTER
DON'T RUSH HIM! GAWD! IF HE DOESN'T WARM UP REALLY WELL, HE COULD GET HURT AGAIN!
CHATTER
OH, THAT WOULD SUCK!
TCH !!
BA
HRAA-AAGH !!
BAM
BAM
WHAP

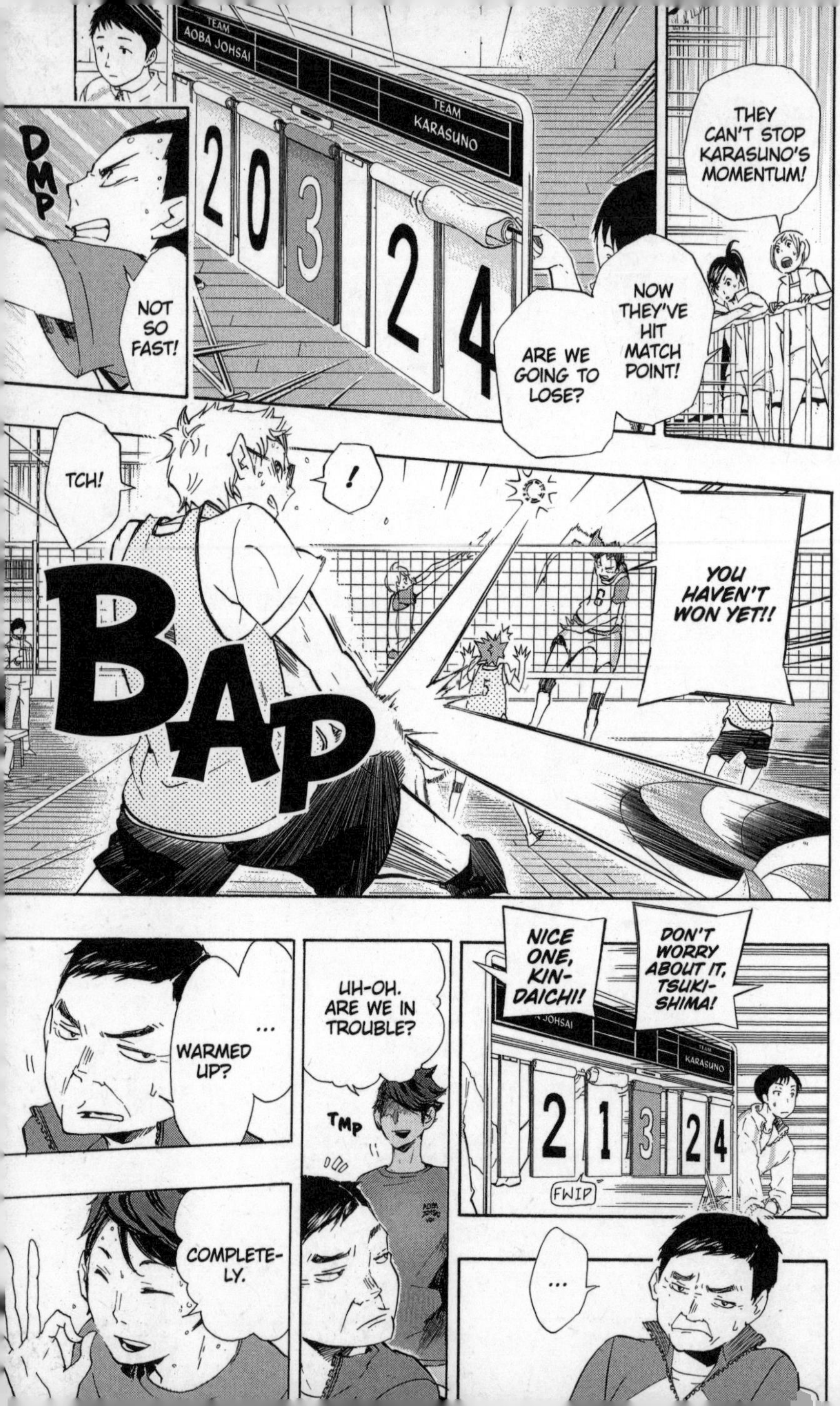

THEY CAN'T STOP KARASUNO'S MOMENTUM!
TEAM AOBA JOHSAI
TEAM KARASUNO
NOW THEY'VE HIT MATCH POINT!
ARE WE GOING TO LOSE?
DMP
NOT SO FAST!
YOU HAVEN'T WON YET!!
!
TCH!
BAP
DON'T WORRY ABOUT IT, TSUKI-SHIMA!
NICE ONE, KIN-DAICHI!
TEAM KARASUNO
FWIP
UH-OH. ARE WE IN TROUBLE?
TMP
... WARMED UP?
...
COMPLETE-LY.

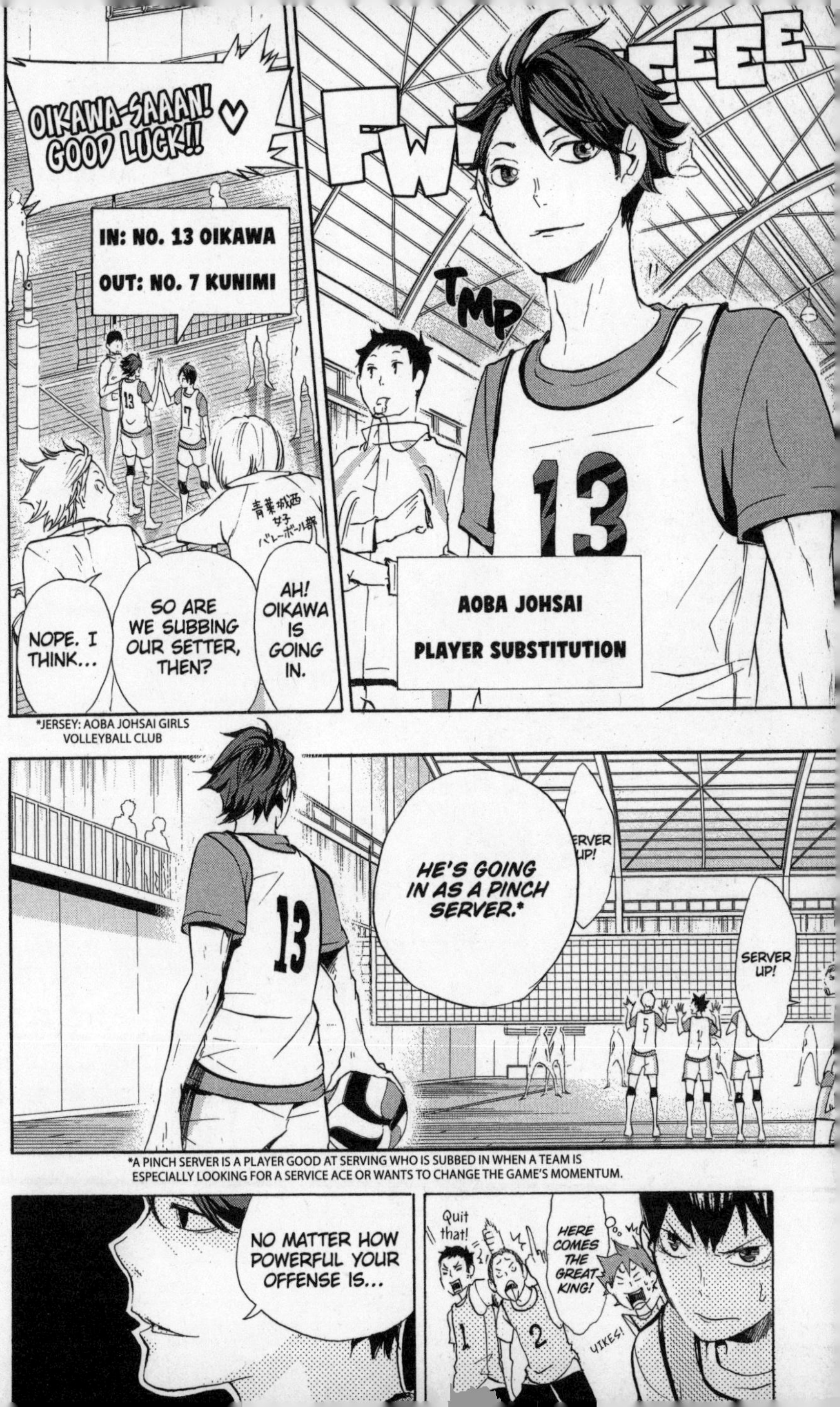
FW EEEE
TMP
AOBA JOHSAI PLAYER SUBSTITUTION
OIKAWA-SAAAN! GOOD LUCK!! ♥
IN: NO. 13 OIKAWA
OUT: NO. 7 KUNIMI
青葉城西 女子 バレーボール部
AH! OIKAWA IS GOING IN.
SO ARE WE SUBBING OUR SETTER, THEN?
NOPE. I THINK...
SERVER UP!
ERVER UP!
HE'S GOING IN AS A PINCH SERVER.*
HERE COMES THE GREAT KING!
Quit that!
YIKES!
NO MATTER HOW POWERFUL YOUR OFFENSE IS...

*JERSEY: AOBA JOHSAI GIRLS VOLLEYBALL CLUB

*A PINCH SERVER IS A PLAYER GOOD AT SERVING WHO IS SUBBED IN WHEN A TEAM IS ESPECIALLY LOOKING FOR A SERVICE ACE OR WANTS TO CHANGE THE GAME'S MOMENTUM.

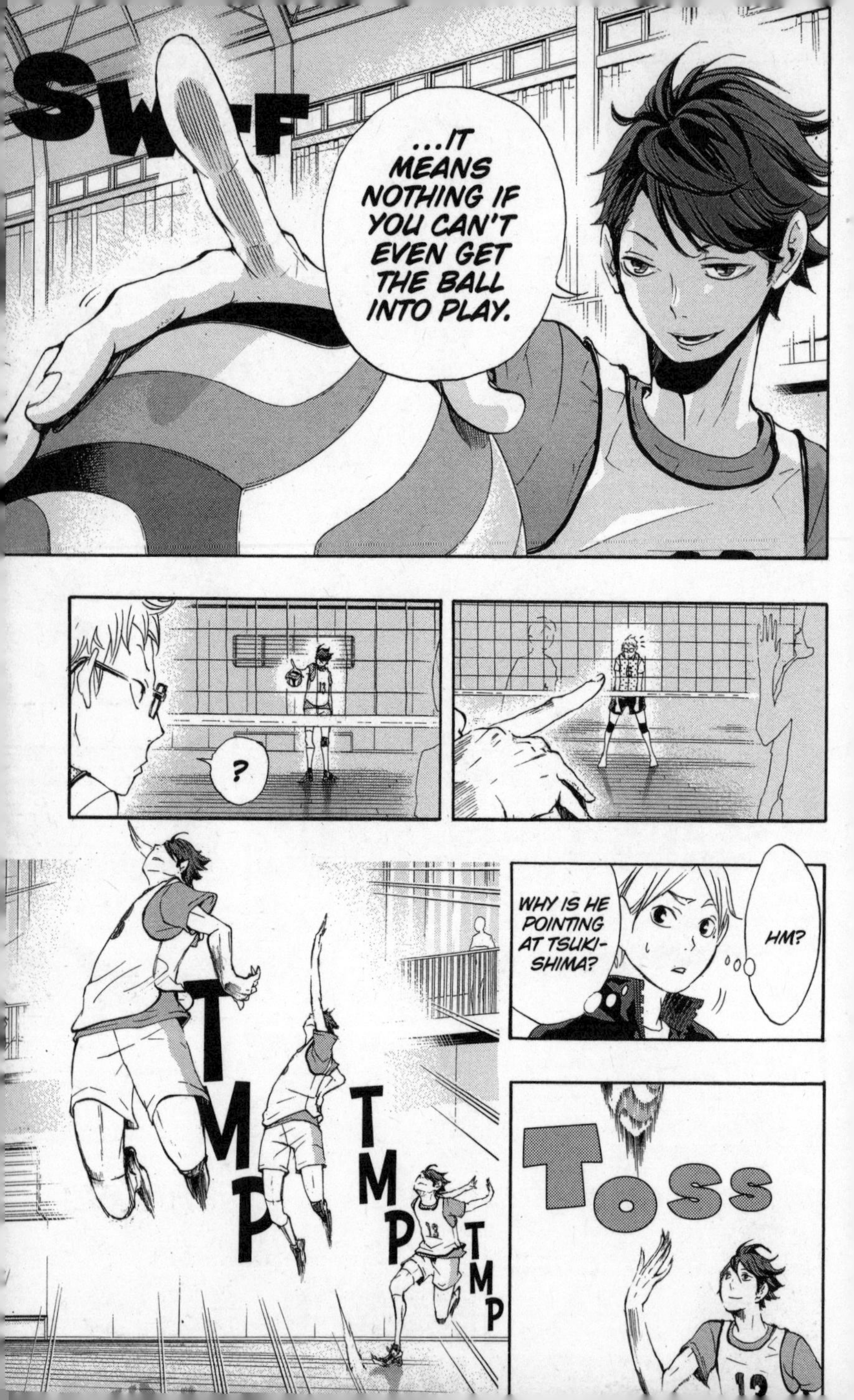
...IT MEANS NOTHING IF YOU CAN'T EVEN GET THE BALL INTO PLAY.
?
HM?
WHY IS HE POINTING AT TSUKISHIMA?
TOSS
TMP
TMP
TMP
TMP

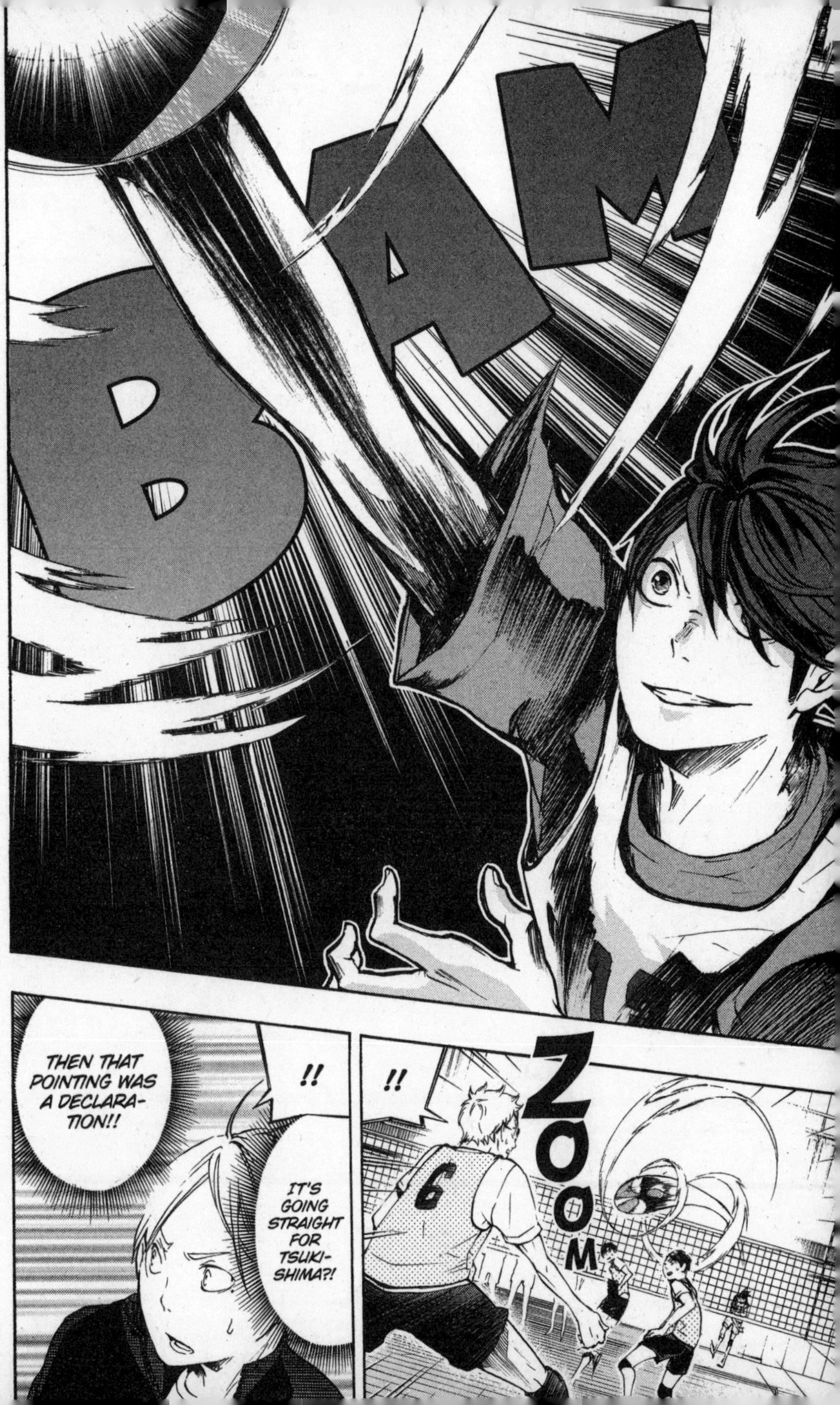
BAM
ZOOM
!!
!!
THEN THAT POINTING WAS A DECLARA-TION!!
IT'S GOING STRAIGHT FOR TSUKI-SHIMA?!

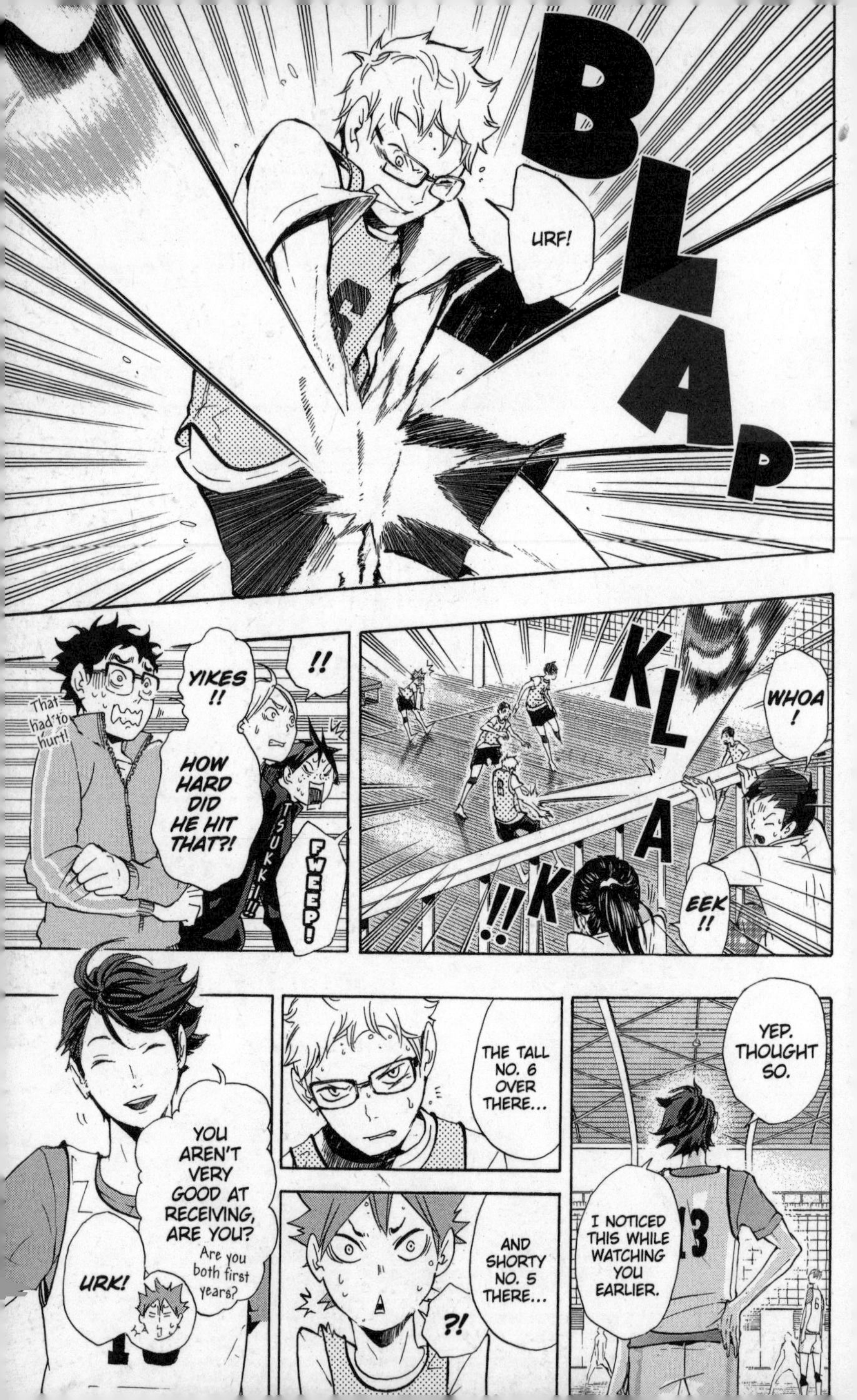
BLAP
URF!
KLAK
WHOA!
EEK!!
!!
!!
YIKES!!
HOW HARD DID HE HIT THAT?!
That had to hurt!
TSUKKI!
FWEEP!
YEP. THOUGHT SO.
I NOTICED THIS WHILE WATCHING YOU EARLIER.
THE TALL NO. 6 OVER THERE...
AND SHORTY NO. 5 THERE...
?!
YOU AREN'T VERY GOOD AT RECEIVING, ARE YOU?
Are you both first years?
URK!

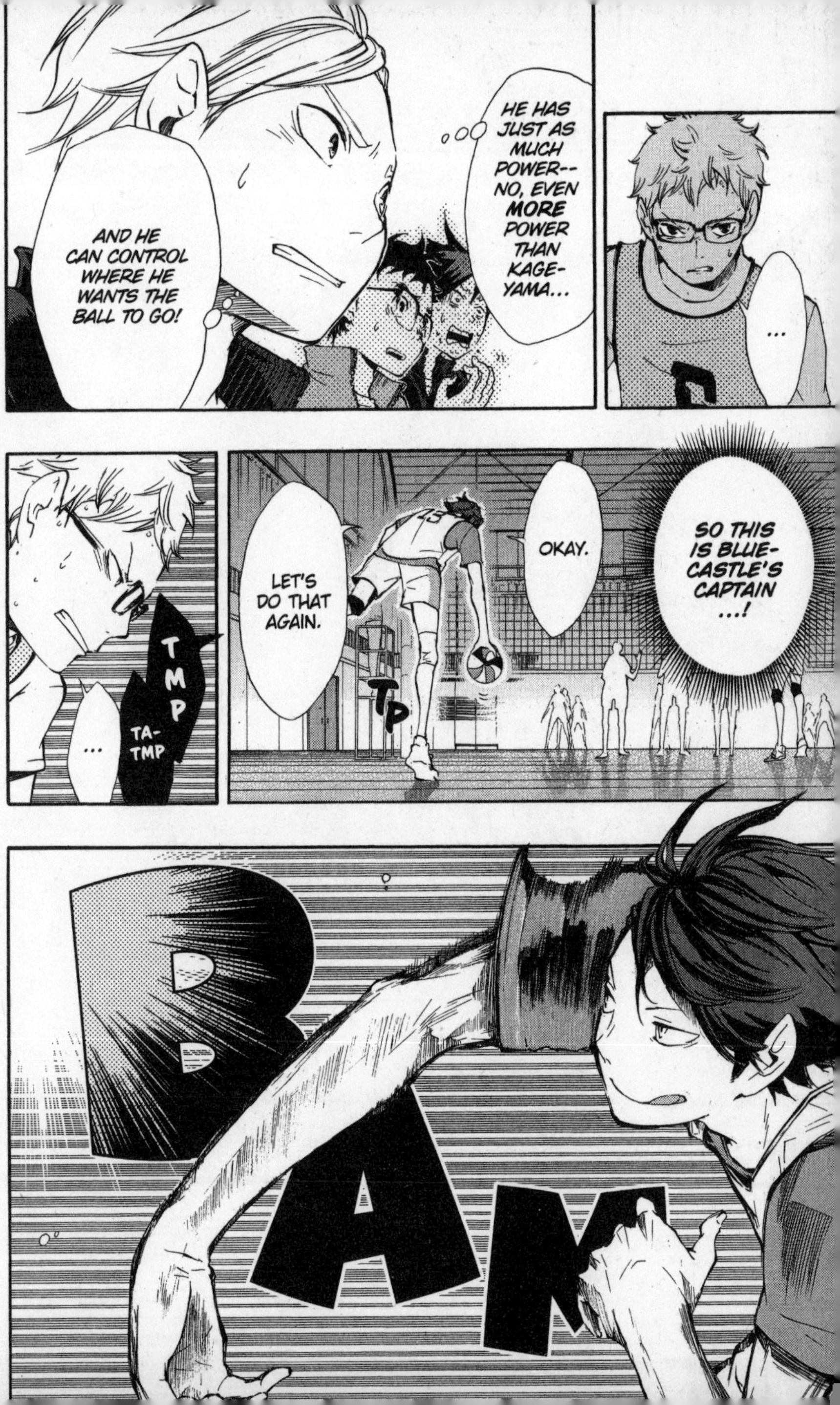
...
HE HAS JUST AS MUCH POWER-- NO, EVEN MORE POWER THAN KAGE-YAMA...
AND HE CAN CONTROL WHERE HE WANTS THE BALL TO GO!
SO THIS IS BLUE-CASTLE'S CAPTAIN ...!
OKAY.
LET'S DO THAT AGAIN.
TP
TMP
TA-TMP
...
BAM

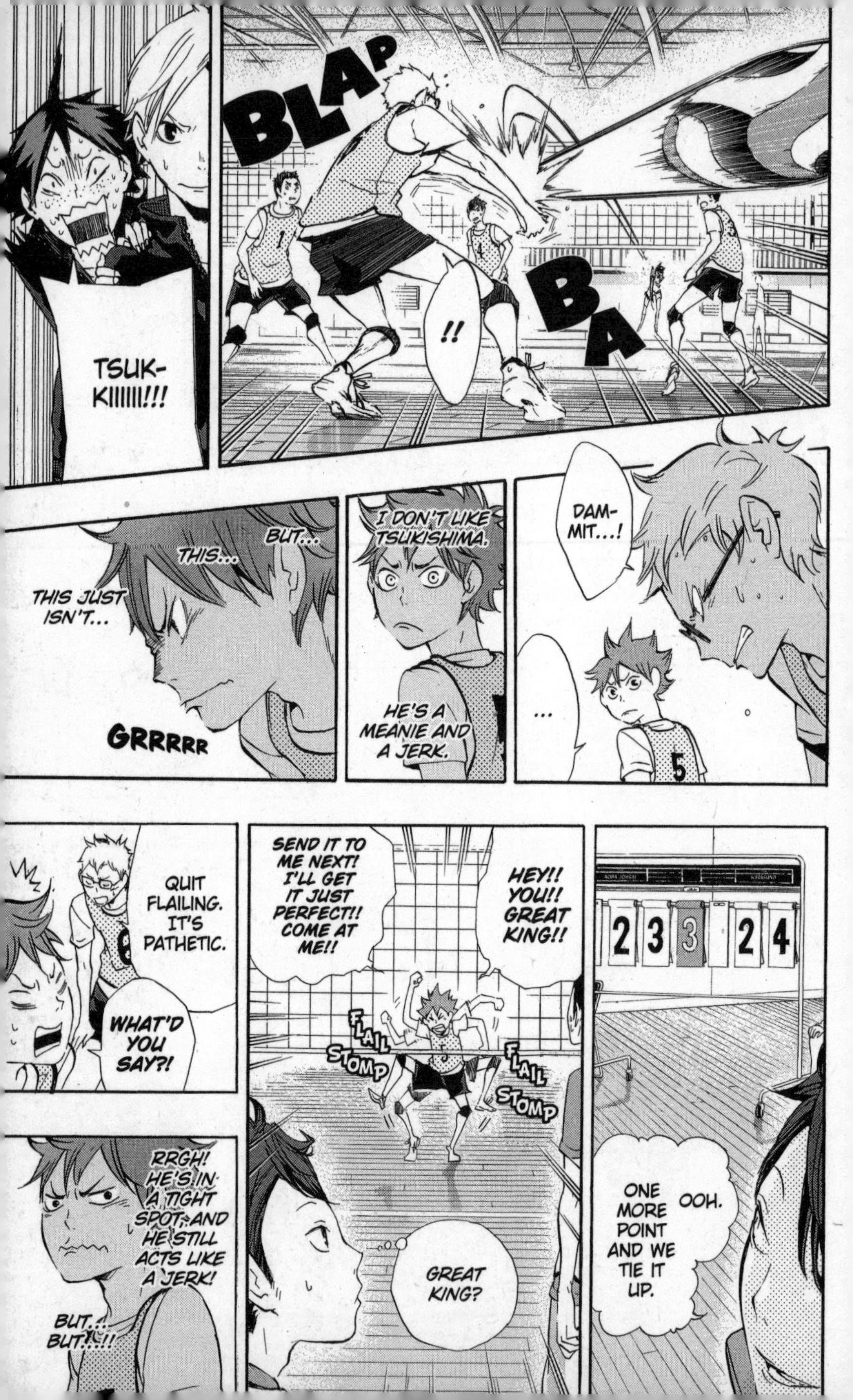
BLAP
!!
BA
TSUK-KIIIIII!!!
DAM-MIT...!
...
I DON'T LIKE TSUKISHIMA.
HE'S A MEANIE AND A JERK.
BUT...
THIS...
THIS JUST ISN'T...
GRRRRR
OOH.
ONE MORE POINT AND WE TIE IT UP.
HEY!! YOU!! GREAT KING!!
SEND IT TO ME NEXT! I'LL GET IT JUST PERFECT!! COME AT ME!!
FLAIL
STOMP
FLAIL
STOMP
GREAT KING?
QUIT FLAILING. IT'S PATHETIC.
WHAT'D YOU SAY?!
RRGH! HE'S IN A TIGHT SPOT, AND HE STILL ACTS LIKE A JERK!
BUT... BUT...!!!

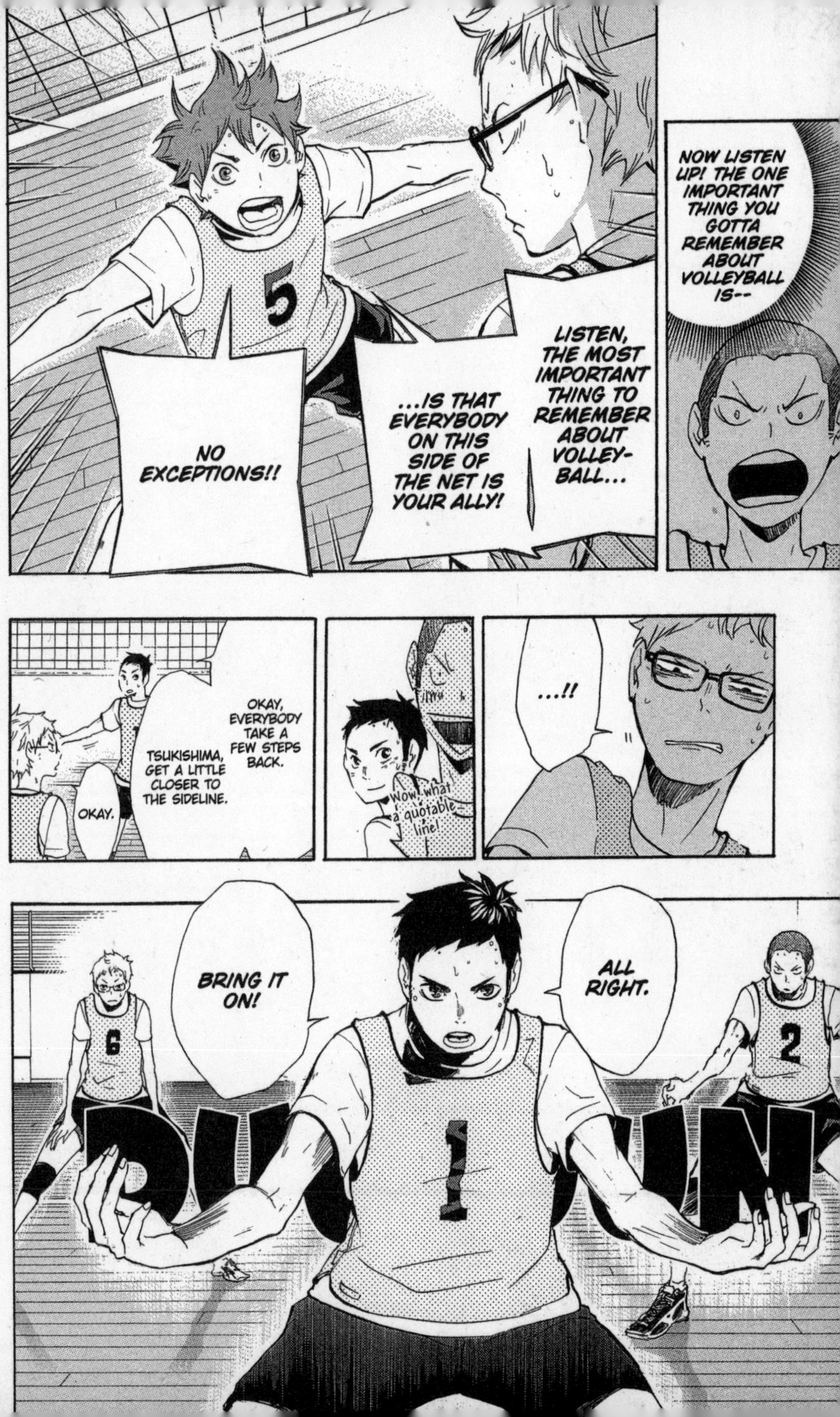
NOW LISTEN UP! THE ONE IMPORTANT THING YOU GOTTA REMEMBER ABOUT VOLLEYBALL IS--
LISTEN, THE MOST IMPORTANT THING TO REMEMBER ABOUT VOLLEY-BALL...
...IS THAT EVERYBODY ON THIS SIDE OF THE NET IS YOUR ALLY!
NO EXCEPTIONS!!
...!!
Wow, what a quotable line!
OKAY, EVERYBODY TAKE A FEW STEPS BACK.
TSUKISHIMA, GET A LITTLE CLOSER TO THE SIDELINE.
OKAY.
ALL RIGHT.
BRING IT ON!

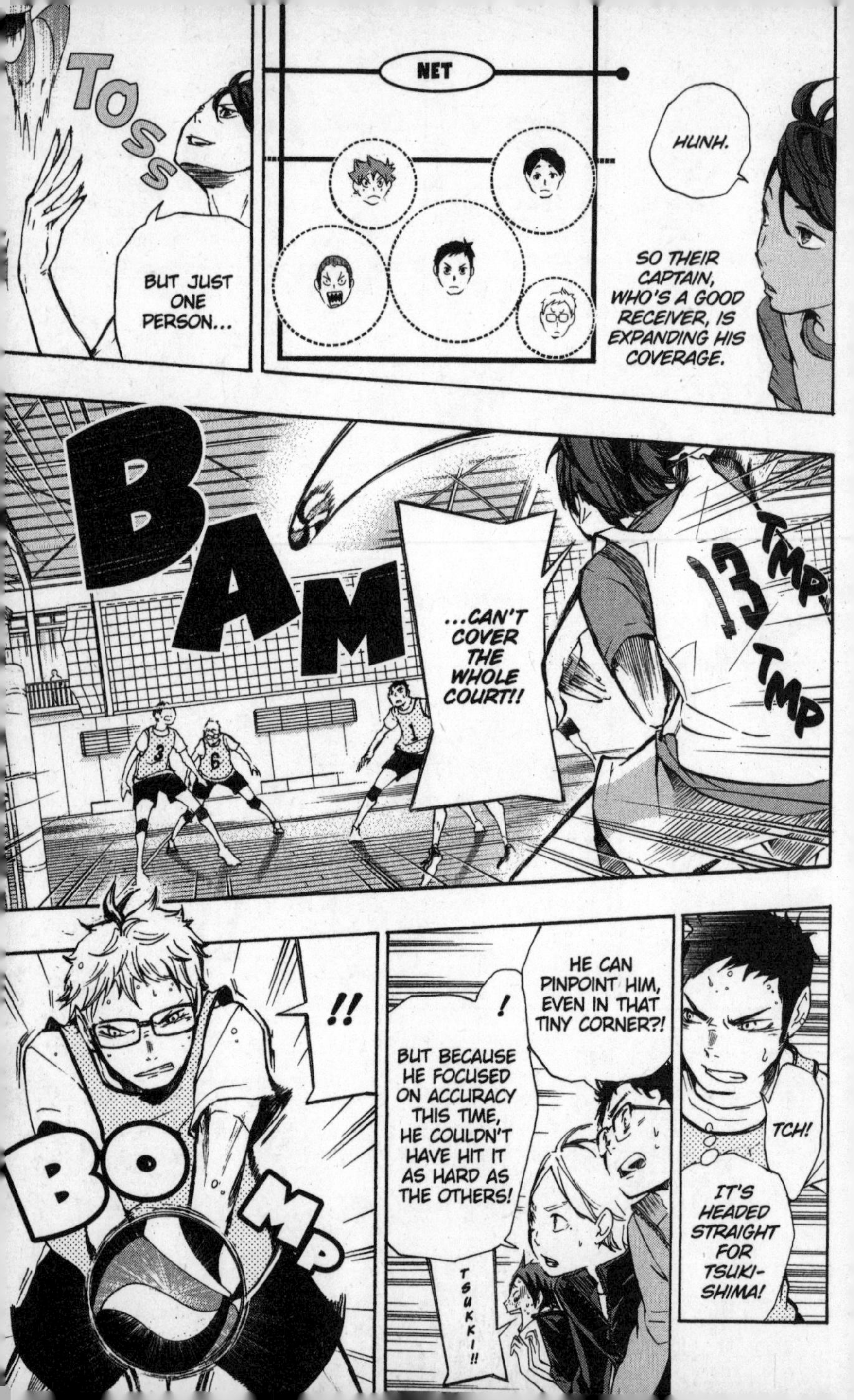
HUNH.
SO THEIR CAPTAIN, WHO'S A GOOD RECEIVER, IS EXPANDING HIS COVERAGE.
NET
TOSS
BUT JUST ONE PERSON...
TMP TMP
BAM
...CAN'T COVER THE WHOLE COURT!!
TCH!
IT'S HEADED STRAIGHT FOR TSUKI-SHIMA!
HE CAN PINPOINT HIM, EVEN IN THAT TINY CORNER?!
!
BUT BECAUSE HE FOCUSED ON ACCURACY THIS TIME, HE COULDN'T HAVE HIT IT AS HARD AS THE OTHERS!
TSUKKI!!
!!
BOMP

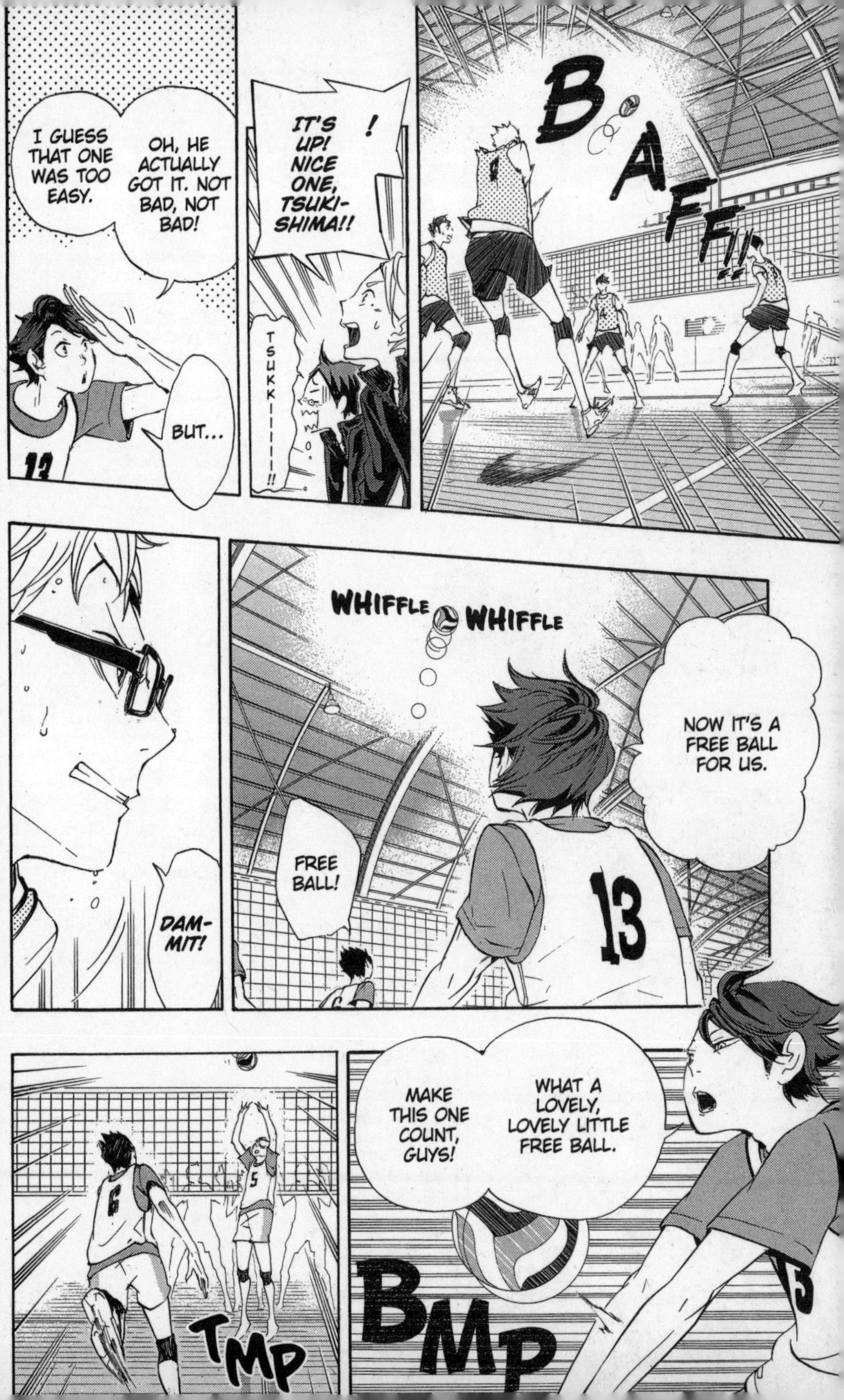
BAFF!!
!
IT'S UP! NICE ONE, TSUKISHIMA!!
TSUKK-----!!
OH, HE ACTUALLY GOT IT. NOT BAD, NOT BAD!
I GUESS THAT ONE WAS TOO EASY.
BUT...
WHIFFLE WHIFFLE
NOW IT'S A FREE BALL FOR US.
FREE BALL!
DAM-MIT!
WHAT A LOVELY, LOVELY LITTLE FREE BALL.
MAKE THIS ONE COUNT, GUYS!
BMP
TMP

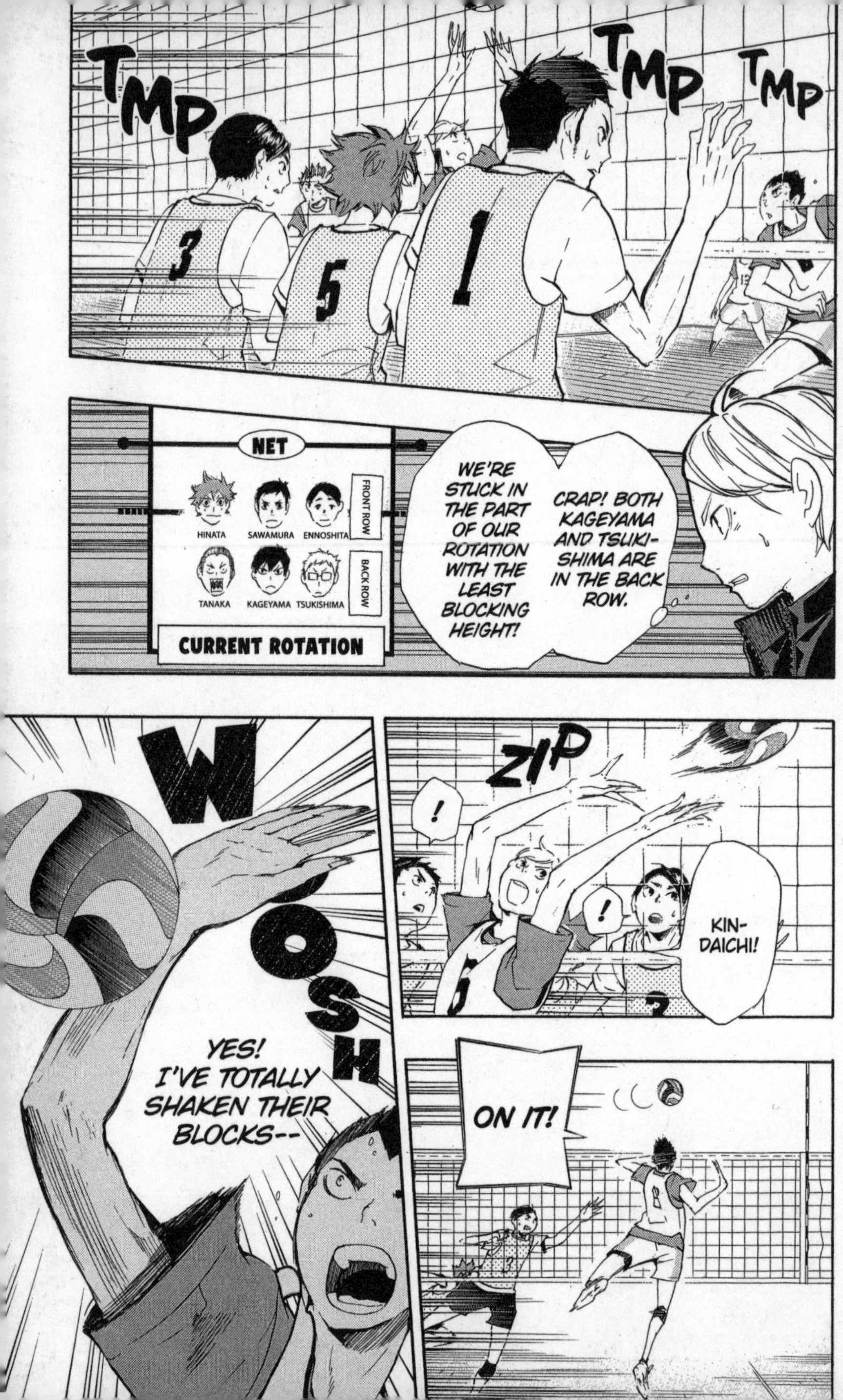
TMP TMP
TMP
CRAP! BOTH KAGEYAMA AND TSUKISHIMA ARE IN THE BACK ROW.
WE'RE STUCK IN THE PART OF OUR ROTATION WITH THE LEAST BLOCKING HEIGHT!
NET
FRONT ROW
ENNOSHITA
SAWAMURA
HINATA
BACK ROW
TSUKISHIMA
KAGEYAMA
TANAKA
CURRENT ROTATION
ZIP
KIN-DAICHI!
!
!
ON IT!
WHOOSH
YES! I'VE TOTALLY SHAKEN THEIR BLOCKS--

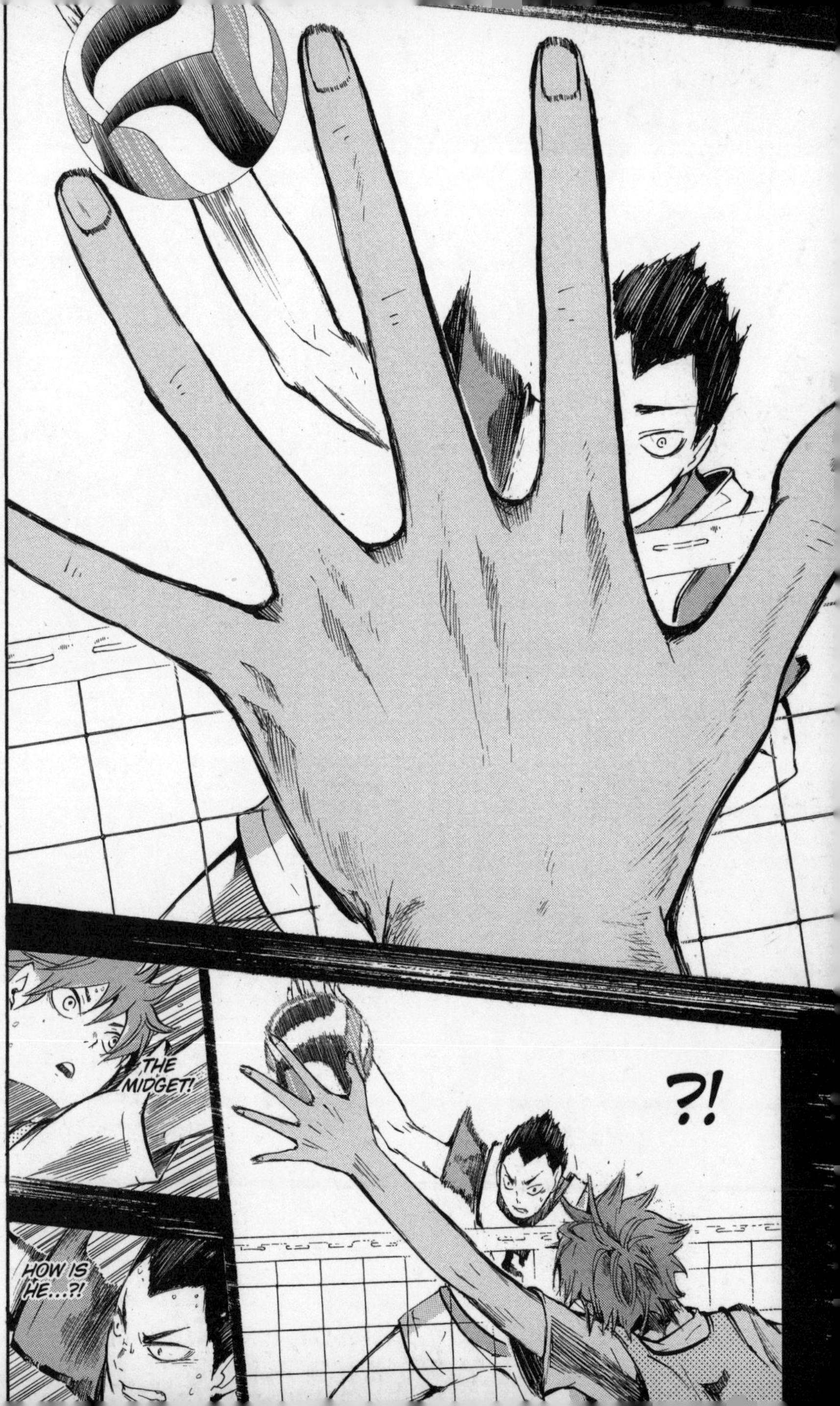
?!
THE MIDGET!
HOW IS HE...?!

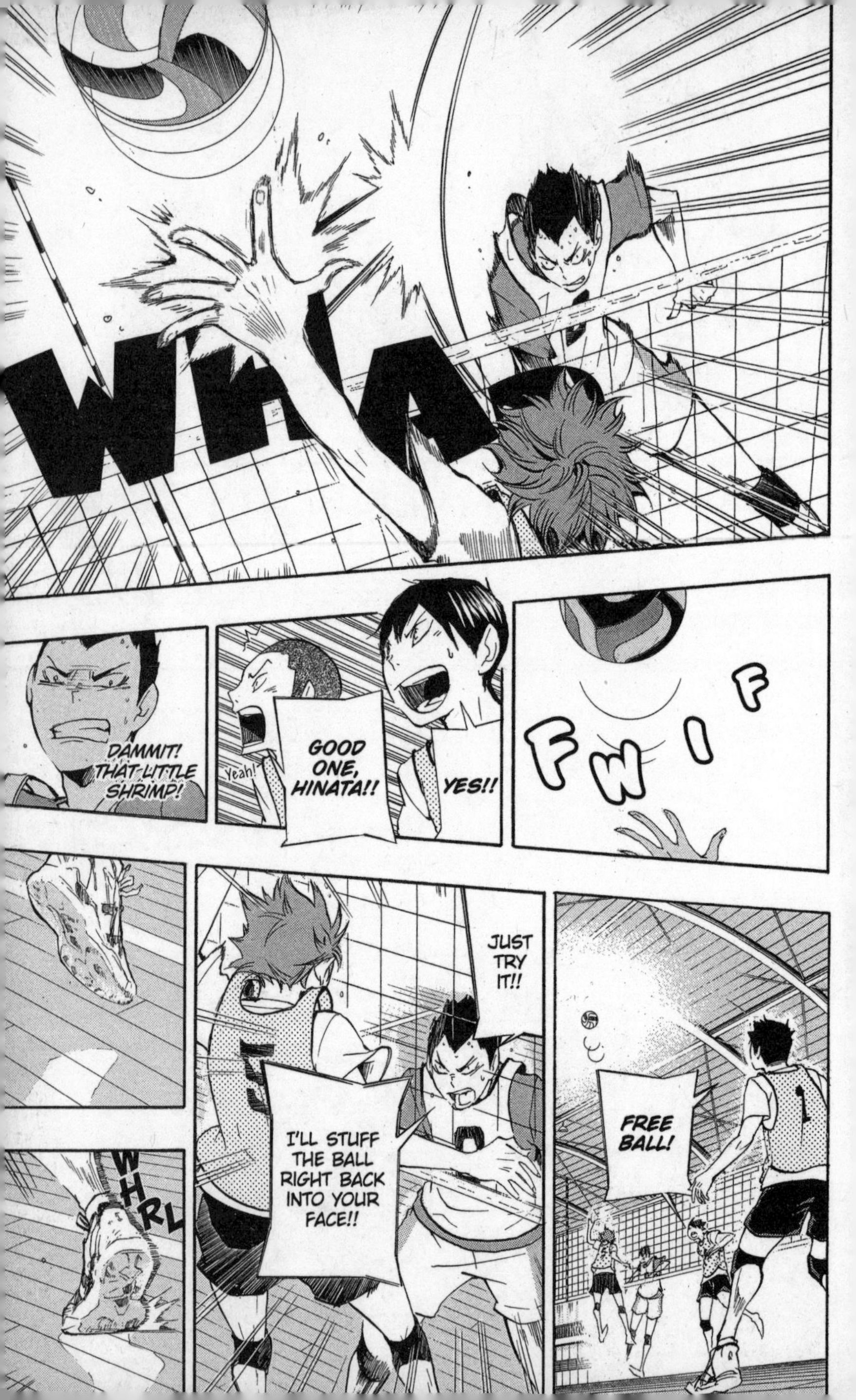
WHA
FWIF
YES!!
GOOD ONE, HINATA!!
Yeah!
DAMMIT! THAT LITTLE SHRIMP!
FREE BALL!
JUST TRY IT!!
I'LL STUFF THE BALL RIGHT BACK INTO YOUR FACE!!
WHRL

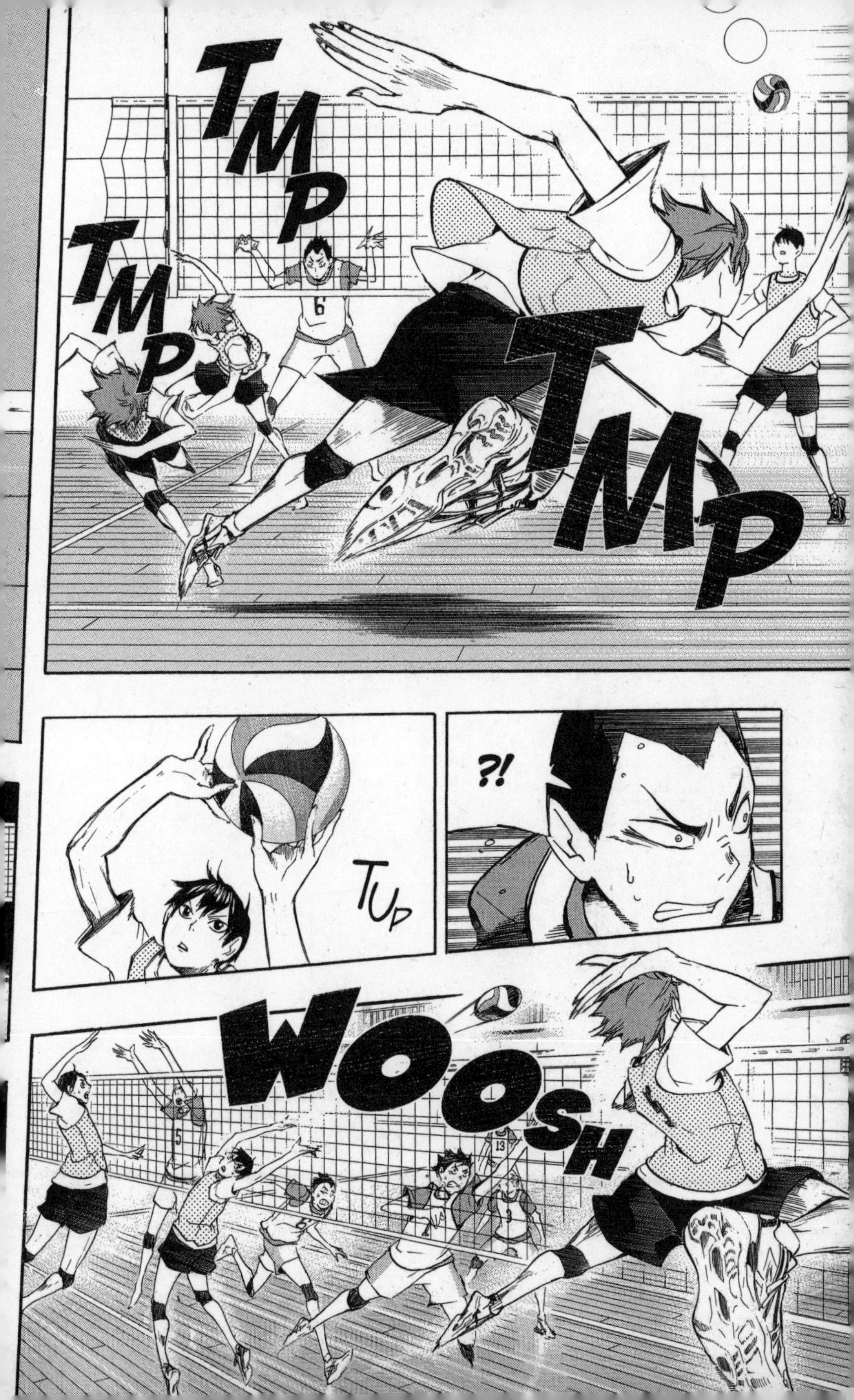
TMP
TMP
TMP
?!
TUP
WOOSH

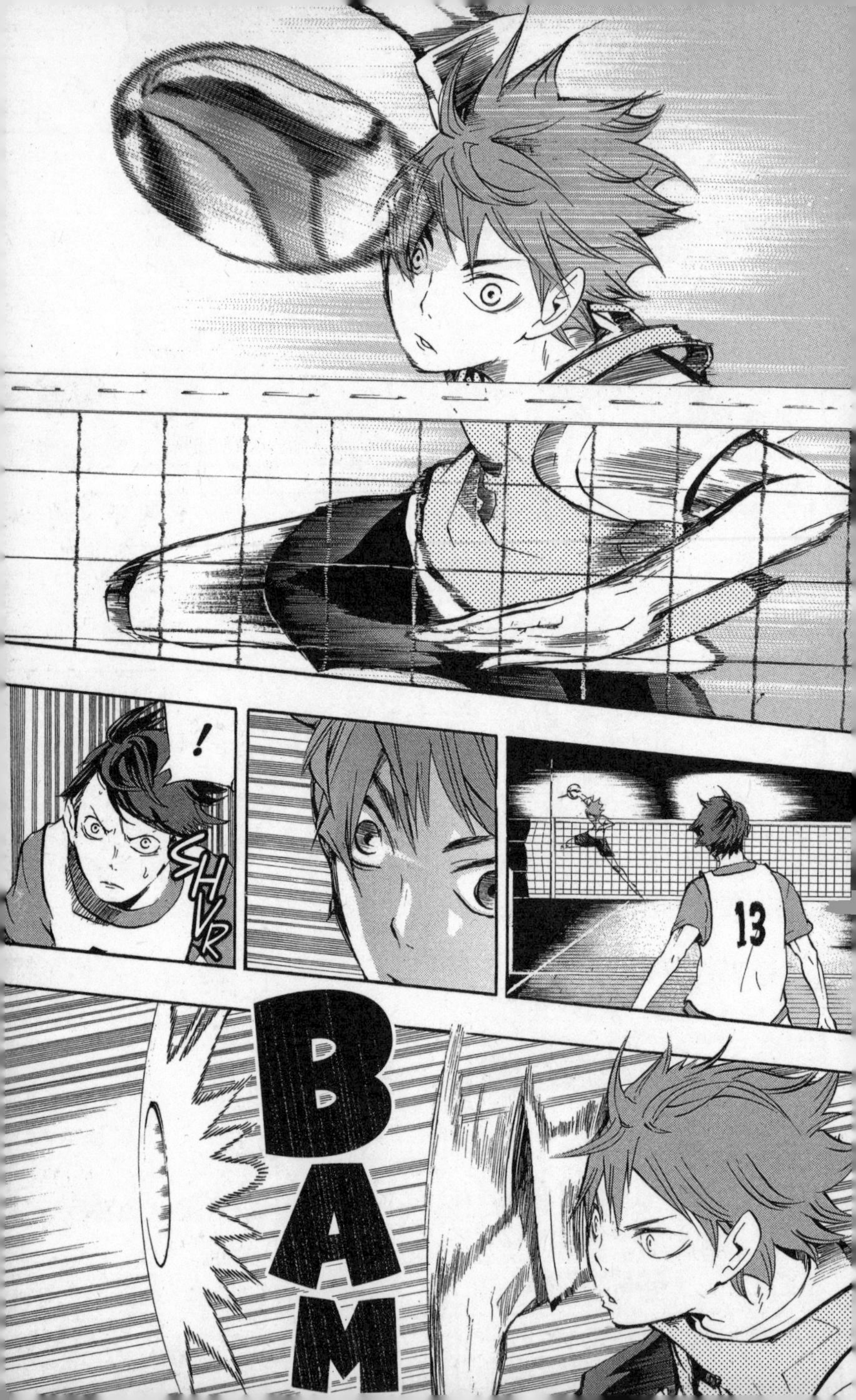
13
!
SHVR
BAM

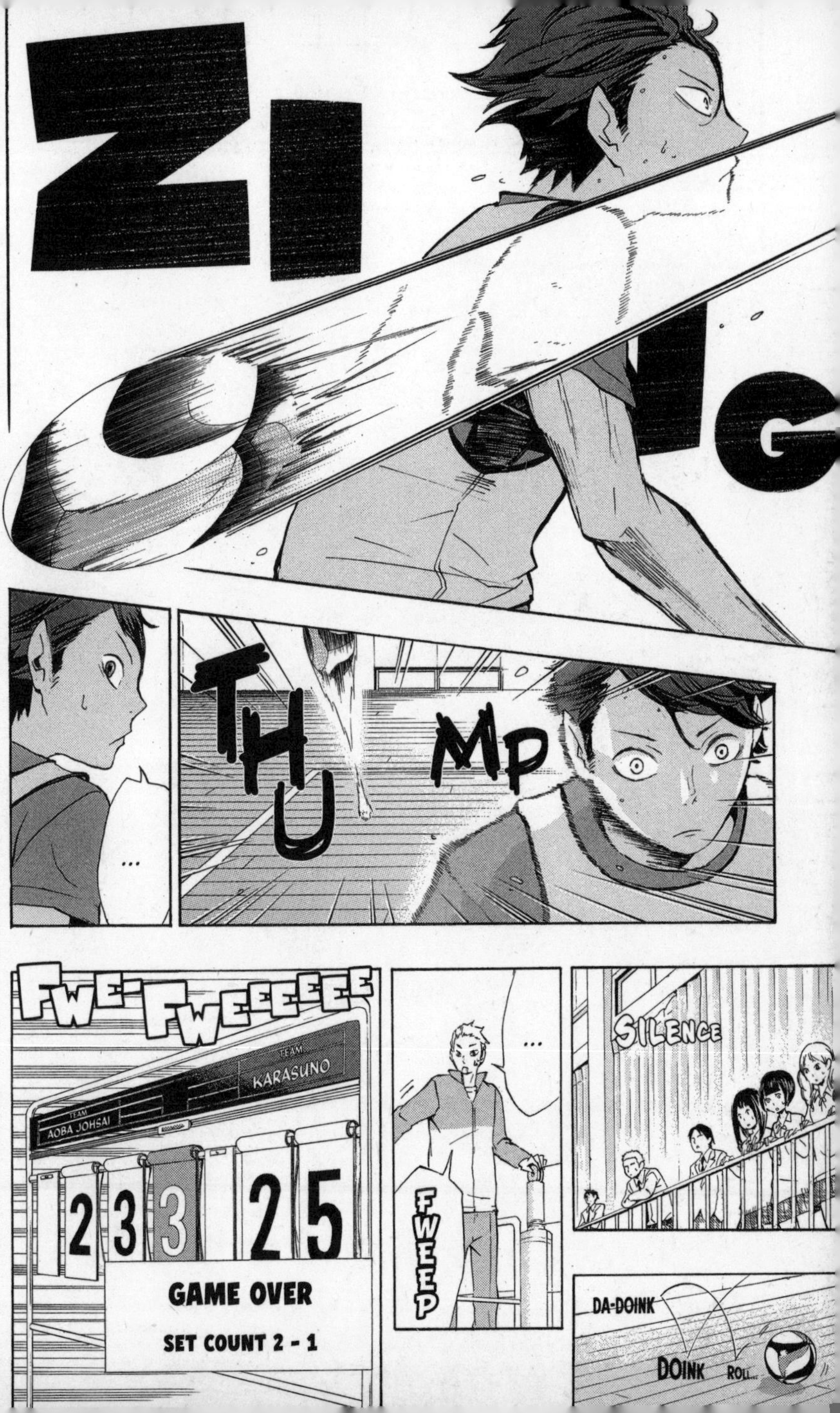

ZING
THUMP
...
SILENCE
DA-DOINK
DOINK
ROLL...
...
FWEEP
FWE-FWEEEEEE
TEAM KARASUNO
TEAM AOBA JOHSAI
2 3 3 2 5
GAME OVER
SET COUNT 2 - 1

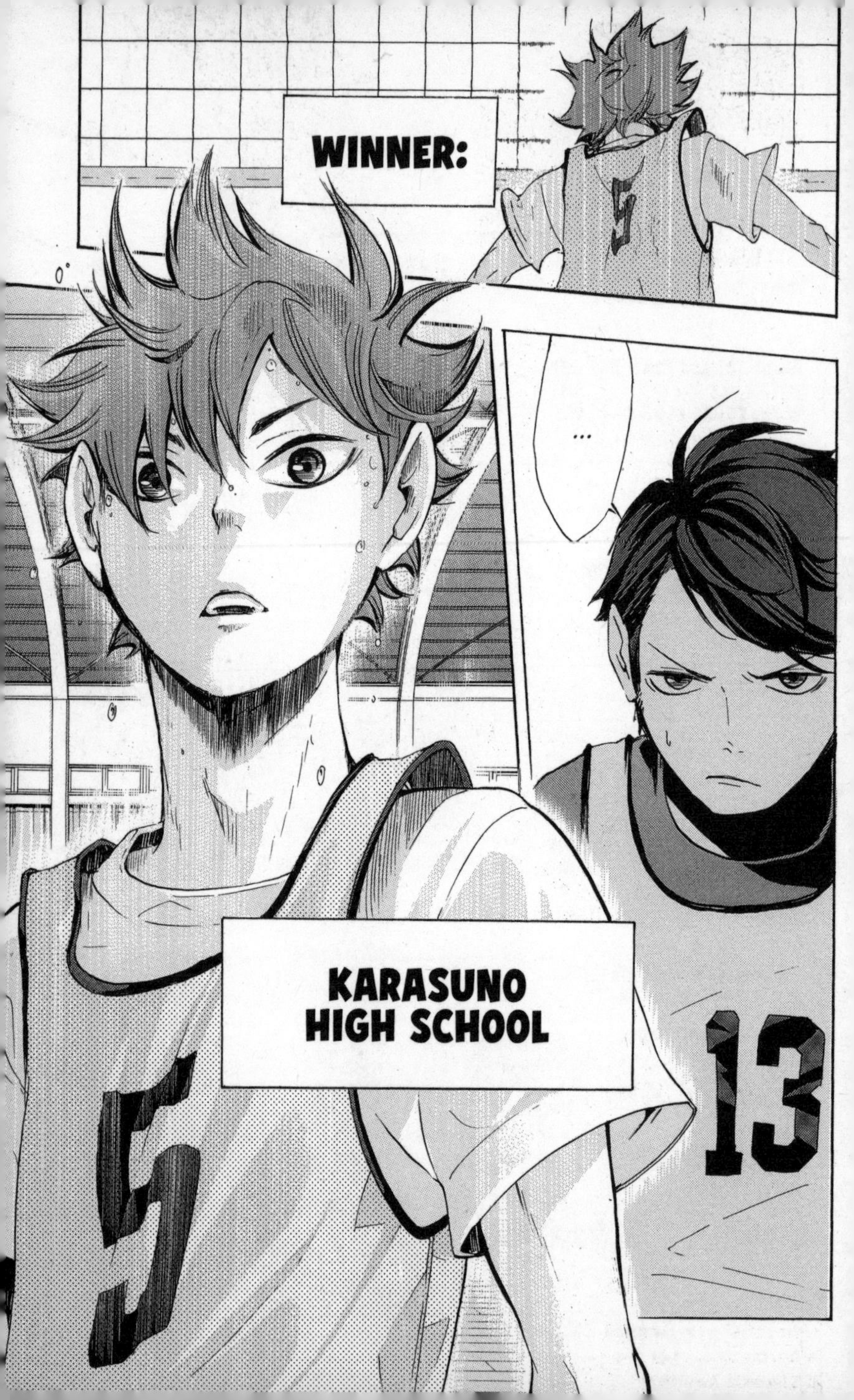
WINNER:
...
KARASUNO HIGH SCHOOL

TOHRU OIKAWA

AOBA JOHSAI HIGH SCHOOL

VOLLEYBALL CLUB CAPTAIN

POSITION:
SETTER

HEIGHT: 6'1"
WEIGHT: 159 LBS.
(AS OF APRIL, 3RD YEAR OF HIGH SCHOOL)

BIRTHDAY: JULY 20

FAVORITE FOOD:
MILK BREAD

CURRENT WORRY:
WHEN HE WENT AND SAID HI TO KARASUNO'S CUTE MANAGER, SHE TOTALLY IGNORED HIM. (SURELY SHE WAS JUST SHY. IT'S NO BIG DEAL, REALLY. DOESN'T BUG HIM AT ALL. NOPE. NUH-UH...)

ABILITY PARAMETERS
(5-POINT SCALE)

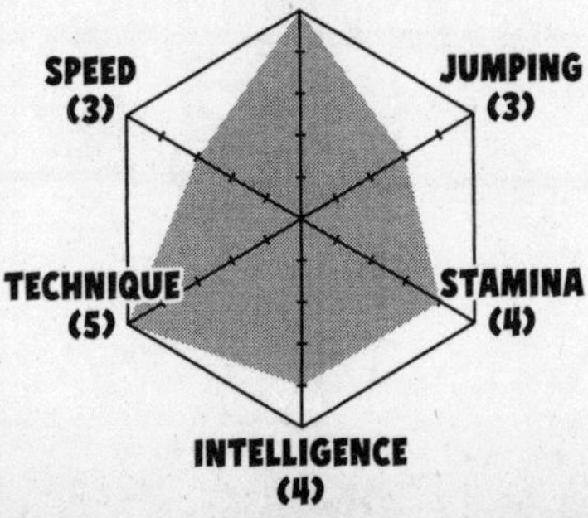
POWER
(5)
JUMPING
(3)
STAMINA
(4)
INTELLIGENCE
(4)
TECHNIQUE
(5)
SPEED
(3)

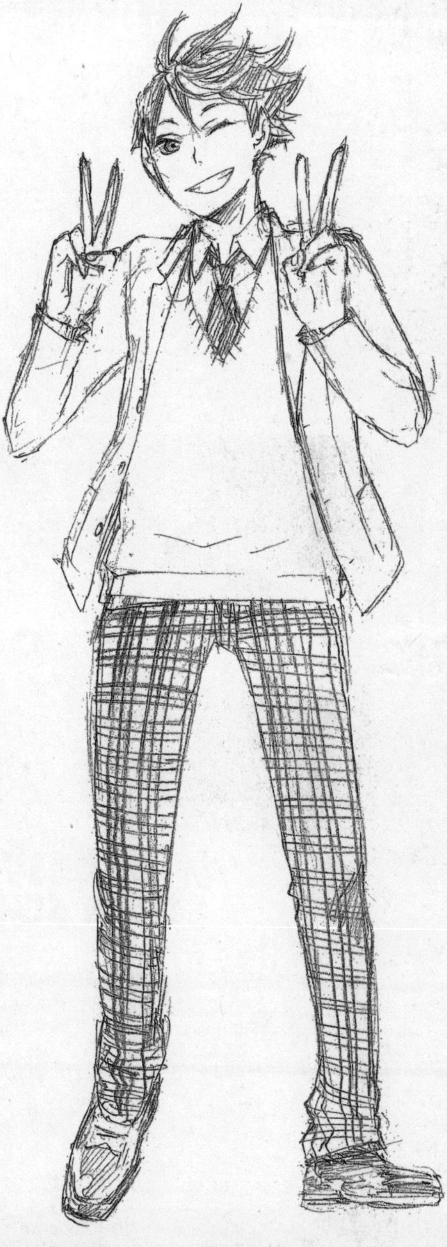

CHAPTER 15: Chemical Reaction

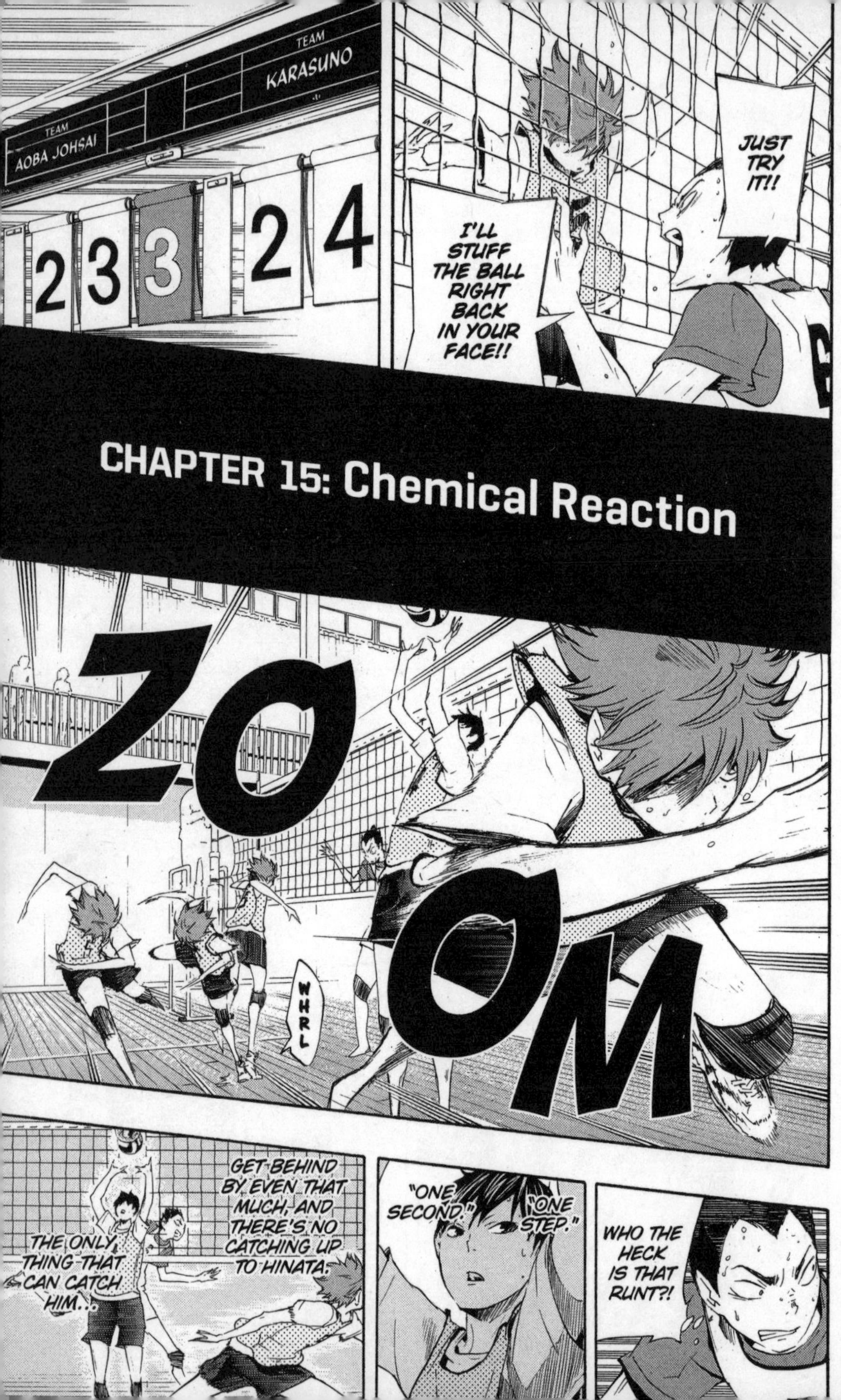
JUST TRY IT!!
I'LL STUFF THE BALL RIGHT BACK IN YOUR FACE!!
TEAM AOBA JOHSAI
TEAM KARASUNO
2 3 3 2 4
CHAPTER 15: Chemical Reaction
ZOOM
WHRL
WHO THE HECK IS THAT RUNT?!
"ONE SECOND."
"ONE STEP."
GET BEHIND BY EVEN THAT MUCH, AND THERE'S NO CATCHING UP TO HINATA.
THE ONLY THING THAT CAN CATCH HIM...

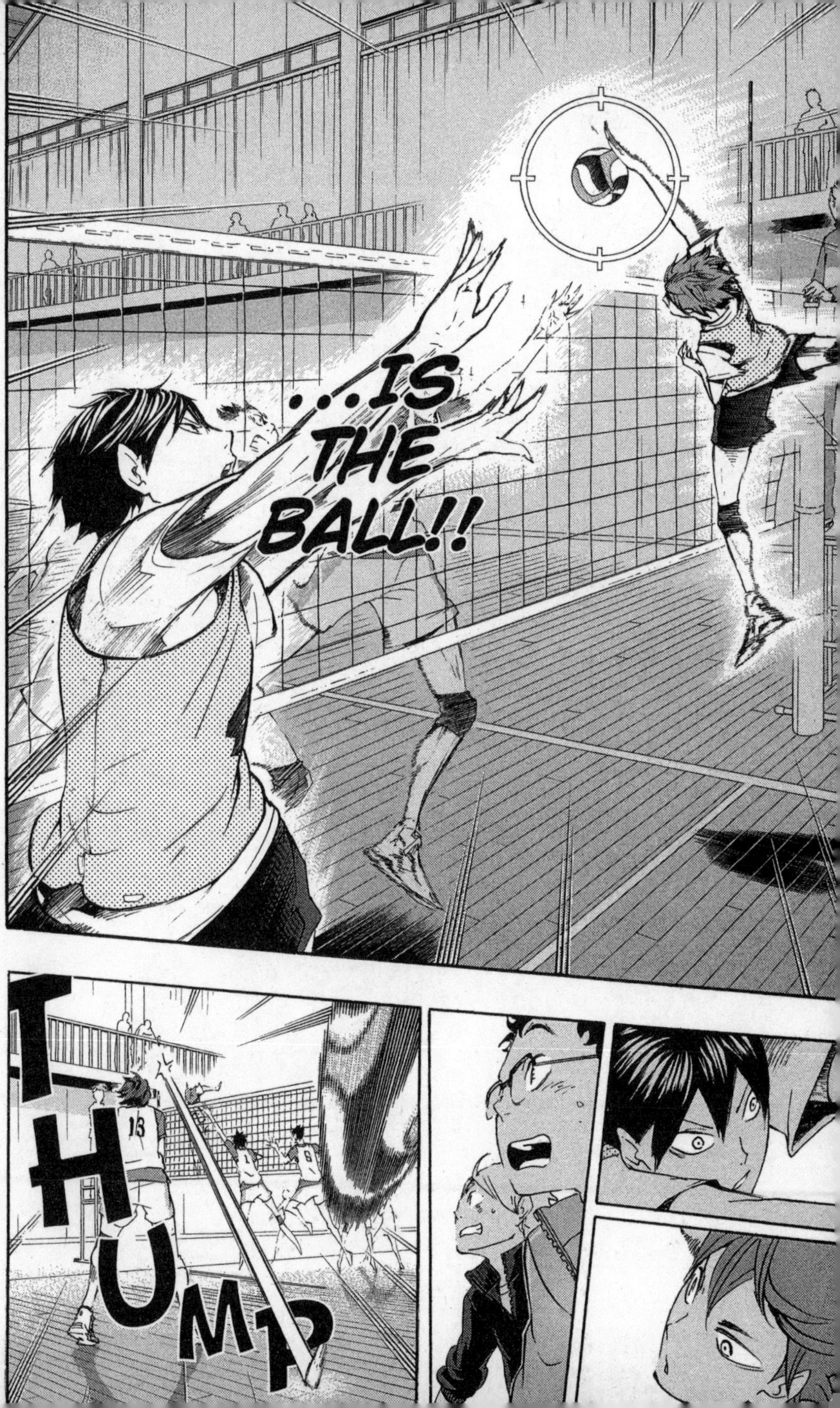
...IS THE BALL!!
THUMP

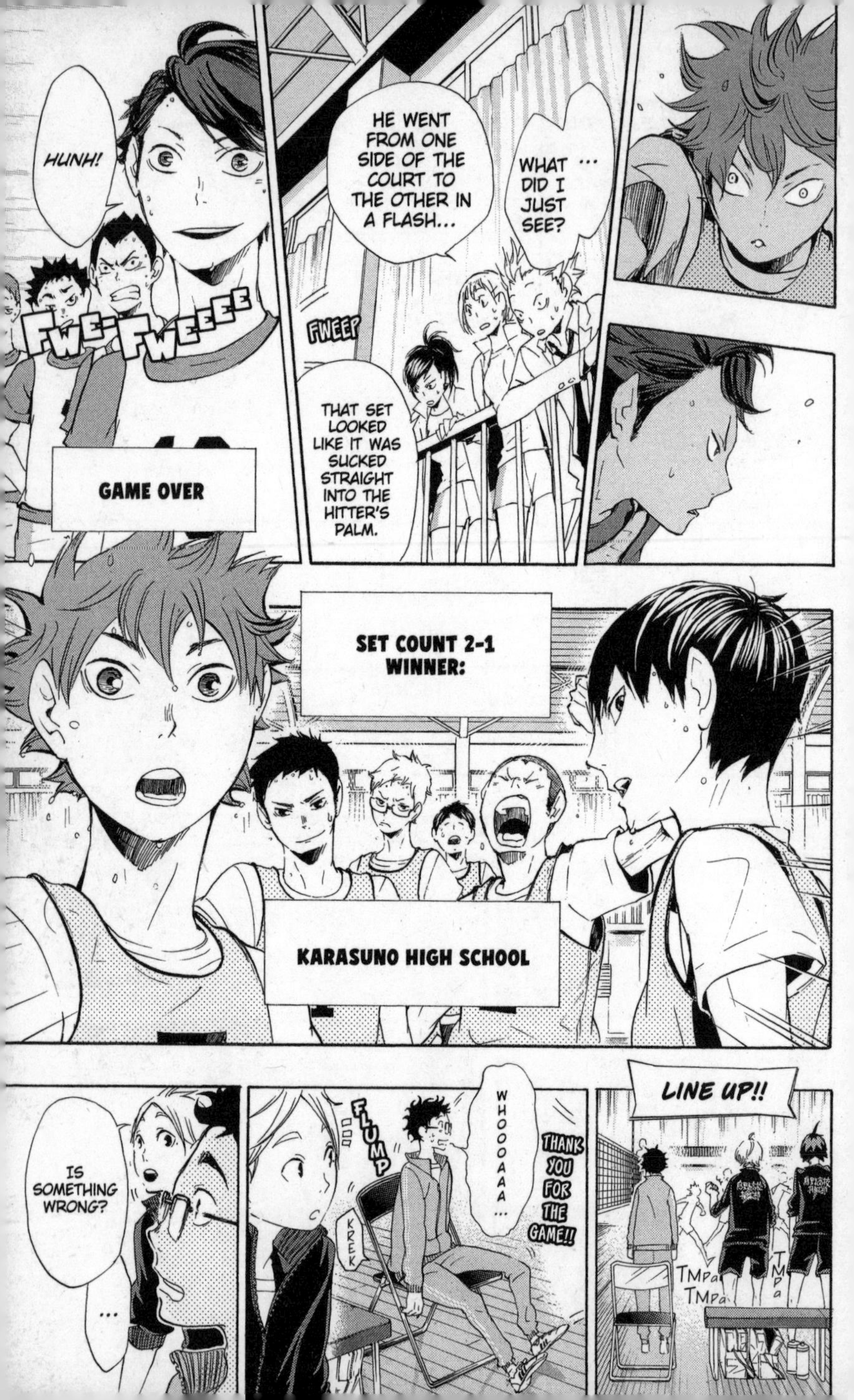

WHAT ... DID I JUST SEE?
HE WENT FROM ONE SIDE OF THE COURT TO THE OTHER IN A FLASH...
FWEEP
THAT SET LOOKED LIKE IT WAS SUCKED STRAIGHT INTO THE HITTER'S PALM.
HUNH!
FWE-FWEEEE
GAME OVER
SET COUNT 2-1
WINNER:
KARASUNO HIGH SCHOOL
LINE UP!!
TMPa TMPa
TMPa
WHOOOAAA...
THANK YOU FOR THE GAME!!
FLUMP
KREK
IS SOMETHING WRONG?
...

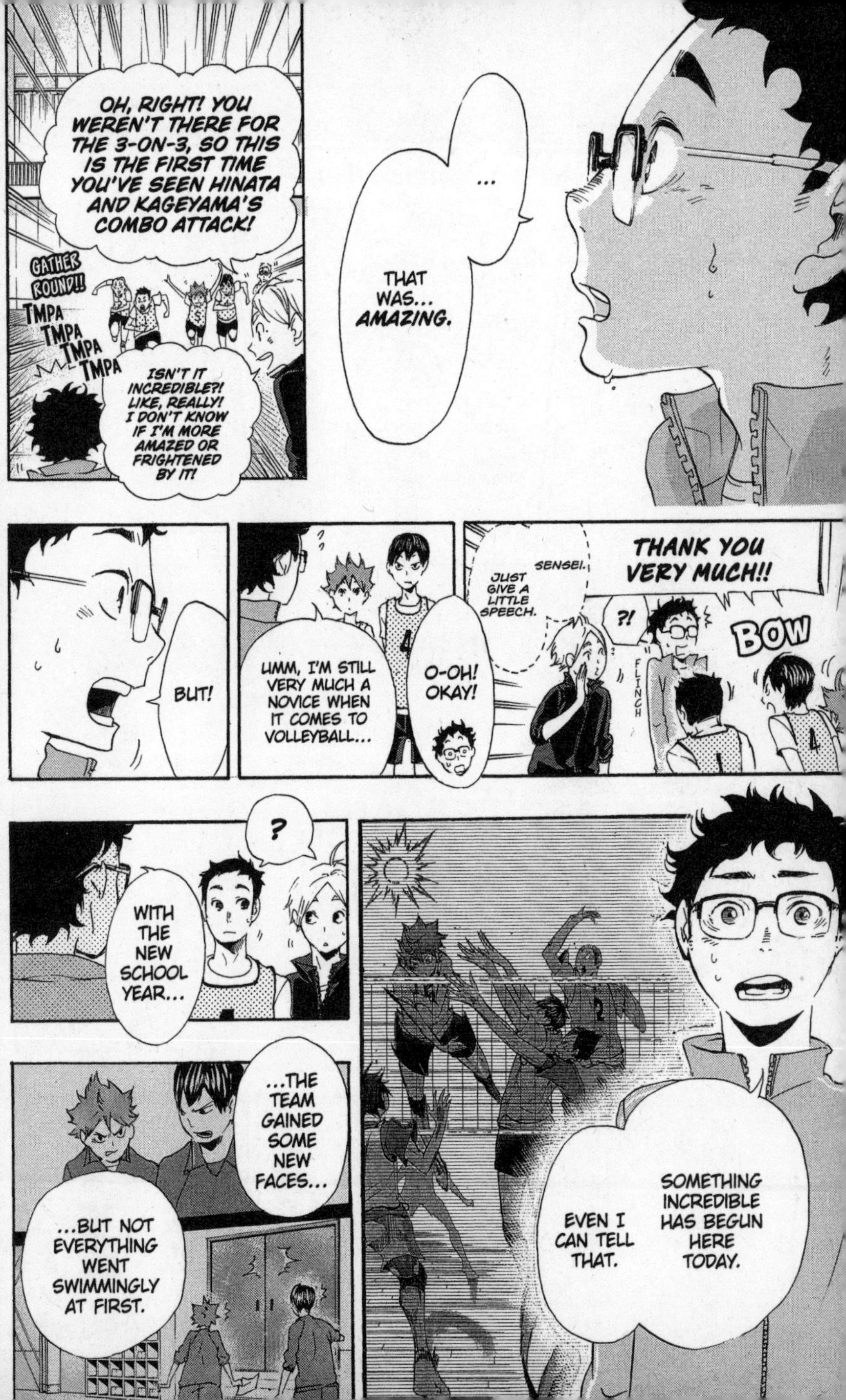
...
THAT WAS... AMAZING.
OH, RIGHT! YOU WEREN'T THERE FOR THE 3-ON-3, SO THIS IS THE FIRST TIME YOU'VE SEEN HINATA AND KAGEYAMA'S COMBO ATTACK!
GATHER ROUND!!
TMPA TMPA TMPA TMPA
ISN'T IT INCREDIBLE?! LIKE, REALLY! I DON'T KNOW IF I'M MORE AMAZED OR FRIGHTENED BY IT!
THANK YOU VERY MUCH!!
BOW
SENSEI.
JUST GIVE A LITTLE SPEECH.
?!
FLINCH
O-OH! OKAY!
UMM, I'M STILL VERY MUCH A NOVICE WHEN IT COMES TO VOLLEYBALL...
BUT!
SOMETHING INCREDIBLE HAS BEGUN HERE TODAY.
EVEN I CAN TELL THAT.
?
WITH THE NEW SCHOOL YEAR...
...THE TEAM GAINED SOME NEW FACES...
...BUT NOT EVERYTHING WENT SWIMMINGLY AT FIRST.

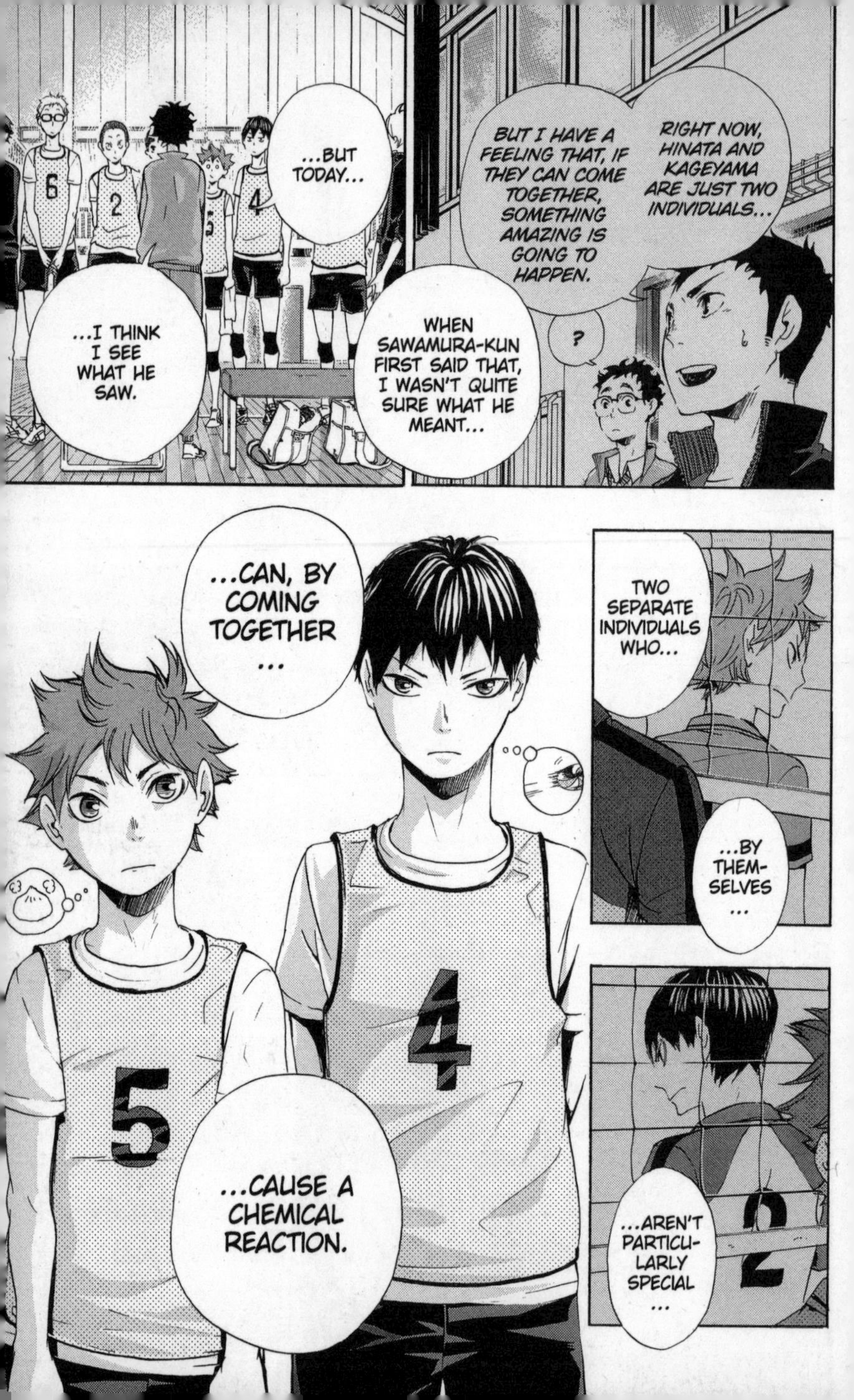
RIGHT NOW, HINATA AND KAGEYAMA ARE JUST TWO INDIVIDUALS...
BUT I HAVE A FEELING THAT, IF THEY CAN COME TOGETHER, SOMETHING AMAZING IS GOING TO HAPPEN.
?
WHEN SAWAMURA-KUN FIRST SAID THAT, I WASN'T QUITE SURE WHAT HE MEANT...
...BUT TODAY...
...I THINK I SEE WHAT HE SAW.
TWO SEPARATE INDIVIDUALS WHO...
...BY THEM-SELVES ...
...AREN'T PARTICU-LARLY SPECIAL ...
...CAN, BY COMING TOGETHER ...
...CAUSE A CHEMICAL REACTION.

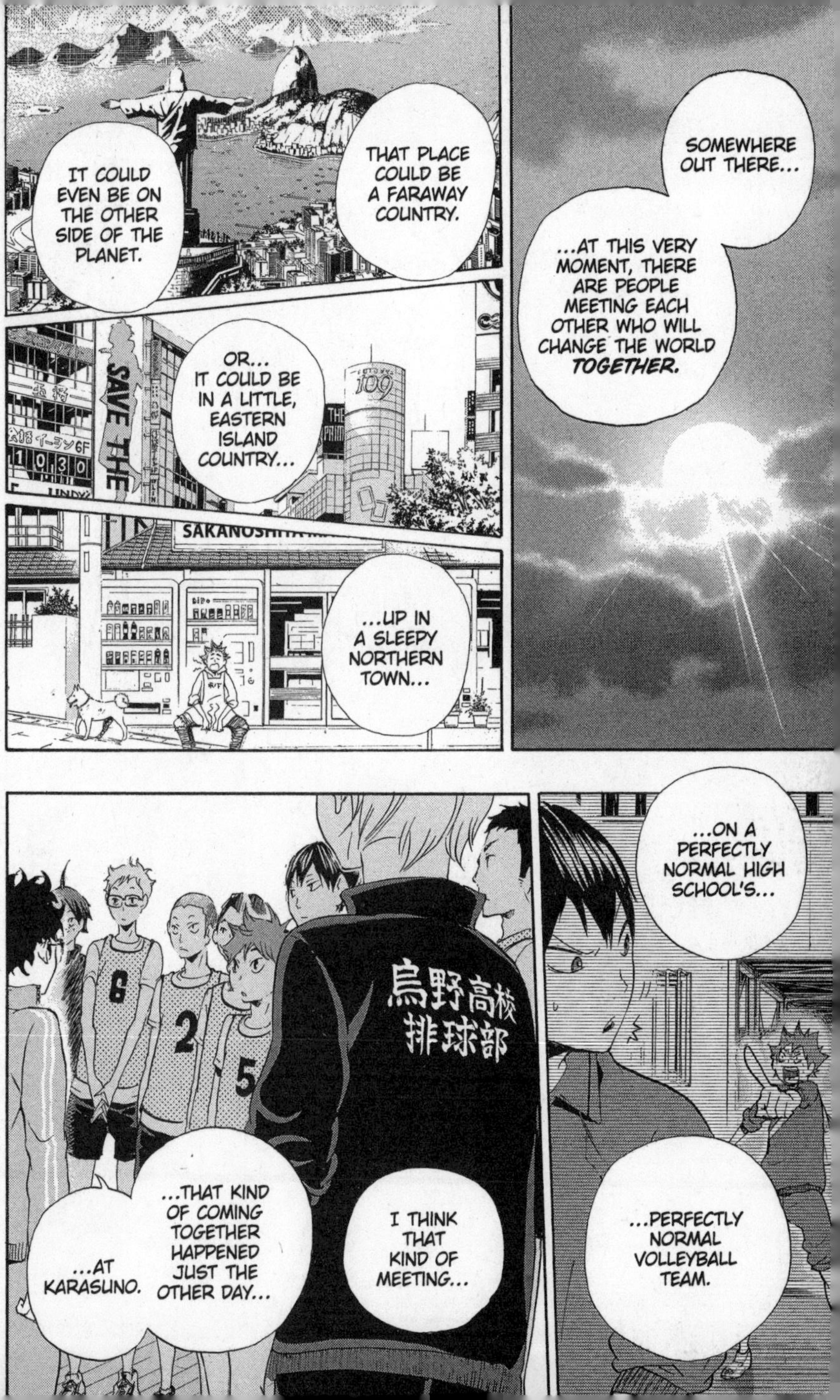
SOMEWHERE OUT THERE...
...AT THIS VERY MOMENT, THERE ARE PEOPLE MEETING EACH OTHER WHO WILL CHANGE THE WORLD *TOGETHER.*
THAT PLACE COULD BE A FARAWAY COUNTRY.
IT COULD EVEN BE ON THE OTHER SIDE OF THE PLANET.
OR... IT COULD BE IN A LITTLE, EASTERN ISLAND COUNTRY...
SAVE THE
109
...UP IN A SLEEPY NORTHERN TOWN...
...ON A PERFECTLY NORMAL HIGH SCHOOL'S...
...PERFECTLY NORMAL VOLLEYBALL TEAM.
烏野高校
排球部
I THINK THAT KIND OF MEETING...
...THAT KIND OF COMING TOGETHER HAPPENED JUST THE OTHER DAY...
...AT KARASUNO.

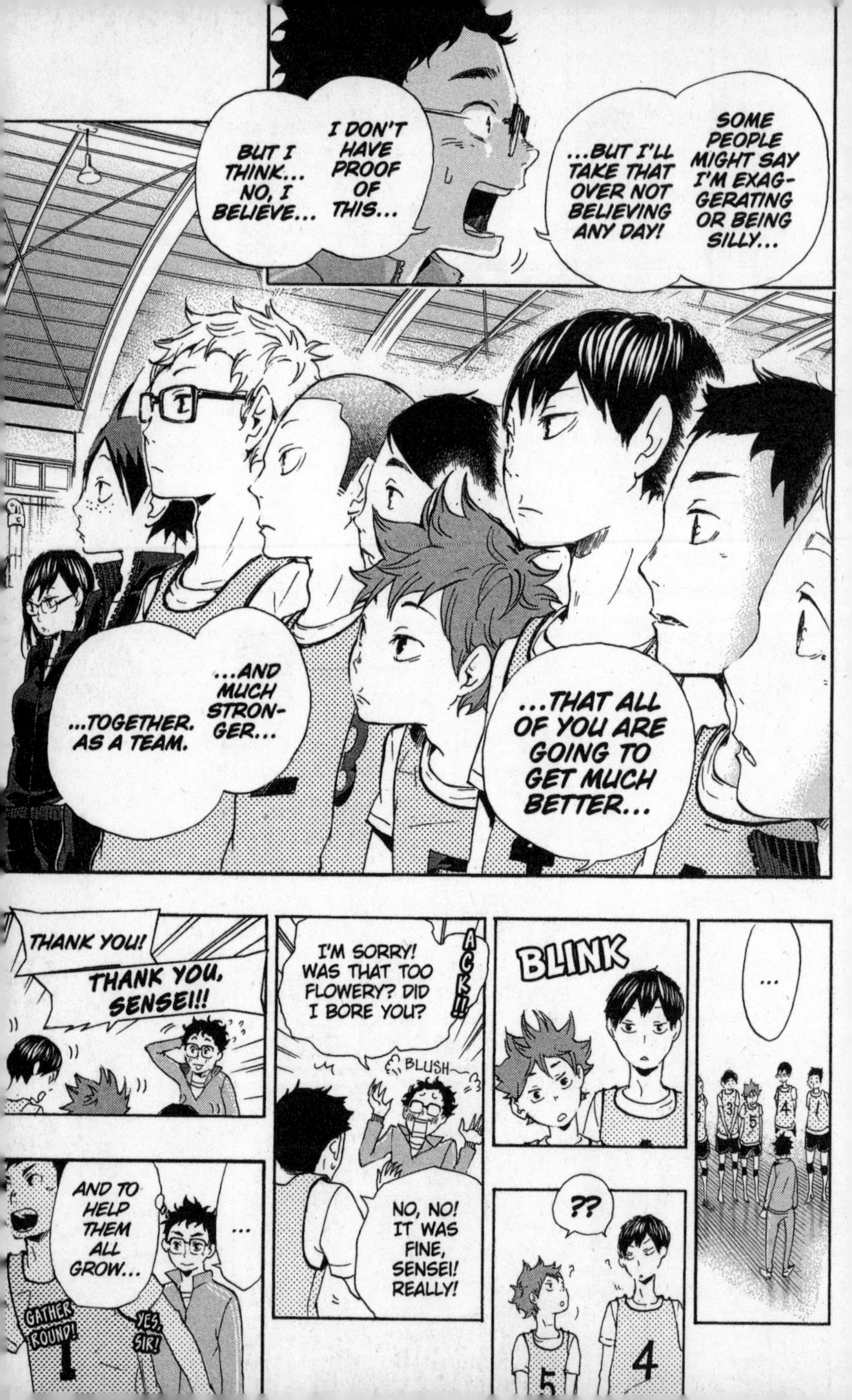
SOME PEOPLE MIGHT SAY I'M EXAG-GERATING OR BEING SILLY...
...BUT I'LL TAKE THAT OVER NOT BELIEVING ANY DAY!
I DON'T HAVE PROOF OF THIS...
BUT I THINK... NO, I BELIEVE...
...THAT ALL OF YOU ARE GOING TO GET MUCH BETTER...
...AND MUCH STRON-GER...
...TOGETHER. AS A TEAM.
...
BLINK
??
ACK!!
I'M SORRY! WAS THAT TOO FLOWERY? DID I BORE YOU?
BLUSH
NO, NO! IT WAS FINE, SENSEI! REALLY!
THANK YOU!
THANK YOU, SENSEI!!
...
AND TO HELP THEM ALL GROW...
YES, SIR!
GATHER ROUND!

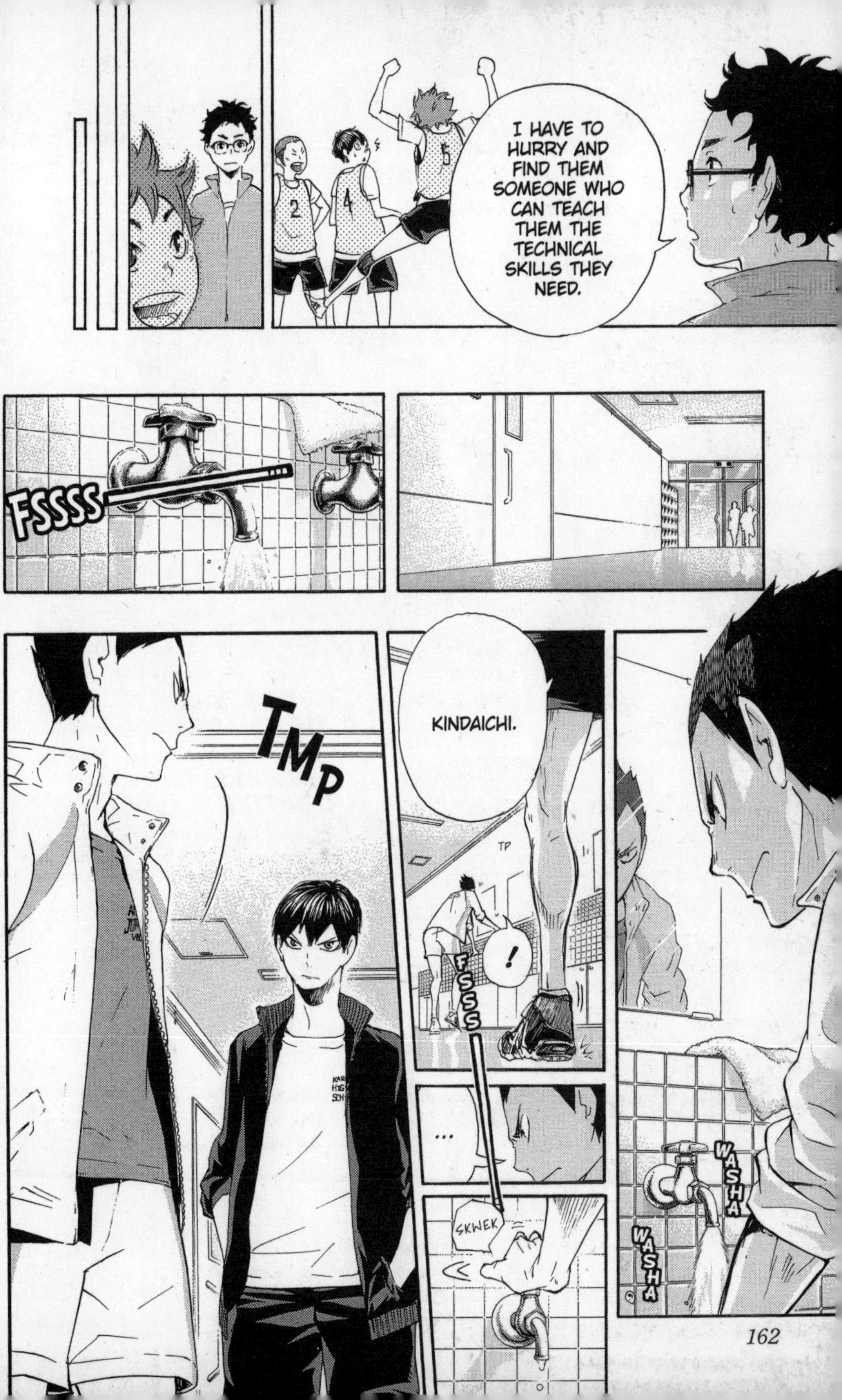
I HAVE TO HURRY AND FIND THEM SOMEONE WHO CAN TEACH THEM THE TECHNICAL SKILLS THEY NEED.
FSSSS
WASHA
WASHA
KINDAICHI.
TP
!
FSSS
...
SKWEK
TMP

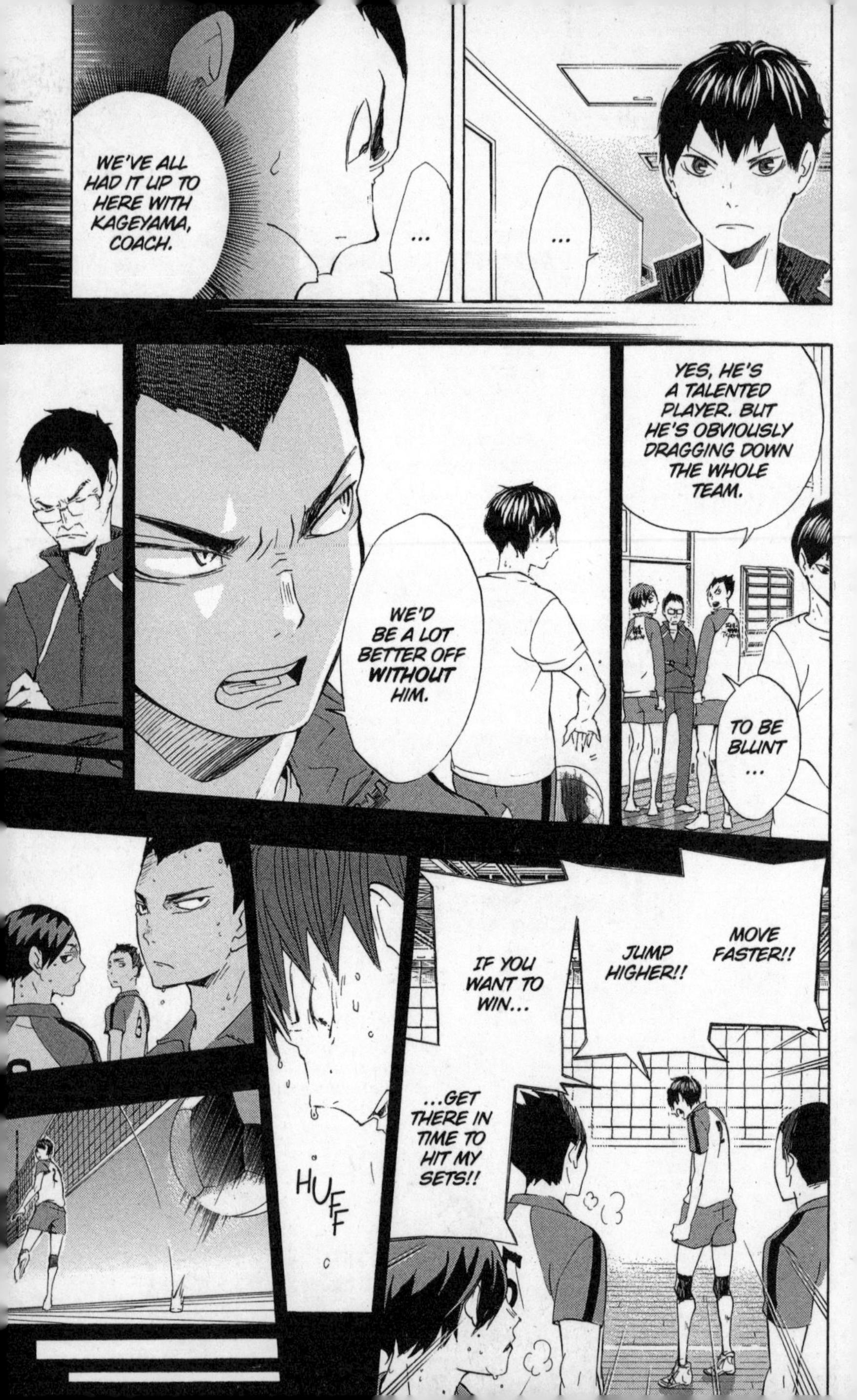
...
...
WE'VE ALL HAD IT UP TO HERE WITH KAGEYAMA, COACH.
YES, HE'S A TALENTED PLAYER. BUT HE'S OBVIOUSLY DRAGGING DOWN THE WHOLE TEAM.
TO BE BLUNT...
WE'D BE A LOT BETTER OFF WITHOUT HIM.
MOVE FASTER!!
JUMP HIGHER!!
IF YOU WANT TO WIN...
...GET THERE IN TIME TO HIT MY SETS!!
HUFF

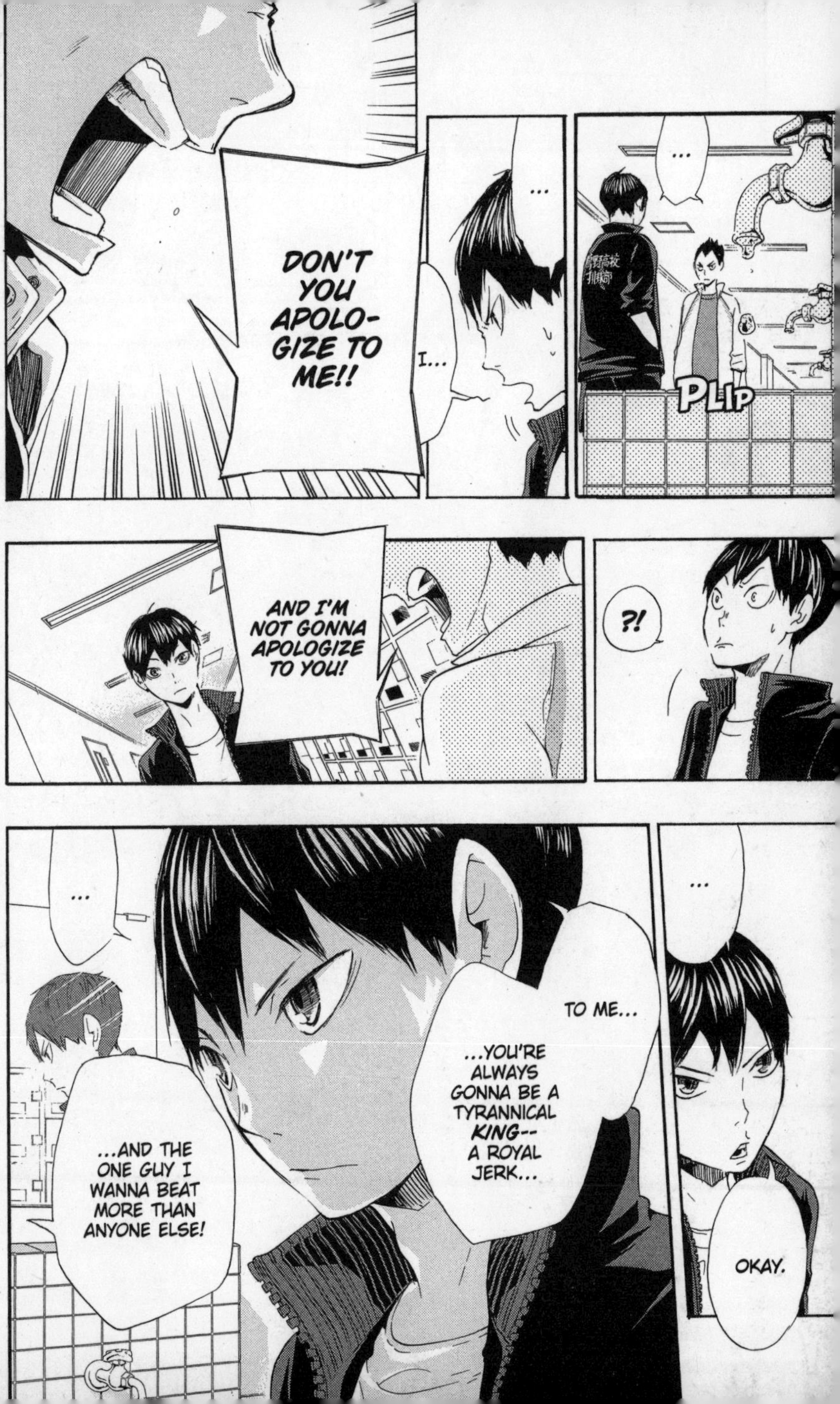
...
PLIP
...
I...
DON'T YOU APOLOGIZE TO ME!!
?!
AND I'M NOT GONNA APOLOGIZE TO YOU!
...
OKAY.
...
TO ME...
...YOU'RE ALWAYS GONNA BE A TYRANNICAL KING-- A ROYAL JERK...
...AND THE ONE GUY I WANNA BEAT MORE THAN ANYONE ELSE!

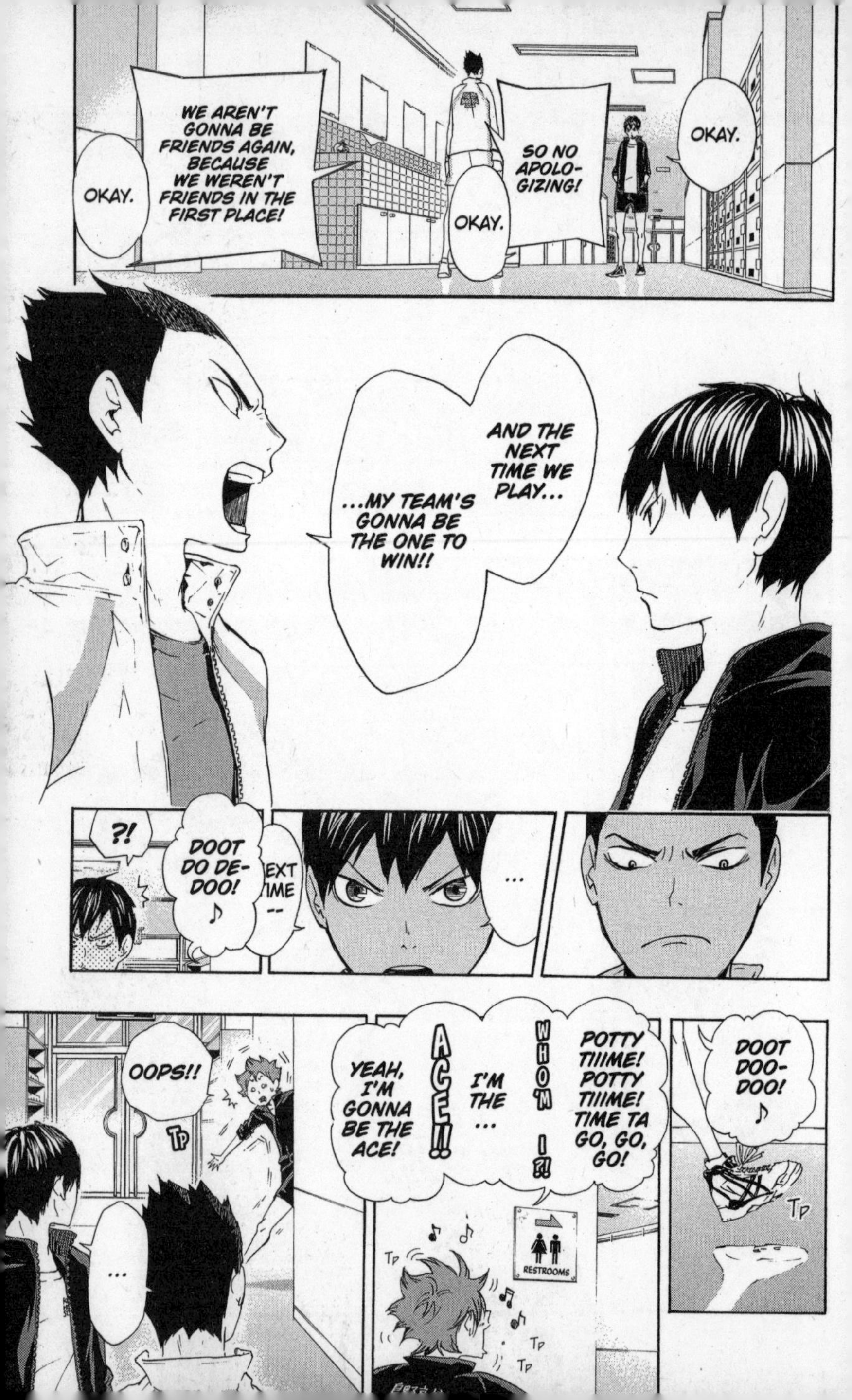
OKAY.
SO NO APOLO-GIZING!
OKAY.
WE AREN'T GONNA BE FRIENDS AGAIN, BECAUSE WE WEREN'T FRIENDS IN THE FIRST PLACE!
OKAY.
AND THE NEXT TIME WE PLAY...
...MY TEAM'S GONNA BE THE ONE TO WIN!!
...
EXT IME --
DOOT DO DE-DOO! ♪
?!
DOOT DOO-DOO! ♪
Tp
POTTY TIIIME! POTTY TIIIME! TIME TA GO, GO, GO!
WHO'M I?!
I'M THE...
ACE!!
YEAH, I'M GONNA BE THE ACE!
RESTROOMS
Tp
Tp
Tp
OOPS!!
Tp
...

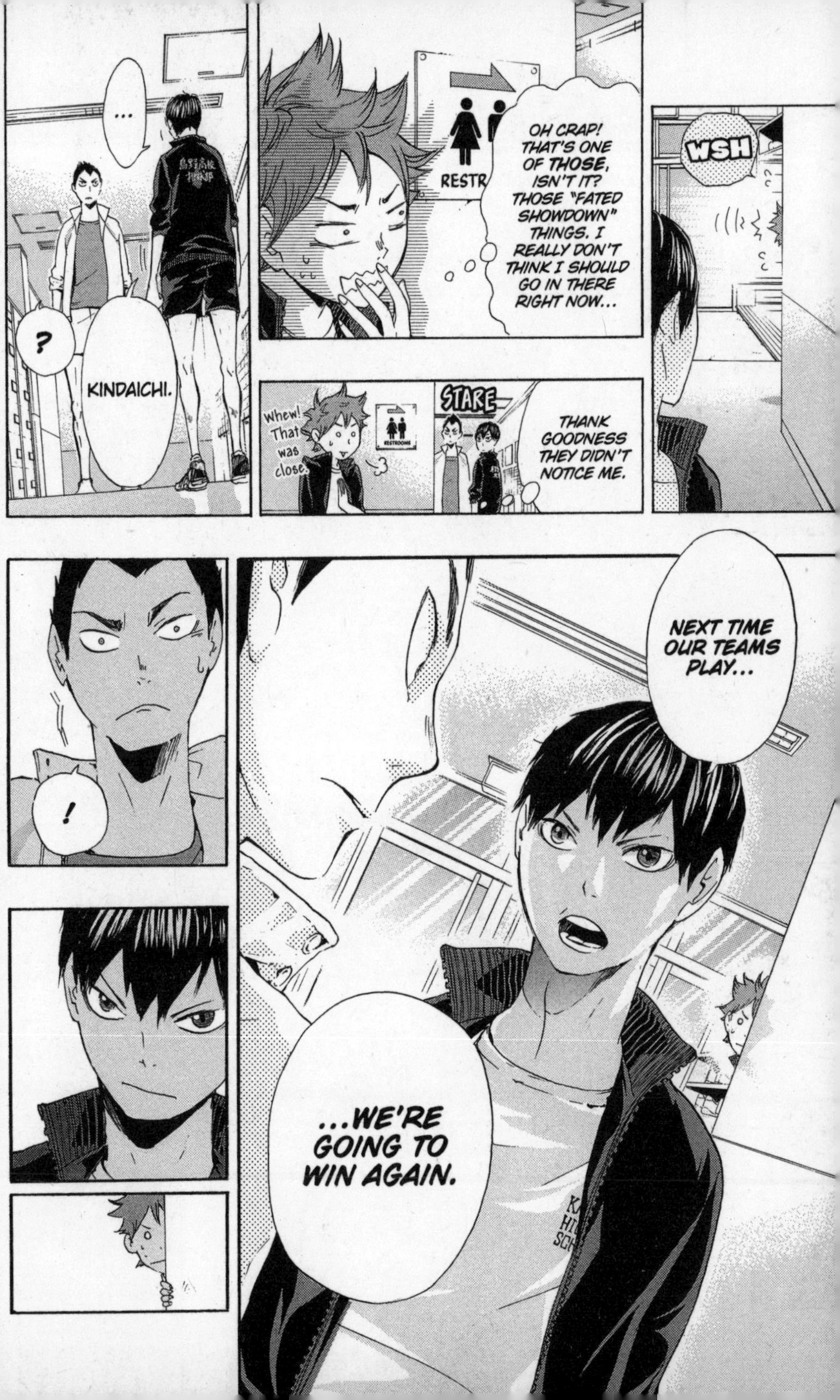
WSH
RESTR
OH CRAP! THAT'S ONE OF THOSE, ISN'T IT? THOSE "FATED SHOWDOWN" THINGS. I REALLY DON'T THINK I SHOULD GO IN THERE RIGHT NOW...
THANK GOODNESS THEY DIDN'T NOTICE ME.
STARE
RESTROOMS
Whew! That was close.
...
?
KINDAICHI.
NEXT TIME OUR TEAMS PLAY...
...WE'RE GOING TO WIN AGAIN.
!

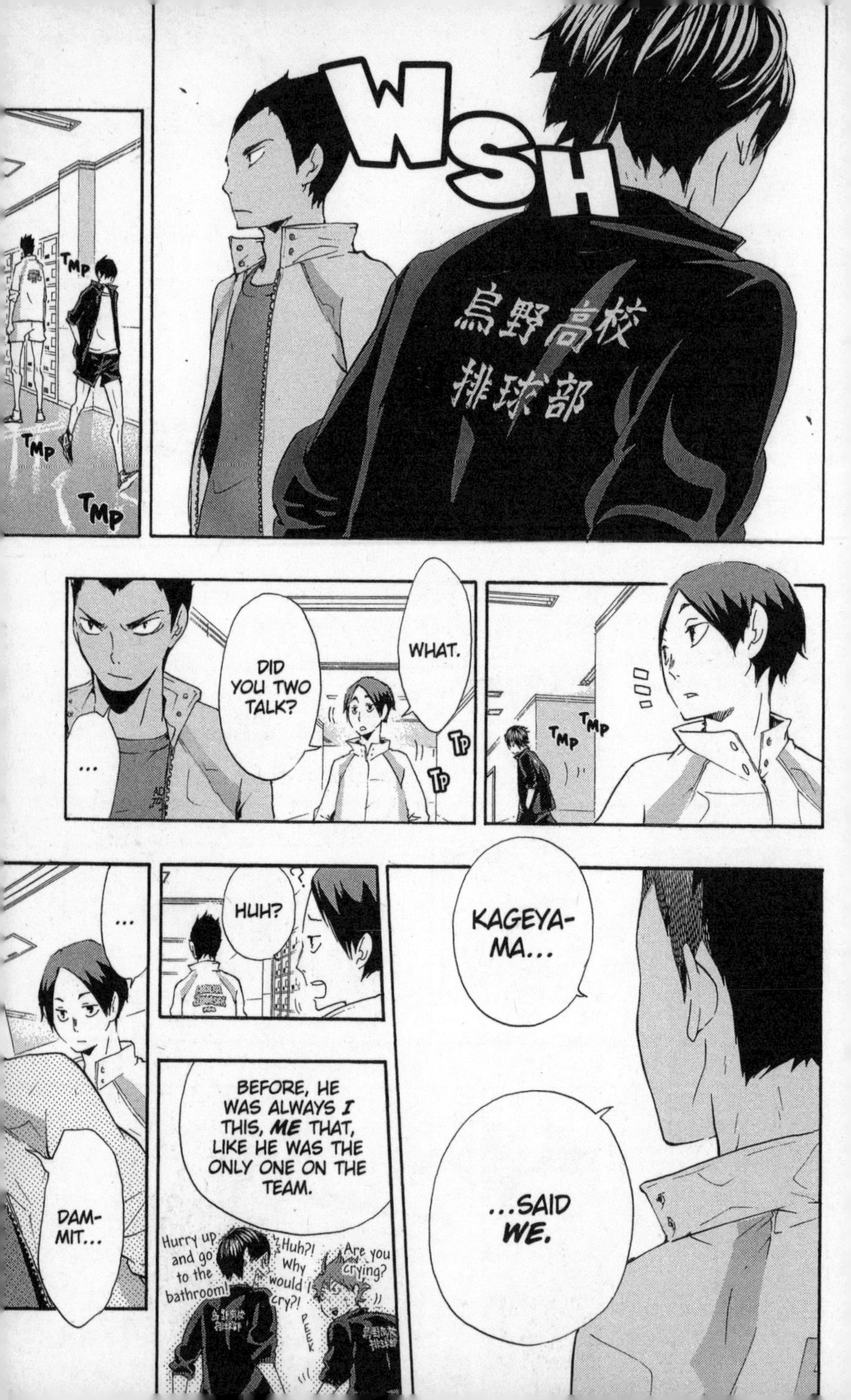
WSH
烏野高校
排球部
TMP
TMP
TMP
TMP
...
TMP
TMP
WHAT.
DID YOU TWO TALK?
Tp
Tp
...
KAGEYAMA...
...SAID WE.
HUH?
BEFORE, HE WAS ALWAYS I THIS, ME THAT, LIKE HE WAS THE ONLY ONE ON THE TEAM.
Are you crying?
Huh?! Why would I cry?!
Hurry up and go to the bathroom!
PEEK
...
DAMMIT...

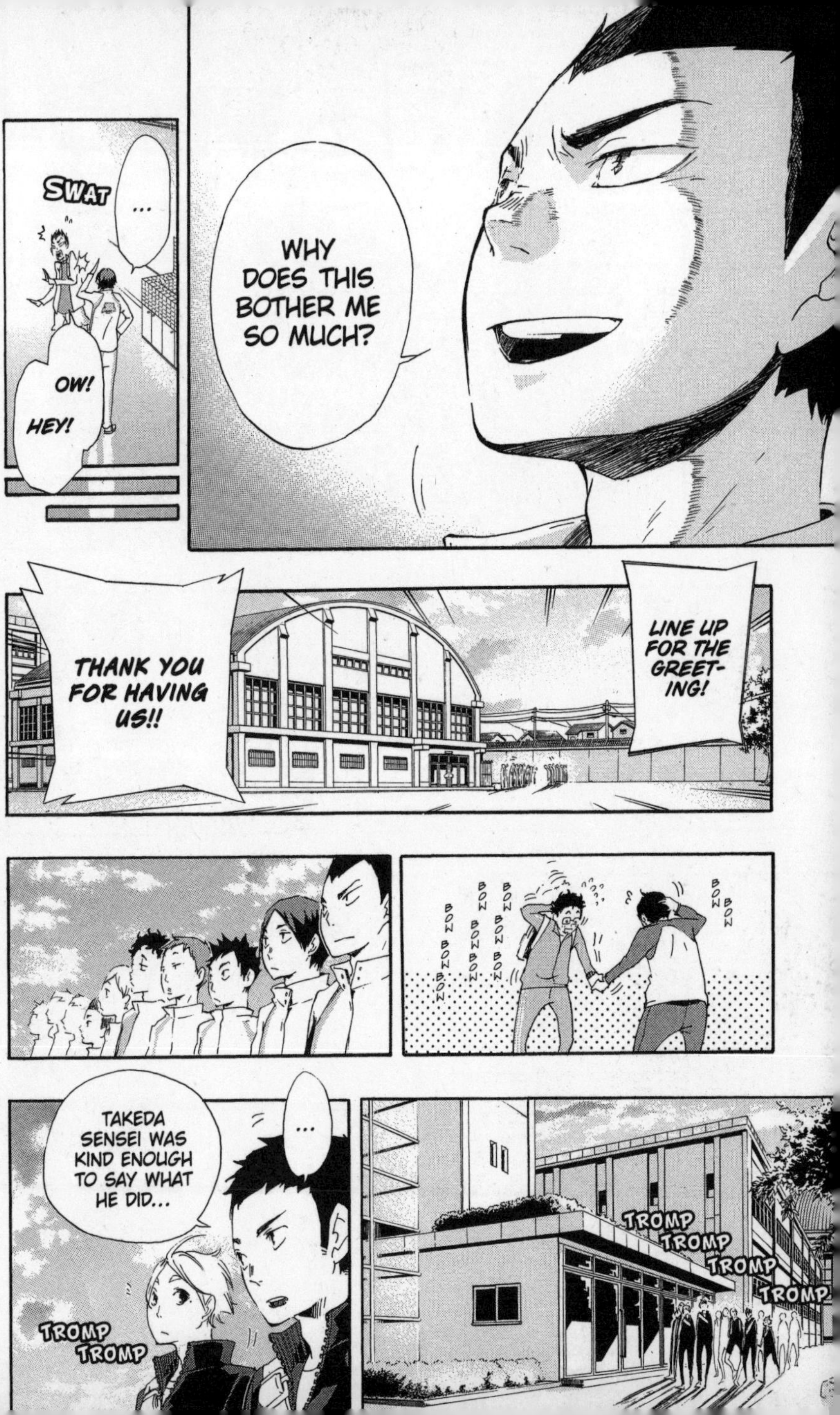
WHY DOES THIS BOTHER ME SO MUCH?
...
SWAT
OW!
HEY!
LINE UP FOR THE GREET-ING!
THANK YOU FOR HAVING US!!
BOW BOW
BOW BOW BOW BOW
BOW BOW BOW BOW
BOW BOW BOW BOW
TROMP TROMP TROMP TROMP
...
TAKEDA SENSEI WAS KIND ENOUGH TO SAY WHAT HE DID...
TROMP TROMP

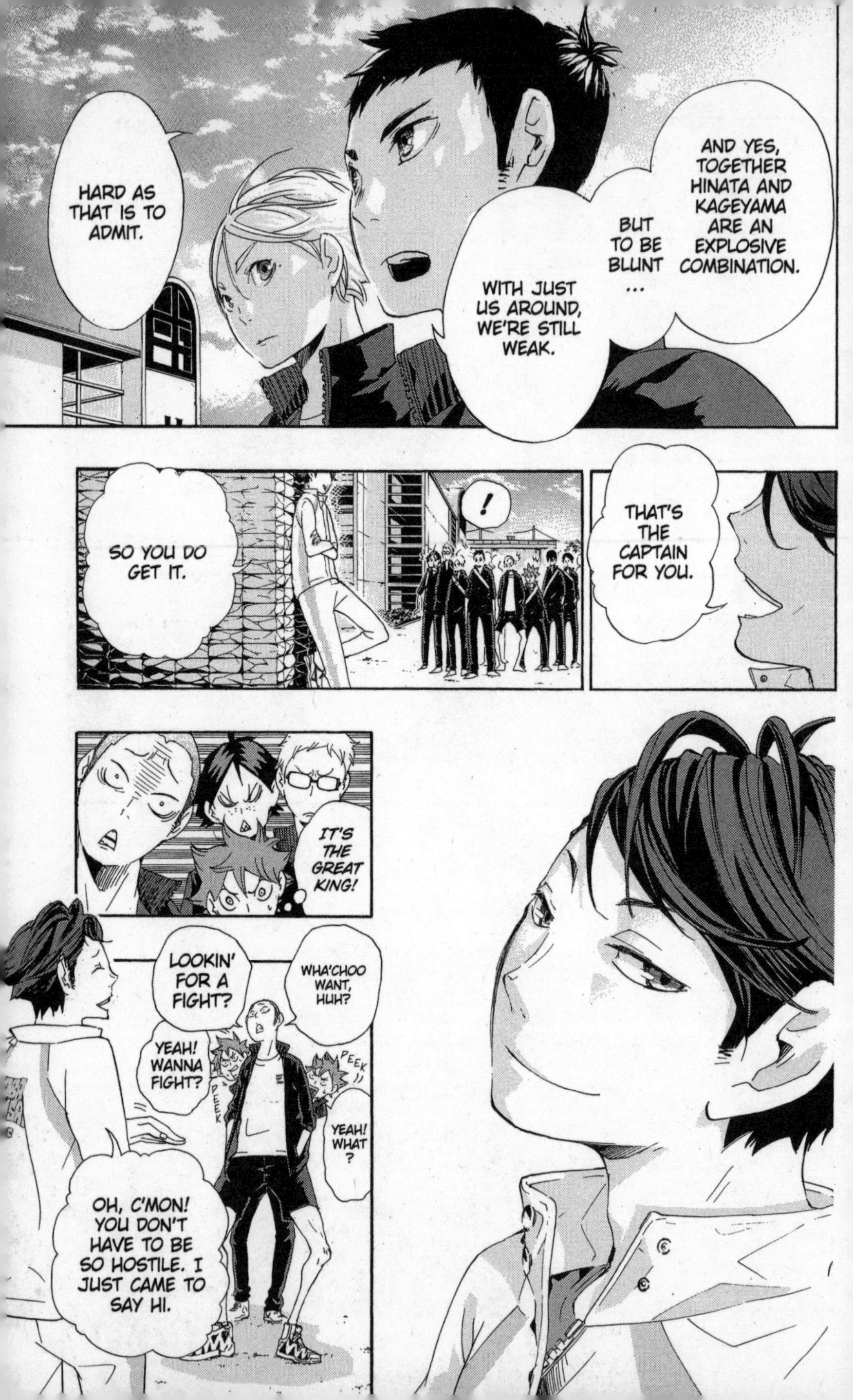
AND YES, TOGETHER HINATA AND KAGEYAMA ARE AN EXPLOSIVE COMBINATION.
BUT TO BE BLUNT ...
WITH JUST US AROUND, WE'RE STILL WEAK.
HARD AS THAT IS TO ADMIT.
THAT'S THE CAPTAIN FOR YOU.
!
SO YOU DO GET IT.
IT'S THE GREAT KING!
WHA'CHOO WANT, HUH?
LOOKIN' FOR A FIGHT?
PEEK
YEAH! WHAT ?
YEAH! WANNA FIGHT?
PEEK
OH, C'MON! YOU DON'T HAVE TO BE SO HOSTILE. I JUST CAME TO SAY HI.

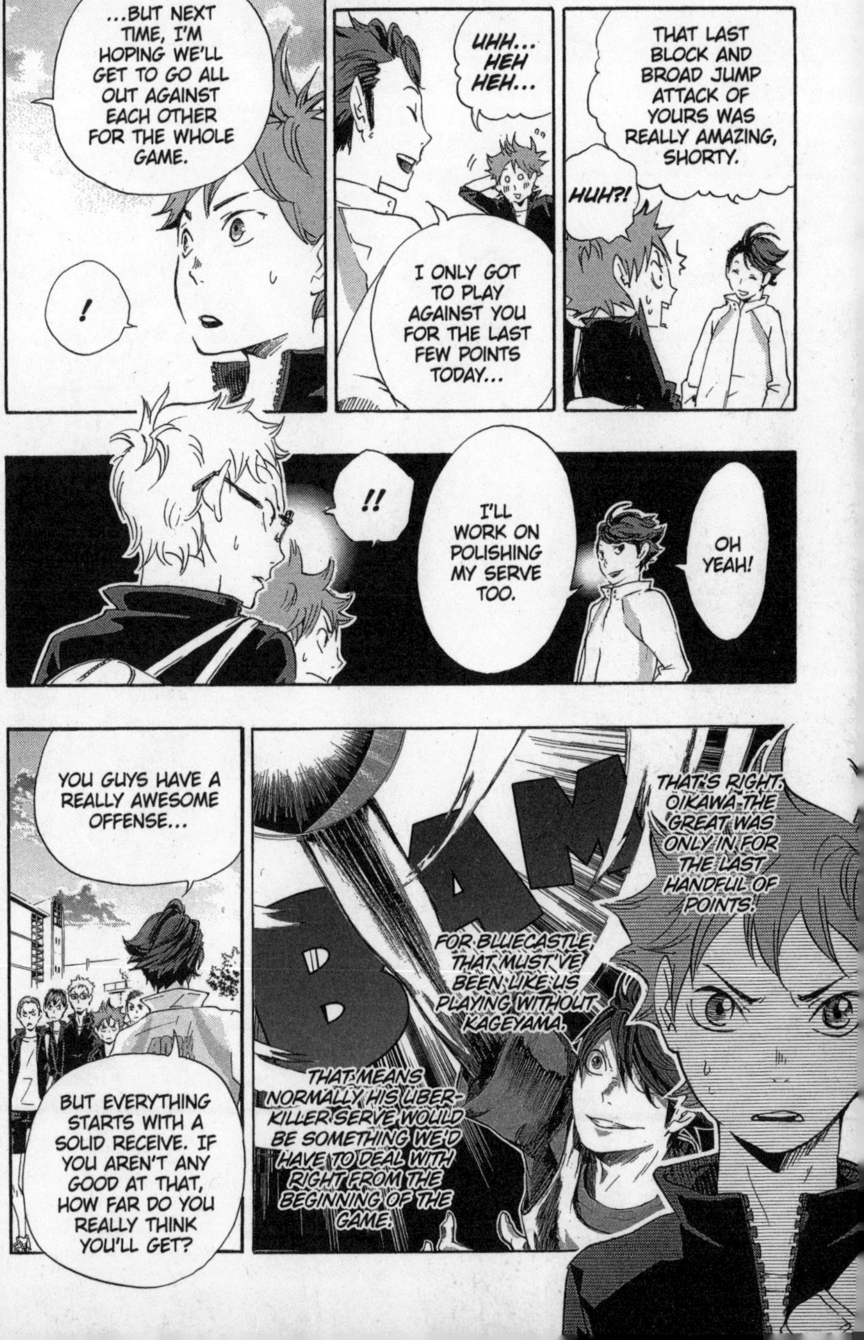
THAT LAST BLOCK AND BROAD JUMP ATTACK OF YOURS WAS REALLY AMAZING, SHORTY.
HUH?!
UHH... HEH HEH...
I ONLY GOT TO PLAY AGAINST YOU FOR THE LAST FEW POINTS TODAY...
...BUT NEXT TIME, I'M HOPING WE'LL GET TO GO ALL OUT AGAINST EACH OTHER FOR THE WHOLE GAME.
!
OH YEAH!
I'LL WORK ON POLISHING MY SERVE TOO.
!!
THAT'S RIGHT, OIKAWA THE GREAT WAS ONLY IN FOR THE LAST HANDFUL OF POINTS.
FOR BLUECASTLE, THAT MUST'VE BEEN LIKE US PLAYING WITHOUT KAGEYAMA.
THAT MEANS NORMALLY HIS LIBER-KILLER SERVE WOULD BE SOMETHING WE'D HAVE TO DEAL WITH RIGHT FROM THE BEGINNING OF THE GAME.
BAM
YOU GUYS HAVE A REALLY AWESOME OFFENSE...
BUT EVERYTHING STARTS WITH A SOLID RECEIVE. IF YOU AREN'T ANY GOOD AT THAT, HOW FAR DO YOU REALLY THINK YOU'LL GET?

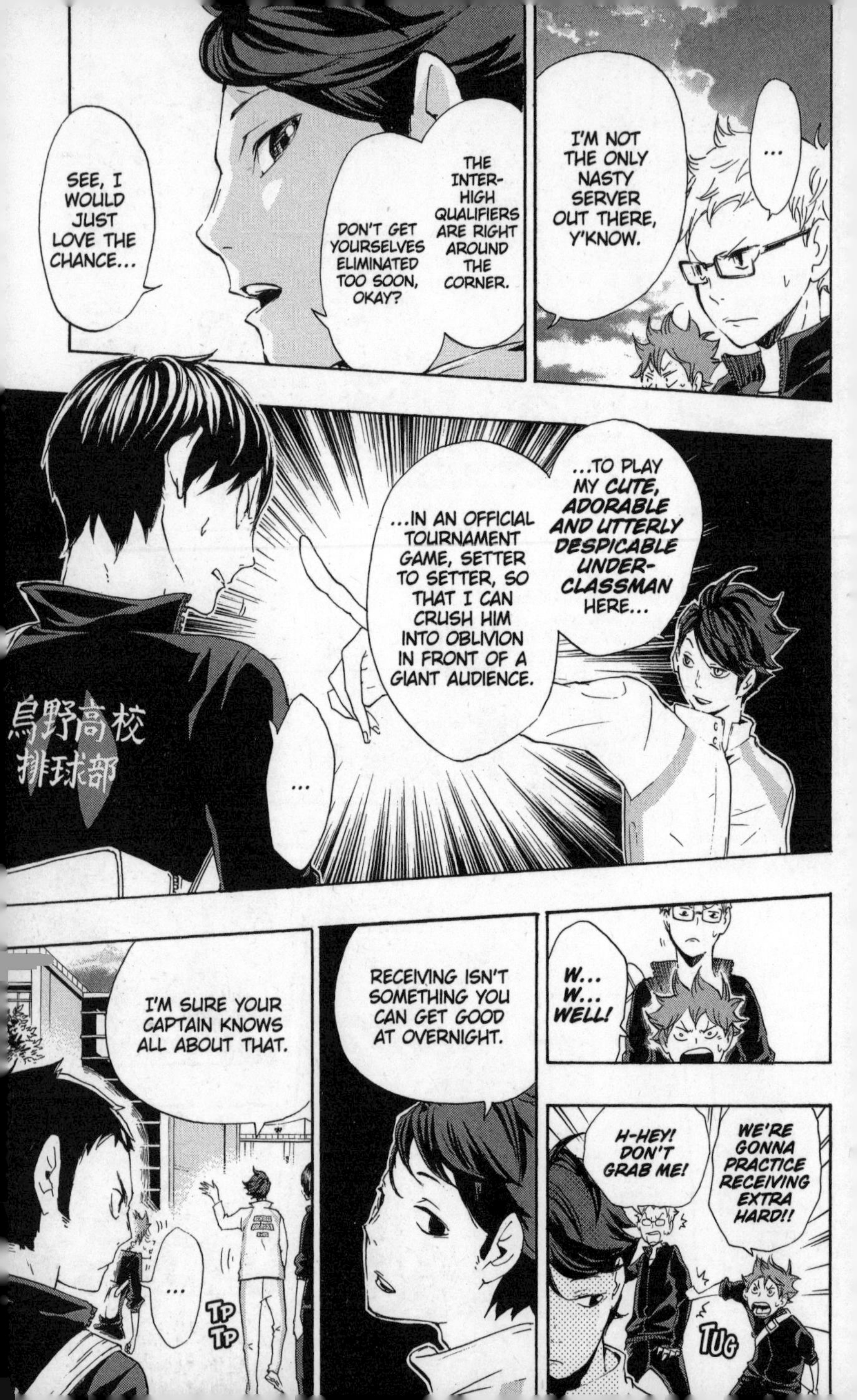
...
I'M NOT THE ONLY NASTY SERVER OUT THERE, Y'KNOW.
THE INTER-HIGH QUALIFIERS ARE RIGHT AROUND THE CORNER.
DON'T GET YOURSELVES ELIMINATED TOO SOON, OKAY?
SEE, I WOULD JUST LOVE THE CHANCE...
...TO PLAY MY CUTE, ADORABLE AND UTTERLY DESPICABLE UNDER-CLASSMAN HERE...
...IN AN OFFICIAL TOURNAMENT GAME, SETTER TO SETTER, SO THAT I CAN CRUSH HIM INTO OBLIVION IN FRONT OF A GIANT AUDIENCE.
烏野高校
排球部
...
W... W... WELL!
WE'RE GONNA PRACTICE RECEIVING EXTRA HARD!!
H-HEY! DON'T GRAB ME!
TUG
RECEIVING ISN'T SOMETHING YOU CAN GET GOOD AT OVERNIGHT.
I'M SURE YOUR CAPTAIN KNOWS ALL ABOUT THAT.
...
TP
TP

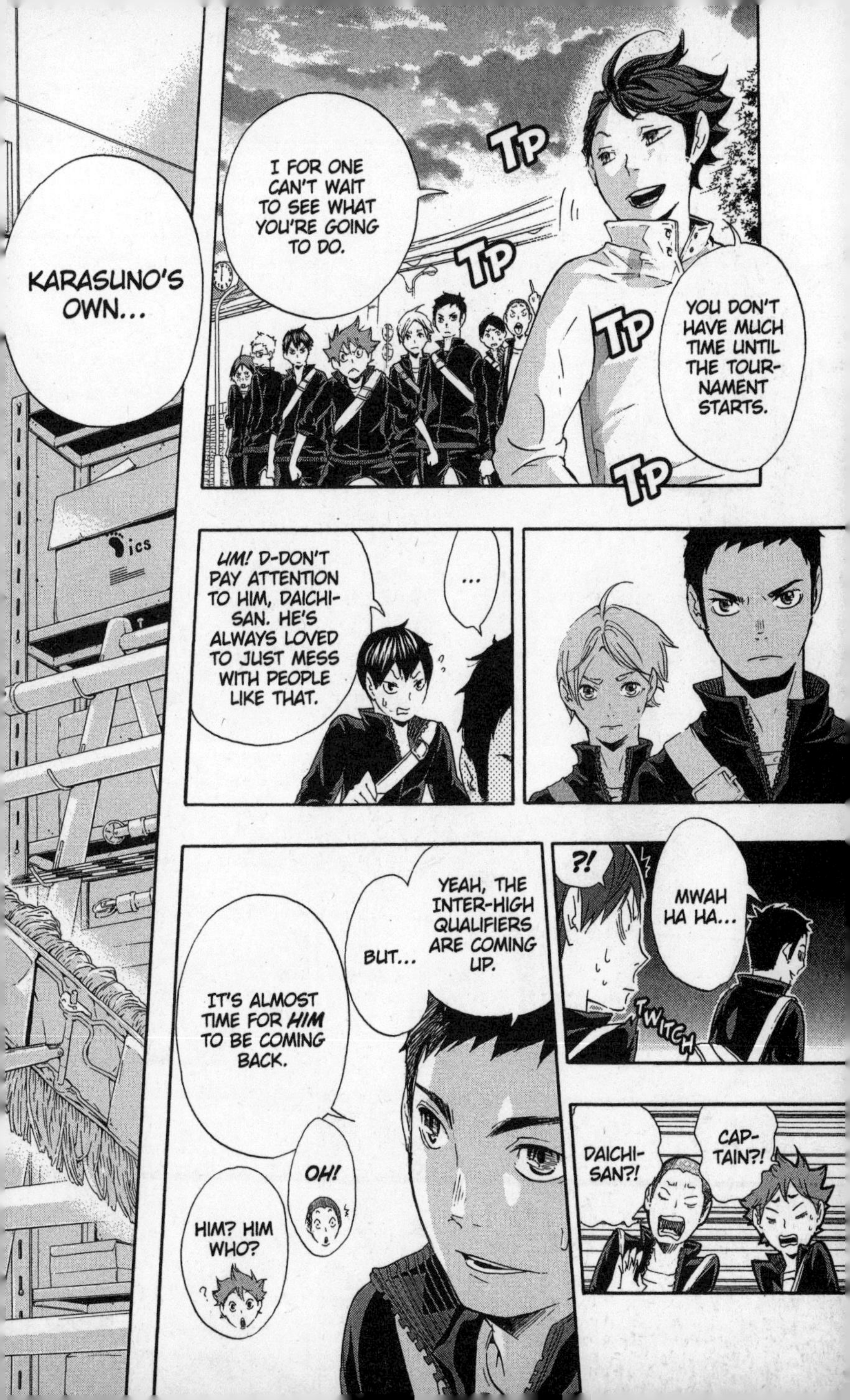

TP
TP
TP
YOU DON'T HAVE MUCH TIME UNTIL THE TOUR-NAMENT STARTS.
TP
I FOR ONE CAN'T WAIT TO SEE WHAT YOU'RE GOING TO DO.
KARASUNO'S OWN...
...
UM! D-DON'T PAY ATTENTION TO HIM, DAICHI-SAN. HE'S ALWAYS LOVED TO JUST MESS WITH PEOPLE LIKE THAT.
MWAH HA HA...
?!
TWITCH
CAP-TAIN?!
DAICHI-SAN?!
YEAH, THE INTER-HIGH QUALIFIERS ARE COMING UP.
BUT...
IT'S ALMOST TIME FOR *HIM* TO BE COMING BACK.
OH!
HIM? HIM WHO?

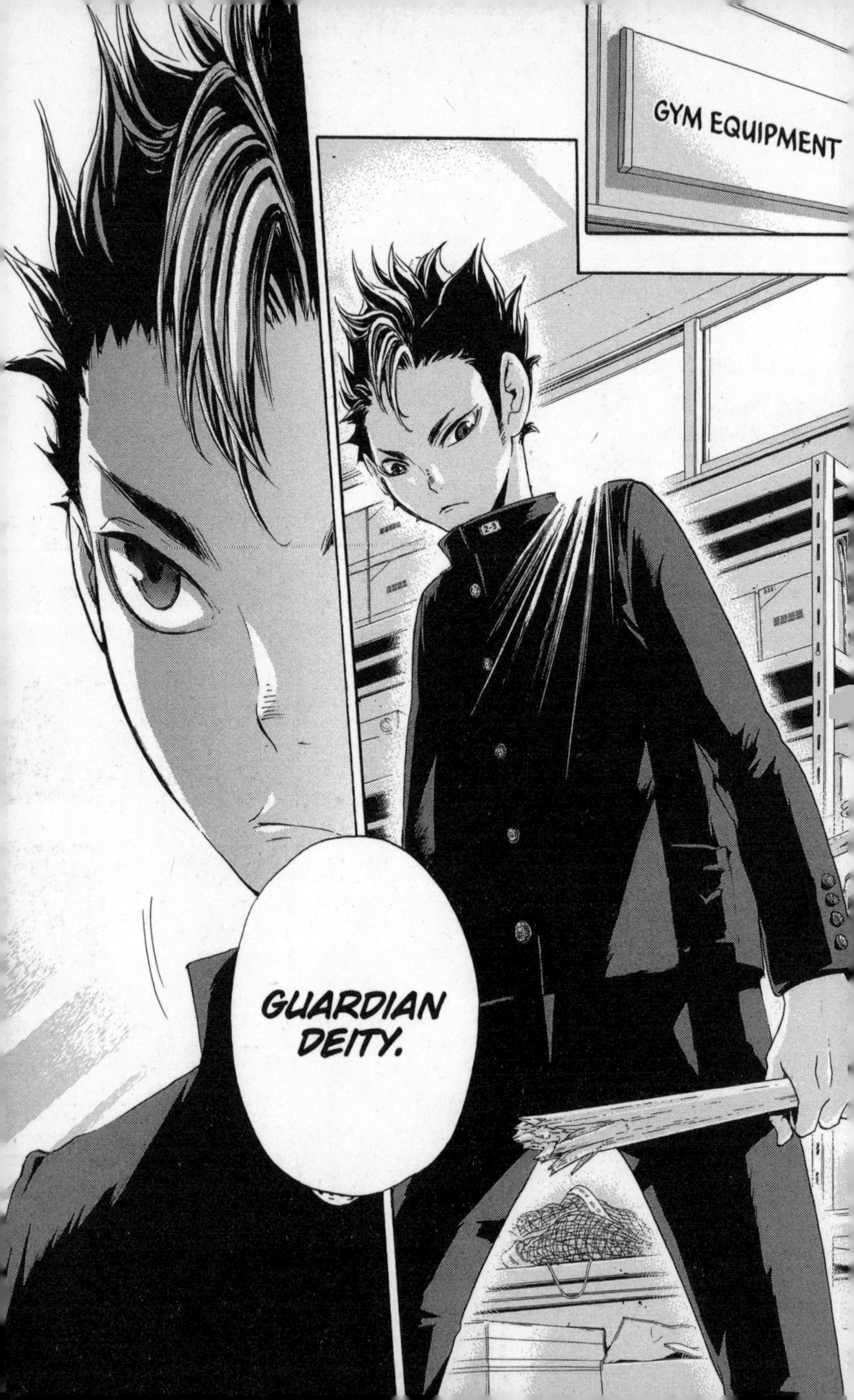
GYM EQUIPMENT
GUARDIAN DEITY.

YUTARO KINDAICHI

AOBA JOHSAI HIGH SCHOOL

POSITION:
MIDDLE BLOCKER

HEIGHT: 6'2"
WEIGHT: 164 LBS.
(AS OF APRIL, 1ST YEAR
OF HIGH SCHOOL)

BIRTHDAY: JUNE 6

FAVORITE FOOD:
GRILLED CORN ON THE COB

CURRENT WORRY:
A GIRL IN HIS CLASS SAID
HE DIDN'T SEEM AS "BIG"
AS HE DID "LONG."

ABILITY PARAMETERS
(5-POINT SCALE)

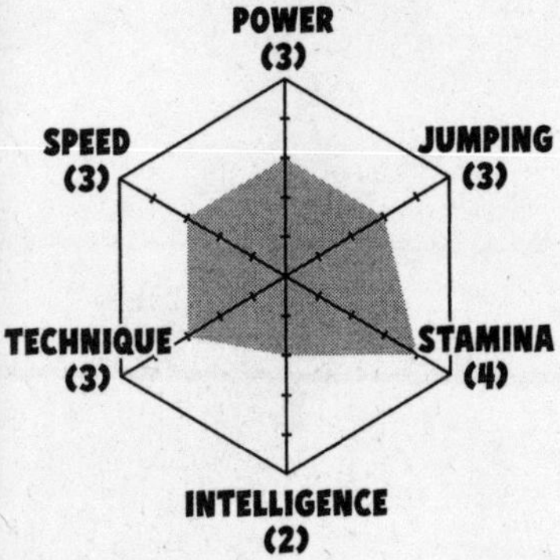
POWER
(3)
JUMPING
(3)
STAMINA
(4)
INTELLIGENCE
(2)
TECHNIQUE
(3)
SPEED
(3)

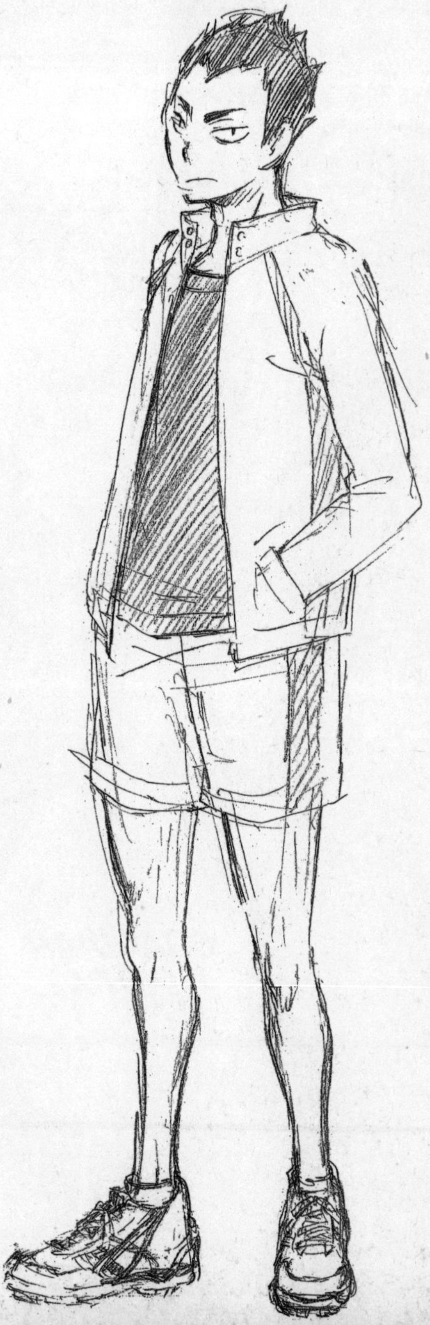

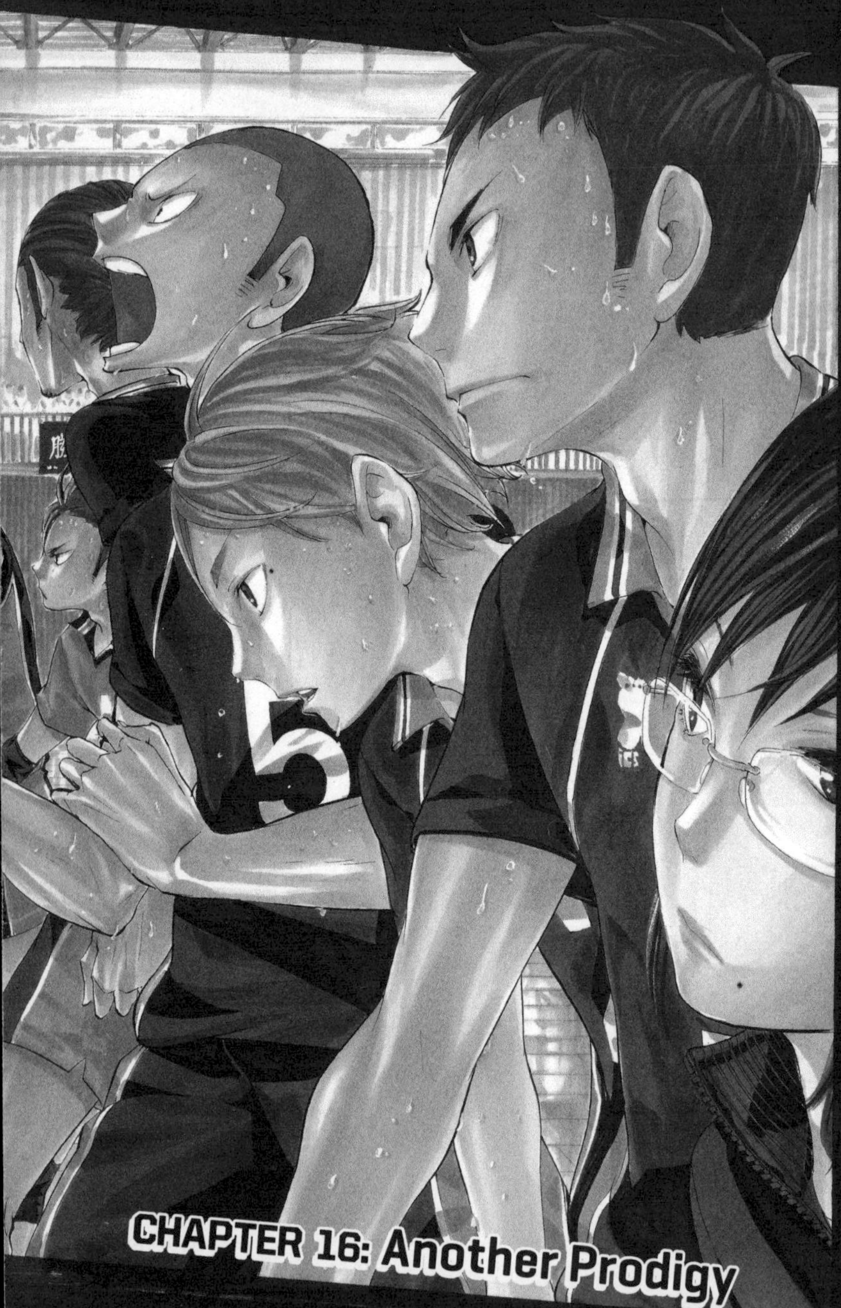

CHAPTER 16: Another Prodigy

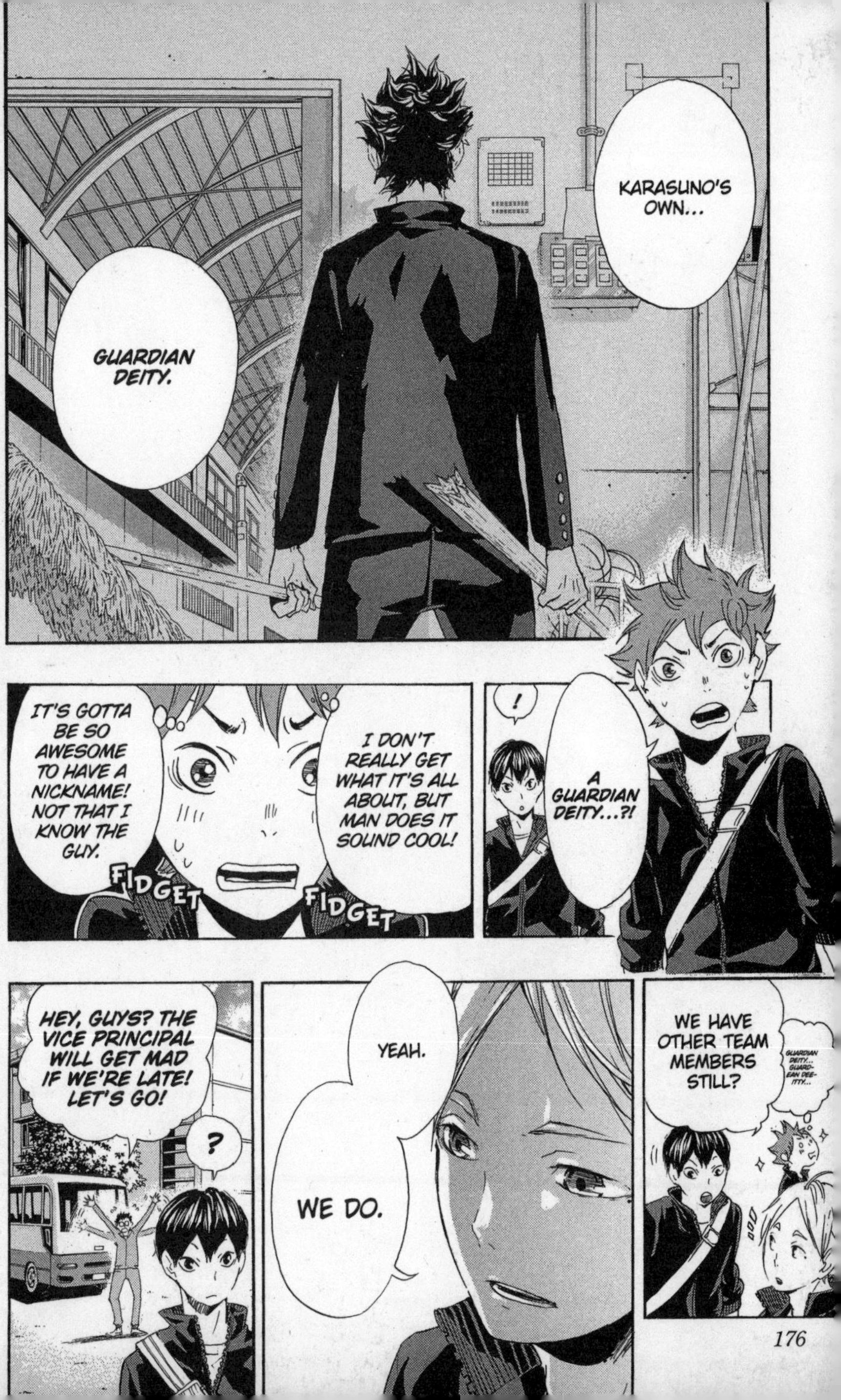
KARASUNO'S OWN...
GUARDIAN DEITY.
!
A GUARDIAN DEITY...?!
I DON'T REALLY GET WHAT IT'S ALL ABOUT, BUT MAN DOES IT SOUND COOL!
IT'S GOTTA BE SO AWESOME TO HAVE A NICKNAME! NOT THAT I KNOW THE GUY.
FIDGET
FIDGET
WE HAVE OTHER TEAM MEMBERS STILL?
GUARDIAN DEITY... GUARD-EAN DEE-ITTY...
YEAH.
WE DO.
HEY, GUYS? THE VICE PRINCIPAL WILL GET MAD IF WE'RE LATE! LET'S GO!
?

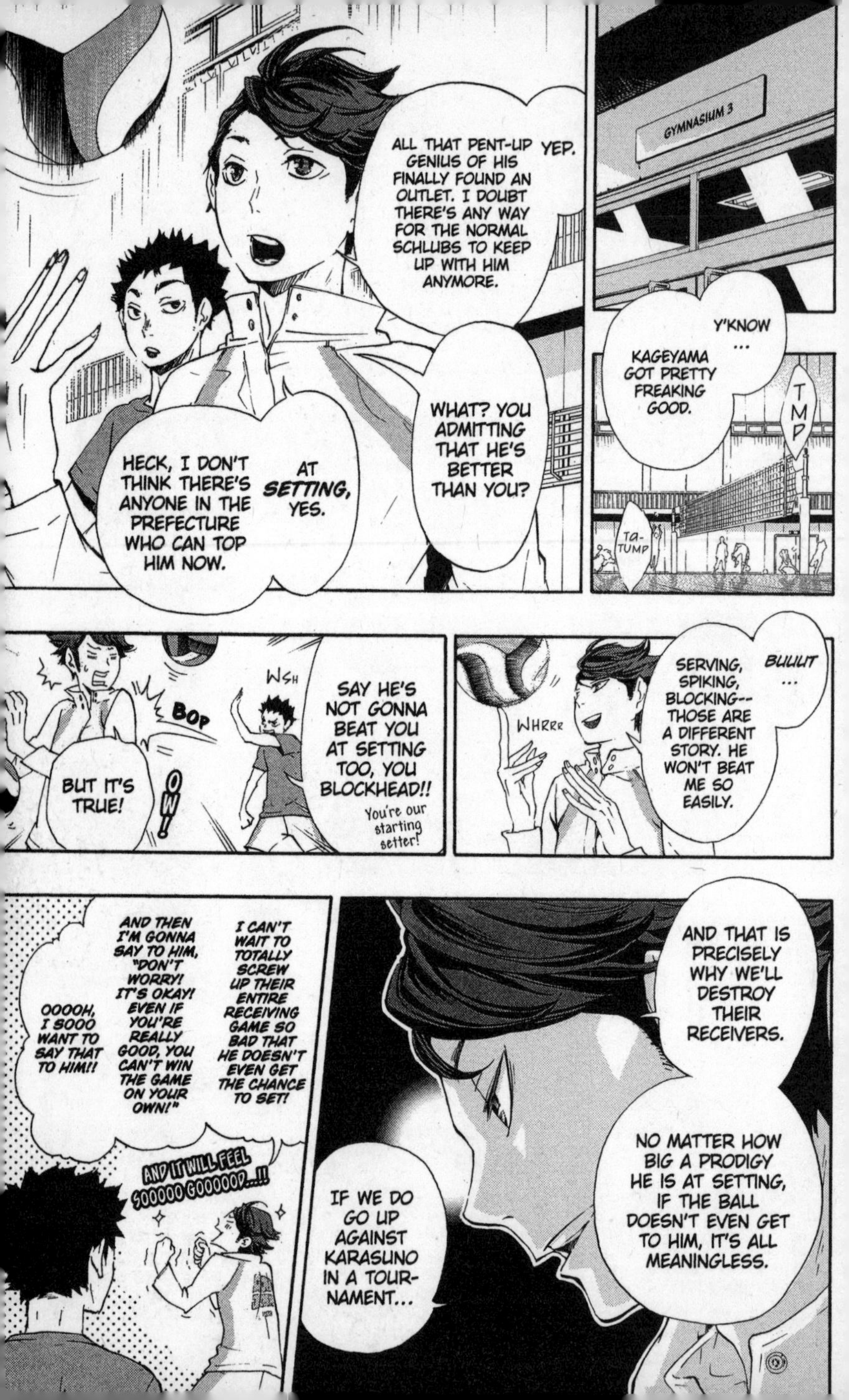
GYMNASIUM 3
Y'KNOW ...
KAGEYAMA GOT PRETTY FREAKING GOOD.
TMP
TA-TUMP
YEP.
ALL THAT PENT-UP GENIUS OF HIS FINALLY FOUND AN OUTLET. I DOUBT THERE'S ANY WAY FOR THE NORMAL SCHLUBS TO KEEP UP WITH HIM ANYMORE.
WHAT? YOU ADMITTING THAT HE'S BETTER THAN YOU?
AT SETTING, YES.
HECK, I DON'T THINK THERE'S ANYONE IN THE PREFECTURE WHO CAN TOP HIM NOW.
BUUUT ...
SERVING, SPIKING, BLOCKING-- THOSE ARE A DIFFERENT STORY. HE WON'T BEAT ME SO EASILY.
WHRRR
SAY HE'S NOT GONNA BEAT YOU AT SETTING TOO, YOU BLOCKHEAD!!
You're our starting setter!
WSH
BOP
OW!
BUT IT'S TRUE!
AND THAT IS PRECISELY WHY WE'LL DESTROY THEIR RECEIVERS.
NO MATTER HOW BIG A PRODIGY HE IS AT SETTING, IF THE BALL DOESN'T EVEN GET TO HIM, IT'S ALL MEANINGLESS.
IF WE DO GO UP AGAINST KARASUNO IN A TOURNAMENT...
I CAN'T WAIT TO TOTALLY SCREW UP THEIR ENTIRE RECEIVING GAME SO BAD THAT HE DOESN'T EVEN GET THE CHANCE TO SET!
AND THEN I'M GONNA SAY TO HIM, "DON'T WORRY! IT'S OKAY! EVEN IF YOU'RE REALLY GOOD, YOU CAN'T WIN THE GAME ON YOUR OWN!"
OOOOH, I SOOO WANT TO SAY THAT TO HIM!!
AND IT WILL FEEL SOOOOO GOOOOOD...!!

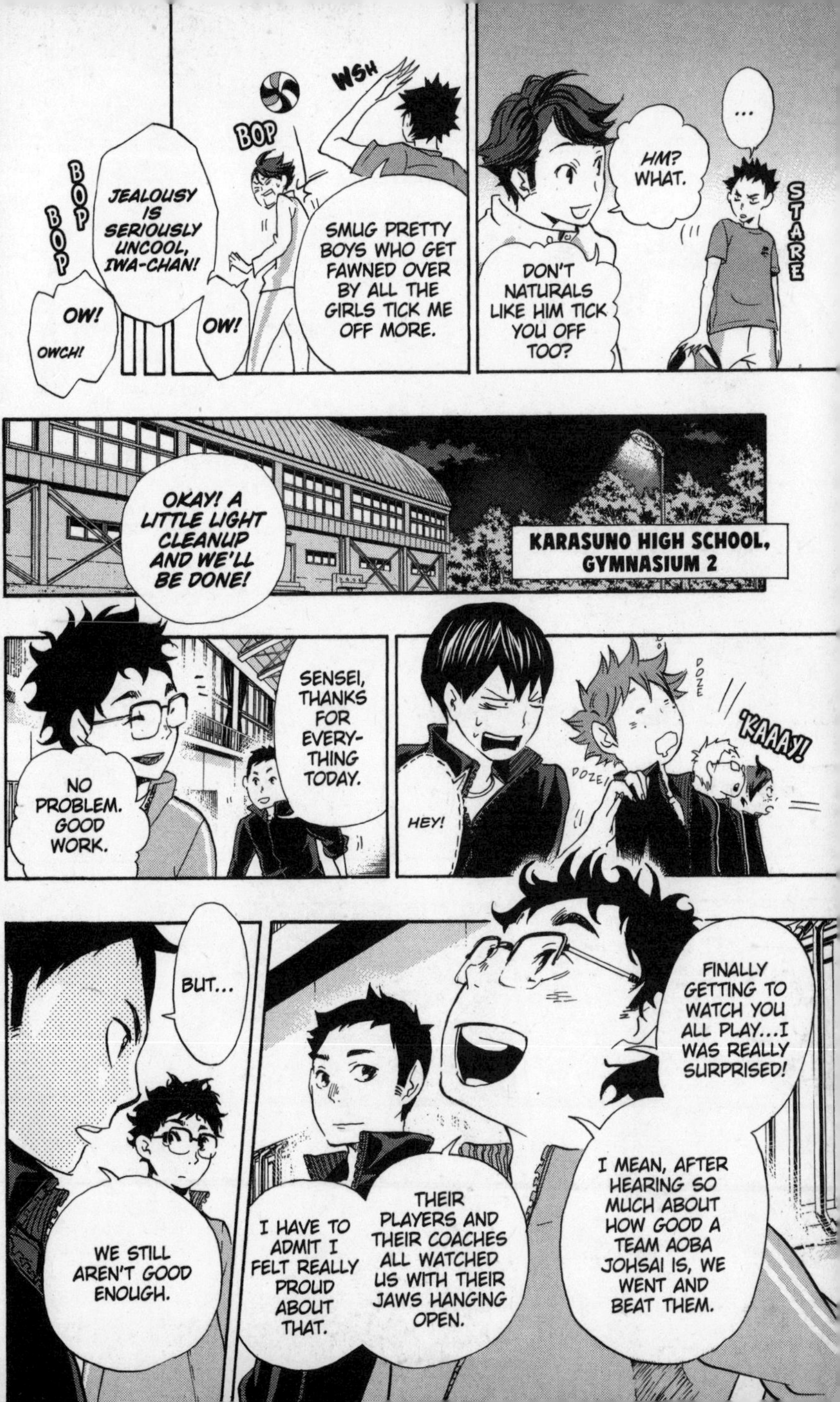
...
STARE
HM? WHAT.
DON'T NATURALS LIKE HIM TICK YOU OFF TOO?
WSH
BOP
SMUG PRETTY BOYS WHO GET FAWNED OVER BY ALL THE GIRLS TICK ME OFF MORE.
JEALOUSY IS SERIOUSLY UNCOOL, IWA-CHAN!
BOP BOP
OW!
OW!
OWCH!
KARASUNO HIGH SCHOOL, GYMNASIUM 2
OKAY! A LITTLE LIGHT CLEANUP AND WE'LL BE DONE!
DOZE
'KAAAY!
DOZE
HEY!
SENSEI, THANKS FOR EVERY-THING TODAY.
NO PROBLEM. GOOD WORK.
FINALLY GETTING TO WATCH YOU ALL PLAY...I WAS REALLY SURPRISED!
I MEAN, AFTER HEARING SO MUCH ABOUT HOW GOOD A TEAM AOBA JOHSAI IS, WE WENT AND BEAT THEM.
THEIR PLAYERS AND THEIR COACHES ALL WATCHED US WITH THEIR JAWS HANGING OPEN.
I HAVE TO ADMIT I FELT REALLY PROUD ABOUT THAT.
BUT...
WE STILL AREN'T GOOD ENOUGH.

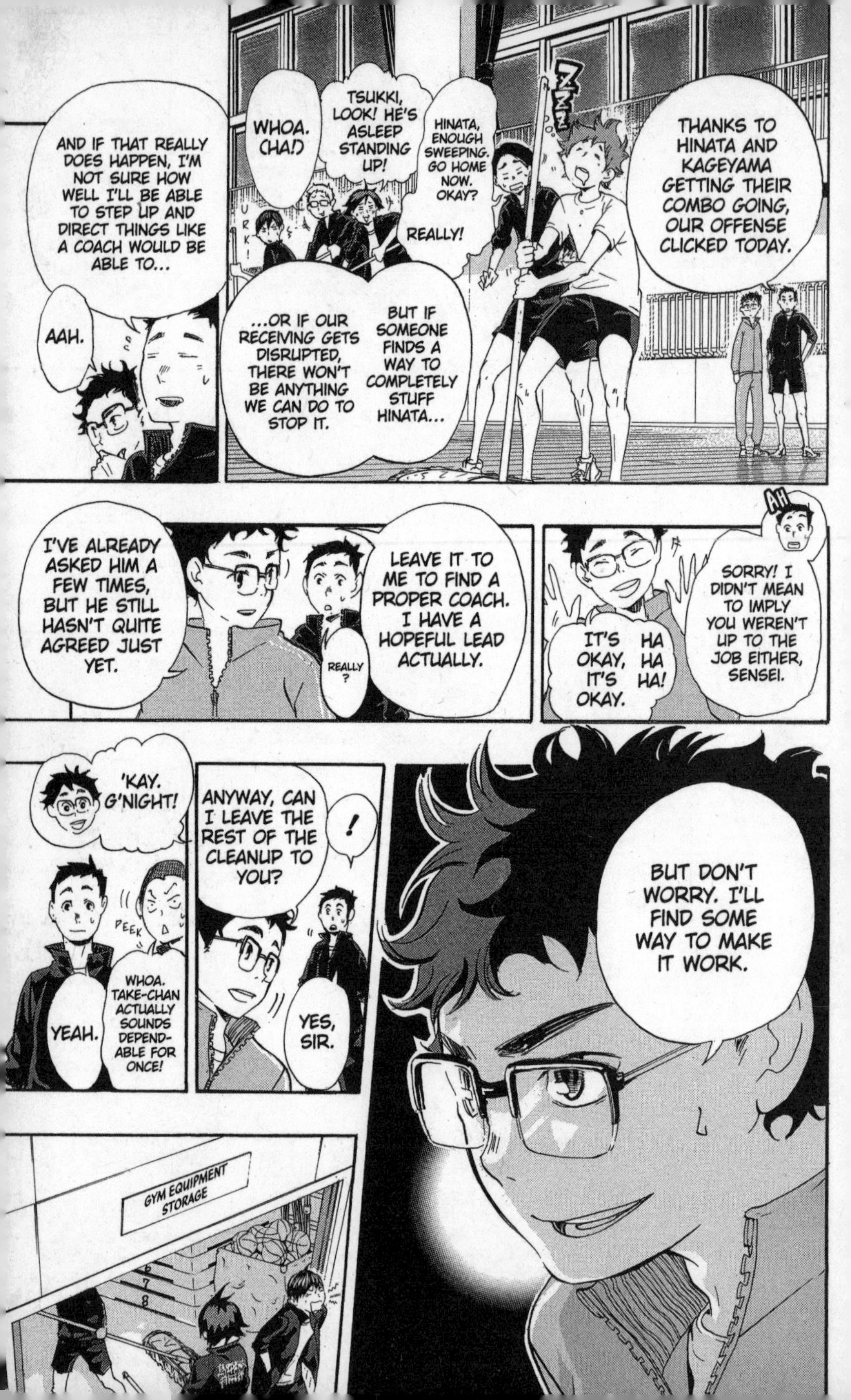
THANKS TO HINATA AND KAGEYAMA GETTING THEIR COMBO GOING, OUR OFFENSE CLICKED TODAY.
ZZZ
HINATA, ENOUGH SWEEPING. GO HOME NOW. OKAY?
REALLY!
TSUKKI, LOOK! HE'S ASLEEP STANDING UP!
WHOA. CHA!D
URK!
BUT IF SOMEONE FINDS A WAY TO COMPLETELY STUFF HINATA...
...OR IF OUR RECEIVING GETS DISRUPTED, THERE WON'T BE ANYTHING WE CAN DO TO STOP IT.
AND IF THAT REALLY DOES HAPPEN, I'M NOT SURE HOW WELL I'LL BE ABLE TO STEP UP AND DIRECT THINGS LIKE A COACH WOULD BE ABLE TO...
AAH.
AH
SORRY! I DIDN'T MEAN TO IMPLY YOU WEREN'T UP TO THE JOB EITHER, SENSEI.
HA HA HA!
IT'S OKAY, IT'S OKAY.
LEAVE IT TO ME TO FIND A PROPER COACH. I HAVE A HOPEFUL LEAD ACTUALLY.
REALLY?
I'VE ALREADY ASKED HIM A FEW TIMES, BUT HE STILL HASN'T QUITE AGREED JUST YET.
BUT DON'T WORRY. I'LL FIND SOME WAY TO MAKE IT WORK.
!
ANYWAY, CAN I LEAVE THE REST OF THE CLEANUP TO YOU?
YES, SIR.
'KAY. G'NIGHT!
PEEK
WHOA. TAKE-CHAN ACTUALLY SOUNDS DEPEND-ABLE FOR ONCE!
YEAH.
GYM EQUIPMENT STORAGE

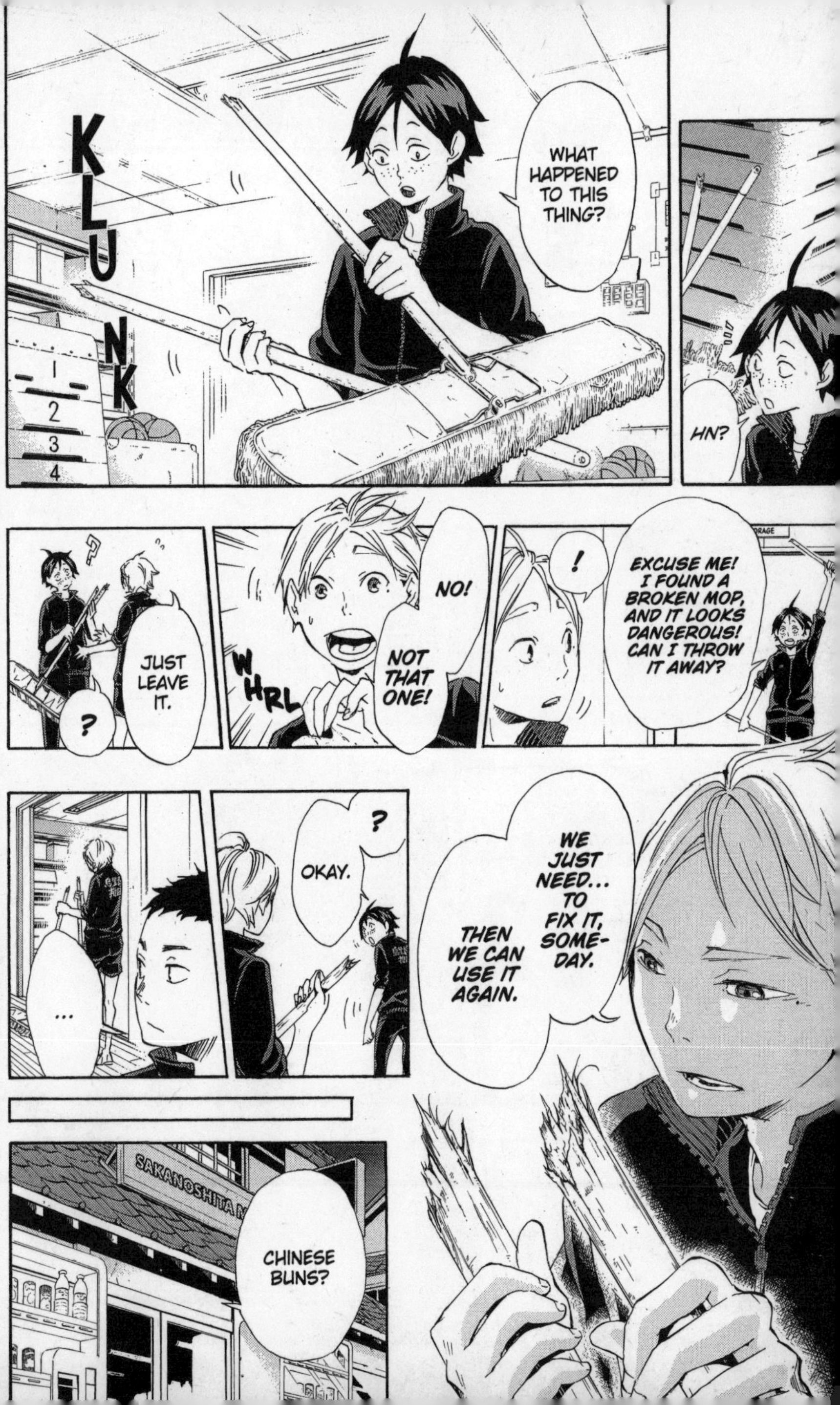
HN?
KLUNK
WHAT HAPPENED TO THIS THING?
EXCUSE ME! I FOUND A BROKEN MOP, AND IT LOOKS DANGEROUS! CAN I THROW IT AWAY?
!
NO!
NOT THAT ONE!
WHRL
?
JUST LEAVE IT.
?
WE JUST NEED... TO FIX IT, SOMEDAY.
THEN WE CAN USE IT AGAIN.
?
OKAY.
...
SAKANOSHITA
CHINESE BUNS?

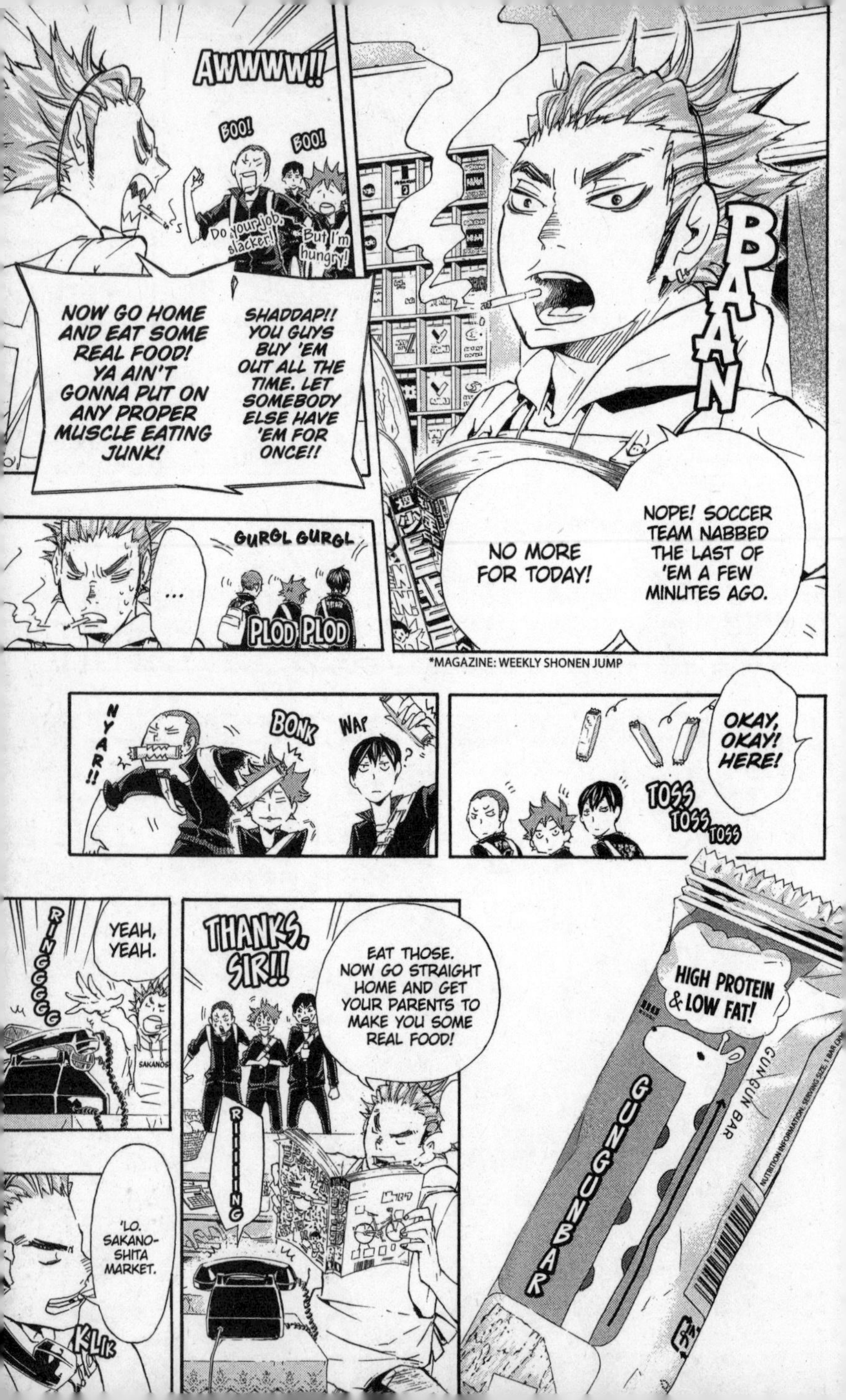
BAAN
NOPE! SOCCER TEAM NABBED THE LAST OF 'EM A FEW MINUTES AGO.
NO MORE FOR TODAY!
AWWWW!!
BOO!
BOO!
But I'm hungry!
Do your job, slacker!!
SHADDAP!! YOU GUYS BUY 'EM OUT ALL THE TIME. LET SOMEBODY ELSE HAVE 'EM FOR ONCE!!
NOW GO HOME AND EAT SOME REAL FOOD! YA AIN'T GONNA PUT ON ANY PROPER MUSCLE EATING JUNK!
GURGL GURGL
...
PLOD PLOD
*MAGAZINE: WEEKLY SHONEN JUMP
OKAY, OKAY! HERE!
TOSS TOSS TOSS
WAP
BONK
NYAR!!
HIGH PROTEIN & LOW FAT!
GUN GUN BAR
GUNGUNBAR
THANKS, SIR!!
EAT THOSE. NOW GO STRAIGHT HOME AND GET YOUR PARENTS TO MAKE YOU SOME REAL FOOD!
RIIIING
YEAH, YEAH.
RINGGGG
'LO. SAKANO-SHITA MARKET.
KLIK

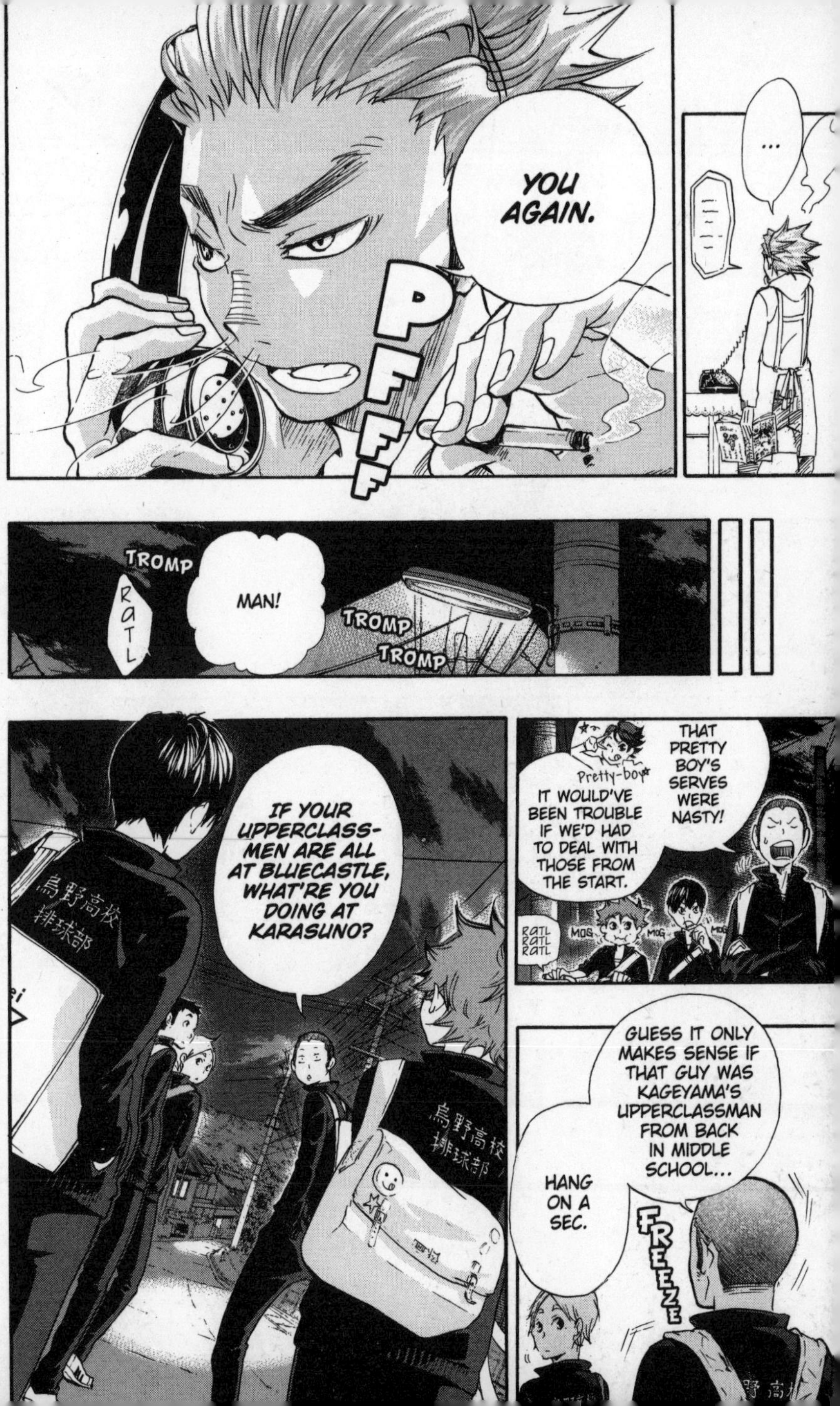
...
YOU AGAIN.
PFFFF
TROMP
RATL
MAN!
TROMP
TROMP
THAT PRETTY BOY'S SERVES WERE NASTY!
Pretty-boy
IT WOULD'VE BEEN TROUBLE IF WE'D HAD TO DEAL WITH THOSE FROM THE START.
MOG
MOG
MOG
RATL RATL RATL
GUESS IT ONLY MAKES SENSE IF THAT GUY WAS KAGEYAMA'S UPPERCLASSMAN FROM BACK IN MIDDLE SCHOOL...
FREEZE
HANG ON A SEC.
IF YOUR UPPERCLASSMEN ARE ALL AT BLUECASTLE, WHAT'RE YOU DOING AT KARASUNO?
烏野高校
排球部
烏野高校
排球部

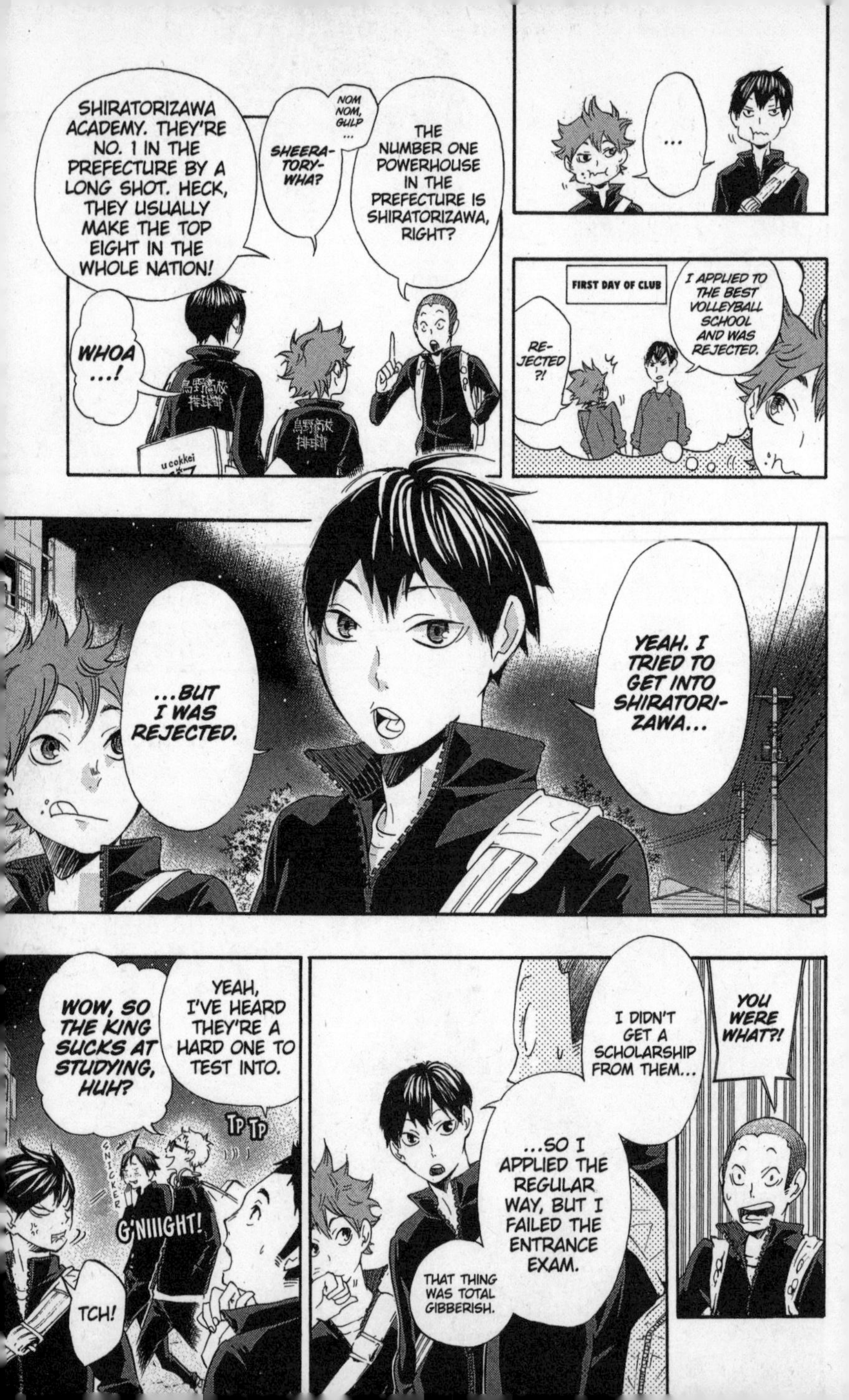
...
FIRST DAY OF CLUB
I APPLIED TO THE BEST VOLLEYBALL SCHOOL AND WAS REJECTED.
RE-JECTED ?!
THE NUMBER ONE POWERHOUSE IN THE PREFECTURE IS SHIRATORIZAWA, RIGHT?
NOM NOM, GULP ...
SHEERA-TORY-WHA?
SHIRATORIZAWA ACADEMY. THEY'RE NO. 1 IN THE PREFECTURE BY A LONG SHOT. HECK, THEY USUALLY MAKE THE TOP EIGHT IN THE WHOLE NATION!
WHOA ...!
YEAH. I TRIED TO GET INTO SHIRATORI-ZAWA...
...BUT I WAS REJECTED.
YOU WERE WHAT?!
I DIDN'T GET A SCHOLARSHIP FROM THEM...
...SO I APPLIED THE REGULAR WAY, BUT I FAILED THE ENTRANCE EXAM.
THAT THING WAS TOTAL GIBBERISH.
YEAH, I'VE HEARD THEY'RE A HARD ONE TO TEST INTO.
WOW, SO THE KING SUCKS AT STUDYING, HUH?
TP TP
SNICKER
G'NIIIGHT!
TCH!

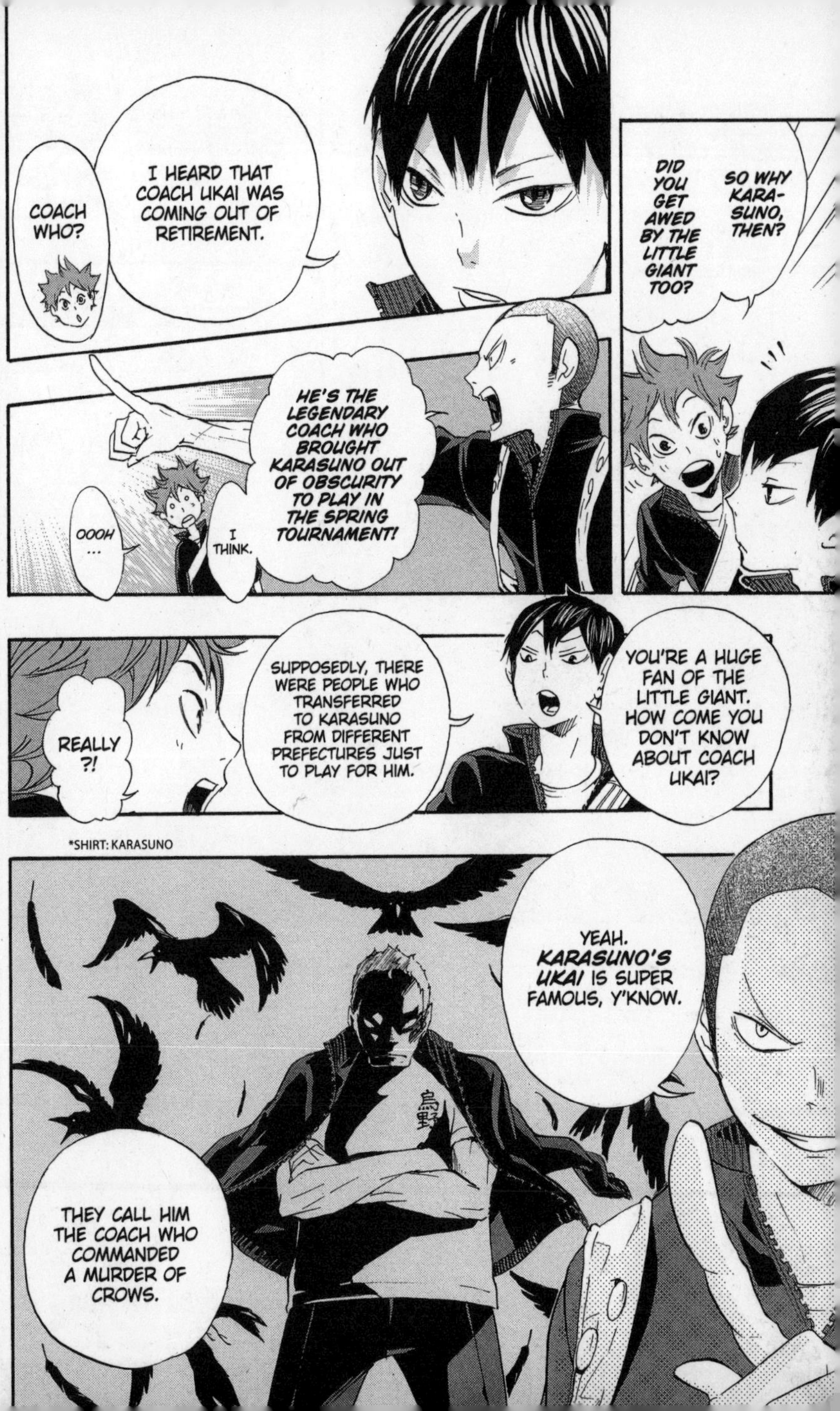
SO WHY KARASUNO, THEN?
DID YOU GET AWED BY THE LITTLE GIANT TOO?
I HEARD THAT COACH UKAI WAS COMING OUT OF RETIREMENT.
COACH WHO?
HE'S THE LEGENDARY COACH WHO BROUGHT KARASUNO OUT OF OBSCURITY TO PLAY IN THE SPRING TOURNAMENT!
I THINK.
OOOH ...
YOU'RE A HUGE FAN OF THE LITTLE GIANT. HOW COME YOU DON'T KNOW ABOUT COACH UKAI?
SUPPOSEDLY, THERE WERE PEOPLE WHO TRANSFERRED TO KARASUNO FROM DIFFERENT PREFECTURES JUST TO PLAY FOR HIM.
REALLY ?!
*SHIRT: KARASUNO
YEAH. KARASUNO'S UKAI IS SUPER FAMOUS, Y'KNOW.
THEY CALL HIM THE COACH WHO COMMANDED A MURDER OF CROWS.

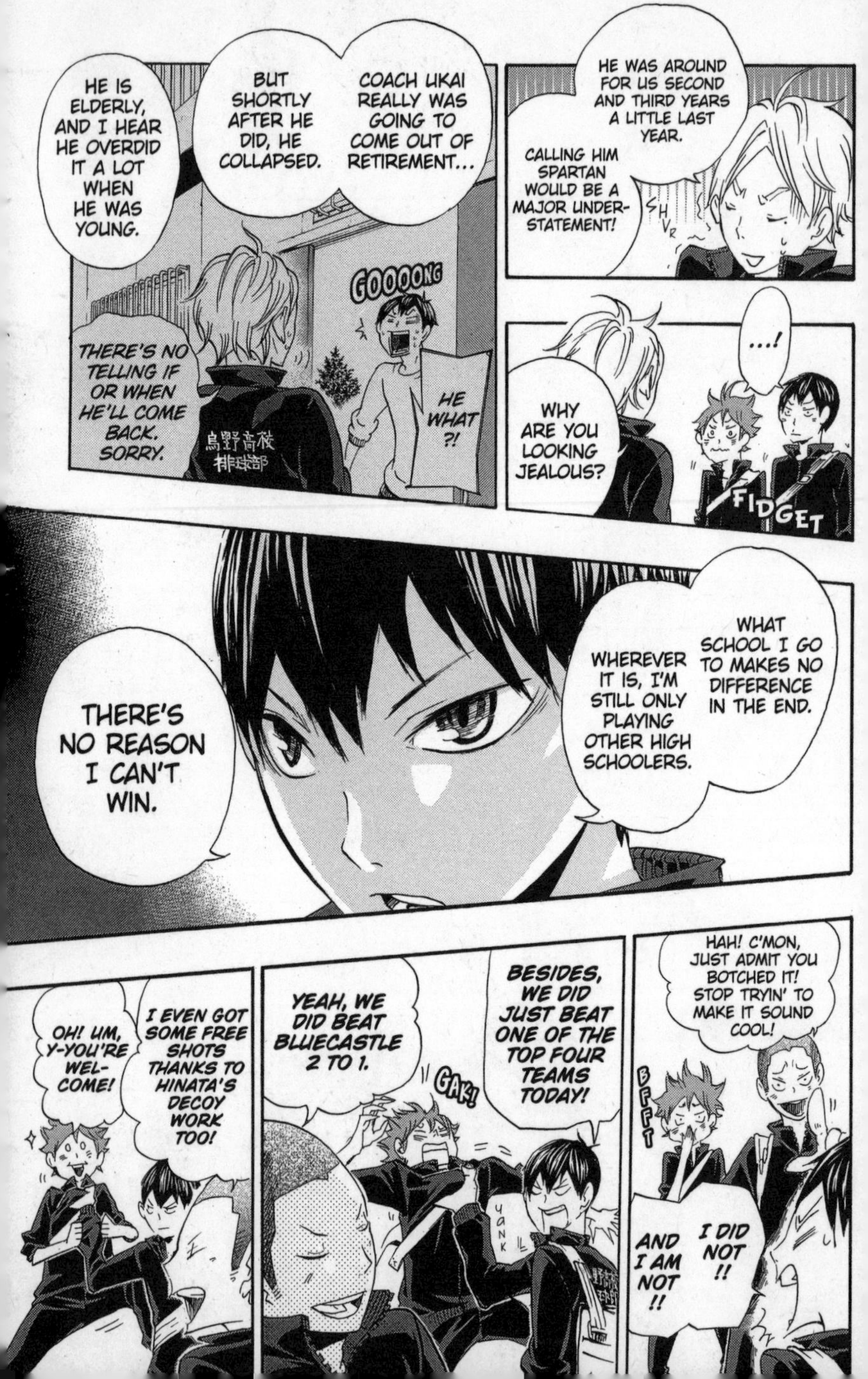
HE WAS AROUND FOR US SECOND AND THIRD YEARS A LITTLE LAST YEAR.
CALLING HIM SPARTAN WOULD BE A MAJOR UNDER-STATEMENT!
SHVR
...!
WHY ARE YOU LOOKING JEALOUS?
FIDGET
COACH UKAI REALLY WAS GOING TO COME OUT OF RETIREMENT...
BUT SHORTLY AFTER HE DID, HE COLLAPSED.
HE IS ELDERLY, AND I HEAR HE OVERDID IT A LOT WHEN HE WAS YOUNG.
GOOOONG
HE WHAT?!
THERE'S NO TELLING IF OR WHEN HE'LL COME BACK. SORRY.
烏野高校
排球部
WHAT SCHOOL I GO TO MAKES NO DIFFERENCE IN THE END.
WHEREVER IT IS, I'M STILL ONLY PLAYING OTHER HIGH SCHOOLERS.
THERE'S NO REASON I CAN'T WIN.
HAH! C'MON, JUST ADMIT YOU BOTCHED IT! STOP TRYIN' TO MAKE IT SOUND COOL!
BFFT
I DID NOT!!
AND I AM NOT!!
BESIDES, WE DID JUST BEAT ONE OF THE TOP FOUR TEAMS TODAY!
YEAH, WE DID BEAT BLUECASTLE 2 TO 1.
GAK!
YANK
I EVEN GOT SOME FREE SHOTS THANKS TO HINATA'S DECOY WORK TOO!
OH! UM, Y-YOU'RE WEL-COME!

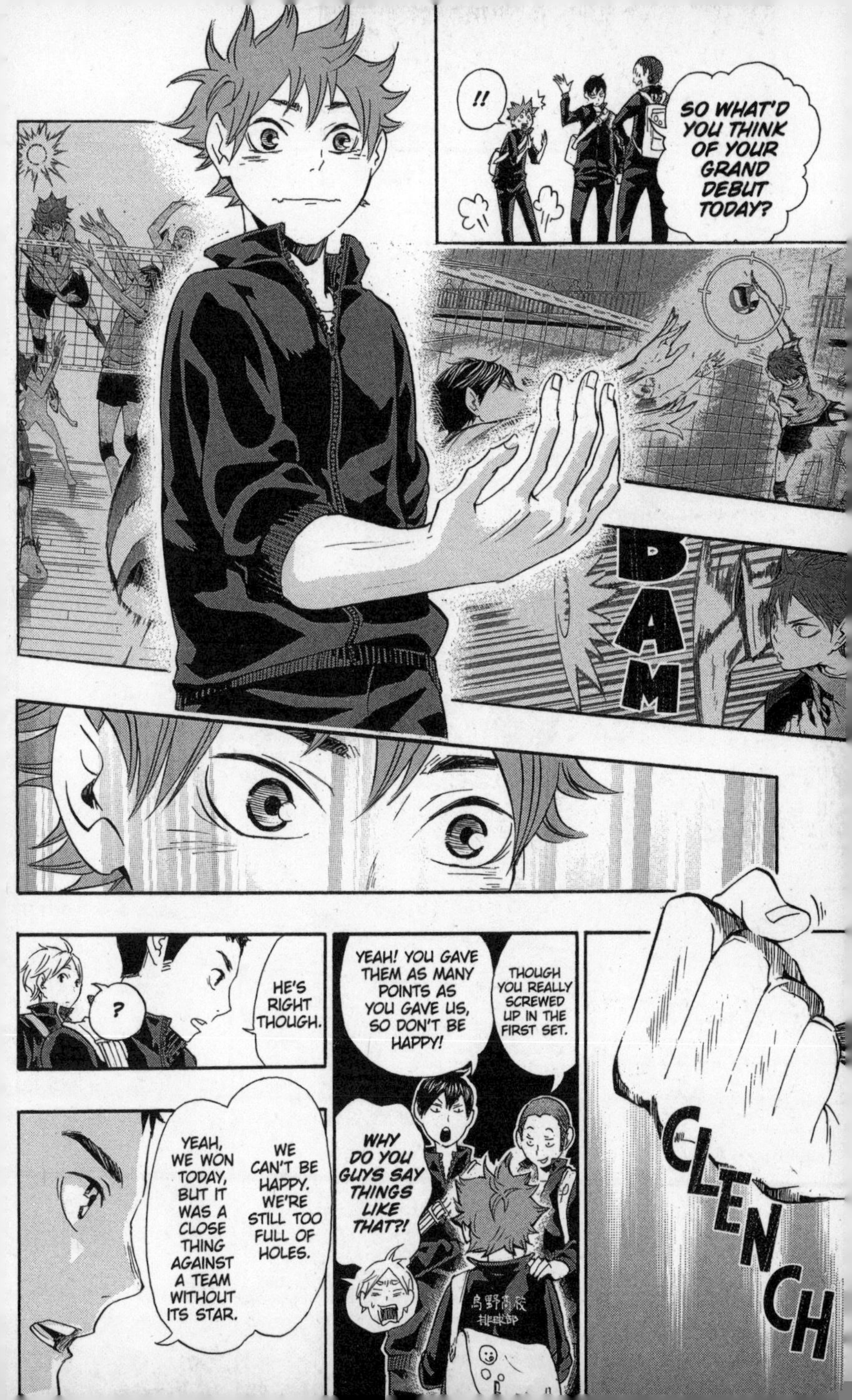
SO WHAT'D YOU THINK OF YOUR GRAND DEBUT TODAY?
!!
BAM
CLENCH
THOUGH YOU REALLY SCREWED UP IN THE FIRST SET.
YEAH! YOU GAVE THEM AS MANY POINTS AS YOU GAVE US, SO DON'T BE HAPPY!
WHY DO YOU GUYS SAY THINGS LIKE THAT?!
HE'S RIGHT THOUGH.
?
WE CAN'T BE HAPPY. WE'RE STILL TOO FULL OF HOLES.
YEAH, WE WON TODAY, BUT IT WAS A CLOSE THING AGAINST A TEAM WITHOUT ITS STAR.

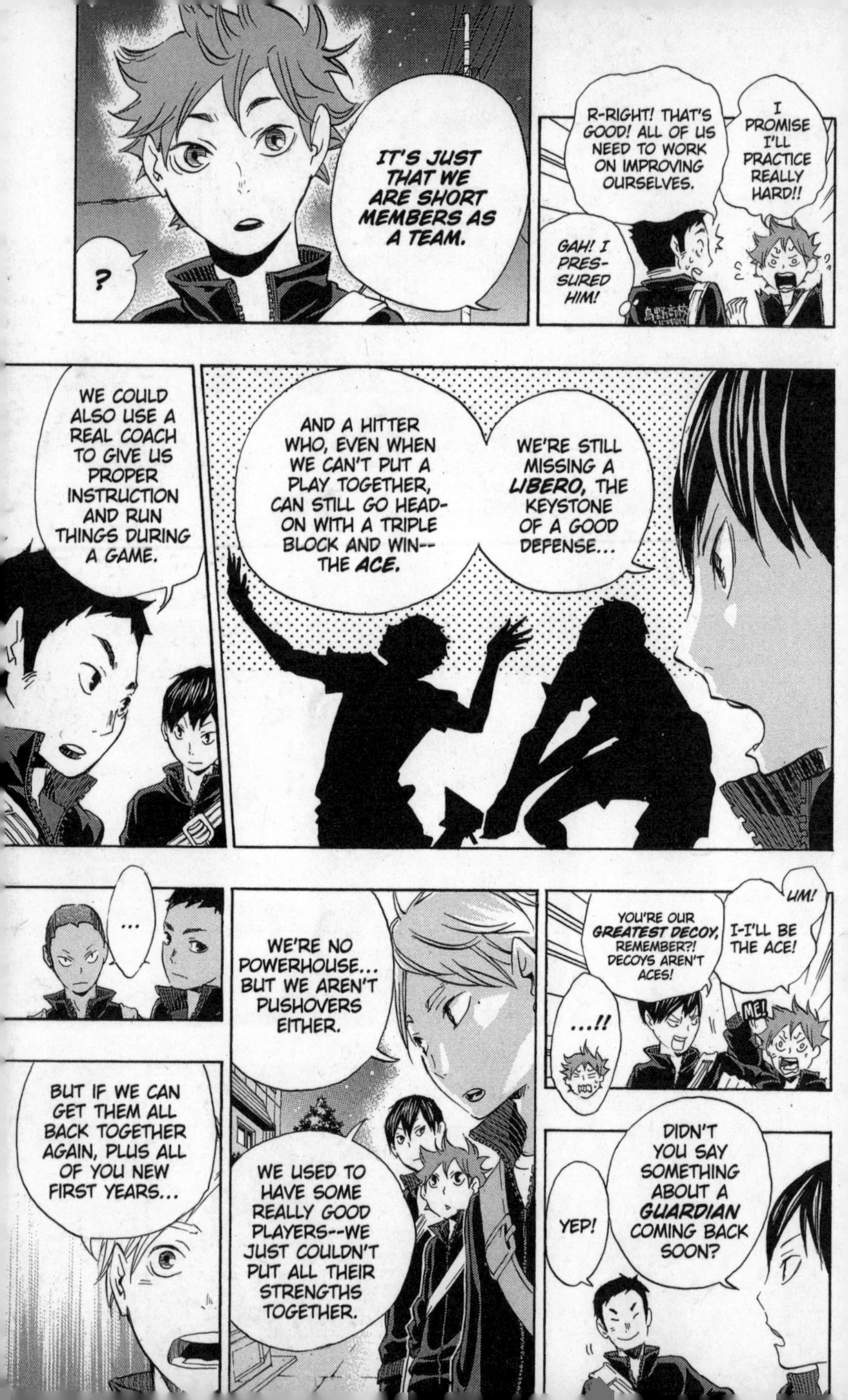
I PROMISE I'LL PRACTICE REALLY HARD!!
R-RIGHT! THAT'S GOOD! ALL OF US NEED TO WORK ON IMPROVING OURSELVES.
GAH! I PRESSURED HIM!
IT'S JUST THAT WE ARE SHORT MEMBERS AS A TEAM.
?
WE'RE STILL MISSING A LIBERO, THE KEYSTONE OF A GOOD DEFENSE...
AND A HITTER WHO, EVEN WHEN WE CAN'T PUT A PLAY TOGETHER, CAN STILL GO HEAD-ON WITH A TRIPLE BLOCK AND WIN-- THE ACE.
WE COULD ALSO USE A REAL COACH TO GIVE US PROPER INSTRUCTION AND RUN THINGS DURING A GAME.
UM!
I-I'LL BE THE ACE!
YOU'RE OUR GREATEST DECOY, REMEMBER?! DECOYS AREN'T ACES!
ME!
...!!
DIDN'T YOU SAY SOMETHING ABOUT A GUARDIAN COMING BACK SOON?
YEP!
WE'RE NO POWERHOUSE... BUT WE AREN'T PUSHOVERS EITHER.
WE USED TO HAVE SOME REALLY GOOD PLAYERS--WE JUST COULDN'T PUT ALL THEIR STRENGTHS TOGETHER.
...
BUT IF WE CAN GET THEM ALL BACK TOGETHER AGAIN, PLUS ALL OF YOU NEW FIRST YEARS...

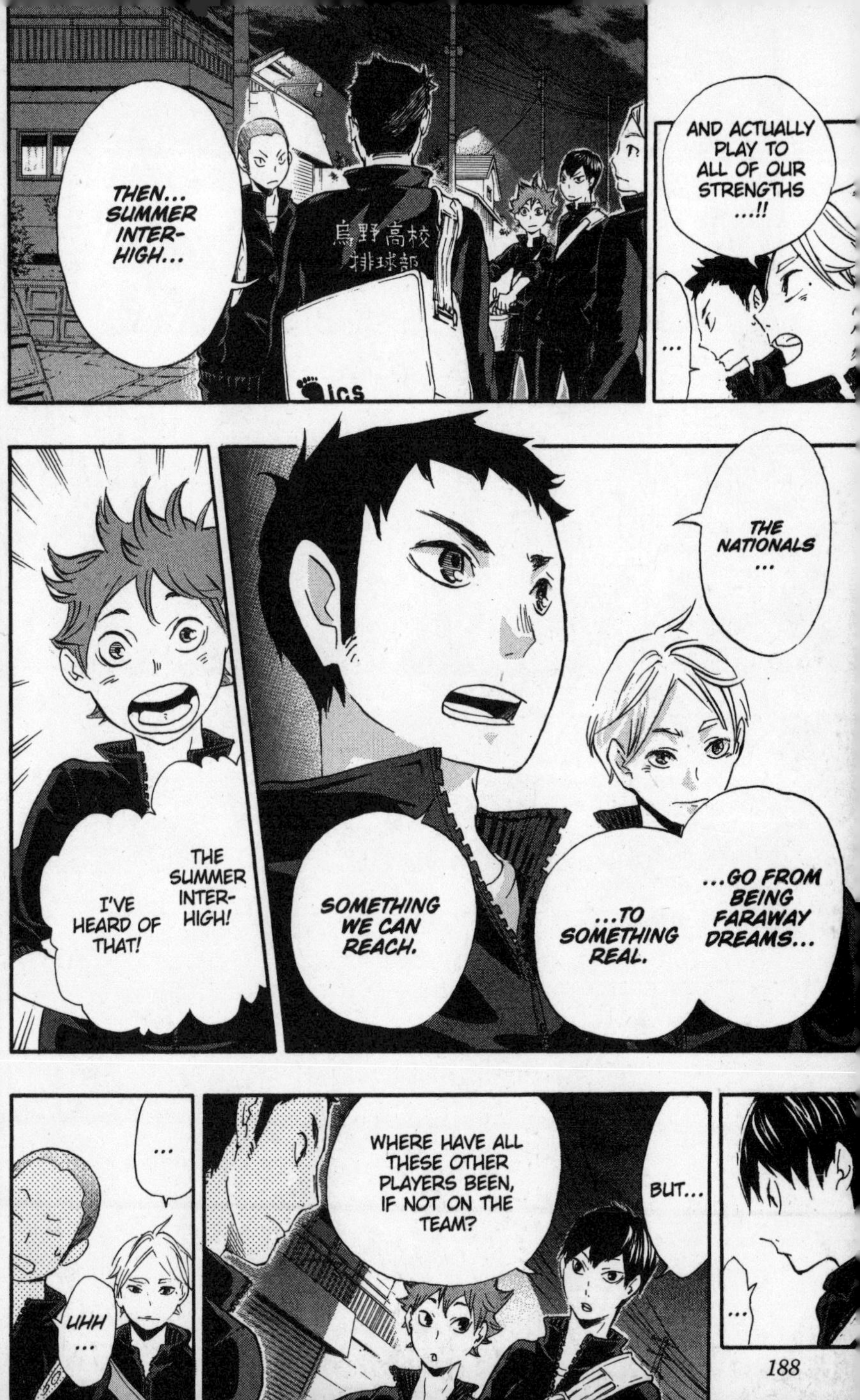
AND ACTUALLY PLAY TO ALL OF OUR STRENGTHS ...!!
...
THEN... SUMMER INTER-HIGH...
THE NATIONALS ...
...GO FROM BEING FARAWAY DREAMS...
...TO SOMETHING REAL.
SOMETHING WE CAN REACH.
THE SUMMER INTER-HIGH!
I'VE HEARD OF THAT!
...
BUT...
WHERE HAVE ALL THESE OTHER PLAYERS BEEN, IF NOT ON THE TEAM?
...
UHH ...

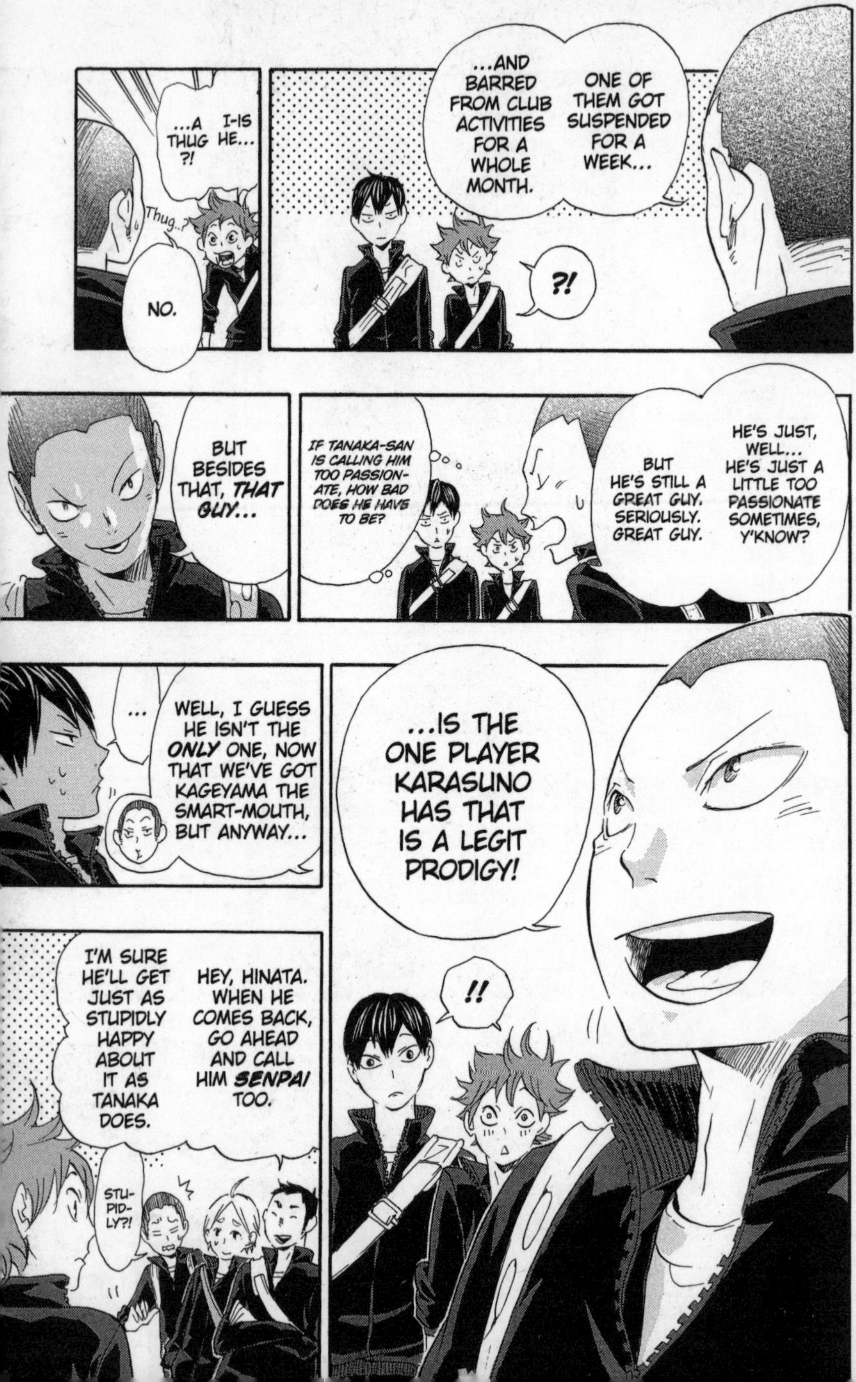
ONE OF THEM GOT SUSPENDED FOR A WEEK...
...AND BARRED FROM CLUB ACTIVITIES FOR A WHOLE MONTH.
?!
I-IS HE... ...A THUG ?!
Thug..?
NO.
HE'S JUST, WELL... HE'S JUST A LITTLE TOO PASSIONATE SOMETIMES, Y'KNOW?
BUT HE'S STILL A GREAT GUY. SERIOUSLY. GREAT GUY.
IF TANAKA-SAN IS CALLING HIM TOO PASSION-ATE, HOW BAD DOES HE HAVE TO BE?
BUT BESIDES THAT, THAT GUY...
...IS THE ONE PLAYER KARASUNO HAS THAT IS A LEGIT PRODIGY!
!!
WELL, I GUESS HE ISN'T THE ONLY ONE, NOW THAT WE'VE GOT KAGEYAMA THE SMART-MOUTH, BUT ANYWAY...
...
HEY, HINATA. WHEN HE COMES BACK, GO AHEAD AND CALL HIM SENPAI TOO.
I'M SURE HE'LL GET JUST AS STUPIDLY HAPPY ABOUT IT AS TANAKA DOES.
STU-PID-LY?!

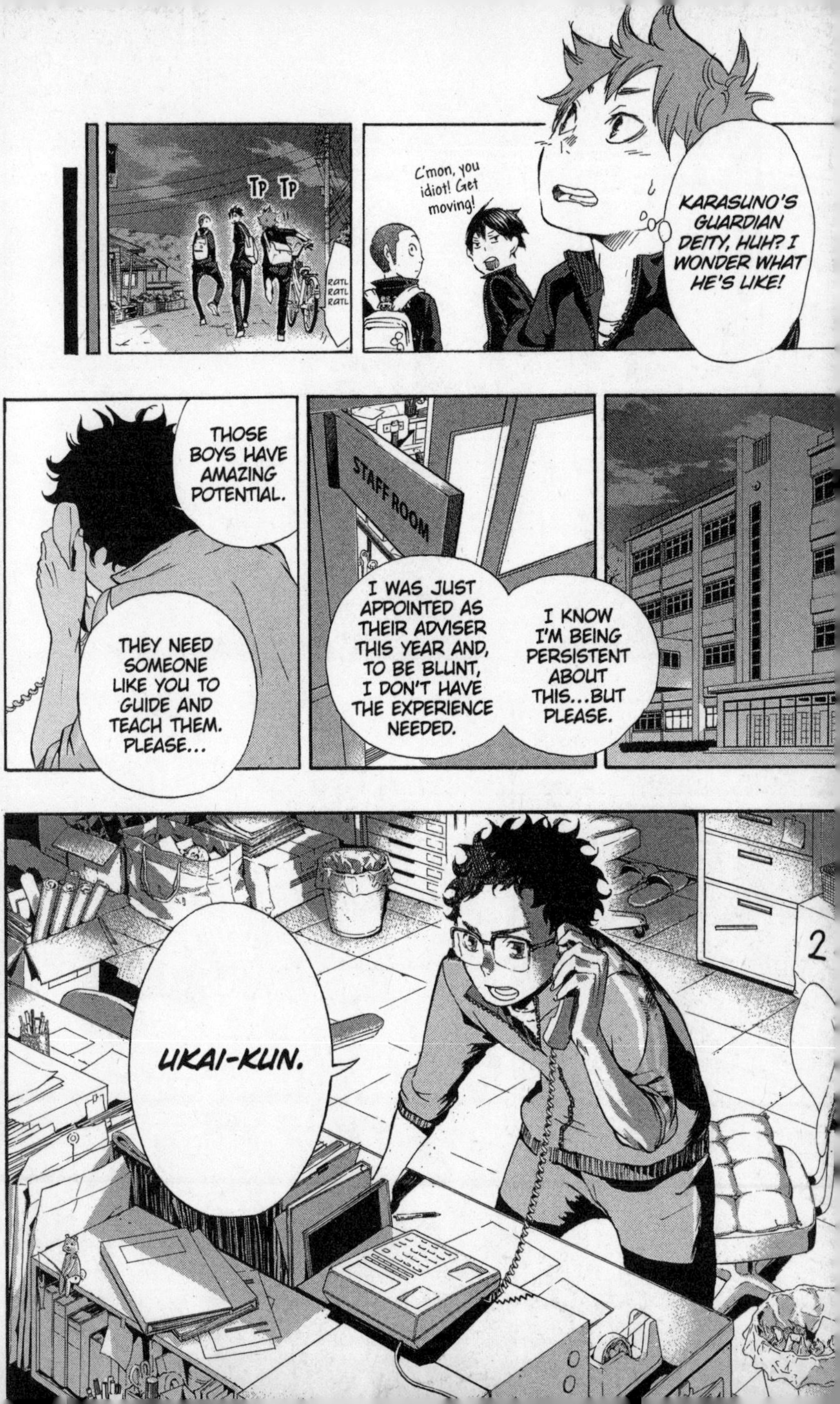
KARASUNO'S GUARDIAN DEITY, HUH? I WONDER WHAT HE'S LIKE!
C'mon, you idiot! Get moving!
Tp Tp
RATL RATL RATL
I KNOW I'M BEING PERSISTENT ABOUT THIS...BUT PLEASE.
STAFF ROOM
I WAS JUST APPOINTED AS THEIR ADVISER THIS YEAR AND, TO BE BLUNT, I DON'T HAVE THE EXPERIENCE NEEDED.
THOSE BOYS HAVE AMAZING POTENTIAL.
THEY NEED SOMEONE LIKE YOU TO GUIDE AND TEACH THEM. PLEASE...
UKAI-KUN.

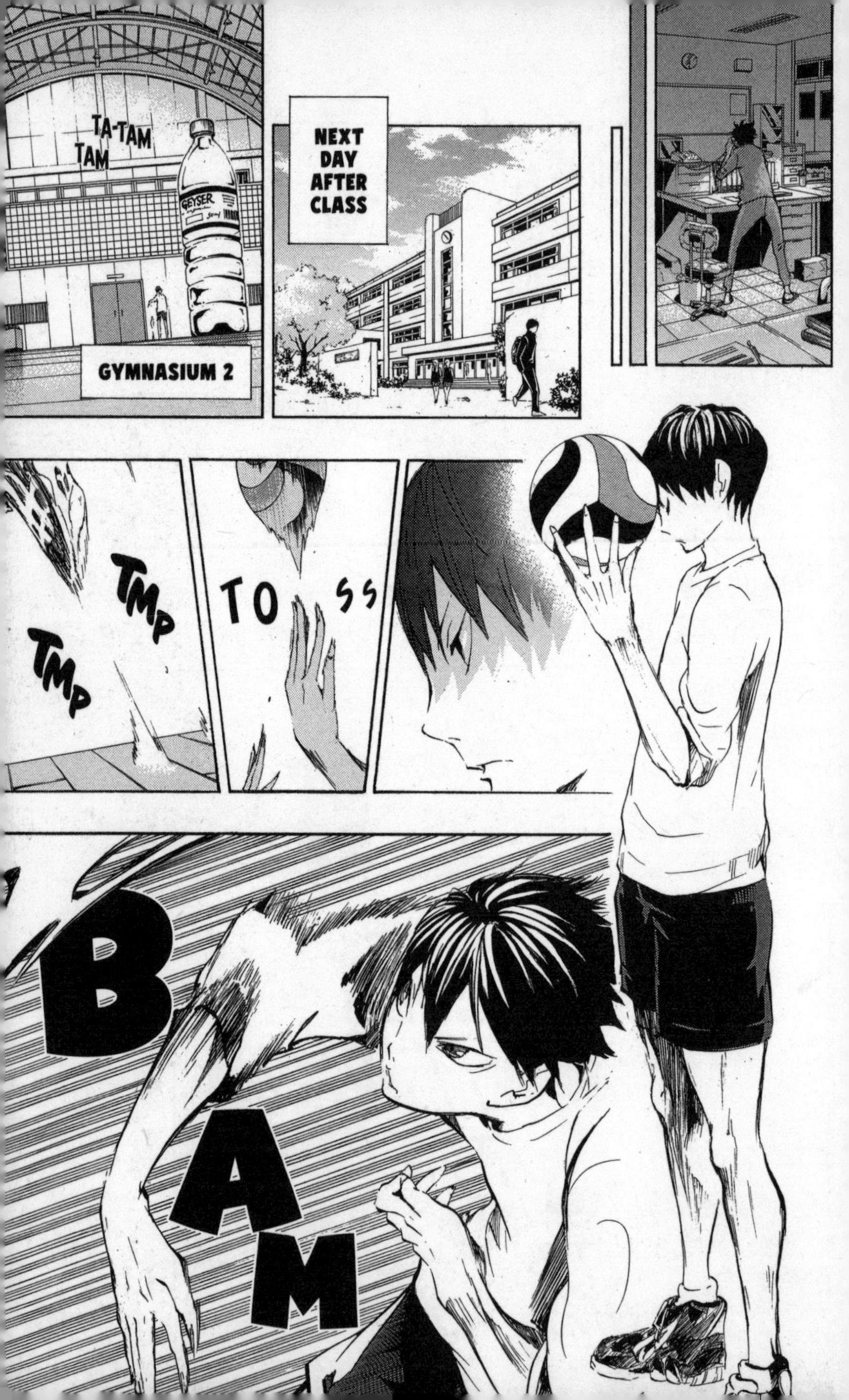
NEXT DAY AFTER CLASS
TA-TAM
TAM
GYMNASIUM 2
TO SS
TMP
TMP
BAM

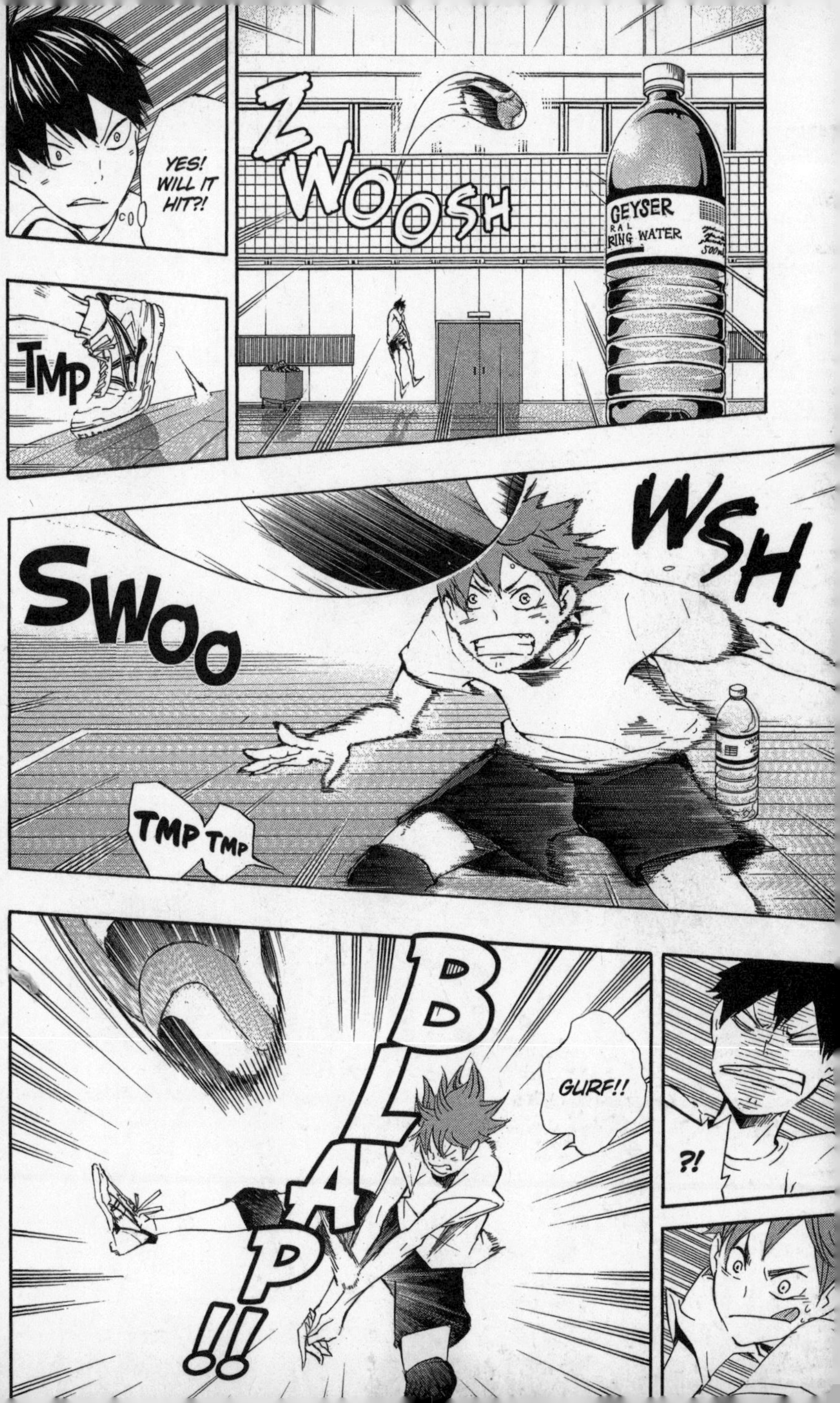
ZWOOSH
GEYSER
RAL
RING WATER
YES! WILL IT HIT?!
TMP
WSH
SWOO
TMP TMP
?!
BLAP!!
GURF!!

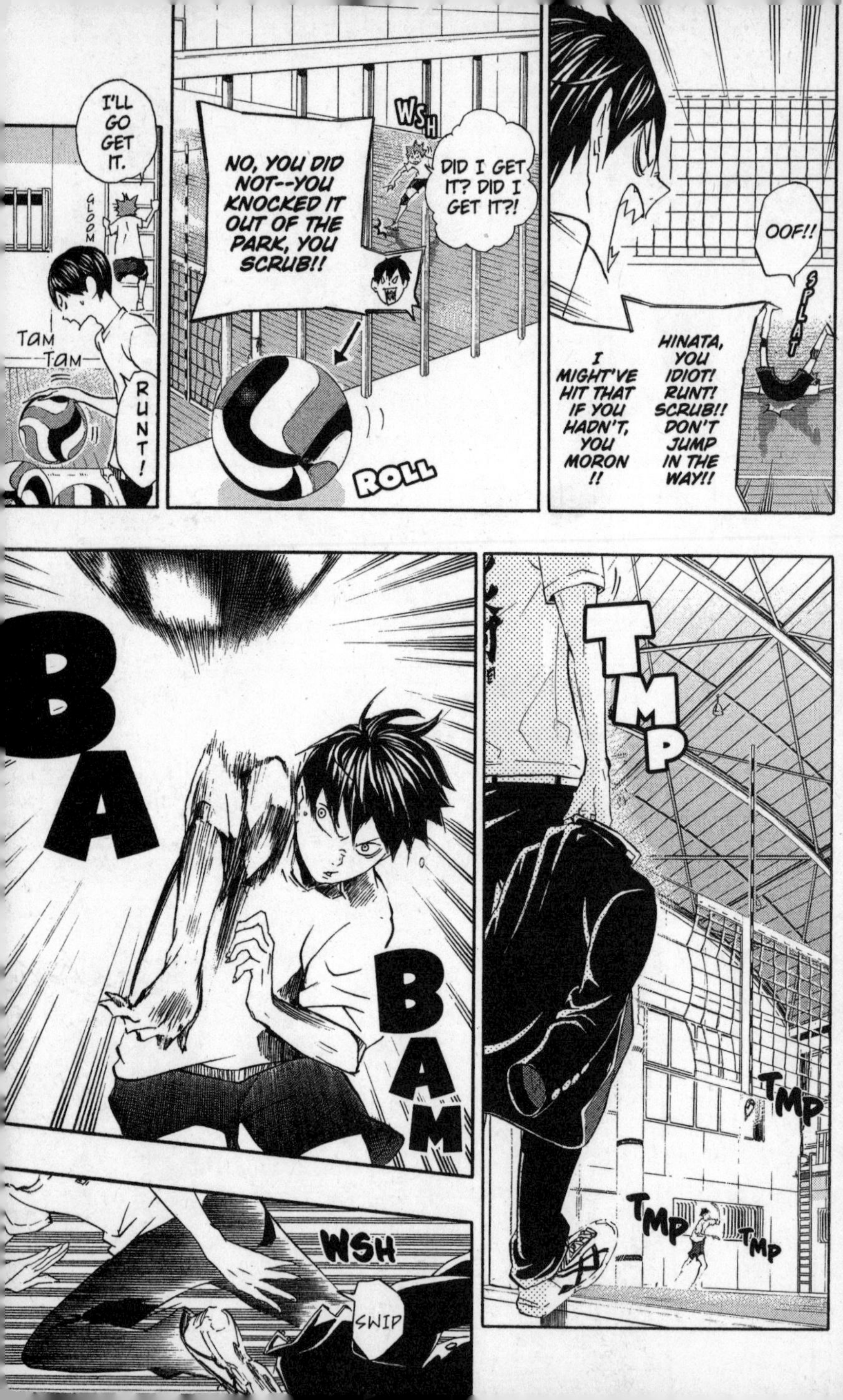
OOF!!
SPLAT
HINATA, YOU IDIOT! RUNT! SCRUB!! DON'T JUMP IN THE WAY!!
I MIGHT'VE HIT THAT IF YOU HADN'T, YOU MORON!!
WSH
DID I GET IT? DID I GET IT?!
NO, YOU DID NOT--YOU KNOCKED IT OUT OF THE PARK, YOU SCRUB!!
ROLL
I'LL GO GET IT.
GLOOM
TAM TAM
RUNT!
TMP
TMP
TMP
TMP
BA
BAM
WSH
SWIP

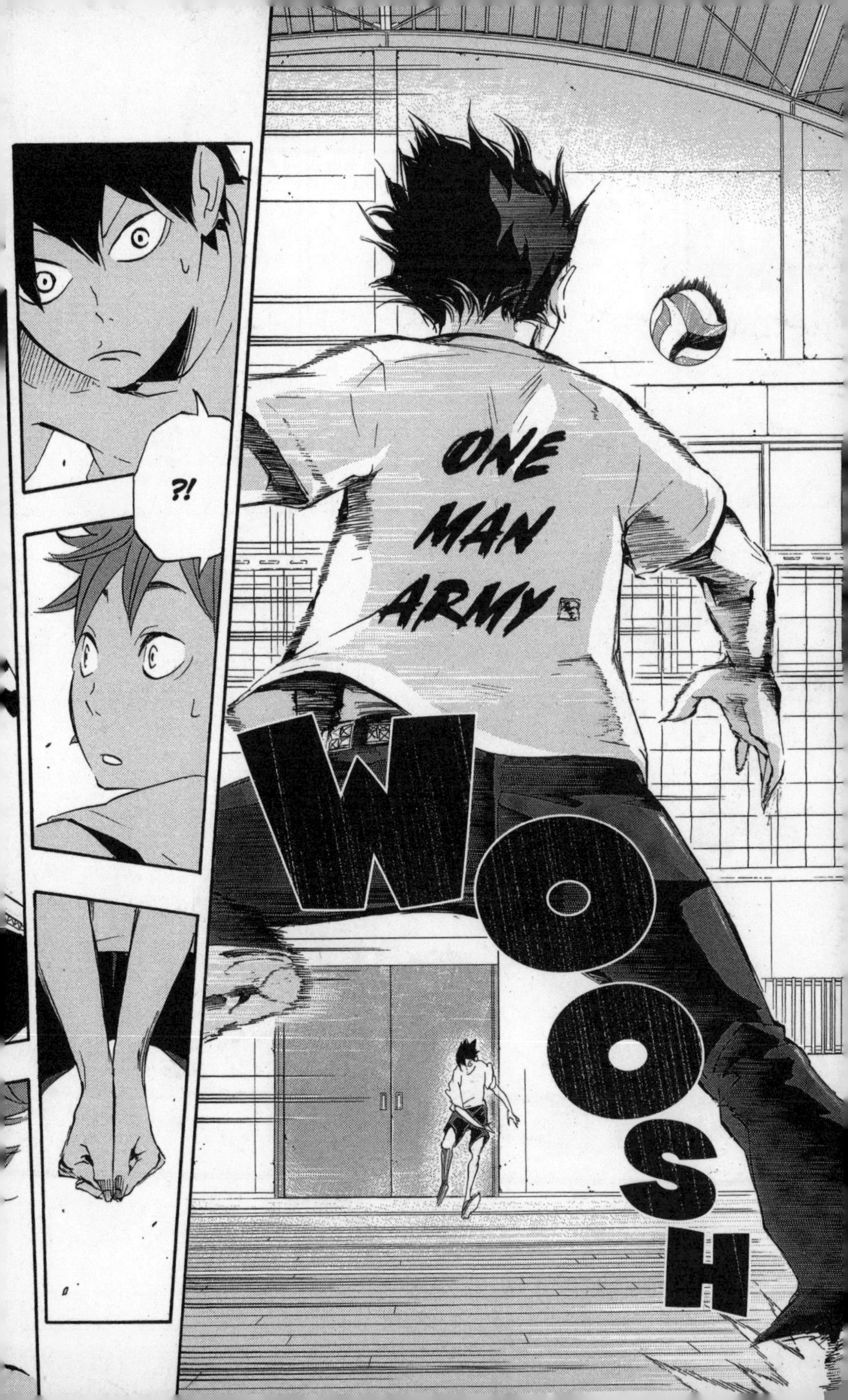

ONE MAN ARMY
WOOOSH
?!

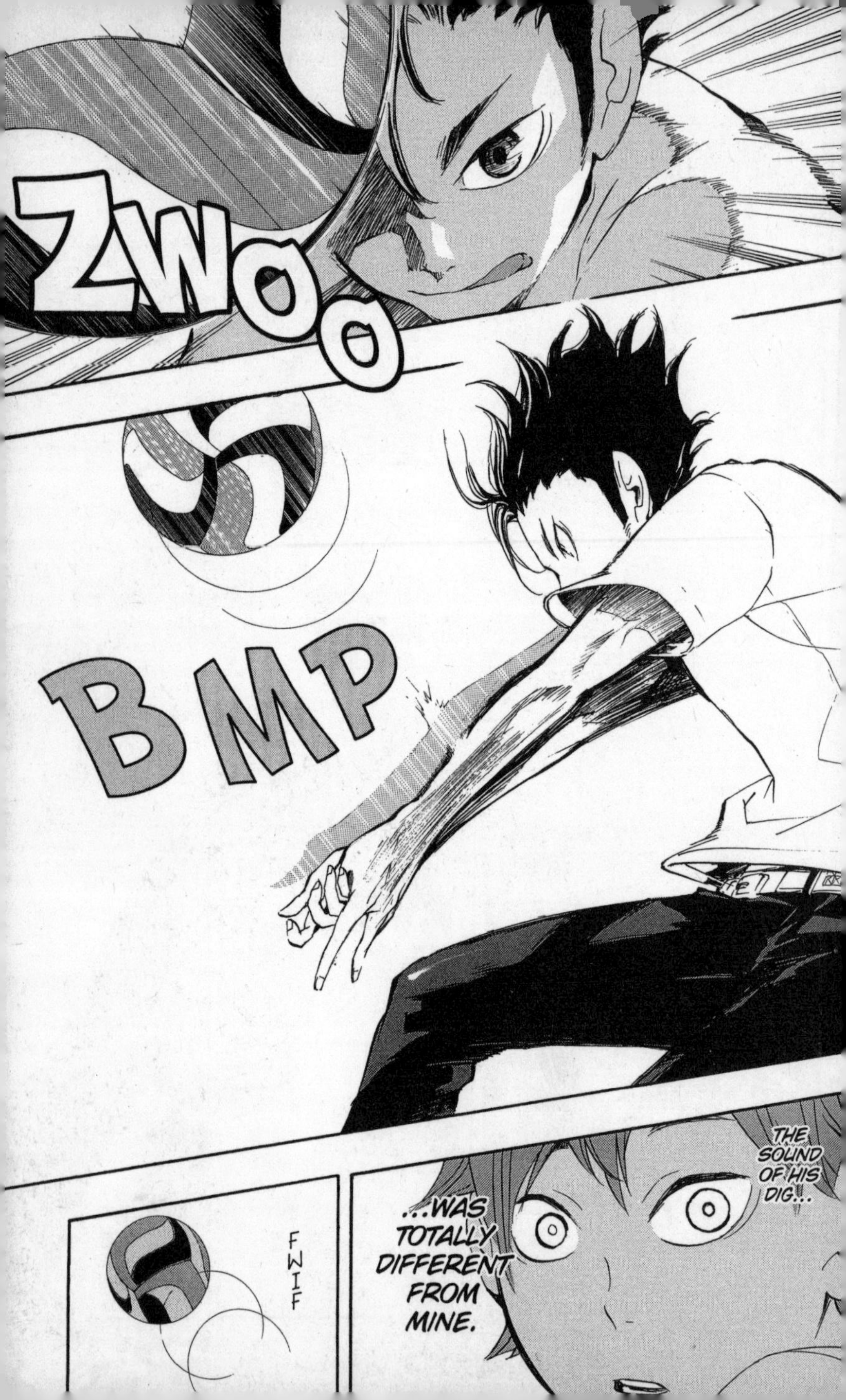
ZWOOO
BMP
THE SOUND OF HIS DIG...
...WAS TOTALLY DIFFERENT FROM MINE.
FWIF

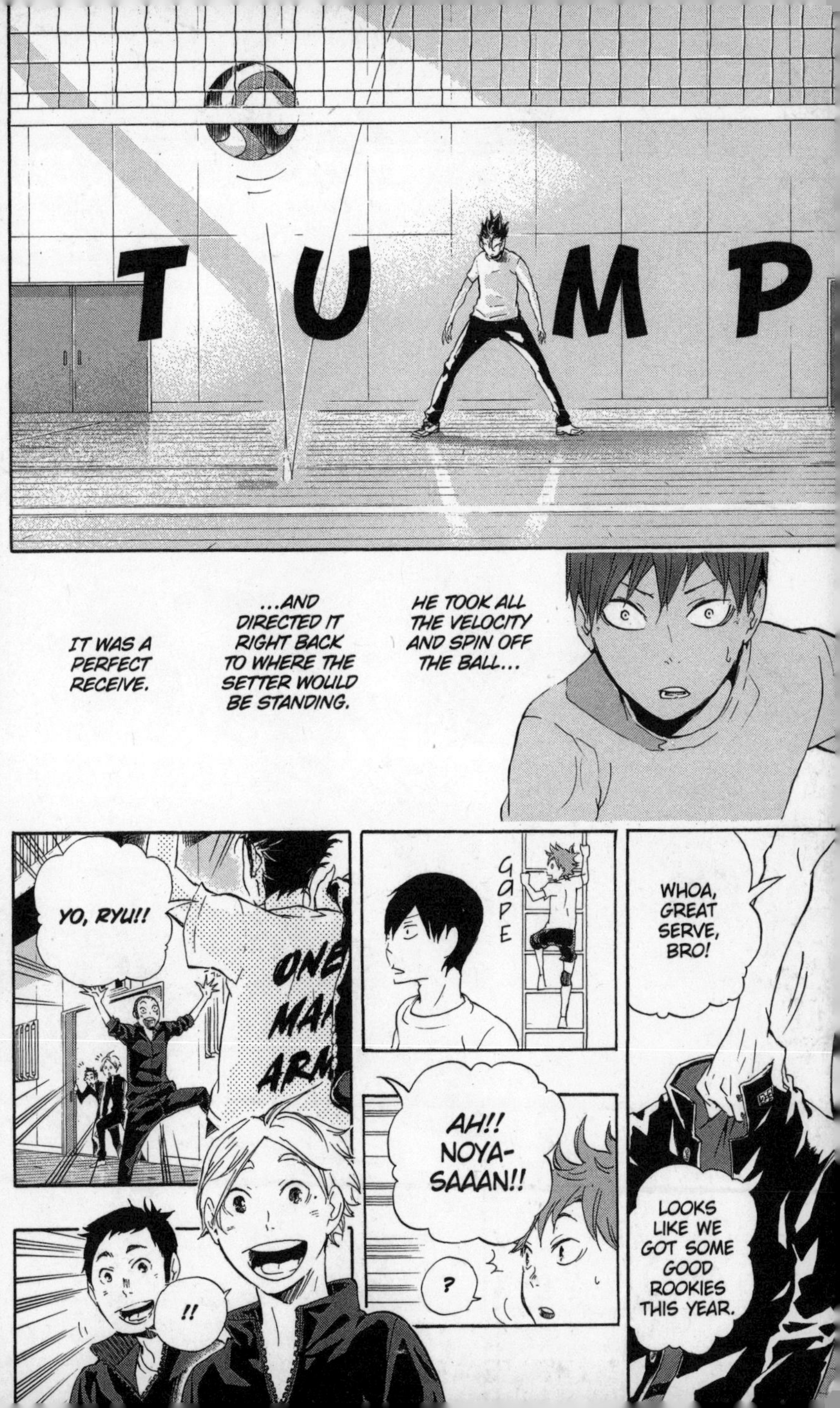
TUMP
HE TOOK ALL THE VELOCITY AND SPIN OFF THE BALL...
...AND DIRECTED IT RIGHT BACK TO WHERE THE SETTER WOULD BE STANDING.
IT WAS A PERFECT RECEIVE.
WHOA, GREAT SERVE, BRO!
LOOKS LIKE WE GOT SOME GOOD ROOKIES THIS YEAR.
GAPE
YO, RYU!!
AH!! NOYA-SAAAN!!
?
!!

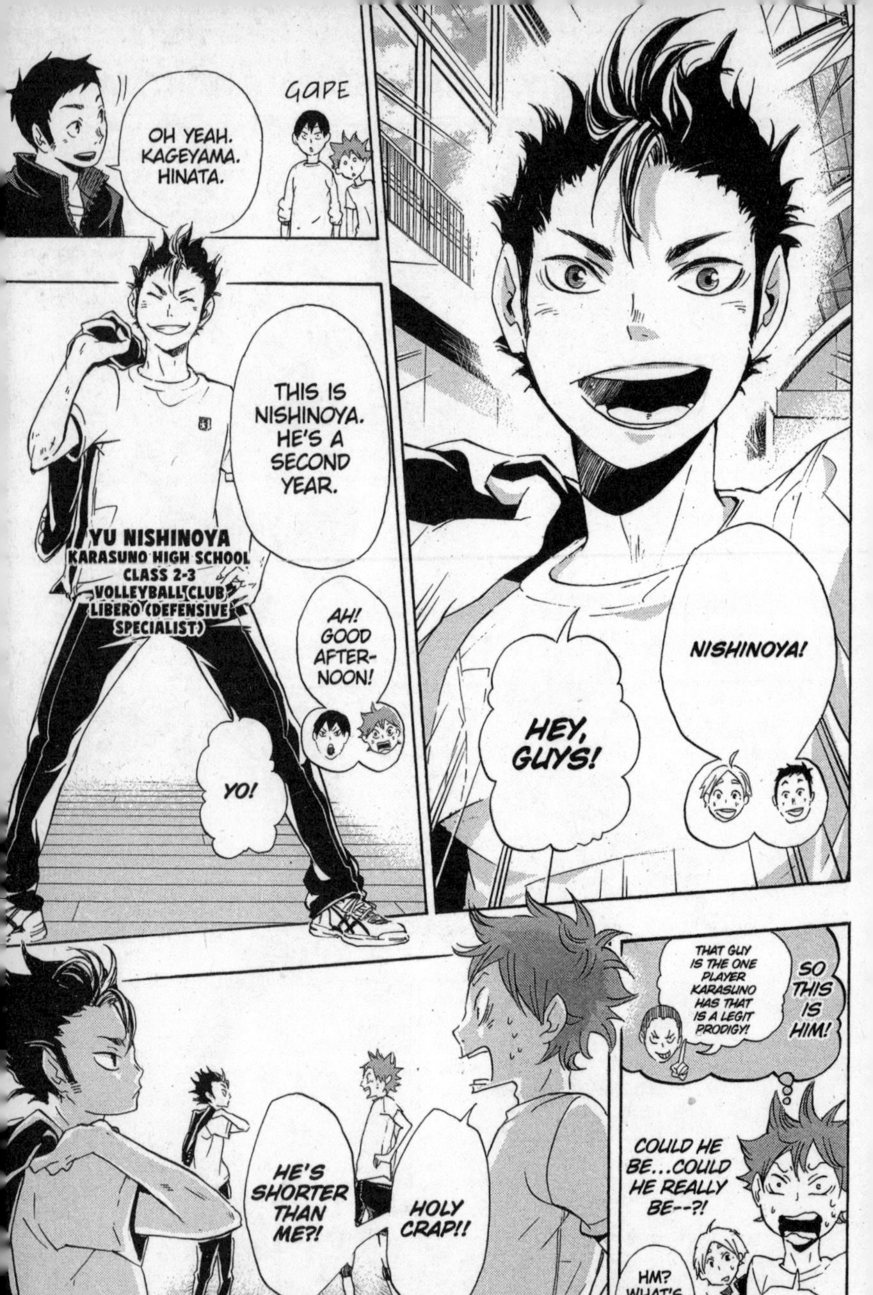
NISHINOYA!
HEY, GUYS!
GAPE
OH YEAH. KAGEYAMA. HINATA.
THIS IS NISHINOYA. HE'S A SECOND YEAR.
YU NISHINOYA KARASUNO HIGH SCHOOL CLASS 2-3 VOLLEYBALL CLUB LIBERO (DEFENSIVE SPECIALIST)
AH! GOOD AFTER-NOON!
YO!
SO THIS IS HIM!
THAT GUY IS THE ONE PLAYER KARASUNO HAS THAT IS A LEGIT PRODIGY!
COULD HE BE...COULD HE REALLY BE--?!
W-WHOA...
HM? WHAT'S WRONG, HINATA?
HOLY CRAP!!
HE'S SHORTER THAN ME?!

HAIKYU!! VOL 2: THE VIEW FROM THE TOP (END)

BONUS STORY: TANAKA SENPAI'S NIGHTMARE

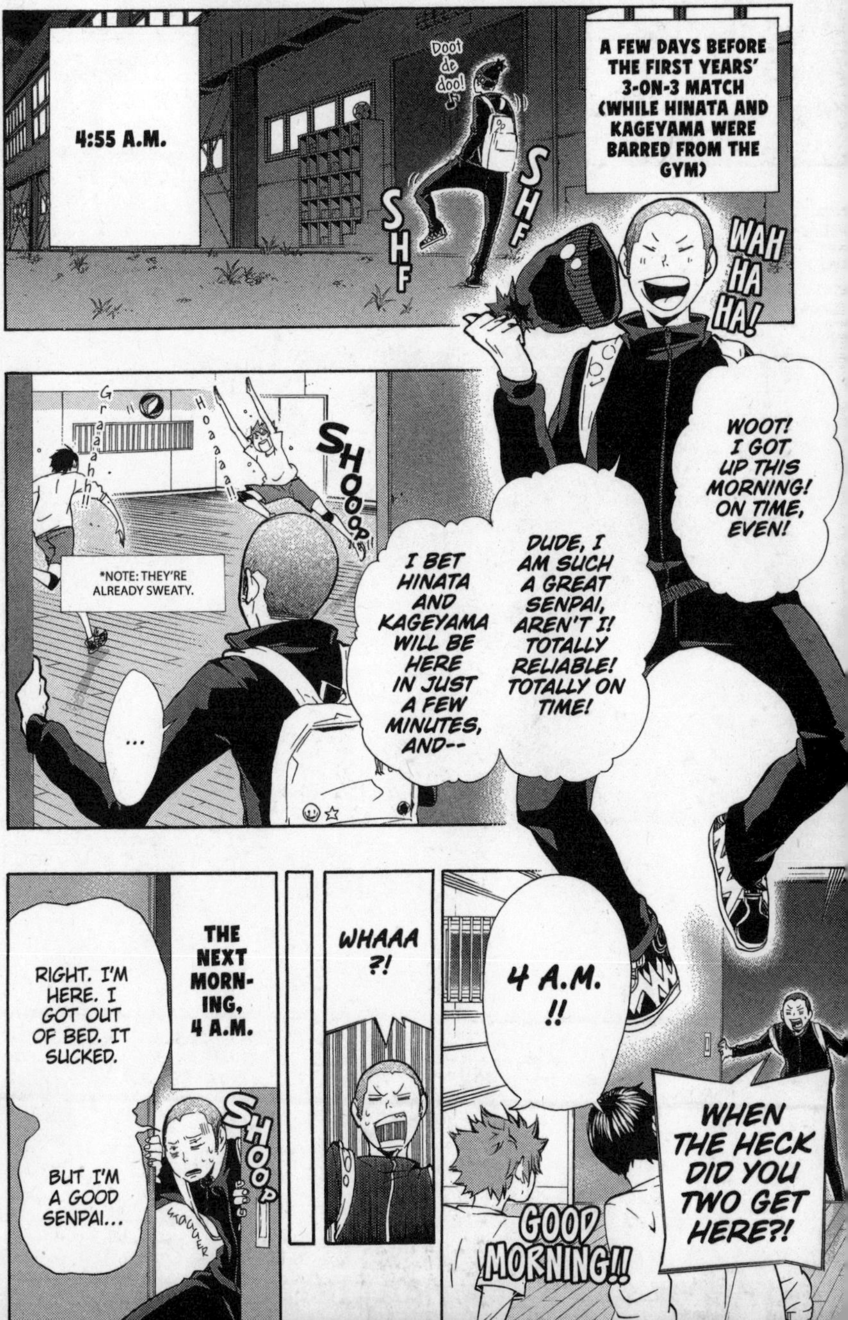

A FEW DAYS BEFORE THE FIRST YEARS' 3-ON-3 MATCH (WHILE HINATA AND KAGEYAMA WERE BARRED FROM THE GYM)
SHF
Doot de doo!
SHF
4:55 A.M.
WAH HA HA!
WOOT! I GOT UP THIS MORNING! ON TIME, EVEN!
DUDE, I AM SUCH A GREAT SENPAI, AREN'T I! TOTALLY RELIABLE! TOTALLY ON TIME!
I BET HINATA AND KAGEYAMA WILL BE HERE IN JUST A FEW MINUTES, AND--
SHOOOOP!!
Hoaaaaa!!
Graaahh!!
*NOTE: THEY'RE ALREADY SWEATY.
...
WHEN THE HECK DID YOU TWO GET HERE?!
GOOD MORNING!!
4 A.M. !!
WHAAA ?!
THE NEXT MORN- ING, 4 A.M.
RIGHT. I'M HERE. I GOT OUT OF BED. IT SUCKED.
SHOOOP
BUT I'M A GOOD SENPAI...
STAGGER

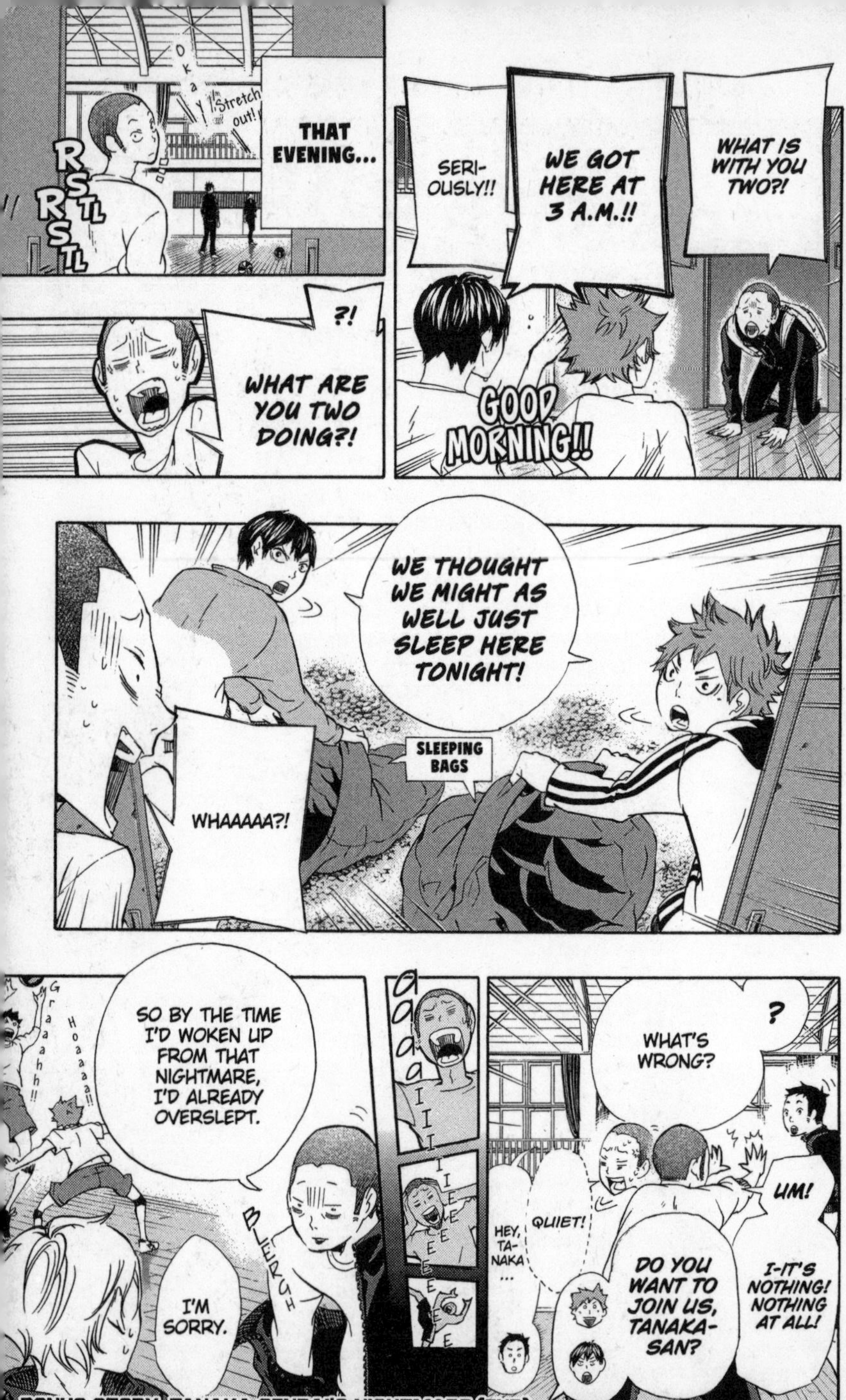
WHAT IS WITH YOU TWO?!
WE GOT HERE AT 3 A.M.!!
SERI-OUSLY!!
GOOD MORNING!!
THAT EVENING...
Okay
Stretch out!
RSTL RSTL
?!
WHAT ARE YOU TWO DOING?!
WE THOUGHT WE MIGHT AS WELL JUST SLEEP HERE TONIGHT!
SLEEPING BAGS
WHAAAAA?!
?
WHAT'S WRONG?
UM!
I-IT'S NOTHING! NOTHING AT ALL!
DO YOU WANT TO JOIN US, TANAKA-SAN?
QUIET!
HEY, TA-NAKA...
aaaaIIIIIEEEEEEEE
BLERGH
SO BY THE TIME I'D WOKEN UP FROM THAT NIGHTMARE, I'D ALREADY OVERSLEPT.
Hoaaaaa!!
Graaahh!!
I'M SORRY.
BONUS STORY: TANAKA SENPAI'S NIGHTMARE (END)

EDITOR'S NOTES

The English edition of Haikyu!! maintains the honorifics used in the original Japanese version. For those of you who are new to these terms, here's a brief explanation to help with your reading experience!

When saying someone's name in Japanese, a suffix is often attached to indicate how familiar the speaker is with the person. Some are more polite and respectful, while others are endearing.

1. ***-kun*** is often used for young men or boys, usually someone you are familiar with.

2. ***-chan*** is used for young children and can be used as a term of endearment.

3. ***-san*** is used for someone you respect or are not close to, or to be polite.

4. ***Senpai*** is used for someone who is older than you or in a higher position or grade in school.

5. ***Kohai*** is used for someone who is younger than you or in a lower position or grade in school.

6. ***Sensei*** means teacher.

7. ***Bluecastle*** is a nickname for Aoba Johsai. It is a combination of *Ao* [blue] and *Joh* [castle].

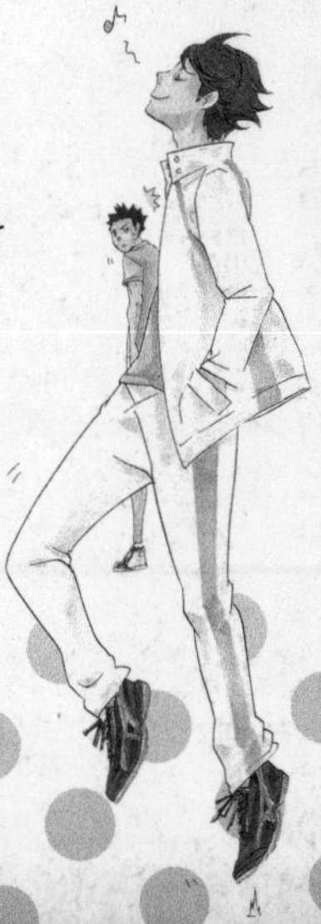